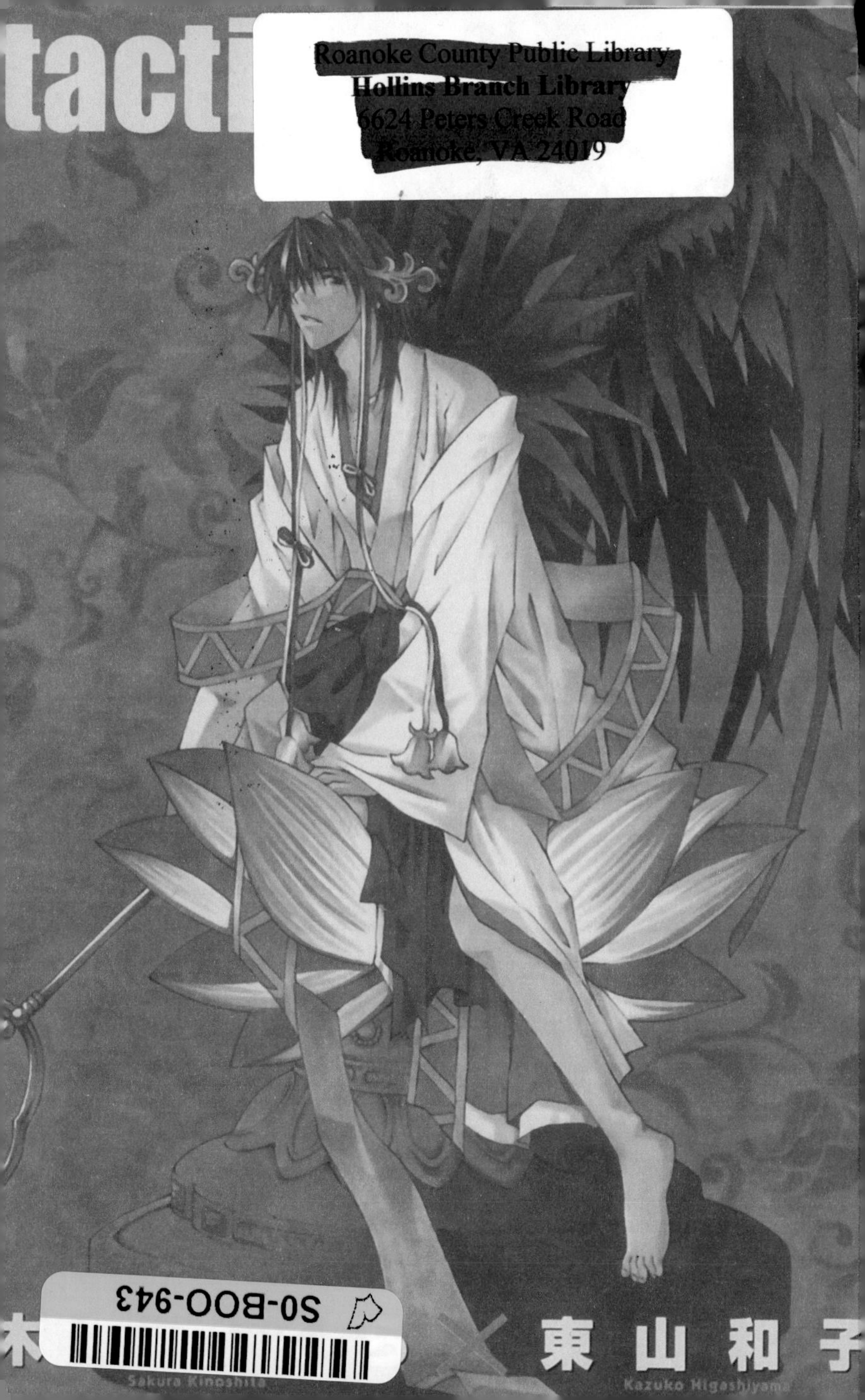
tacti
木
Sakura Kinoshita
東山和子
Kazuko Higashiyama

tactics

Sakura Kinoshita × *Kazuko Higashiyama*

4

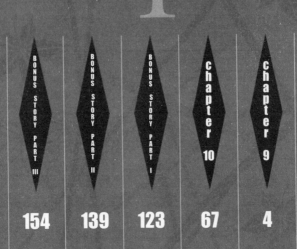

tactics

**Volume 4
by Sakura Kinoshita and
Kazuko Higashiyama**

HAMBURG // LONDON // LOS ANGELES // TOKYO

tactics Volume 4
ART & STORY BY: Sakura Kinoshita × Kazuko Higashiyama

Translation - Christine Schilling
Associate Editor - Lianne Sentar
Copy Editor - Nikhil Burman
Retouch and Lettering - Star Print Brokers
Production Artist - Mike Estacio
Graphic Designer - James Lee

Editor - Lillian Diaz-Przybyl
Digital Imaging Manager - Chris Buford
Pre-Production Supervisor - Erika Terriquez
Production Manager - Elisabeth Brizzi
Managing Editor - Vy Nguyen
Creative Director - Anne Marie Horne
Editor-in-Chief - Rob Tokar
Publisher - Mike Kiley
President and C.O.O. - John Parker
C.E.O. and Chief Creative Officer - Stuart Levy

A  Manga

TOKYOPOP Inc.
5900 Wilshire Blvd. Suite 2000
Los Angeles, CA 90036

E-mail: info@TOKYOPOP.com
Come visit us online at www.TOKYOPOP.com

ISBN: 978-1-59816-963-8

First TOKYOPOP printing: March 2008

10 9 8 7 6 5 4 3 2 1

Printed in the USA

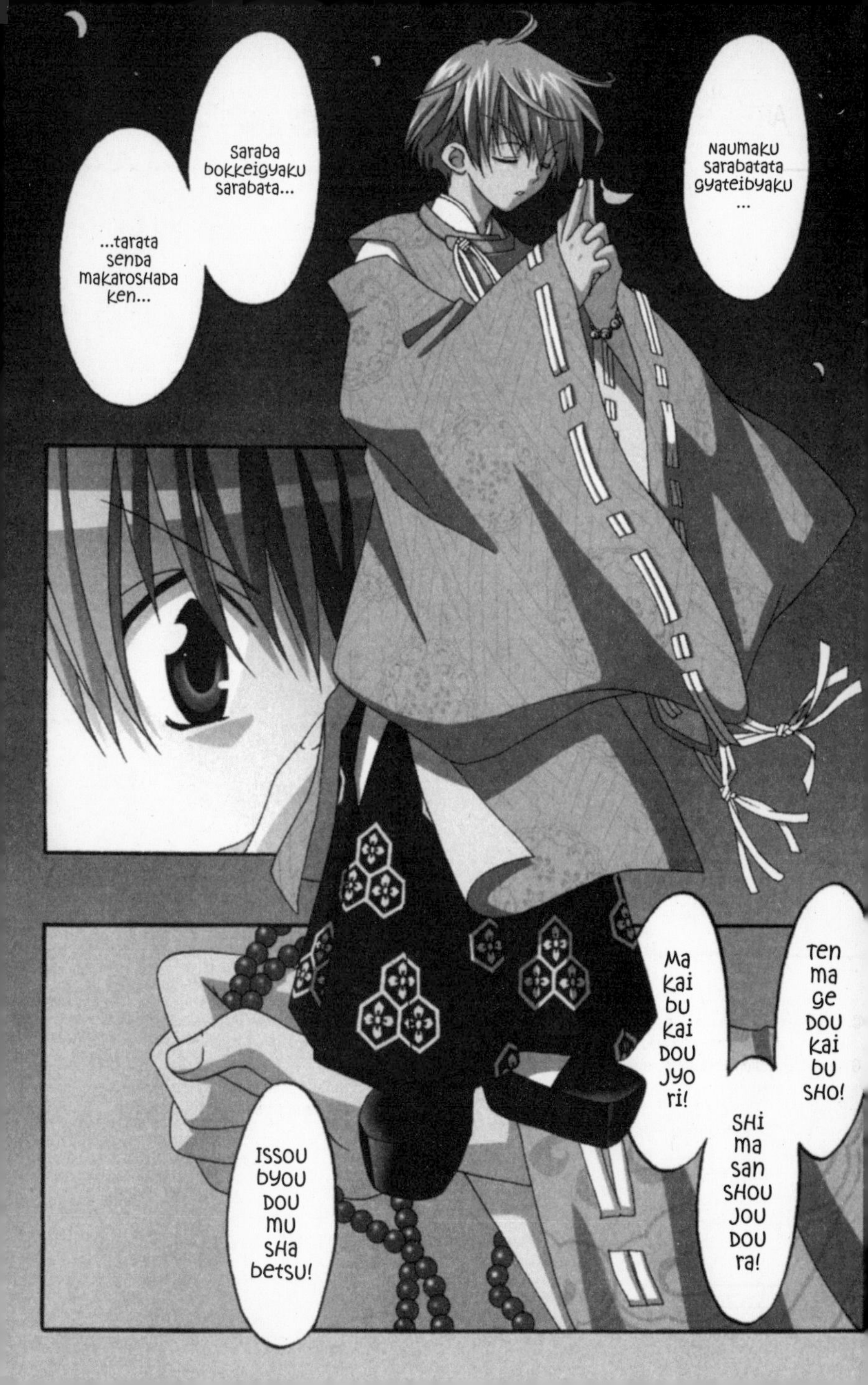

Naumaku sarabatata gyateibyaku ...
Saraba bokkeigyaku sarabata...
...tarata senda makaroshada ken...
Ten ma ge dou kai bu sho!
Ma kai bu kai dou jyo ri!
Shi ma san shou jou dou ra!
Issou byou dou mu sha betsu!

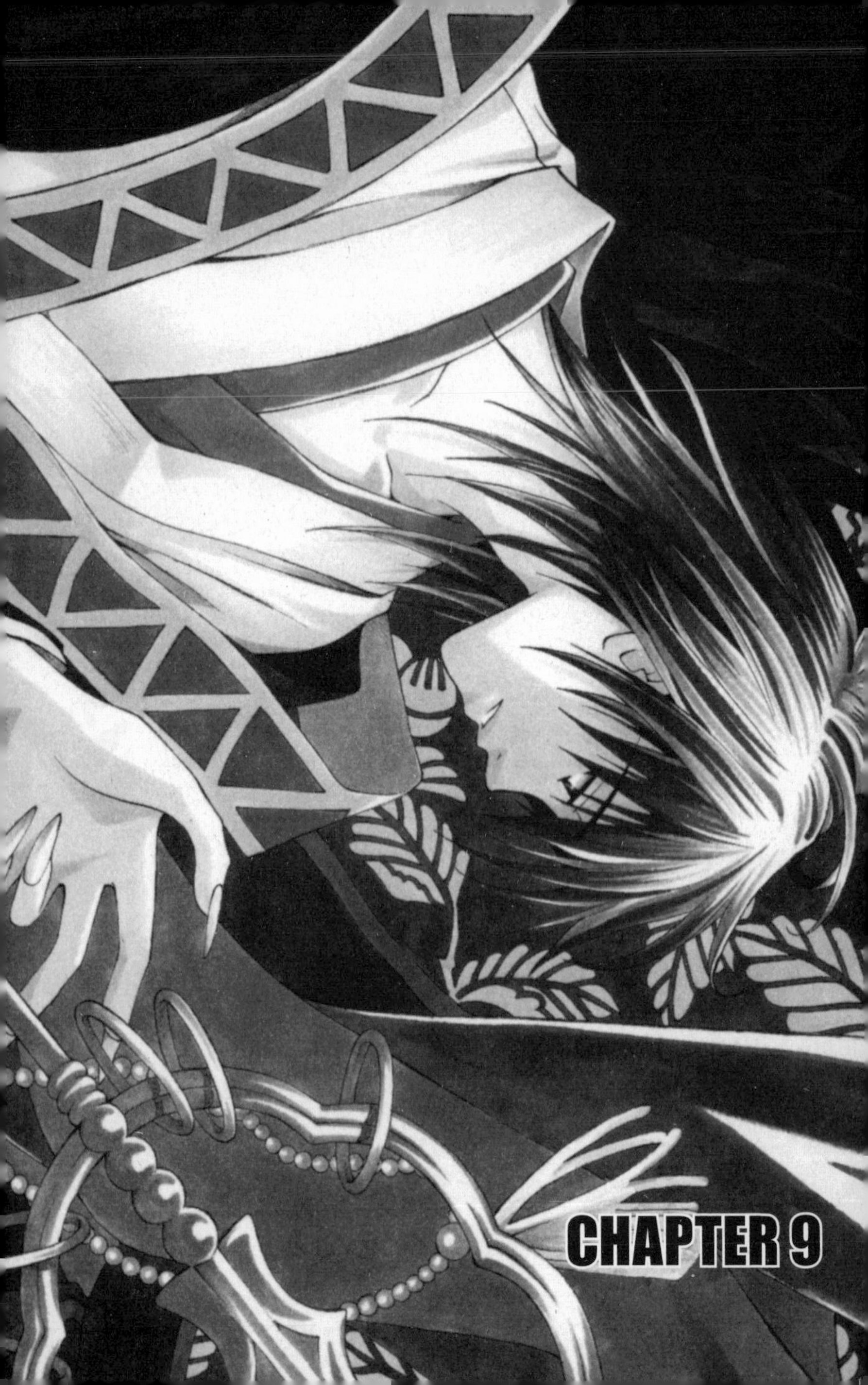
CHAPTER 9

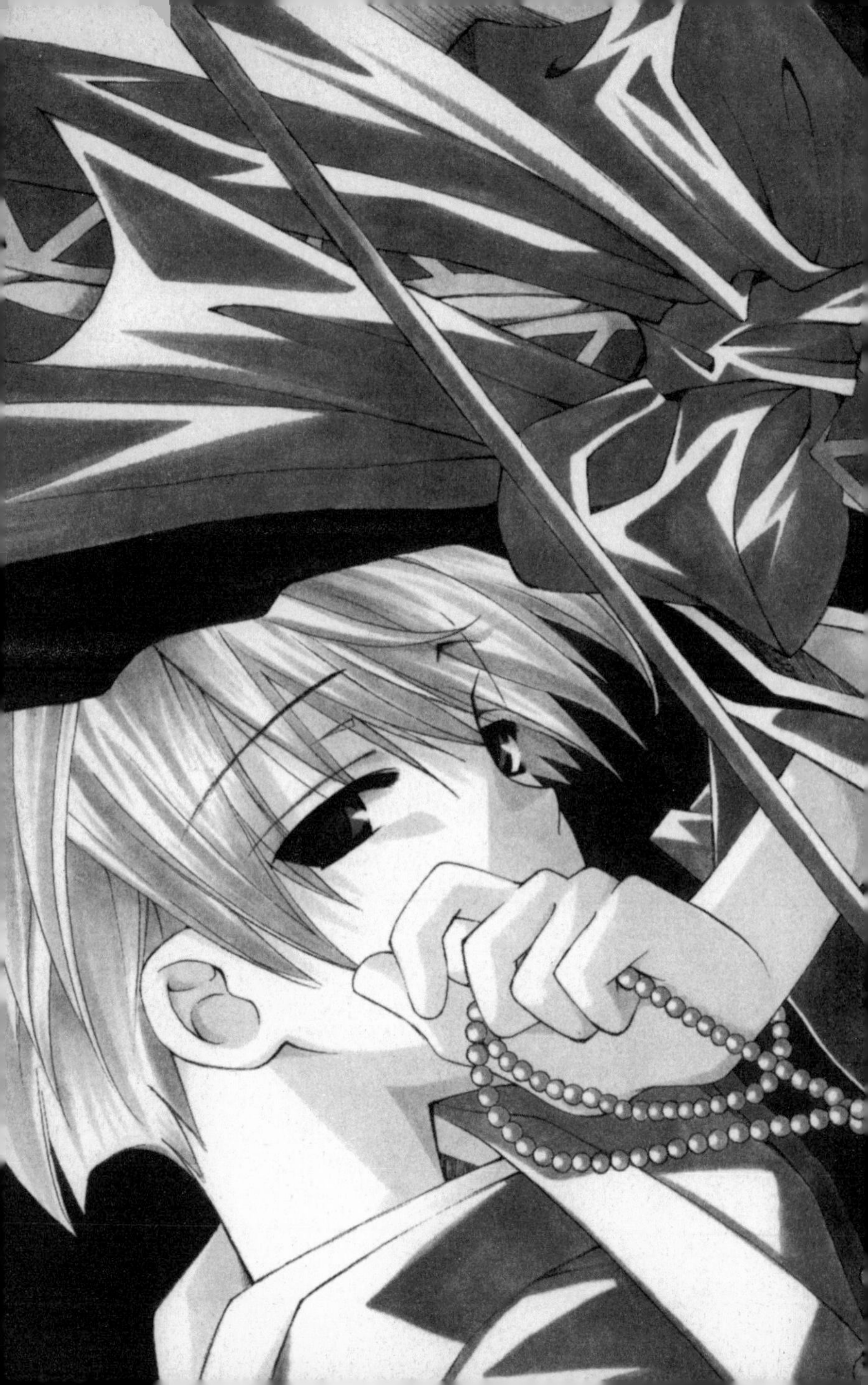

SPECIAL RE-RECORDING!

Sakura Kinoshita and Kazuko Higashiyama's

tactics Drama CD Off-Recording Report!

SINCE WE'RE BAD AT SELF-PORTRAITS, PLEASE ENJOY THE REPLACEMENTS. ♡

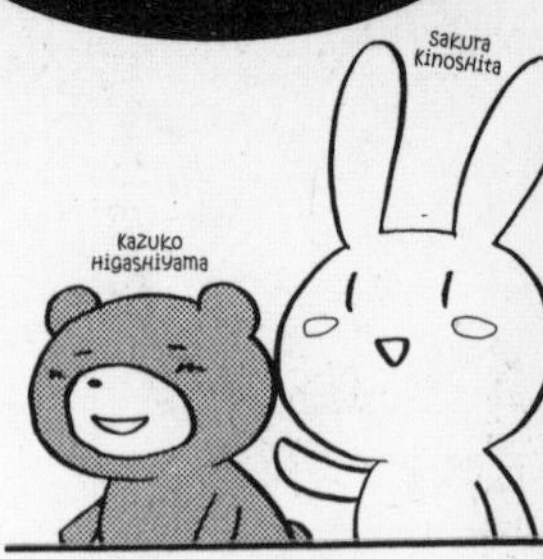

Sakura Kinoshita
Kazuko Higashiyama

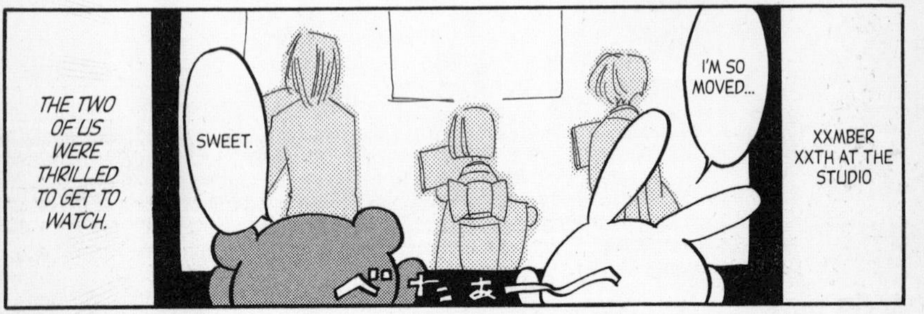

XXMBER XXTH AT THE STUDIO
I'M SO MOVED...
SWEET.
THE TWO OF US WERE THRILLED TO GET TO WATCH.

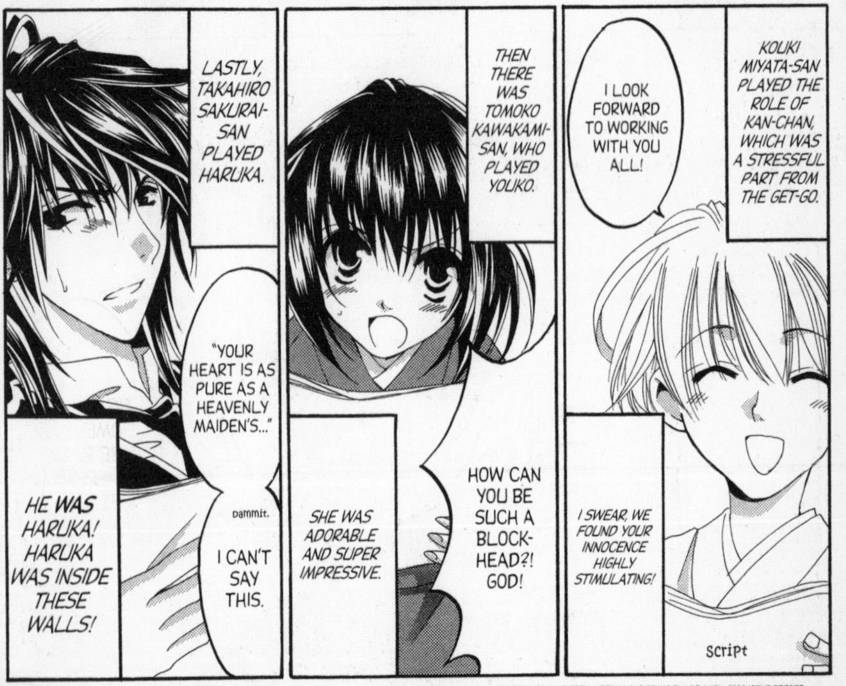

KOUKI MIYATA-SAN PLAYED THE ROLE OF KAN-CHAN, WHICH WAS A STRESSFUL PART FROM THE GET-GO.
I LOOK FORWARD TO WORKING WITH YOU ALL!
I SWEAR, WE FOUND YOUR INNOCENCE HIGHLY STIMULATING!
Script
THEN THERE WAS TOMOKO KAWAKAMI-SAN, WHO PLAYED YOUKO.
HOW CAN YOU BE SUCH A BLOCKHEAD?! GOD!
SHE WAS ADORABLE AND SUPER IMPRESSIVE.
LASTLY, TAKAHIRO SAKURAI-SAN PLAYED HARUKA.
"YOUR HEART IS AS PURE AS A HEAVENLY MAIDEN'S..."
Dammit.
I CAN'T SAY THIS.
HE WAS HARUKA! HARUKA WAS INSIDE THESE WALLS!

※ THIS MANGA WAS SERIALIZED IN THE COMIC BLADE APRIL 2003 ISSUE BEFORE THE COMIC BLADE DRAMA CD SERIES OF "TACTICS" VOLUME 1 WENT ON SALE.

★ MORE ON PAGE 70!

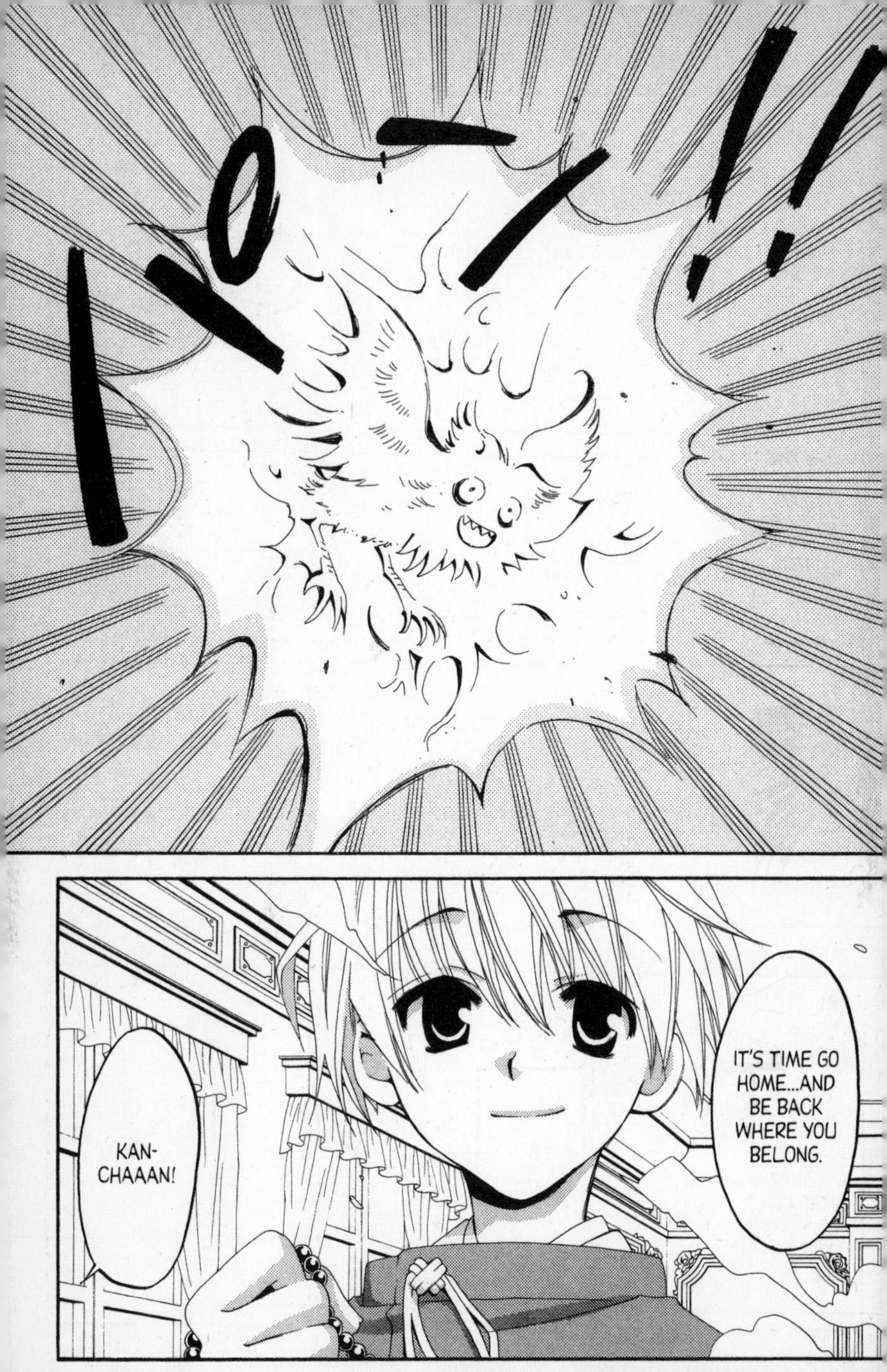
IT'S TIME GO HOME...AND BE BACK WHERE YOU BELONG.
KAN-CHAAAN!

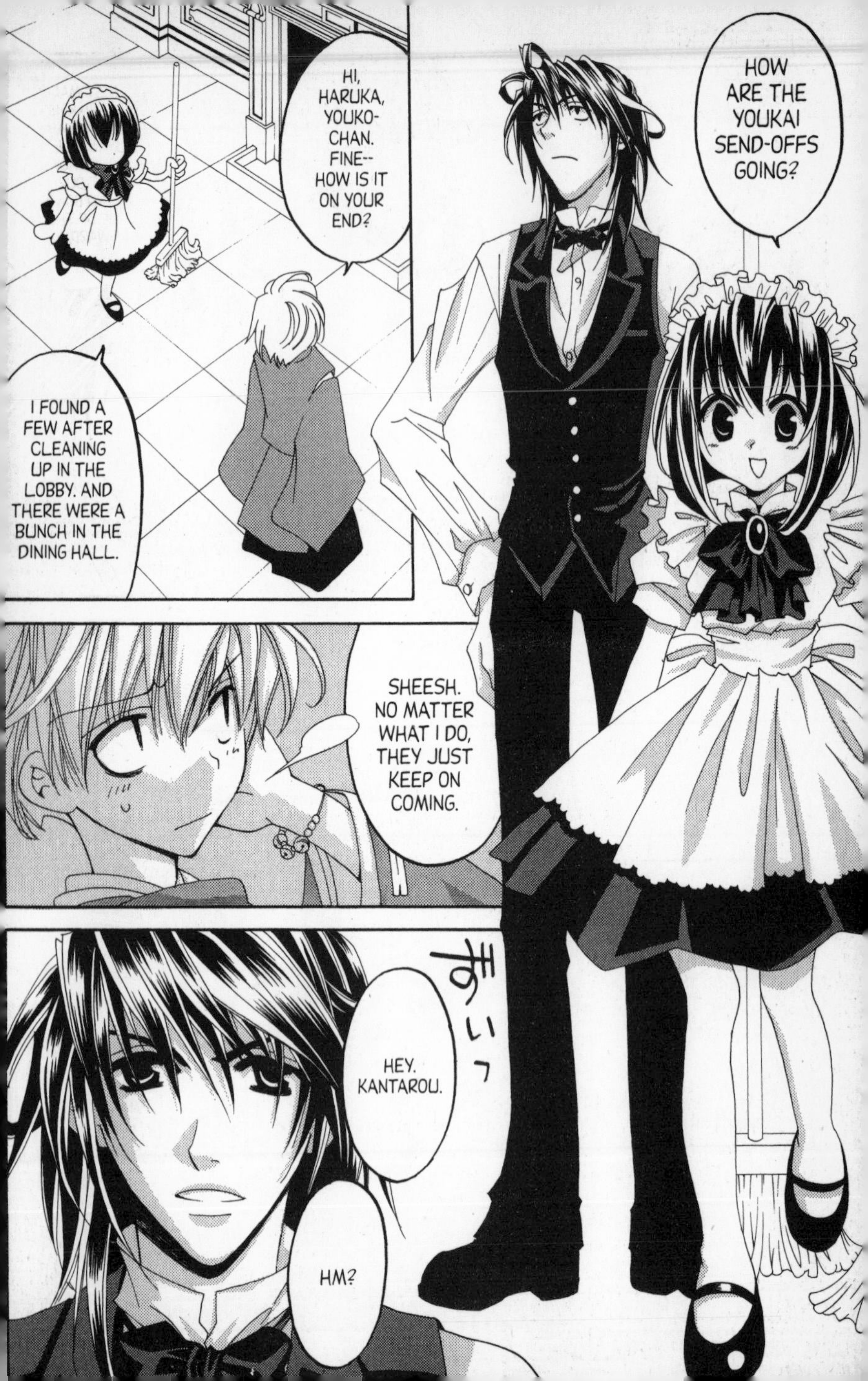
HOW ARE THE YOUKAI SEND-OFFS GOING?
HI, HARUKA, YOUKO-CHAN. FINE--HOW IS IT ON YOUR END?
I FOUND A FEW AFTER CLEANING UP IN THE LOBBY. AND THERE WERE A BUNCH IN THE DINING HALL.
SHEESH. NO MATTER WHAT I DO, THEY JUST KEEP ON COMING.
すいっ
HEY. KANTAROU.
HM?

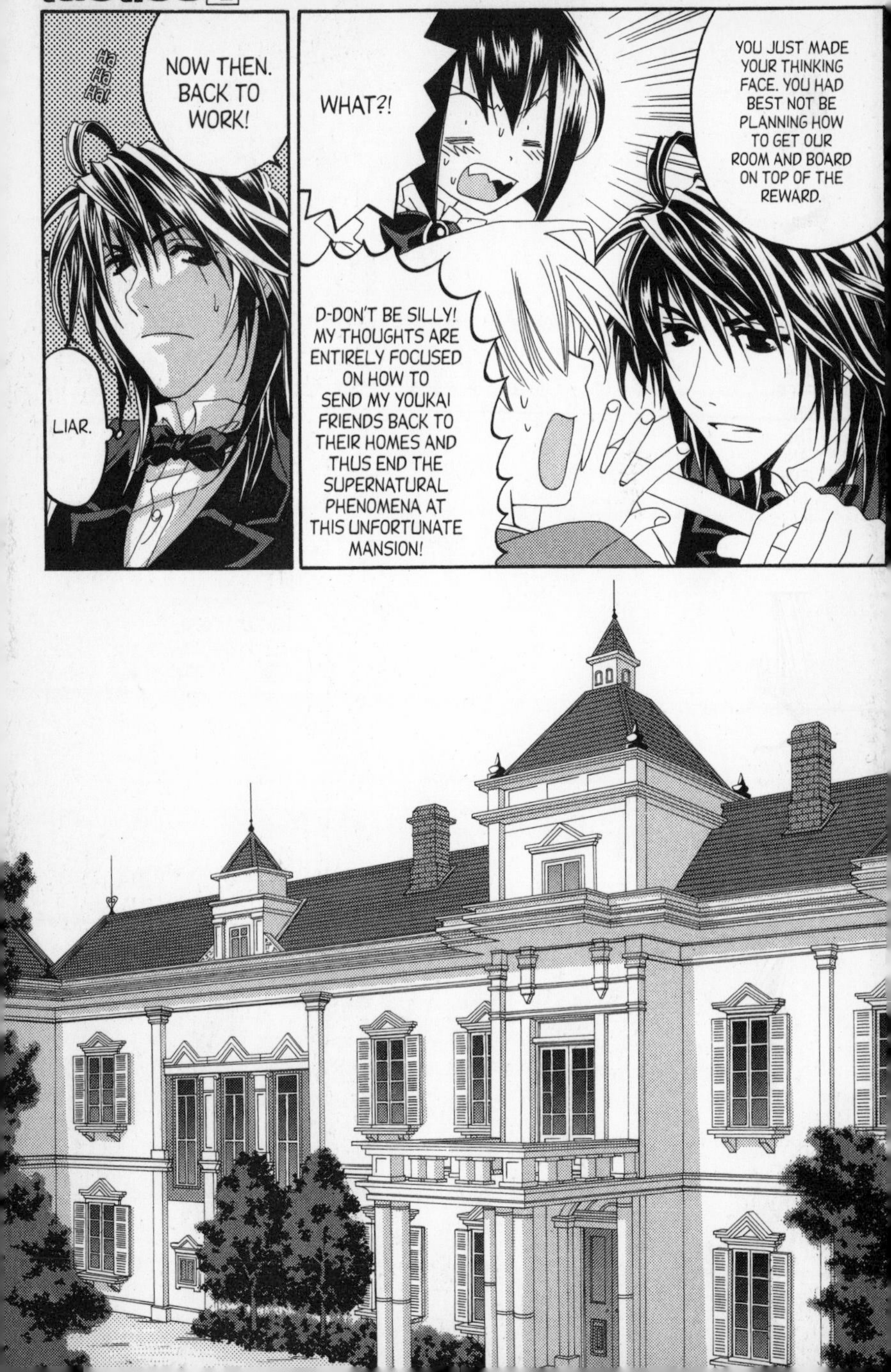
YOU JUST MADE YOUR THINKING FACE. YOU HAD BEST NOT BE PLANNING HOW TO GET OUR ROOM AND BOARD ON TOP OF THE REWARD.
WHAT?!
D-DON'T BE SILLY! MY THOUGHTS ARE ENTIRELY FOCUSED ON HOW TO SEND MY YOUKAI FRIENDS BACK TO THEIR HOMES AND THUS END THE SUPERNATURAL PHENOMENA AT THIS UNFORTUNATE MANSION!
HA HA HA!
NOW THEN. BACK TO WORK!
LIAR.

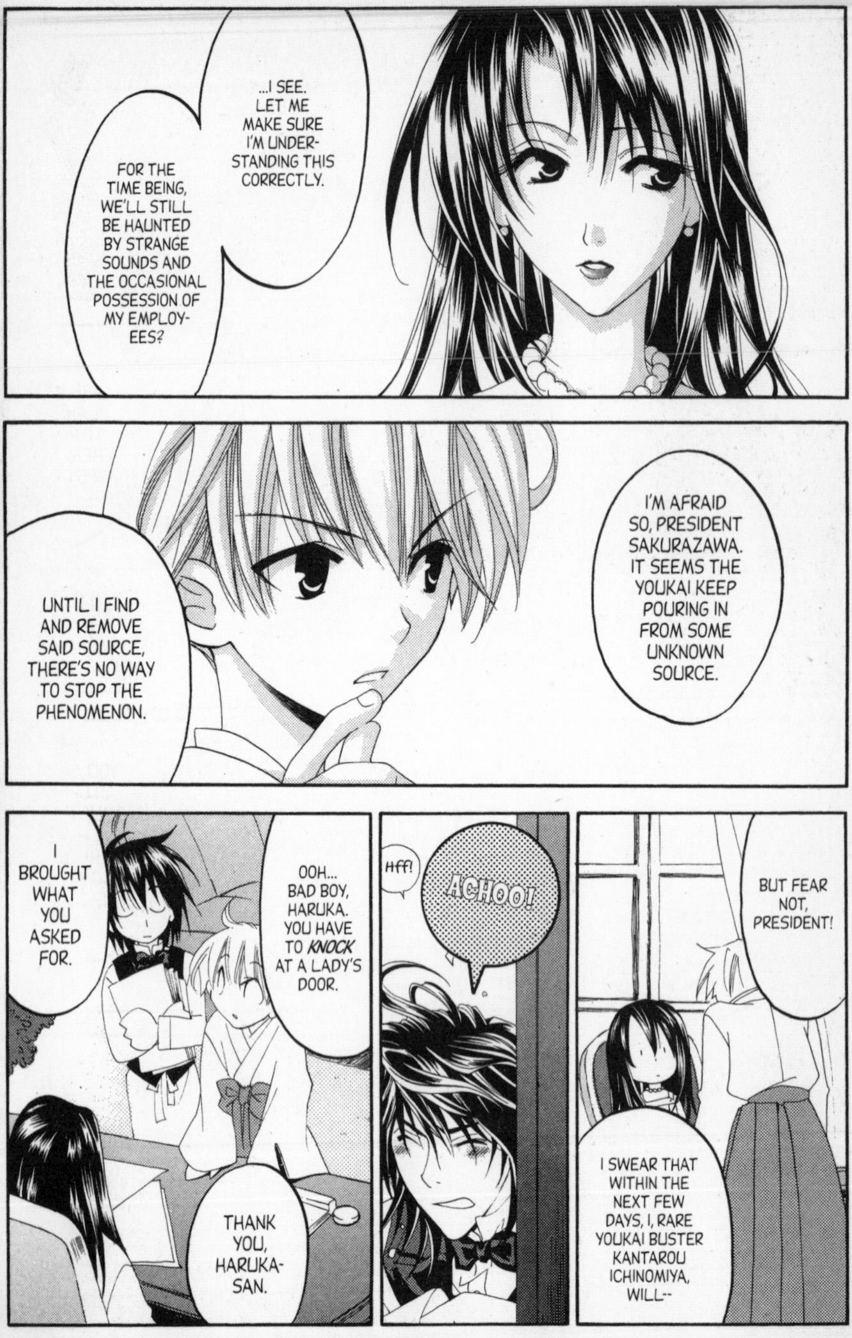
...I SEE. LET ME MAKE SURE I'M UNDER-STANDING THIS CORRECTLY.
FOR THE TIME BEING, WE'LL STILL BE HAUNTED BY STRANGE SOUNDS AND THE OCCASIONAL POSSESSION OF MY EMPLOY-EES?
I'M AFRAID SO, PRESIDENT SAKURAZAWA. IT SEEMS THE YOUKAI KEEP POURING IN FROM SOME UNKNOWN SOURCE.
UNTIL I FIND AND REMOVE SAID SOURCE, THERE'S NO WAY TO STOP THE PHENOMENON.
BUT FEAR NOT, PRESIDENT!
I SWEAR THAT WITHIN THE NEXT FEW DAYS, I, RARE YOUKAI BUSTER KANTAROU ICHINOMIYA, WILL--
ACHOO!
Hff!
OOH... BAD BOY, HARUKA. YOU HAVE TO *KNOCK* AT A LADY'S DOOR.
I BROUGHT WHAT YOU ASKED FOR.
THANK YOU, HARUKA-SAN.

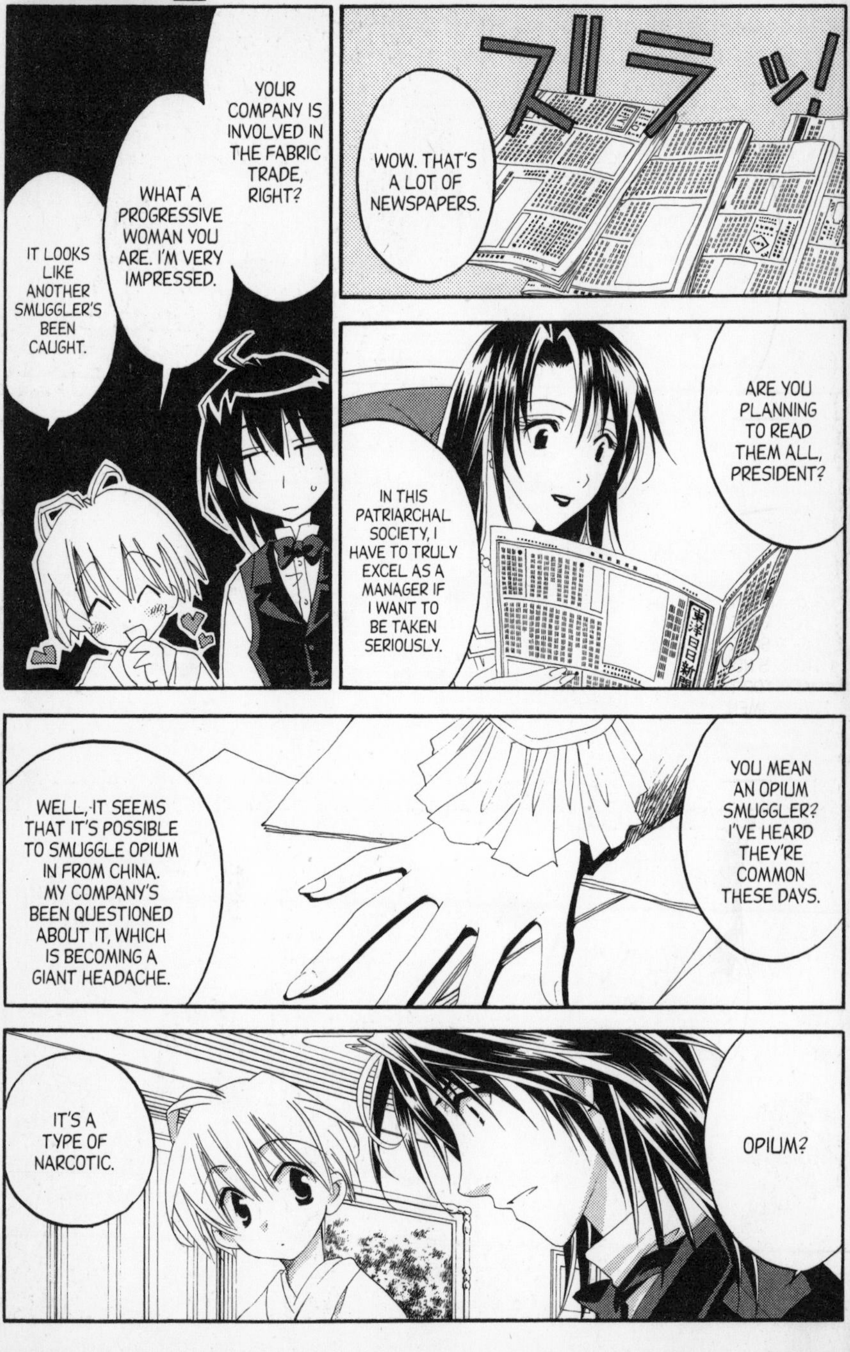
ズラッ!
WOW. THAT'S A LOT OF NEWSPAPERS.
ARE YOU PLANNING TO READ THEM ALL, PRESIDENT?
IN THIS PATRIARCHAL SOCIETY, I HAVE TO TRULY EXCEL AS A MANAGER IF I WANT TO BE TAKEN SERIOUSLY.
YOUR COMPANY IS INVOLVED IN THE FABRIC TRADE, RIGHT?
WHAT A PROGRESSIVE WOMAN YOU ARE. I'M VERY IMPRESSED.
IT LOOKS LIKE ANOTHER SMUGGLER'S BEEN CAUGHT.
YOU MEAN AN OPIUM SMUGGLER? I'VE HEARD THEY'RE COMMON THESE DAYS.
WELL, IT SEEMS THAT IT'S POSSIBLE TO SMUGGLE OPIUM IN FROM CHINA. MY COMPANY'S BEEN QUESTIONED ABOUT IT, WHICH IS BECOMING A GIANT HEADACHE.
OPIUM?
IT'S A TYPE OF NARCOTIC.

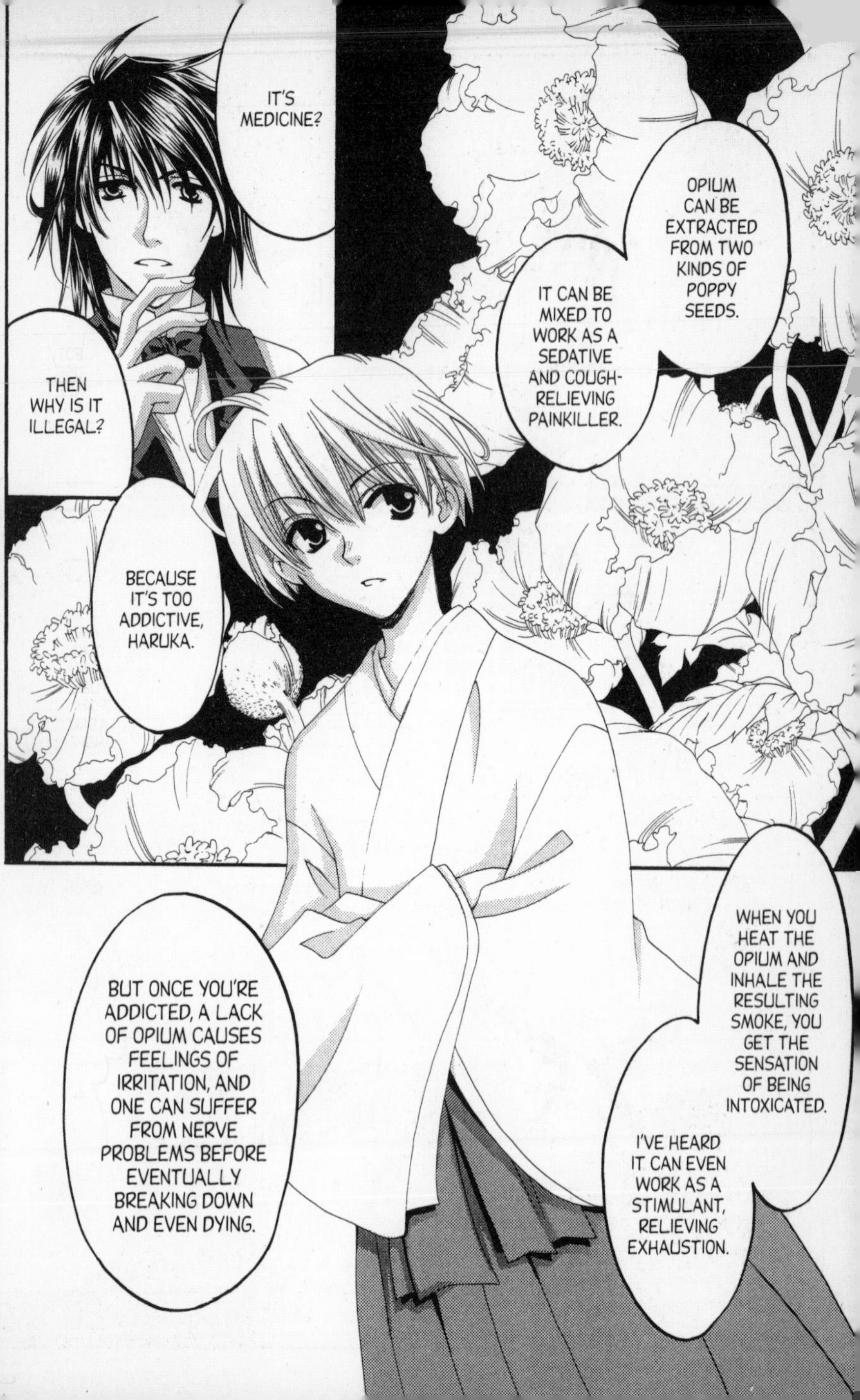

OPIUM CAN BE EXTRACTED FROM TWO KINDS OF POPPY SEEDS.
IT CAN BE MIXED TO WORK AS A SEDATIVE AND COUGH-RELIEVING PAINKILLER.
IT'S MEDICINE?
THEN WHY IS IT ILLEGAL?
BECAUSE IT'S TOO ADDICTIVE, HARUKA.
WHEN YOU HEAT THE OPIUM AND INHALE THE RESULTING SMOKE, YOU GET THE SENSATION OF BEING INTOXICATED.
I'VE HEARD IT CAN EVEN WORK AS A STIMULANT, RELIEVING EXHAUSTION.
BUT ONCE YOU'RE ADDICTED, A LACK OF OPIUM CAUSES FEELINGS OF IRRITATION, AND ONE CAN SUFFER FROM NERVE PROBLEMS BEFORE EVENTUALLY BREAKING DOWN AND EVEN DYING.

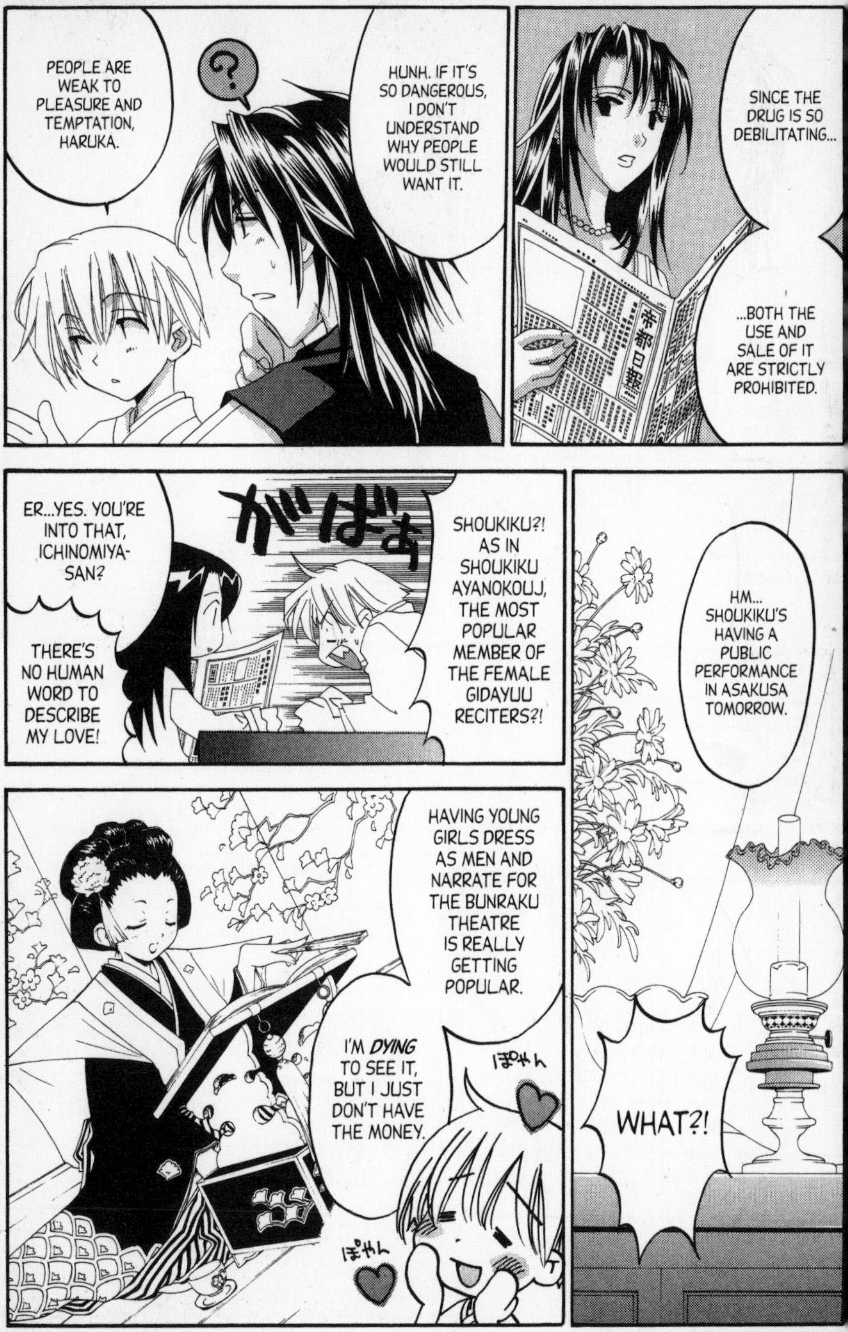
SINCE THE DRUG IS SO DEBILITATING...
...BOTH THE USE AND SALE OF IT ARE STRICTLY PROHIBITED.
HUNH. IF IT'S SO DANGEROUS, I DON'T UNDERSTAND WHY PEOPLE WOULD STILL WANT IT.
?
PEOPLE ARE WEAK TO PLEASURE AND TEMPTATION, HARUKA.
HM... SHOUKIKU'S HAVING A PUBLIC PERFORMANCE IN ASAKUSA TOMORROW.
WHAT?!
がばっ
SHOUKIKU?! AS IN SHOUKIKU AYANOKOUJ, THE MOST POPULAR MEMBER OF THE FEMALE GIDAYUU RECITERS?!
ER...YES. YOU'RE INTO THAT, ICHINOMIYA-SAN?
THERE'S NO HUMAN WORD TO DESCRIBE MY LOVE!
HAVING YOUNG GIRLS DRESS AS MEN AND NARRATE FOR THE BUNRAKU THEATRE IS REALLY GETTING POPULAR.
ぽやん
I'M *DYING* TO SEE IT, BUT I JUST DON'T HAVE THE MONEY.
ぽやん

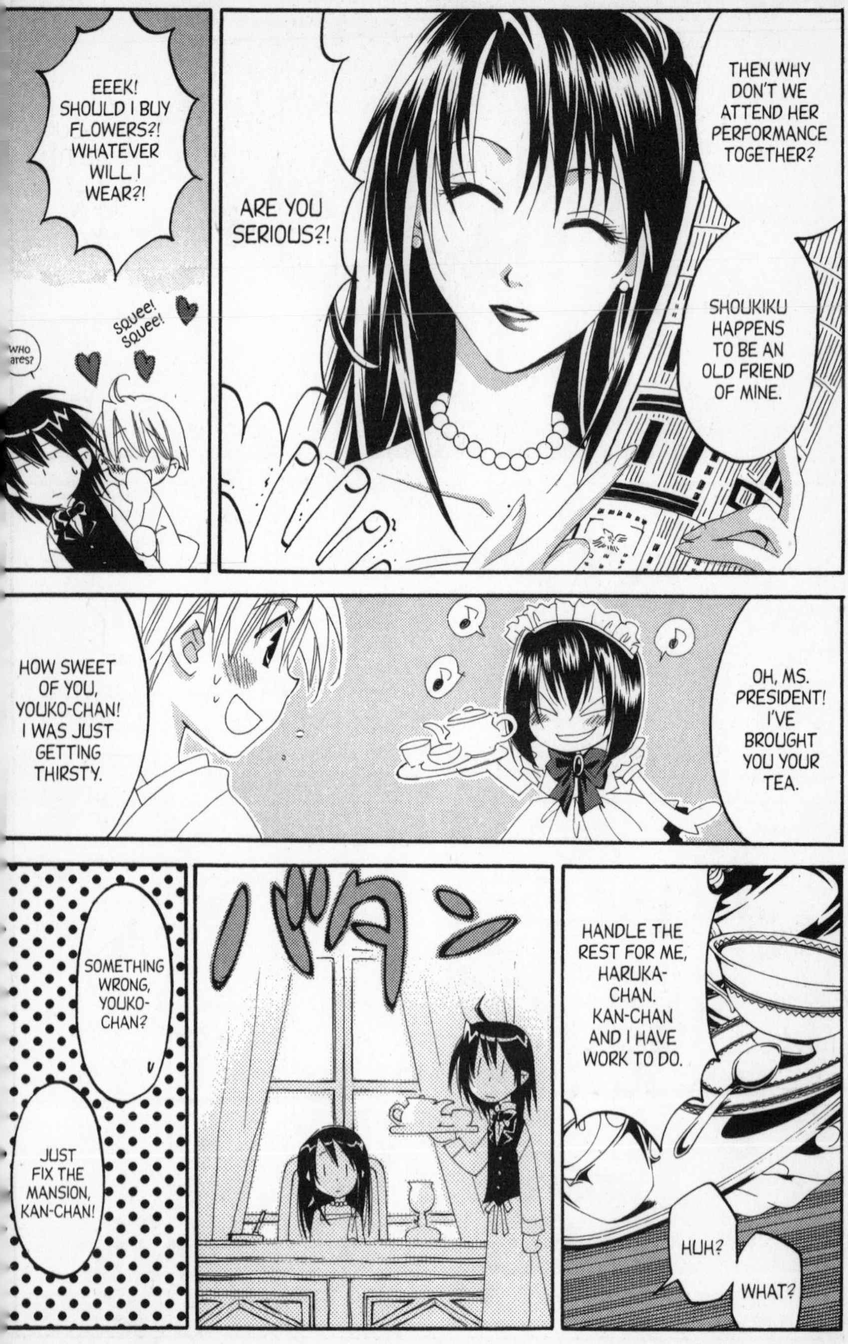
THEN WHY DON'T WE ATTEND HER PERFORMANCE TOGETHER?
SHOUKIKU HAPPENS TO BE AN OLD FRIEND OF MINE.
ARE YOU SERIOUS?!
EEEK! SHOULD I BUY FLOWERS?! WHATEVER WILL I WEAR?!
SQUEE! SQUEE!
WHO ares?
OH, MS. PRESIDENT! I'VE BROUGHT YOU YOUR TEA.
HOW SWEET OF YOU, YOUKO-CHAN! I WAS JUST GETTING THIRSTY.
HANDLE THE REST FOR ME, HARUKA-CHAN. KAN-CHAN AND I HAVE WORK TO DO.
HUH?
WHAT?
SOMETHING WRONG, YOUKO-CHAN?
JUST FIX THE MANSION, KAN-CHAN!

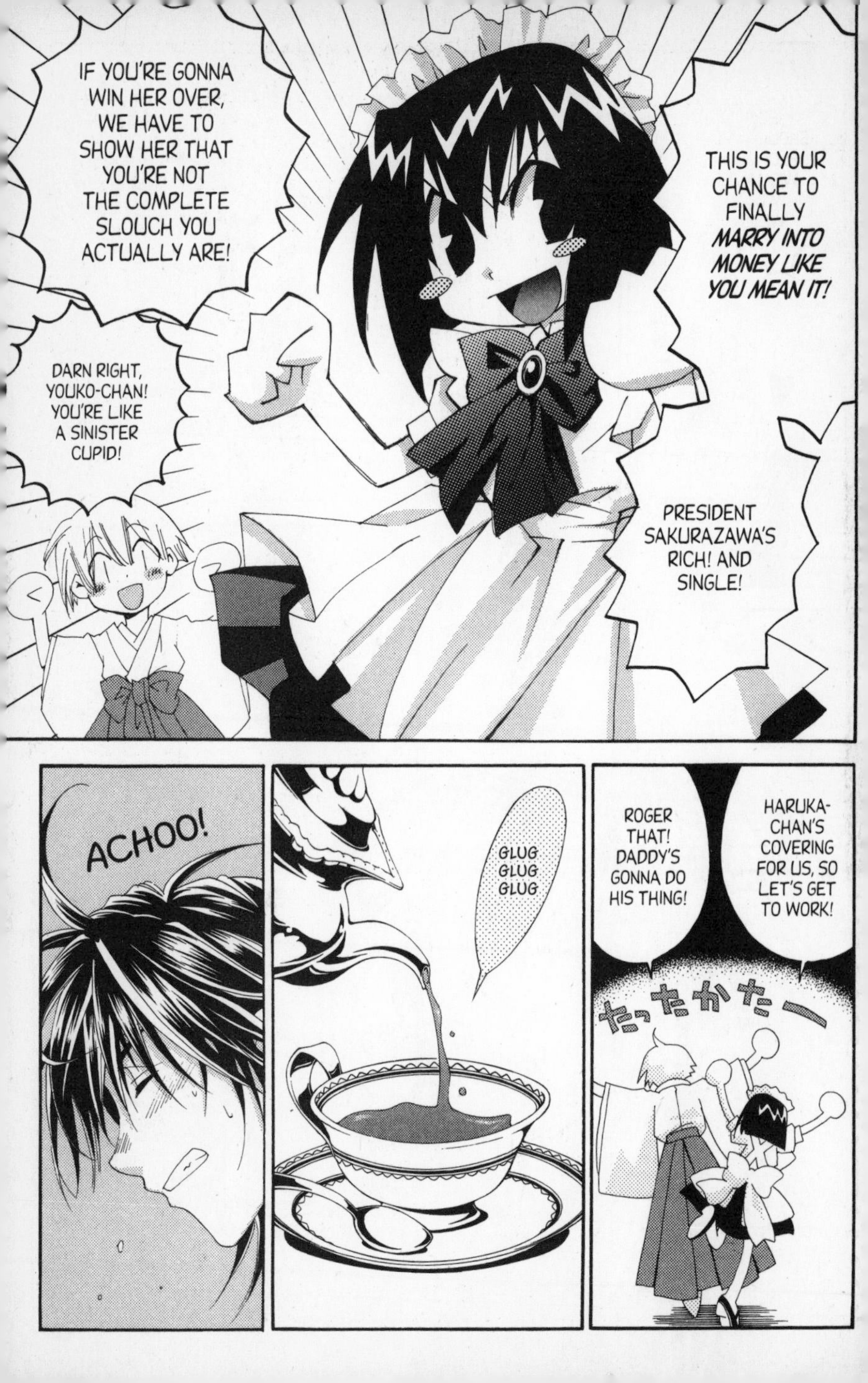

THIS IS YOUR CHANCE TO FINALLY *MARRY INTO MONEY LIKE YOU MEAN IT!*
PRESIDENT SAKURAZAWA'S RICH! AND SINGLE!
IF YOU'RE GONNA WIN HER OVER, WE HAVE TO SHOW HER THAT YOU'RE NOT THE COMPLETE SLOUCH YOU ACTUALLY ARE!
DARN RIGHT, YOUKO-CHAN! YOU'RE LIKE A SINISTER CUPID!
HARUKA-CHAN'S COVERING FOR US, SO LET'S GET TO WORK!
ROGER THAT! DADDY'S GONNA DO HIS THING!
たったかたー
GLUG GLUG GLUG
ACHOO!

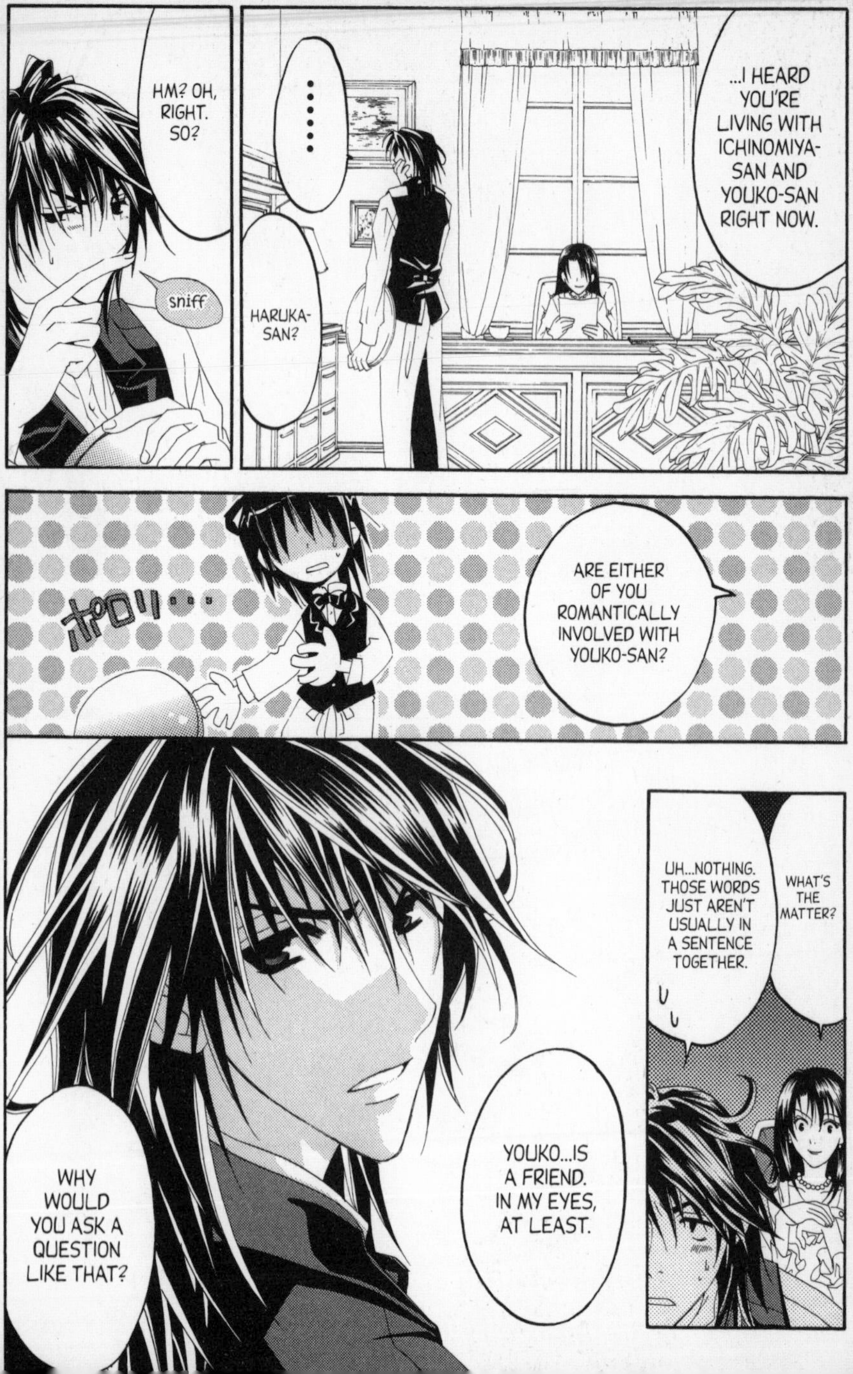
...I HEARD YOU'RE LIVING WITH ICHINOMIYA-SAN AND YOUKO-SAN RIGHT NOW.
......
HARUKA-SAN?
HM? OH, RIGHT. SO?
sniff
ARE EITHER OF YOU ROMANTICALLY INVOLVED WITH YOUKO-SAN?
ポロリ...
WHAT'S THE MATTER?
UH...NOTHING. THOSE WORDS JUST AREN'T USUALLY IN A SENTENCE TOGETHER.
YOUKO...IS A FRIEND. IN MY EYES, AT LEAST.
WHY WOULD YOU ASK A QUESTION LIKE THAT?

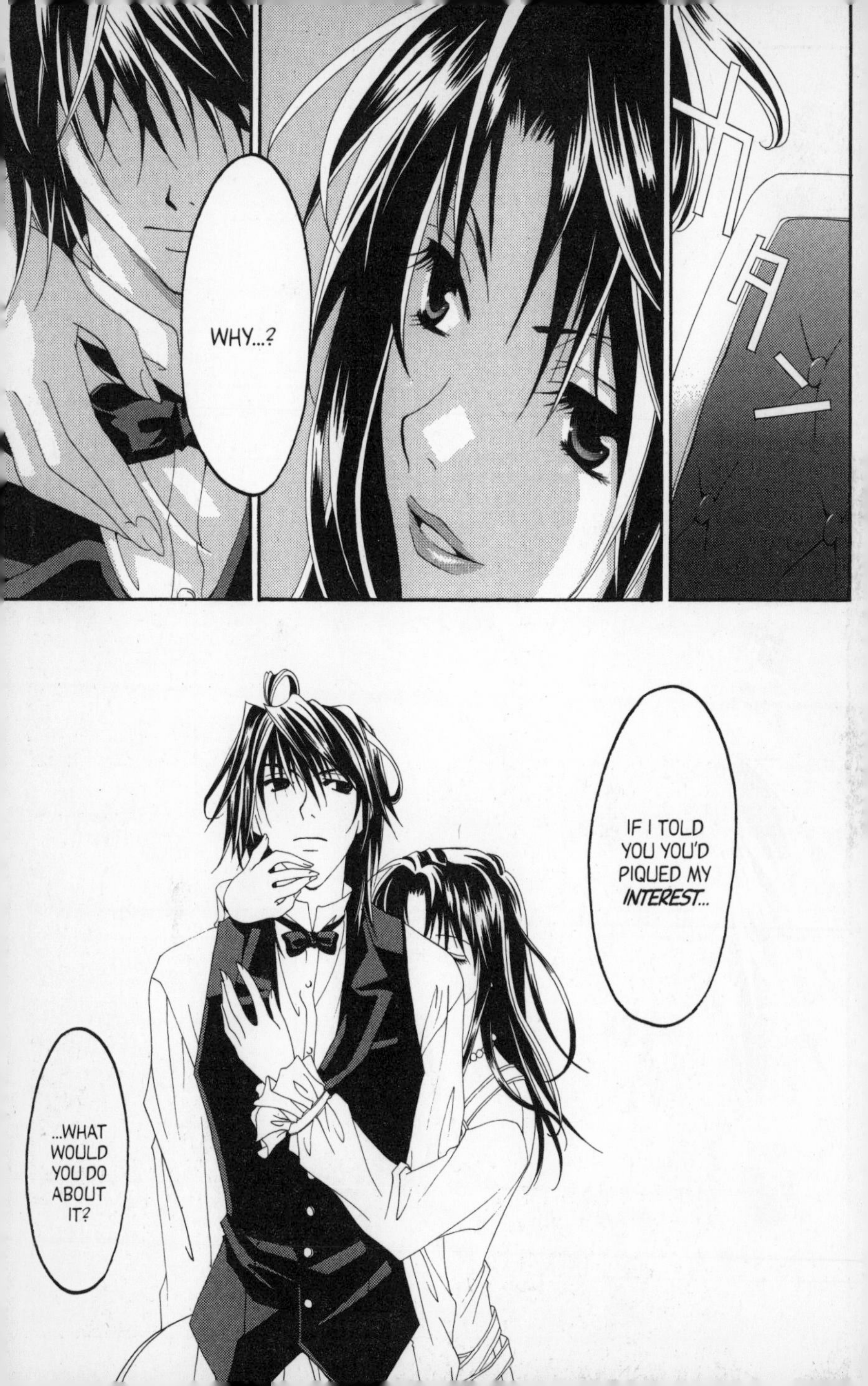
WHY...?
IF I TOLD YOU YOU'D PIQUED MY *INTEREST*...
...WHAT WOULD YOU DO ABOUT IT?

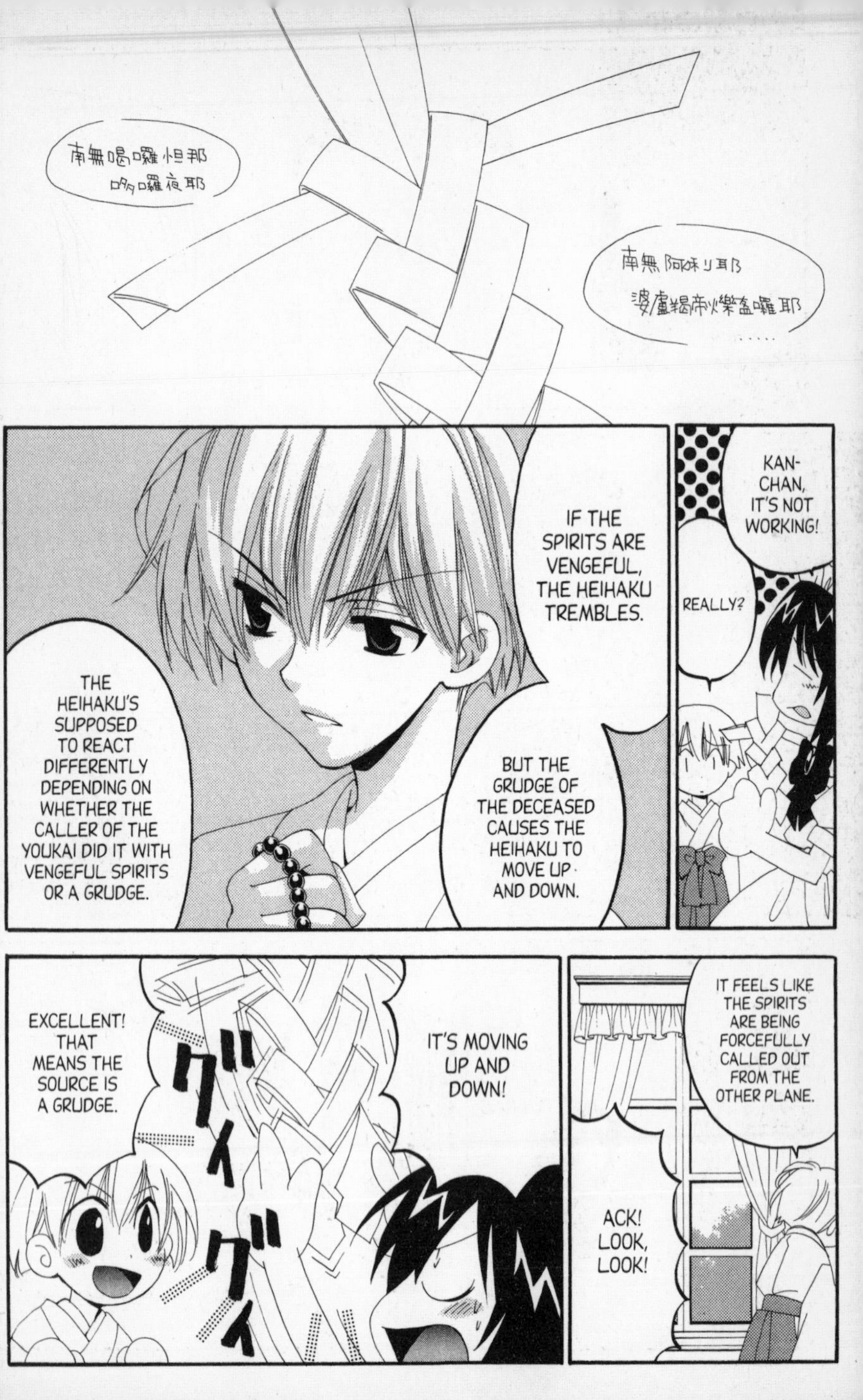

南無喝囉怛那 哆囉夜耶
南無阿唎耶 婆盧羯帝爍鉢囉耶 ……
KAN-CHAN, IT'S NOT WORKING!
REALLY?
IF THE SPIRITS ARE VENGEFUL, THE HEIHAKU TREMBLES.
BUT THE GRUDGE OF THE DECEASED CAUSES THE HEIHAKU TO MOVE UP AND DOWN.
THE HEIHAKU'S SUPPOSED TO REACT DIFFERENTLY DEPENDING ON WHETHER THE CALLER OF THE YOUKAI DID IT WITH VENGEFUL SPIRITS OR A GRUDGE.
IT FEELS LIKE THE SPIRITS ARE BEING FORCEFULLY CALLED OUT FROM THE OTHER PLANE.
ACK! LOOK, LOOK!
IT'S MOVING UP AND DOWN!
グイグイグイ
EXCELLENT! THAT MEANS THE SOURCE IS A GRUDGE.

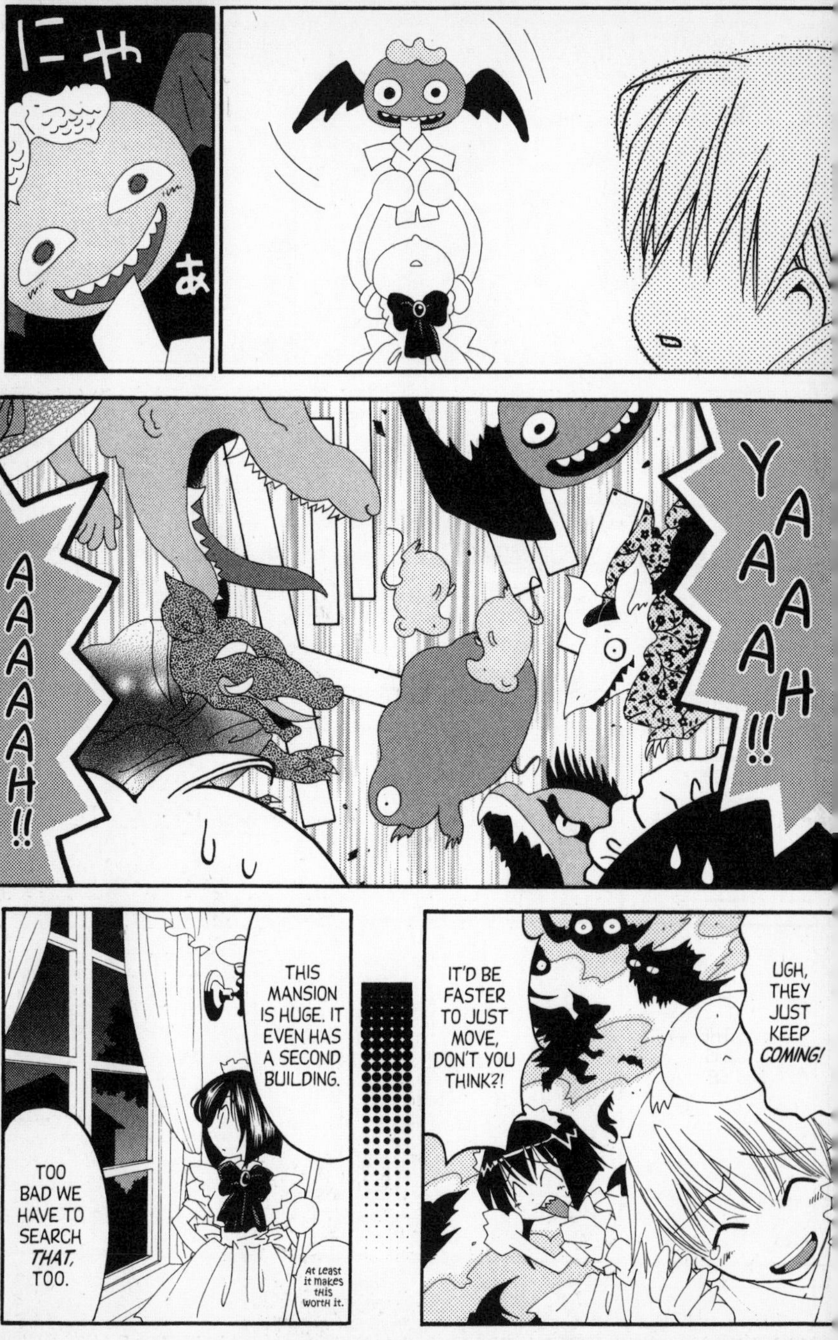
にゃ
あ
YAAAAH!!
AAAAAAH!!
UGH, THEY JUST KEEP COMING!
IT'D BE FASTER TO JUST MOVE, DON'T YOU THINK?!
THIS MANSION IS HUGE. IT EVEN HAS A SECOND BUILDING.
TOO BAD WE HAVE TO SEARCH THAT, TOO.
At least it makes this worth it.

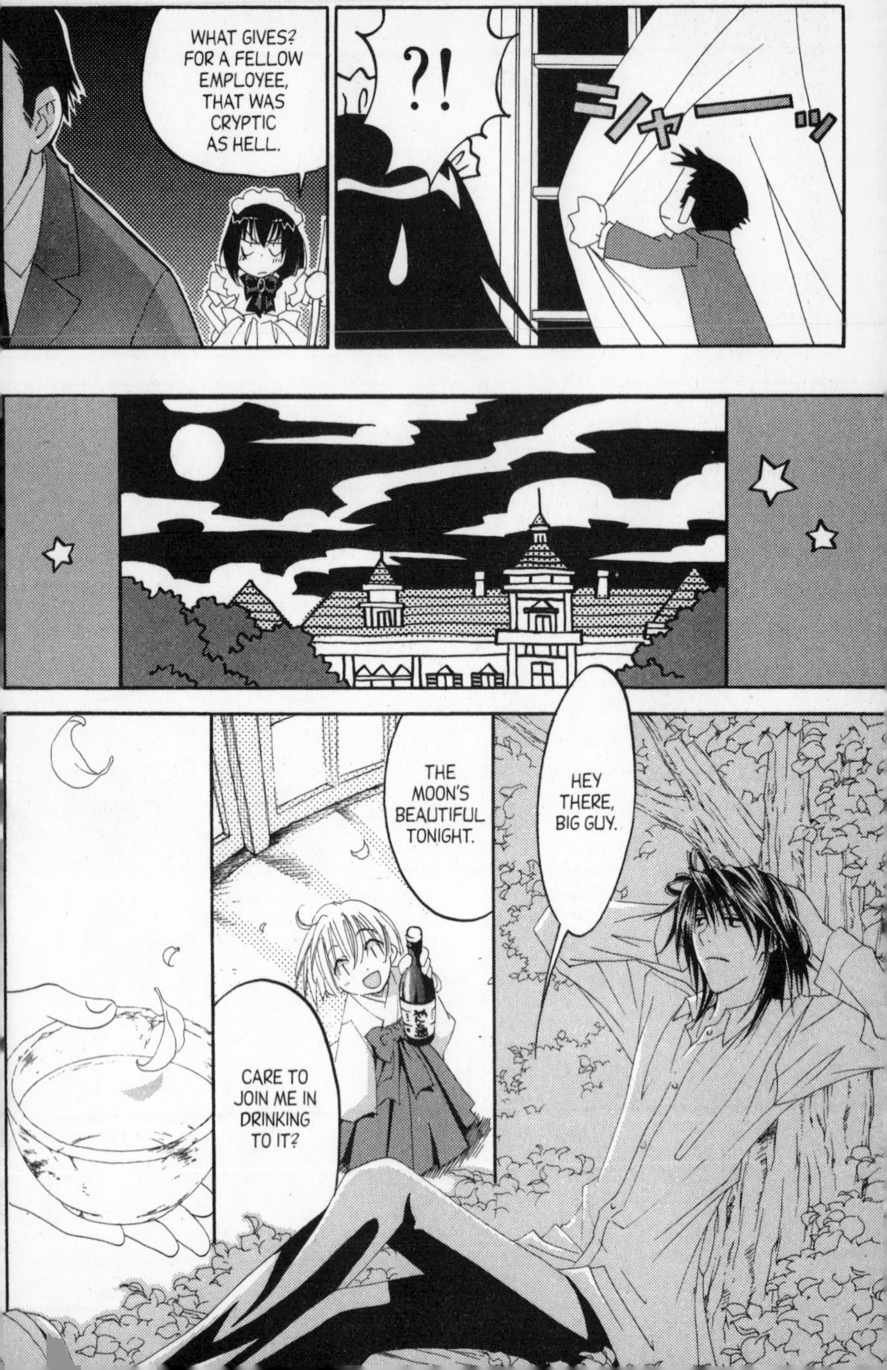
シャーーッ
?!
WHAT GIVES? FOR A FELLOW EMPLOYEE, THAT WAS CRYPTIC AS HELL.
HEY THERE, BIG GUY.
THE MOON'S BEAUTIFUL TONIGHT.
CARE TO JOIN ME IN DRINKING TO IT?

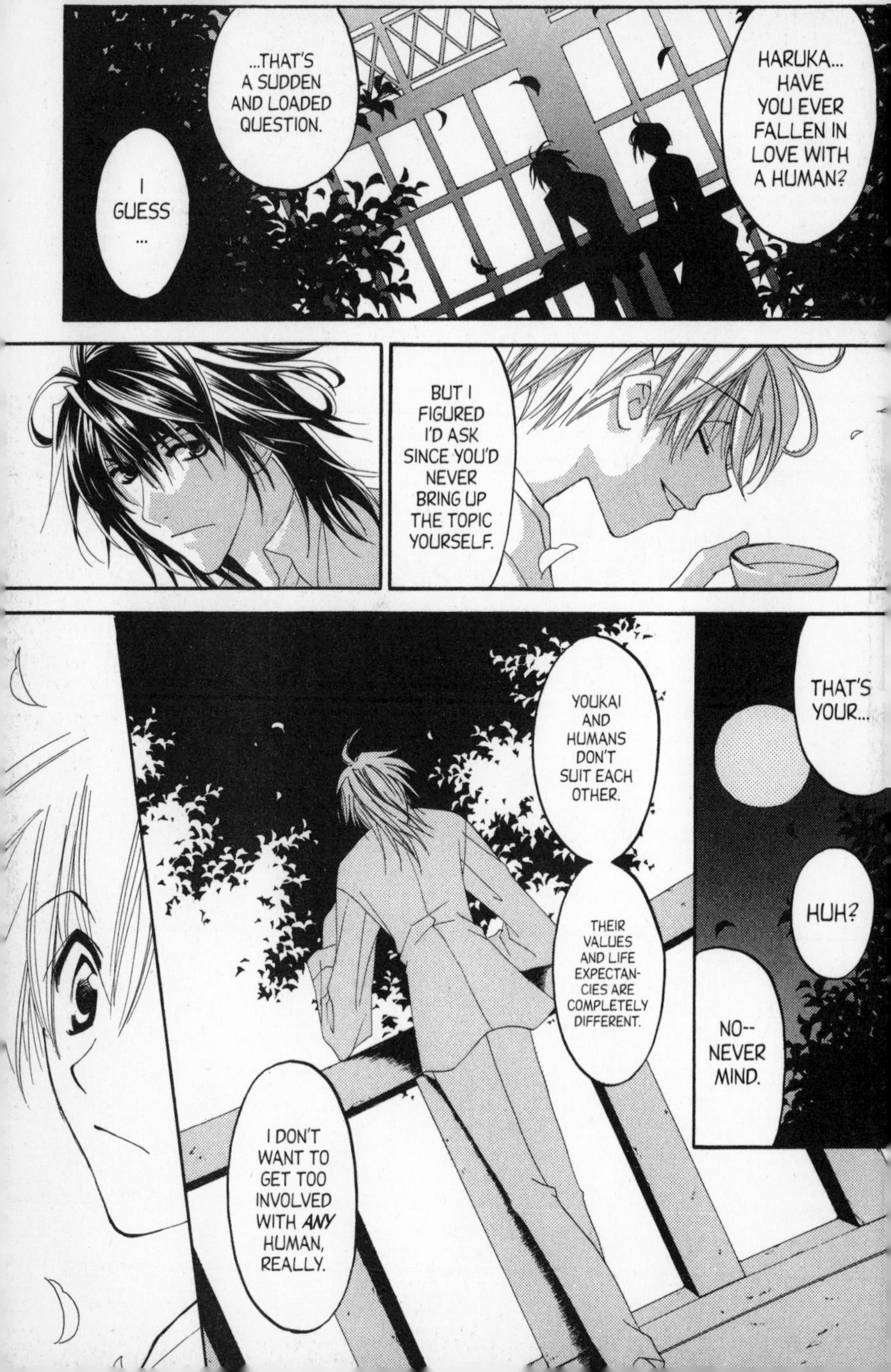
HARUKA... HAVE YOU EVER FALLEN IN LOVE WITH A HUMAN?
...THAT'S A SUDDEN AND LOADED QUESTION.
I GUESS ...
BUT I FIGURED I'D ASK SINCE YOU'D NEVER BRING UP THE TOPIC YOURSELF.
THAT'S YOUR...
HUH?
NO-- NEVER MIND.
YOUKAI AND HUMANS DON'T SUIT EACH OTHER.
THEIR VALUES AND LIFE EXPECTANCIES ARE COMPLETELY DIFFERENT.
I DON'T WANT TO GET TOO INVOLVED WITH *ANY* HUMAN, REALLY.

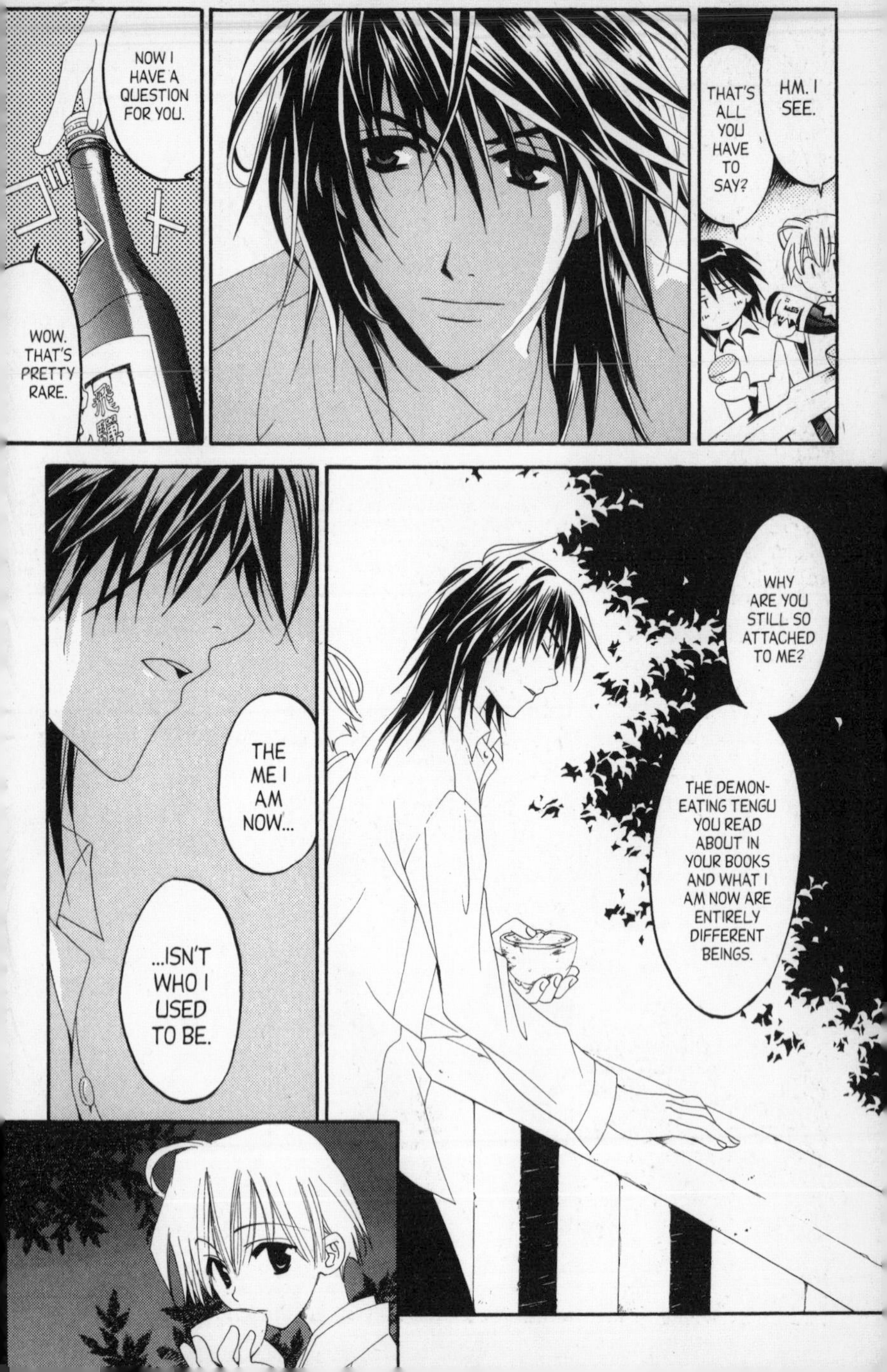
HM. I SEE.
THAT'S ALL YOU HAVE TO SAY?
NOW I HAVE A QUESTION FOR YOU.
ゴト
WOW. THAT'S PRETTY RARE.
WHY ARE YOU STILL SO ATTACHED TO ME?
THE DEMON-EATING TENGU YOU READ ABOUT IN YOUR BOOKS AND WHAT I AM NOW ARE ENTIRELY DIFFERENT BEINGS.
THE ME I AM NOW...
...ISN'T WHO I USED TO BE.

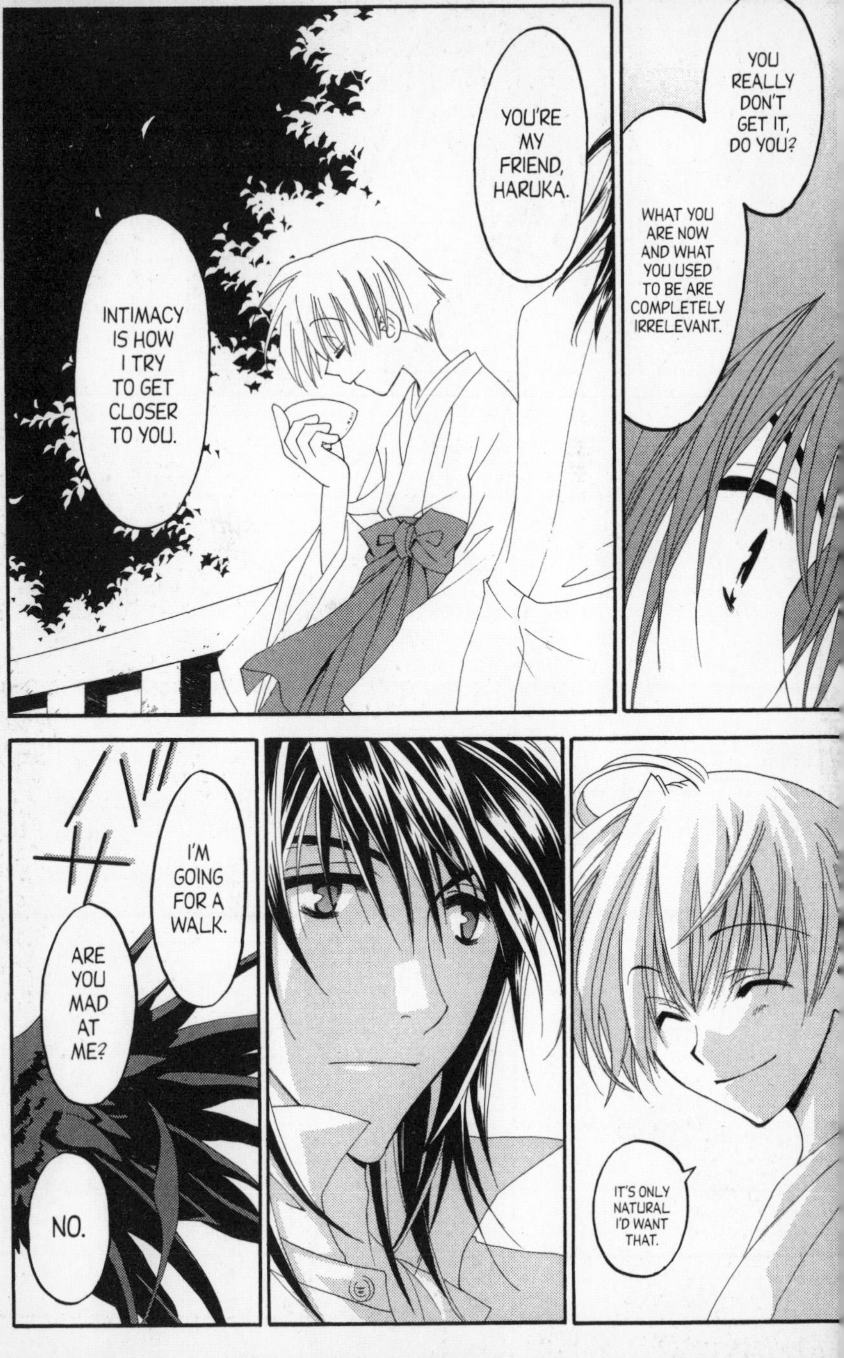
YOU REALLY DON'T GET IT, DO YOU?
WHAT YOU ARE NOW AND WHAT YOU USED TO BE ARE COMPLETELY IRRELEVANT.
YOU'RE MY FRIEND, HARUKA.
INTIMACY IS HOW I TRY TO GET CLOSER TO YOU.
IT'S ONLY NATURAL I'D WANT THAT.
I'M GOING FOR A WALK.
ARE YOU MAD AT ME?
NO.

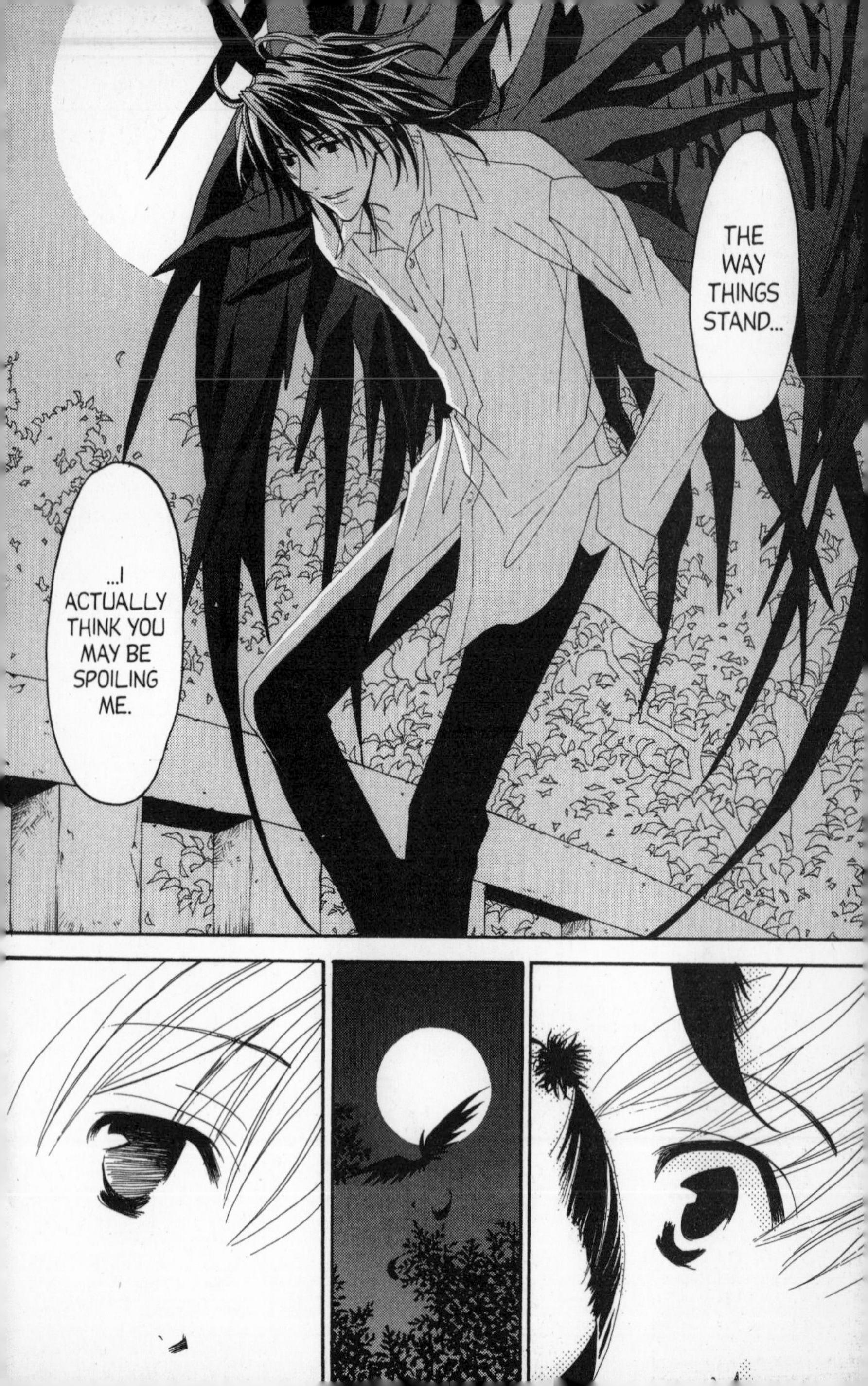
THE WAY THINGS STAND...
...I ACTUALLY THINK YOU MAY BE SPOILING ME.

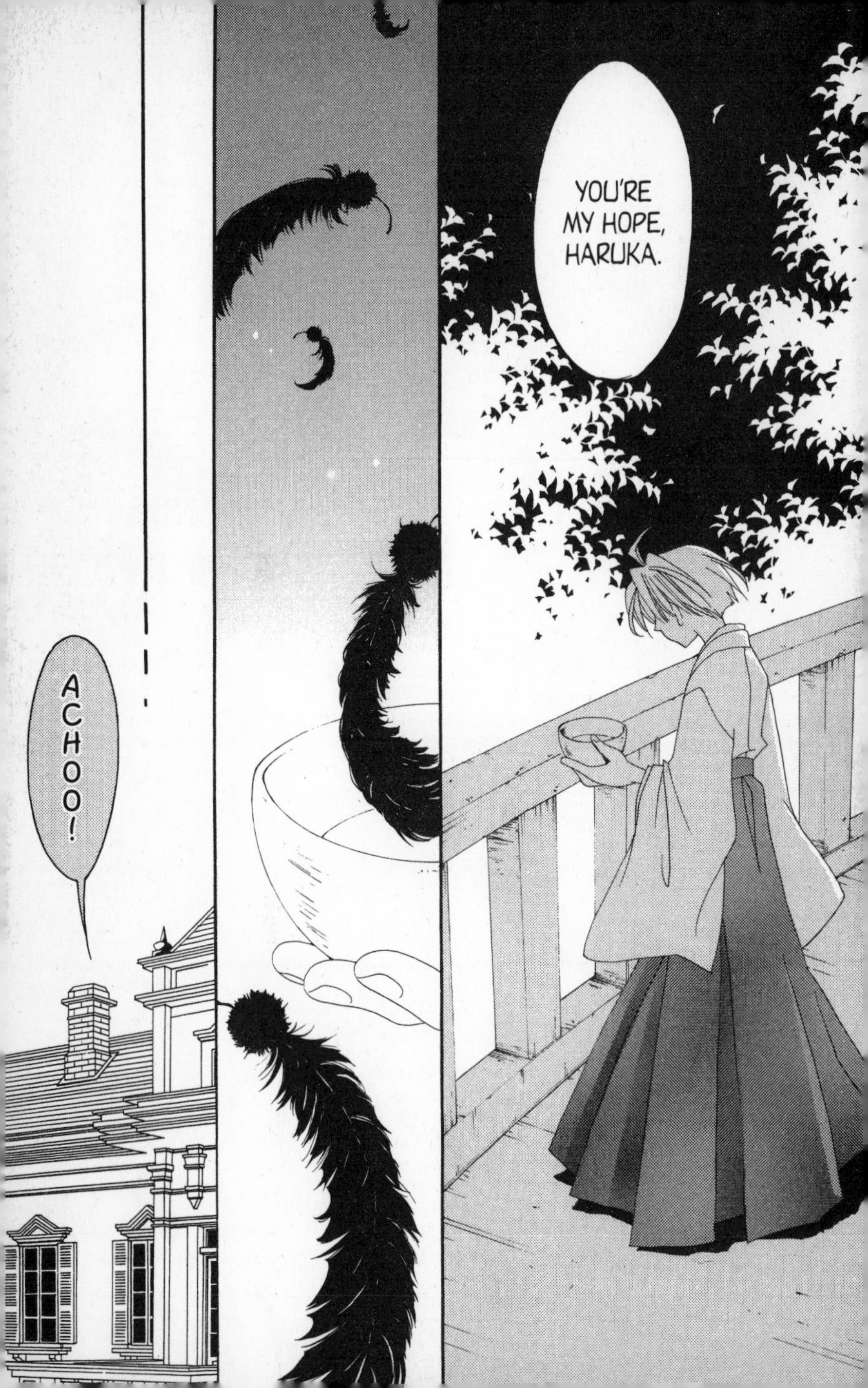
YOU'RE MY HOPE, HARUKA.
ACHOO!

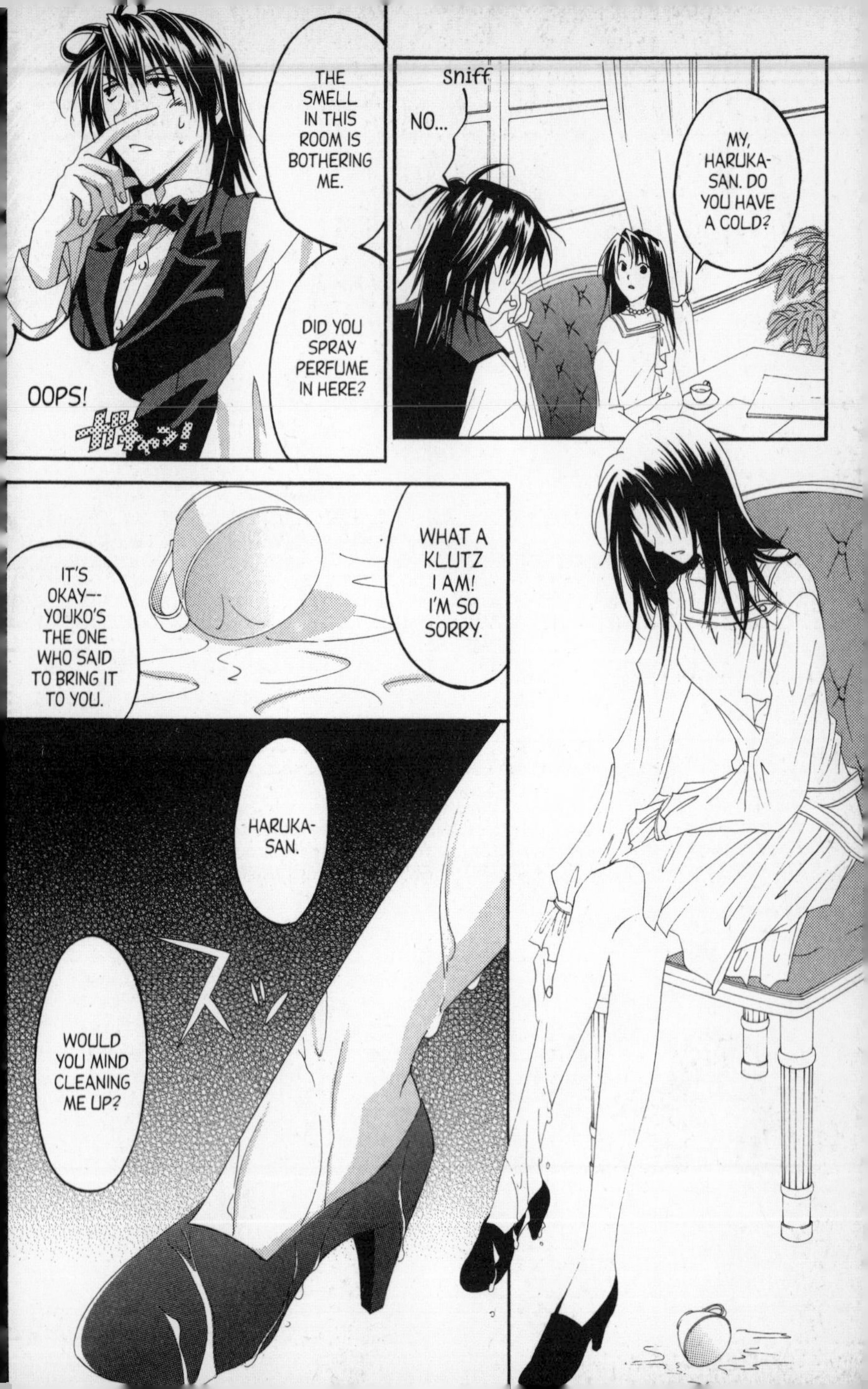
MY, HARUKA-SAN. DO YOU HAVE A COLD?
sniff
NO...
THE SMELL IN THIS ROOM IS BOTHERING ME.
DID YOU SPRAY PERFUME IN HERE?
OOPS!
WHAT A KLUTZ I AM! I'M SO SORRY.
IT'S OKAY--YOUKO'S THE ONE WHO SAID TO BRING IT TO YOU.
HARUKA-SAN.
WOULD YOU MIND CLEANING ME UP?

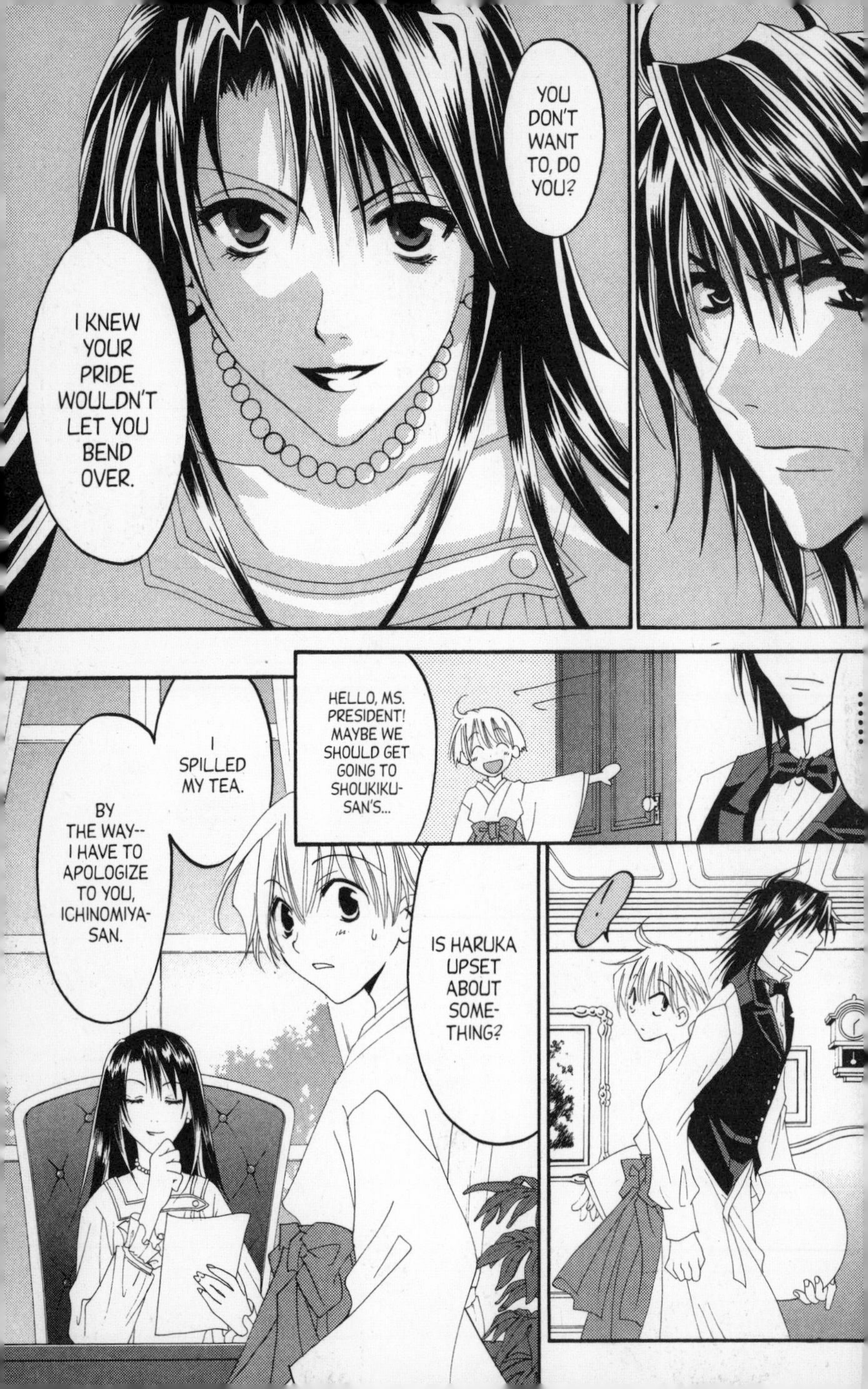
YOU DON'T WANT TO, DO YOU?
I KNEW YOUR PRIDE WOULDN'T LET YOU BEND OVER.
HELLO, MS. PRESIDENT! MAYBE WE SHOULD GET GOING TO SHOUKIKU-SAN'S...
IS HARUKA UPSET ABOUT SOME-THING?
I SPILLED MY TEA.
BY THE WAY-- I HAVE TO APOLOGIZE TO YOU, ICHINOMIYA-SAN.

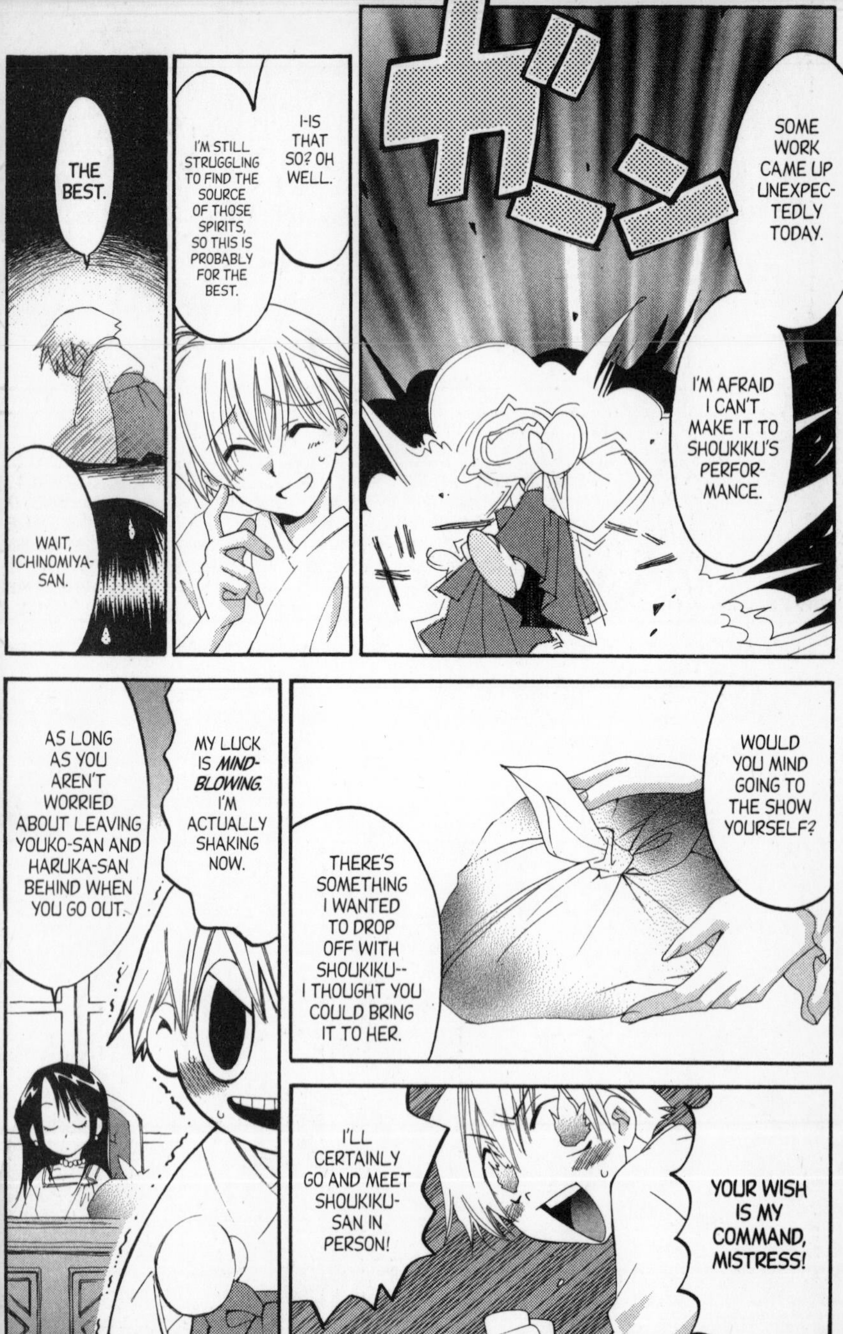
ガーン
SOME WORK CAME UP UNEXPEC-TEDLY TODAY.
I'M AFRAID I CAN'T MAKE IT TO SHOUKIKU'S PERFOR-MANCE.
I-IS THAT SO? OH WELL.
I'M STILL STRUGGLING TO FIND THE SOURCE OF THOSE SPIRITS, SO THIS IS PROBABLY FOR THE BEST.
THE BEST.
WAIT, ICHINOMIYA-SAN.
WOULD YOU MIND GOING TO THE SHOW YOURSELF?
THERE'S SOMETHING I WANTED TO DROP OFF WITH SHOUKIKU-- I THOUGHT YOU COULD BRING IT TO HER.
YOUR WISH IS MY COMMAND, MISTRESS!
I'LL CERTAINLY GO AND MEET SHOUKIKU-SAN IN PERSON!
MY LUCK IS *MIND-BLOWING.* I'M ACTUALLY SHAKING NOW.
AS LONG AS YOU AREN'T WORRIED ABOUT LEAVING YOUKO-SAN AND HARUKA-SAN BEHIND WHEN YOU GO OUT.

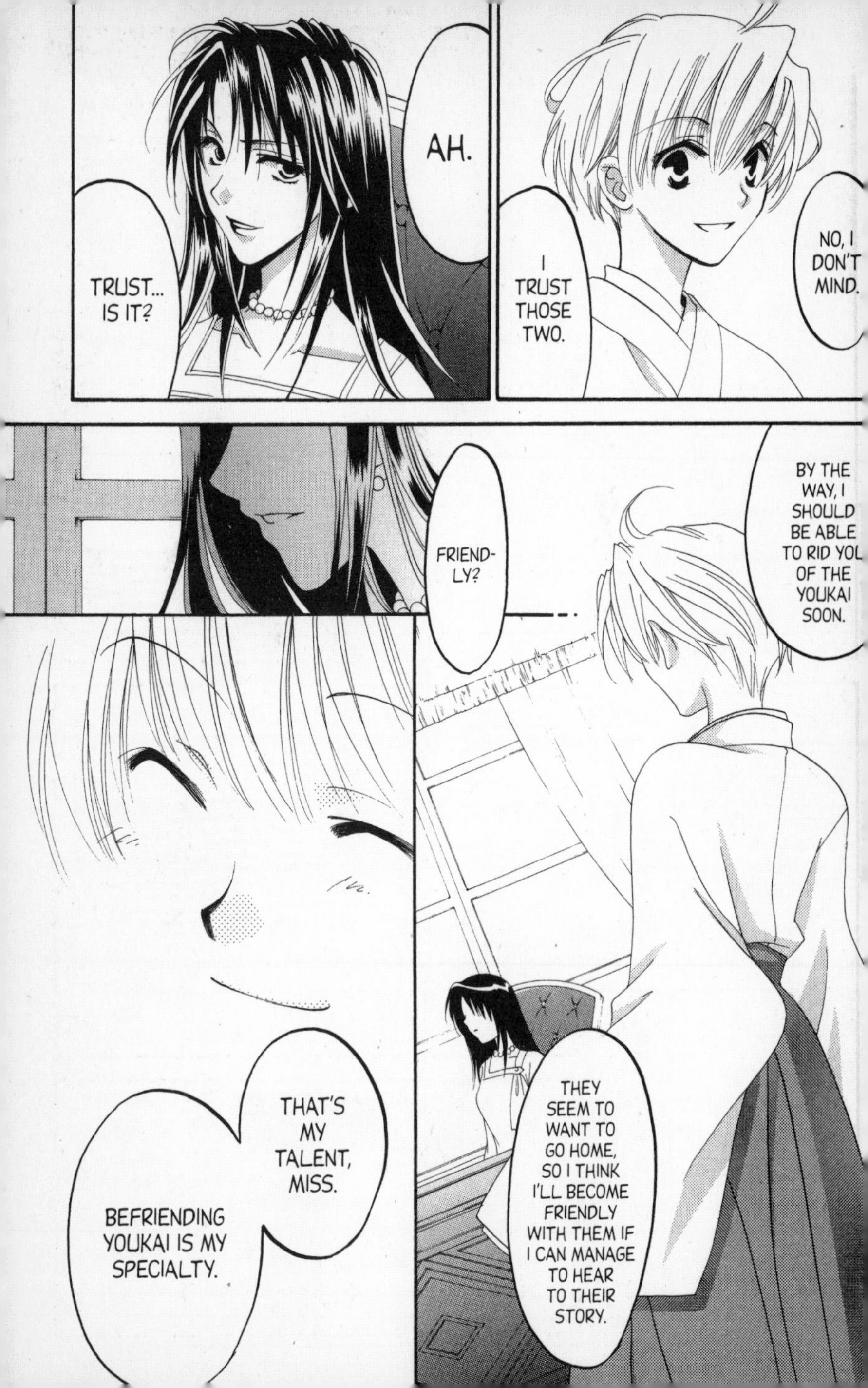
NO, I DON'T MIND.
I TRUST THOSE TWO.
AH.
TRUST... IS IT?
BY THE WAY, I SHOULD BE ABLE TO RID YOU OF THE YOUKAI SOON.
FRIEND-LY?
THEY SEEM TO WANT TO GO HOME, SO I THINK I'LL BECOME FRIENDLY WITH THEM IF I CAN MANAGE TO HEAR TO THEIR STORY.
THAT'S MY TALENT, MISS.
BEFRIENDING YOUKAI IS MY SPECIALTY.

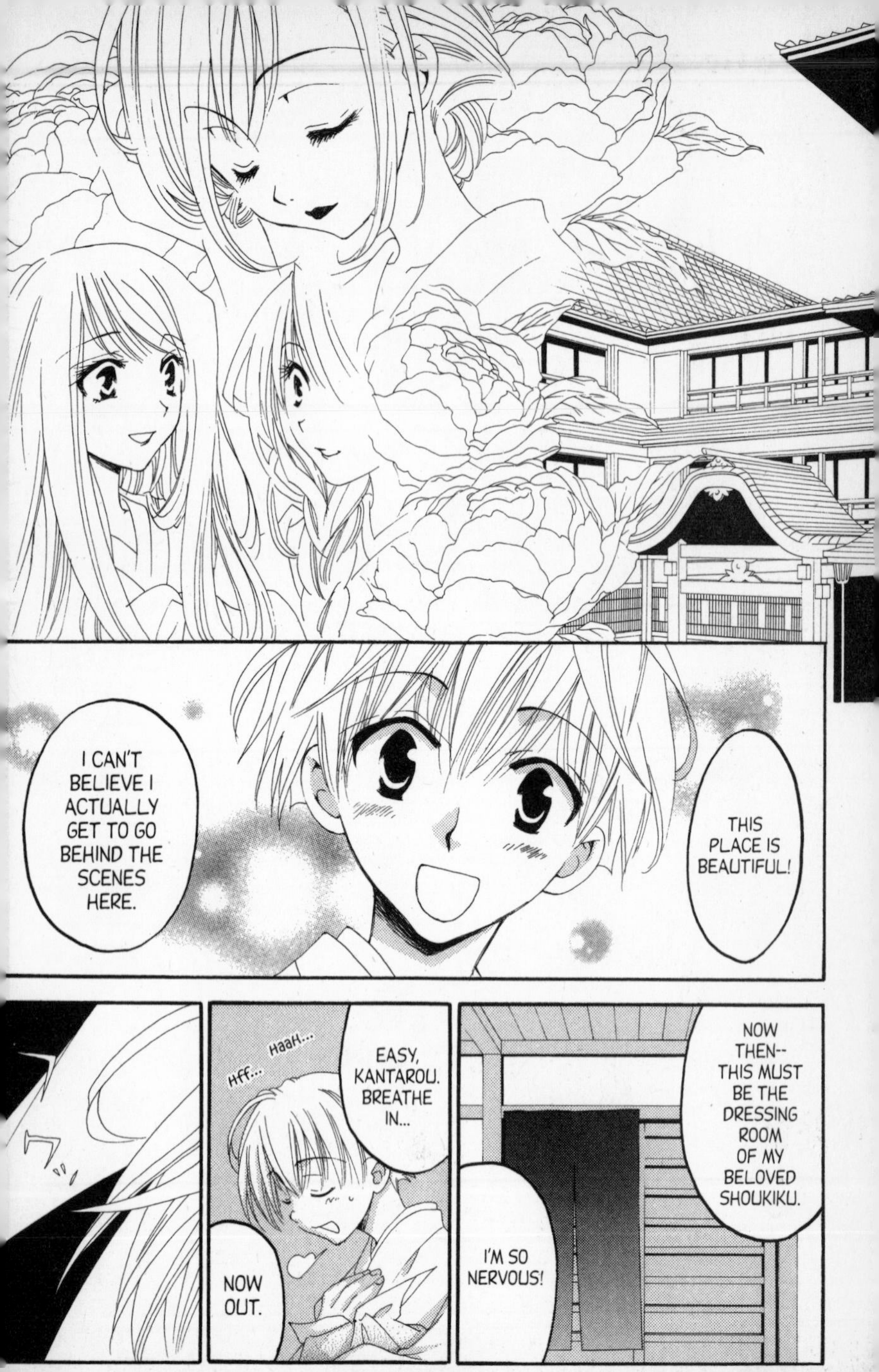
THIS PLACE IS BEAUTIFUL!
I CAN'T BELIEVE I ACTUALLY GET TO GO BEHIND THE SCENES HERE.
NOW THEN-- THIS MUST BE THE DRESSING ROOM OF MY BELOVED SHOUKIKU.
I'M SO NERVOUS!
EASY, KANTAROU. BREATHE IN...
Haah...
Hff...
NOW OUT.

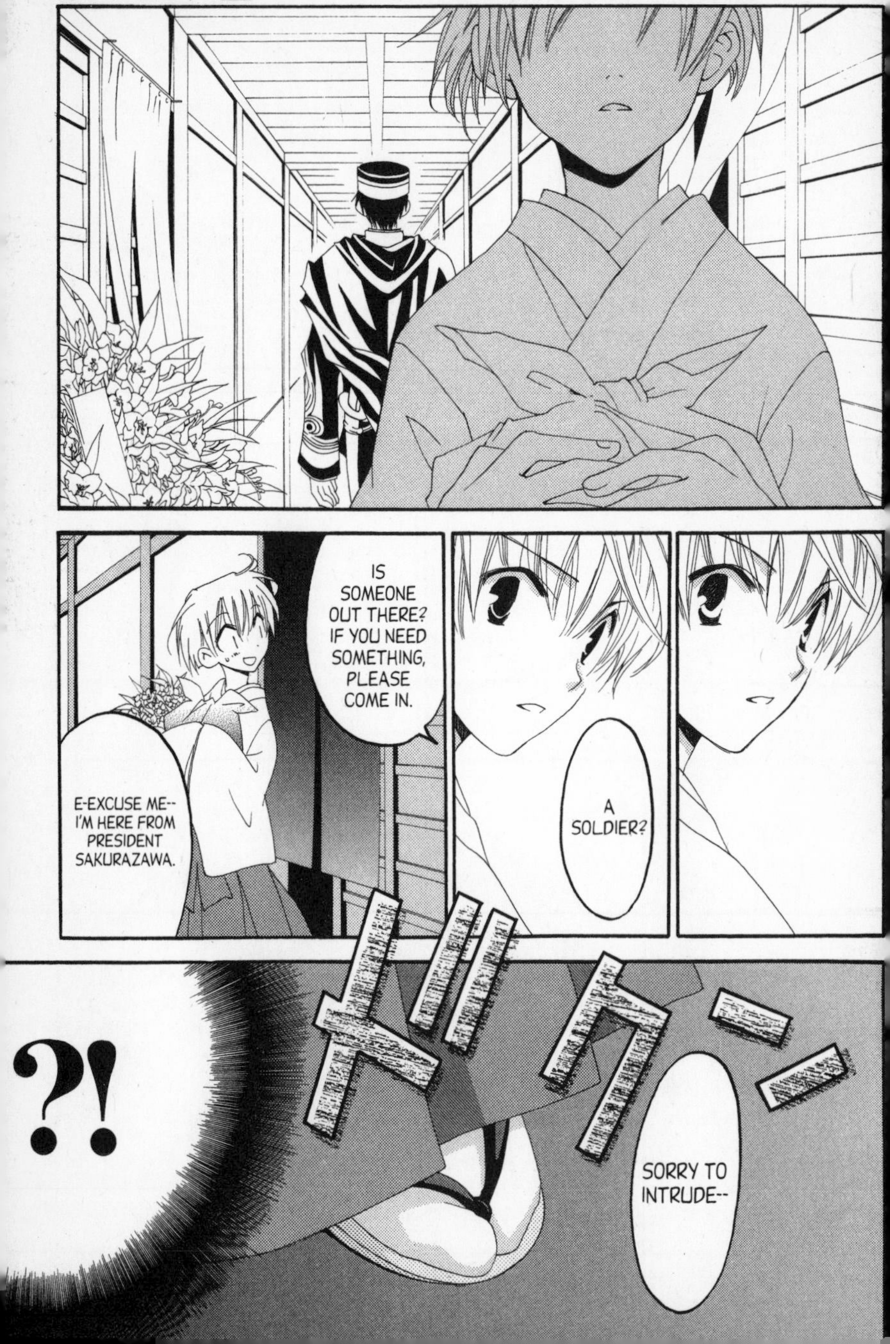
A SOLDIER?
IS SOMEONE OUT THERE? IF YOU NEED SOMETHING, PLEASE COME IN.
E-EXCUSE ME-- I'M HERE FROM PRESIDENT SAKURAZAWA.
SORRY TO INTRUDE--
?!

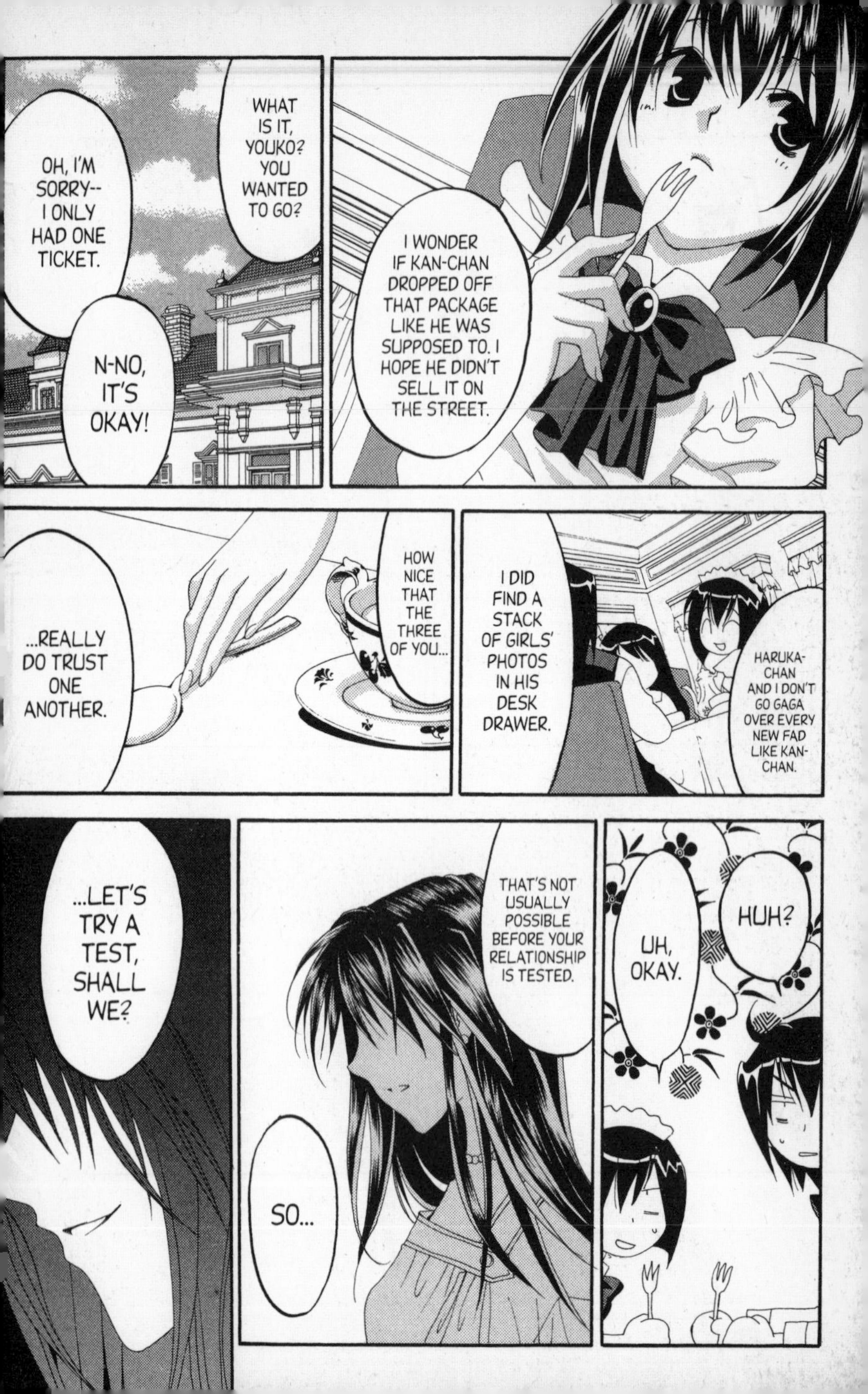
I WONDER IF KAN-CHAN DROPPED OFF THAT PACKAGE LIKE HE WAS SUPPOSED TO. I HOPE HE DIDN'T SELL IT ON THE STREET.
WHAT IS IT, YOUKO? YOU WANTED TO GO?
OH, I'M SORRY-- I ONLY HAD ONE TICKET.
N-NO, IT'S OKAY!
HARUKA-CHAN AND I DON'T GO GAGA OVER EVERY NEW FAD LIKE KAN-CHAN.
I DID FIND A STACK OF GIRLS' PHOTOS IN HIS DESK DRAWER.
HOW NICE THAT THE THREE OF YOU...
...REALLY DO TRUST ONE ANOTHER.
HUH?
UH, OKAY.
THAT'S NOT USUALLY POSSIBLE BEFORE YOUR RELATIONSHIP IS TESTED.
SO...
...LET'S TRY A TEST, SHALL WE?

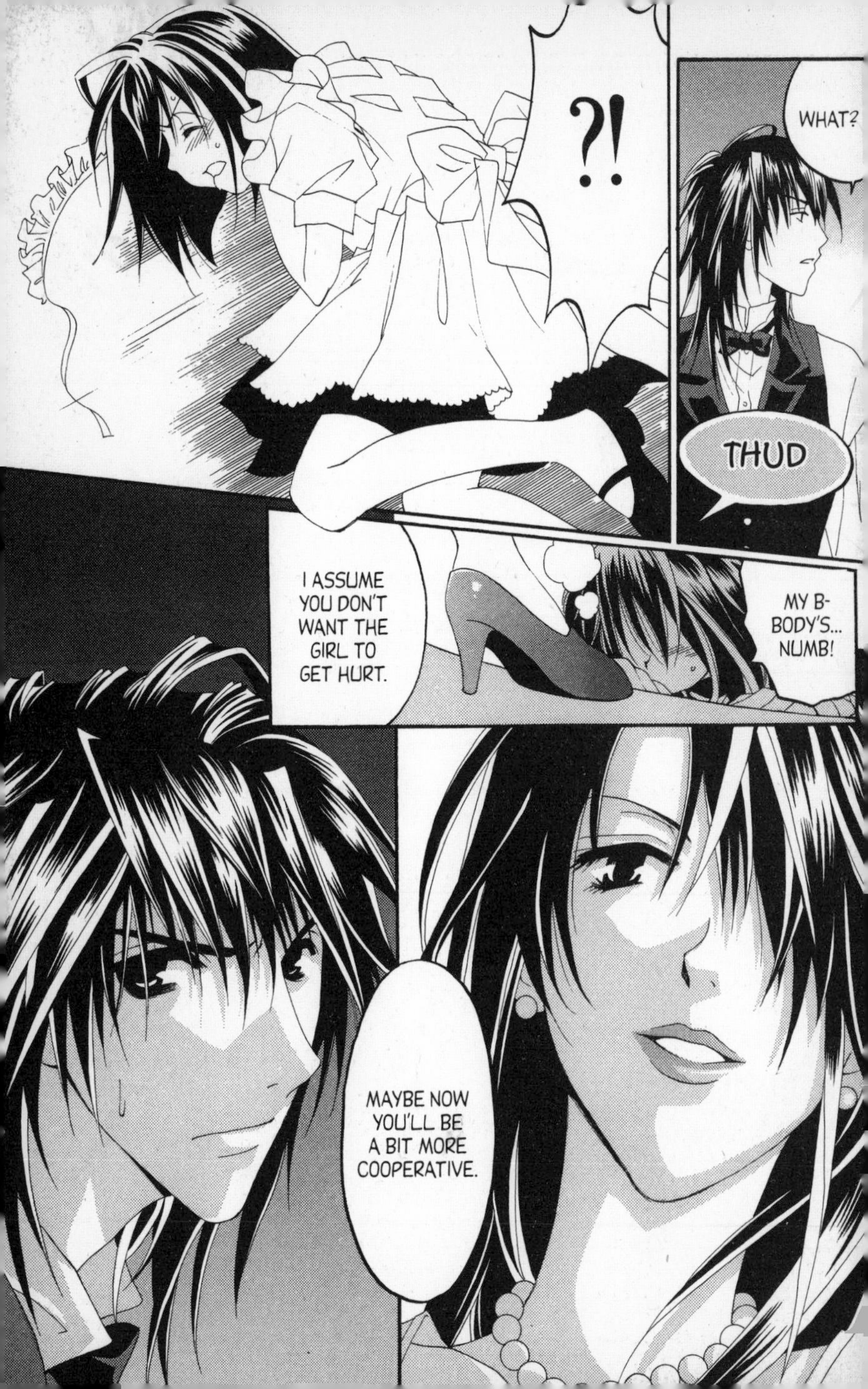
WHAT?
THUD
?!
MY B-BODY'S... NUMB!
I ASSUME YOU DON'T WANT THE GIRL TO GET HURT.
MAYBE NOW YOU'LL BE A BIT MORE COOPERATIVE.

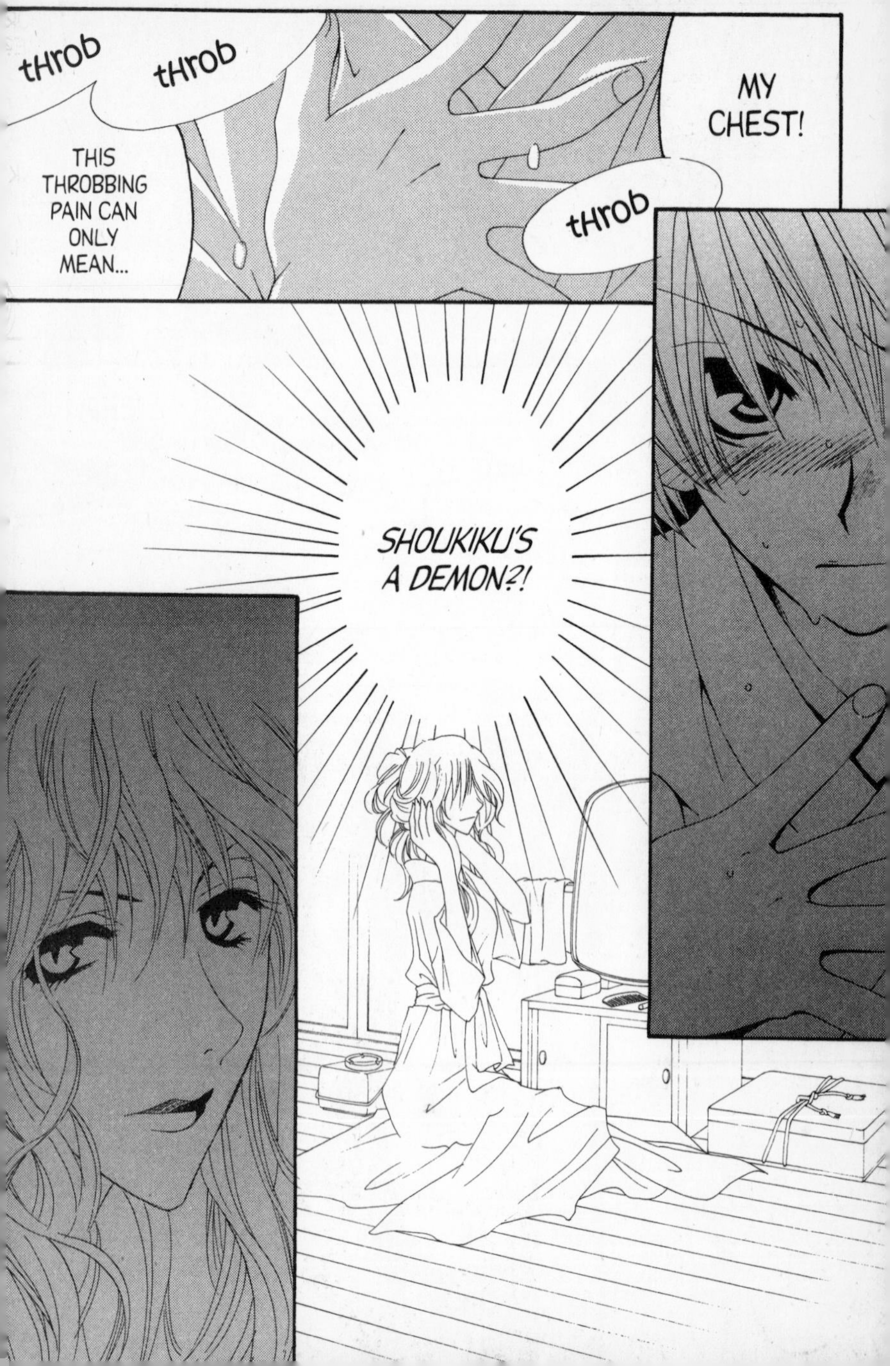
MY CHEST!
tHrob
tHrob
tHrob
THIS THROBBING PAIN CAN ONLY MEAN...
SHOUKIKU'S A DEMON?!

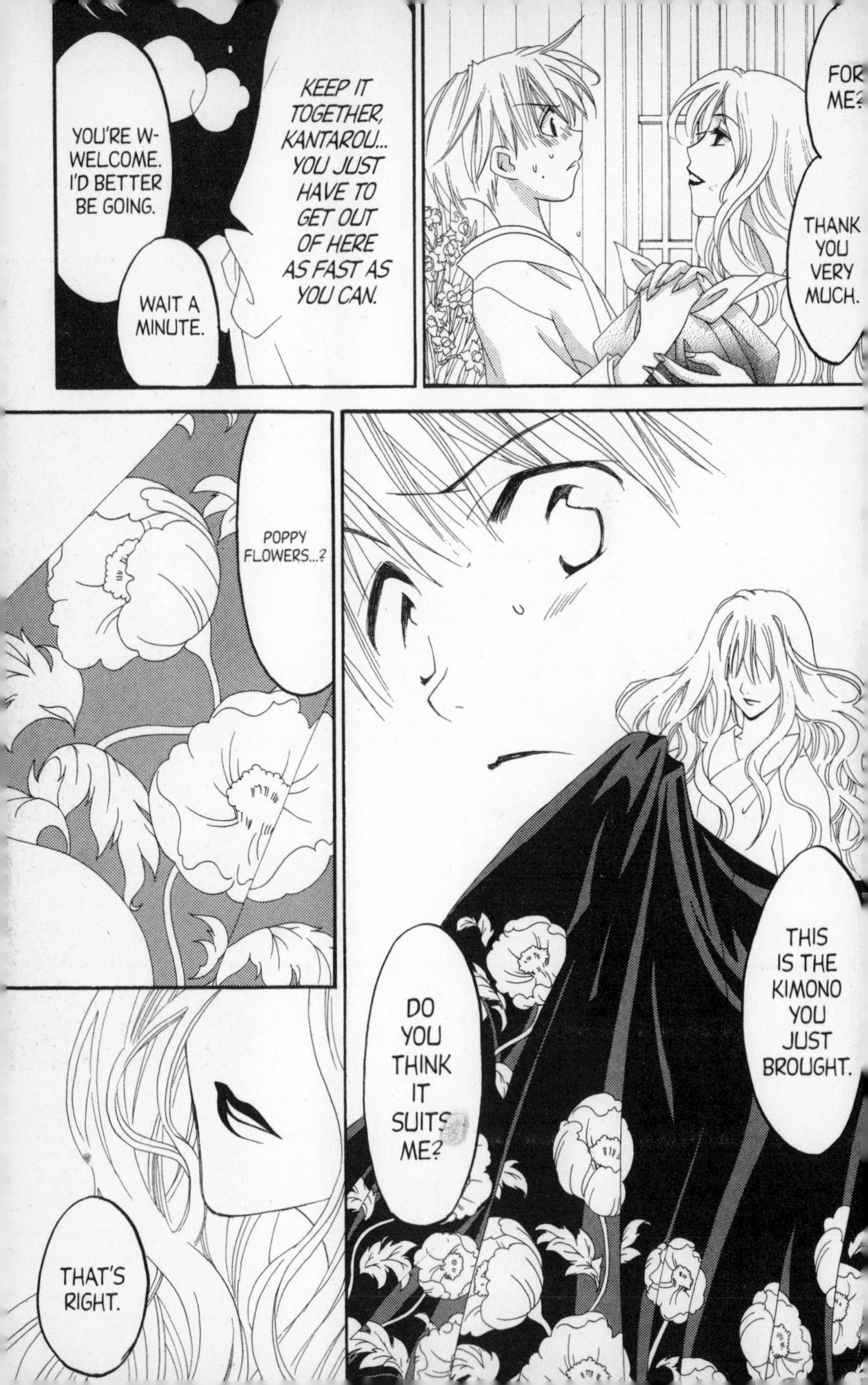
FOR ME?
THANK YOU VERY MUCH.
KEEP IT TOGETHER, KANTAROU... YOU JUST HAVE TO GET OUT OF HERE AS FAST AS YOU CAN.
YOU'RE W-WELCOME. I'D BETTER BE GOING.
WAIT A MINUTE.
THIS IS THE KIMONO YOU JUST BROUGHT.
DO YOU THINK IT SUITS ME?
POPPY FLOWERS...?
THAT'S RIGHT.

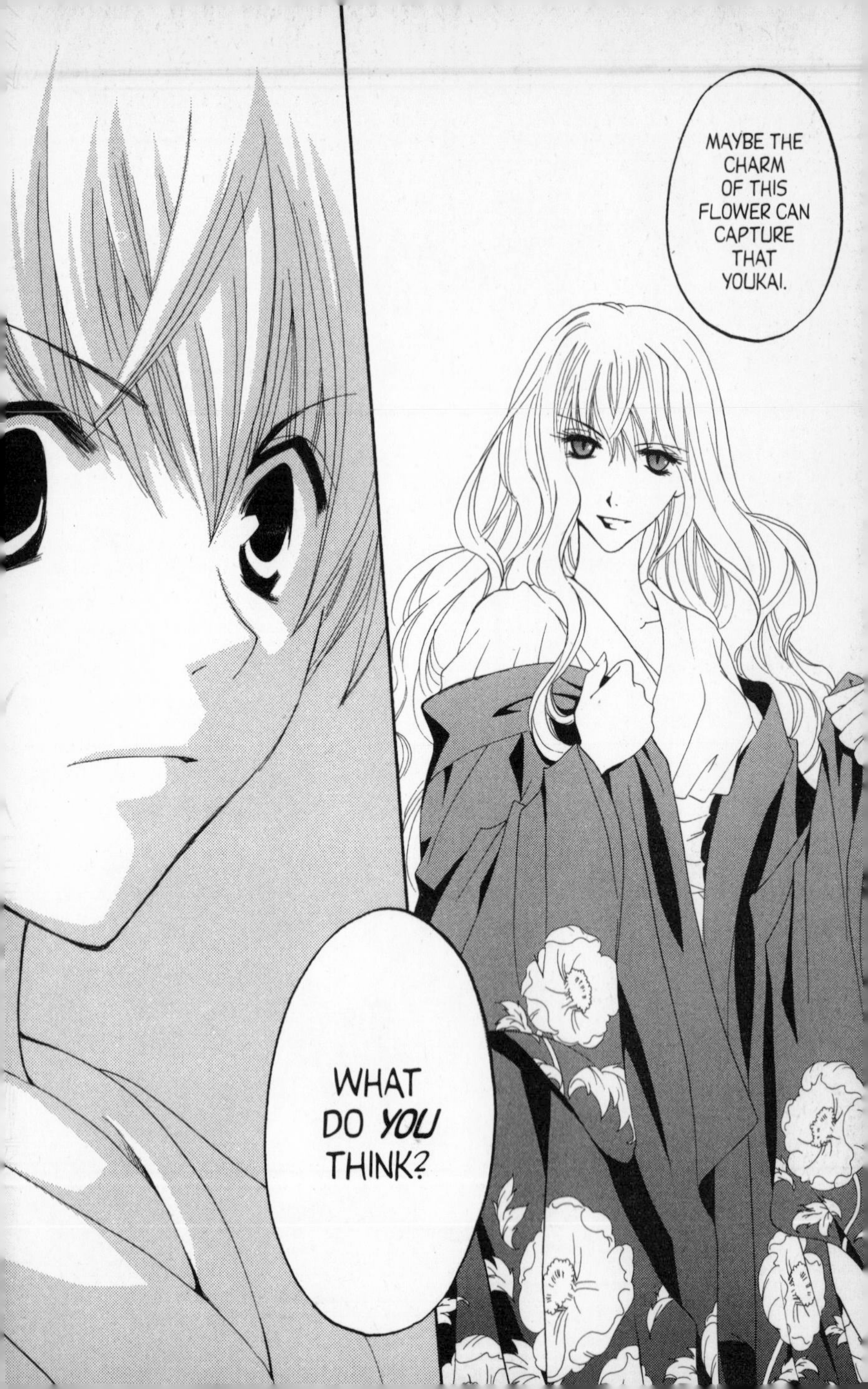
MAYBE THE CHARM OF THIS FLOWER CAN CAPTURE THAT YOUKAI.
WHAT DO *YOU* THINK?

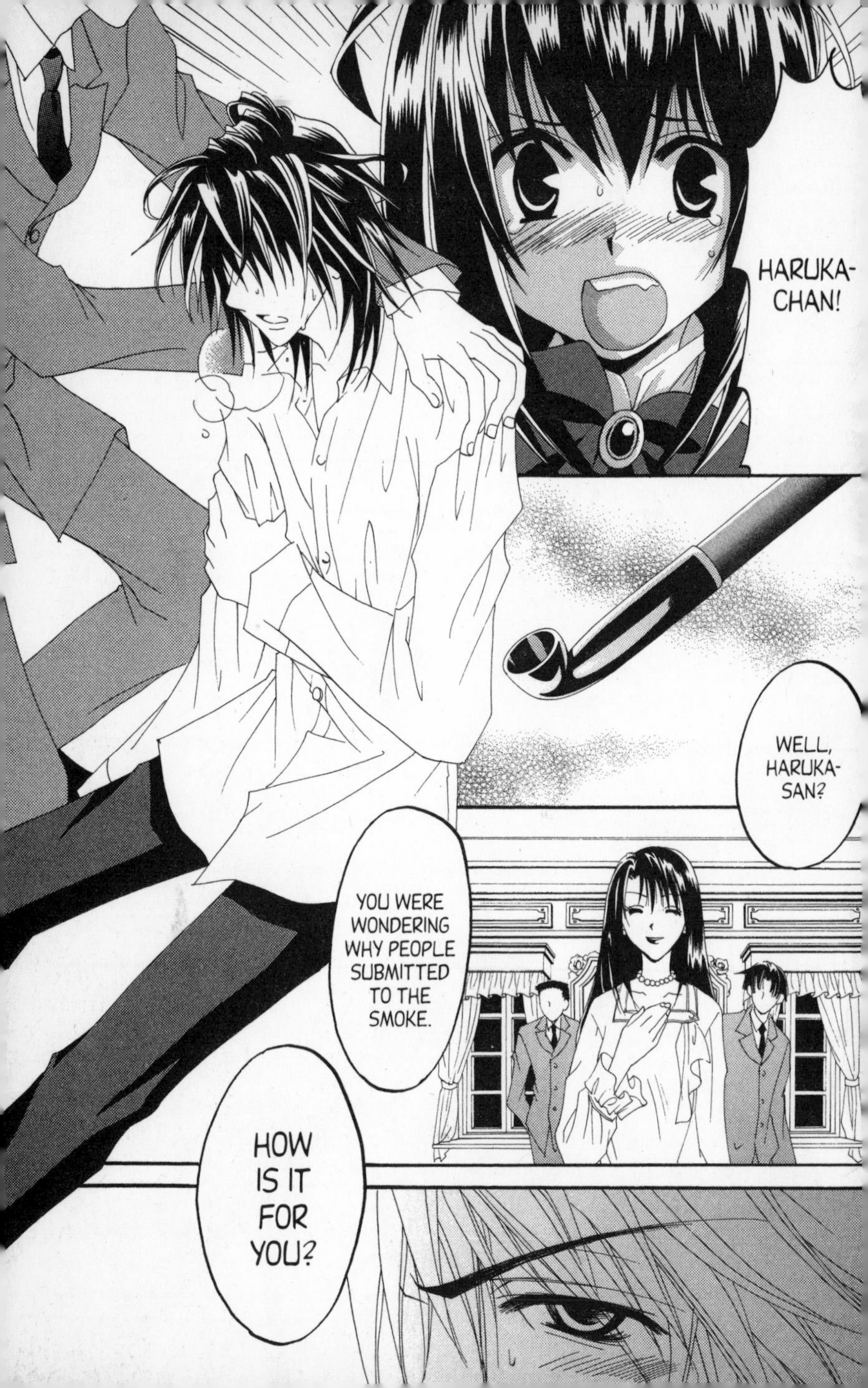
HARUKA-CHAN!
WELL, HARUKA-SAN?
YOU WERE WONDERING WHY PEOPLE SUBMITTED TO THE SMOKE.
HOW IS IT FOR YOU?

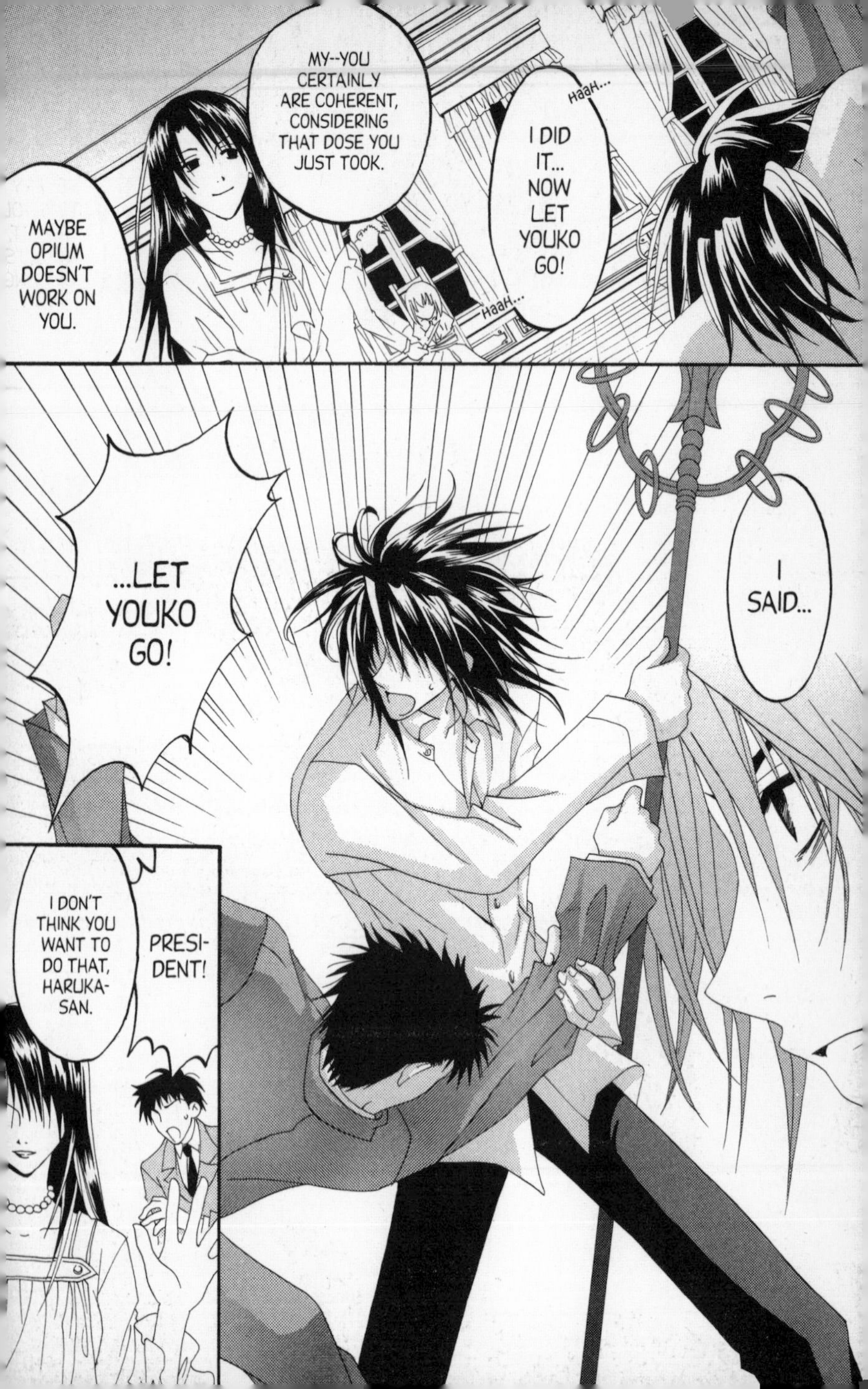
HAAH...
I DID IT... NOW LET YOUKO GO!
HAAH...
MY--YOU CERTAINLY ARE COHERENT, CONSIDERING THAT DOSE YOU JUST TOOK.
MAYBE OPIUM DOESN'T WORK ON YOU.
I SAID...
...LET YOUKO GO!
PRESI-DENT!
I DON'T THINK YOU WANT TO DO THAT, HARUKA-SAN.

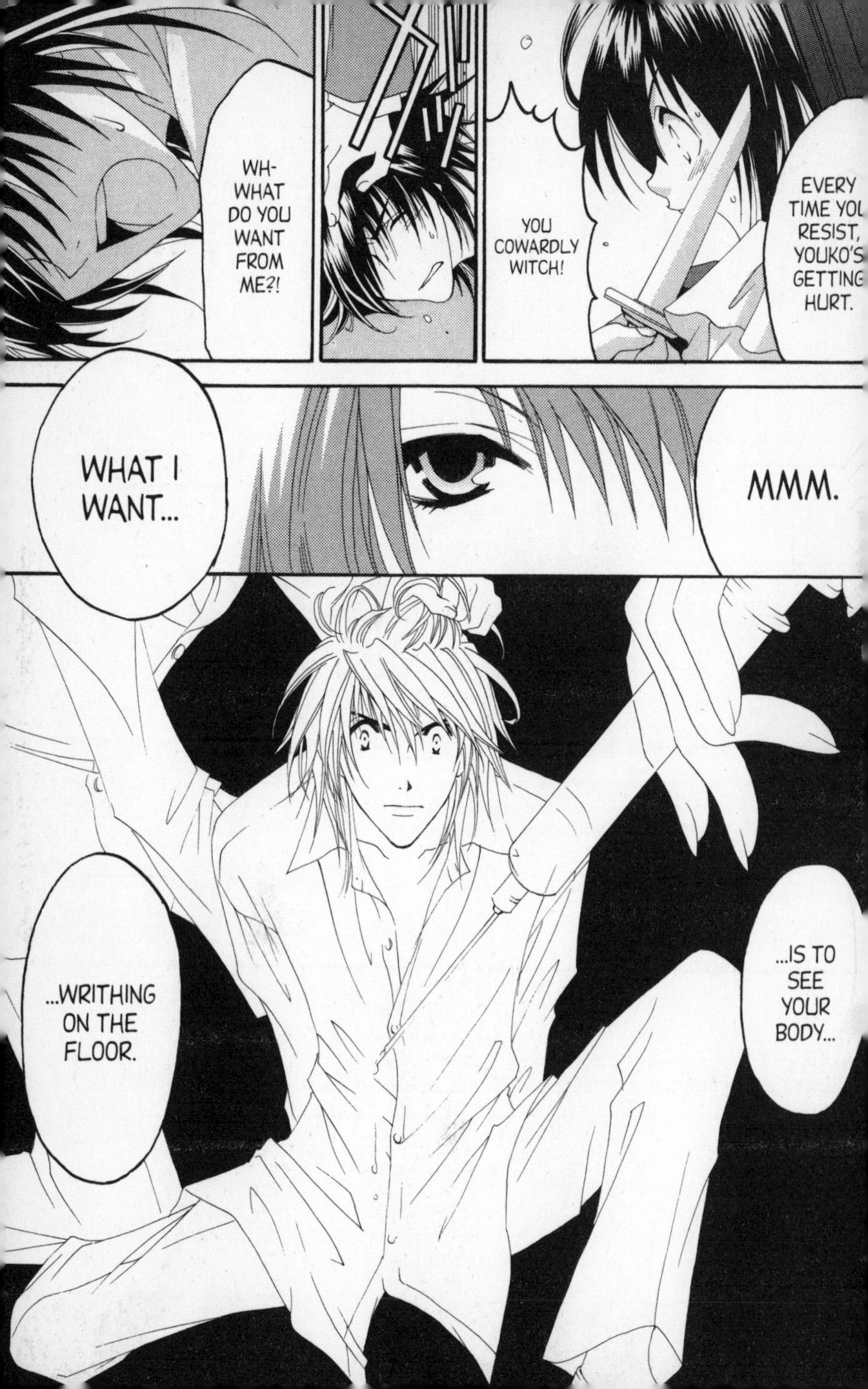
EVERY TIME YOU RESIST, YOUKO'S GETTING HURT.
YOU COWARDLY WITCH!
WH- WHAT DO YOU WANT FROM ME?!
MMM.
WHAT I WANT...
...IS TO SEE YOUR BODY...
...WRITHING ON THE FLOOR.

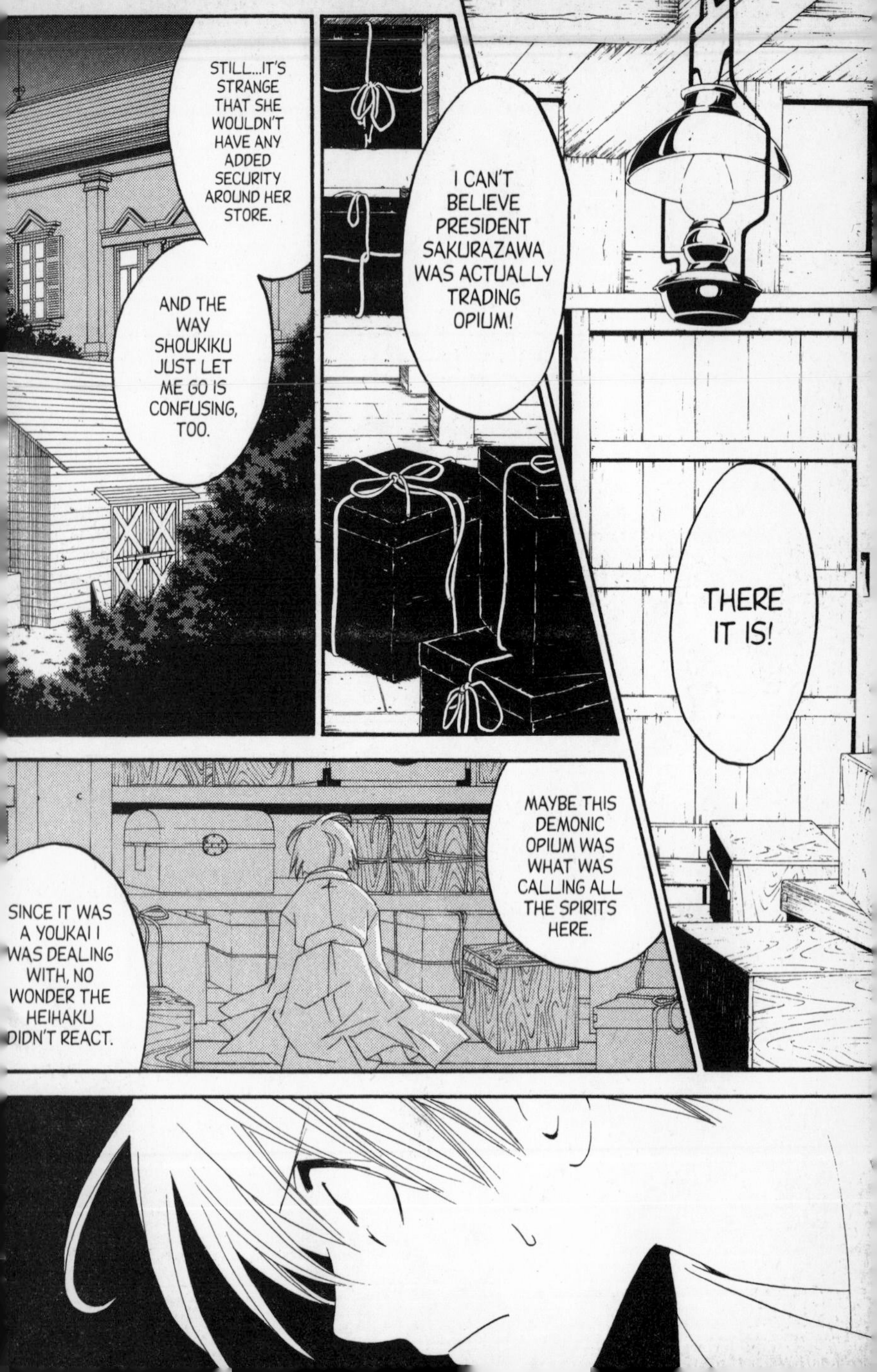
THERE IT IS!
I CAN'T BELIEVE PRESIDENT SAKURAZAWA WAS ACTUALLY TRADING OPIUM!
STILL...IT'S STRANGE THAT SHE WOULDN'T HAVE ANY ADDED SECURITY AROUND HER STORE.
AND THE WAY SHOUKIKU JUST LET ME GO IS CONFUSING, TOO.
MAYBE THIS DEMONIC OPIUM WAS WHAT WAS CALLING ALL THE SPIRITS HERE.
SINCE IT WAS A YOUKAI I WAS DEALING WITH, NO WONDER THE HEIHAKU DIDN'T REACT.

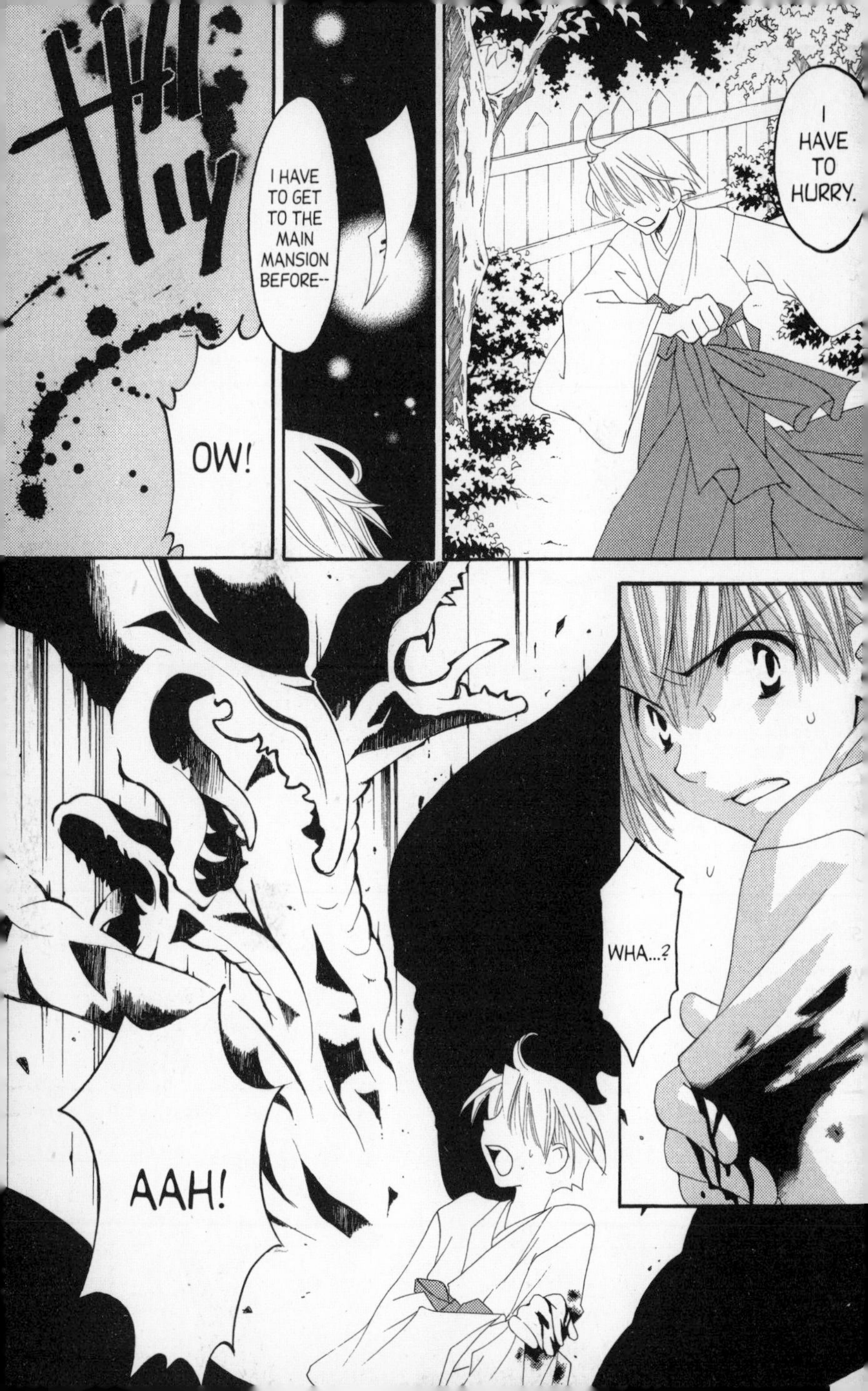
I HAVE TO HURRY.
I HAVE TO GET TO THE MAIN MANSION BEFORE--
OW!
WHA...?
AAH!

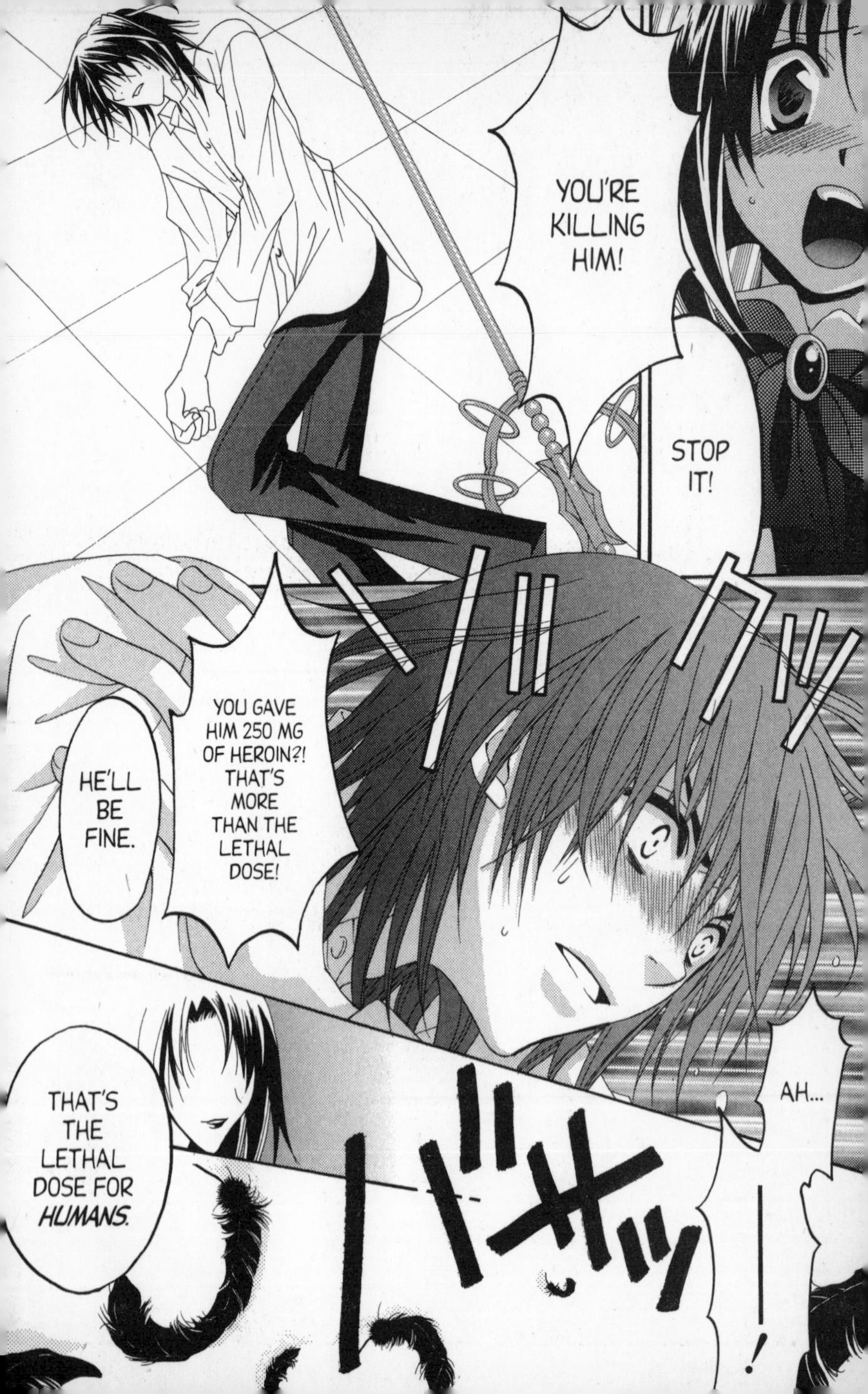
YOU'RE KILLING HIM!
STOP IT!
カッ
YOU GAVE HIM 250 MG OF HEROIN?! THAT'S MORE THAN THE LETHAL DOSE!
HE'LL BE FINE.
AH...
THAT'S THE LETHAL DOSE FOR *HUMANS*.
ドサッ
!

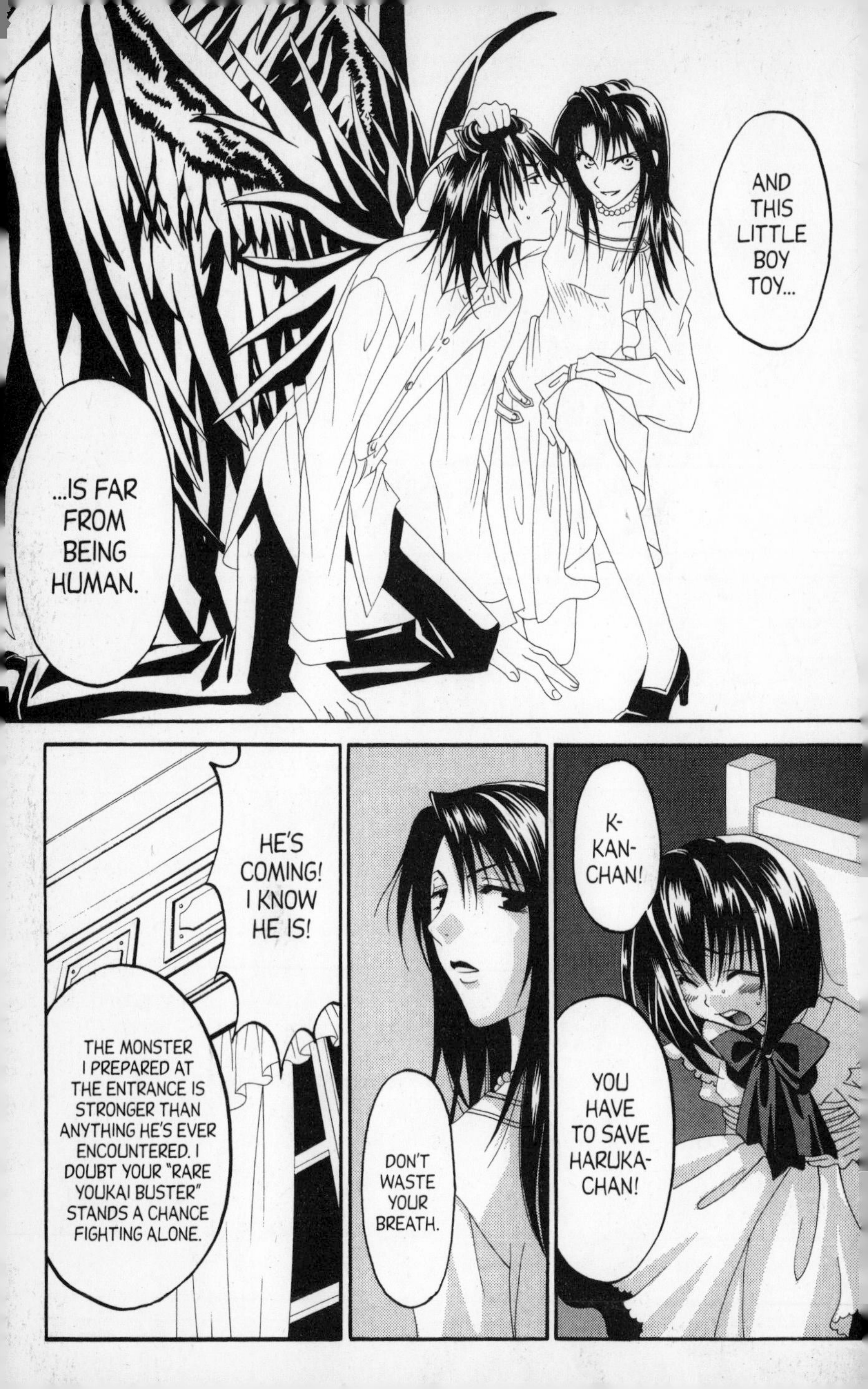
AND THIS LITTLE BOY TOY...
...IS FAR FROM BEING HUMAN.
K-KAN-CHAN!
YOU HAVE TO SAVE HARUKA-CHAN!
DON'T WASTE YOUR BREATH.
HE'S COMING! I KNOW HE IS!
THE MONSTER I PREPARED AT THE ENTRANCE IS STRONGER THAN ANYTHING HE'S EVER ENCOUNTERED. I DOUBT YOUR "RARE YOUKAI BUSTER" STANDS A CHANCE FIGHTING ALONE.

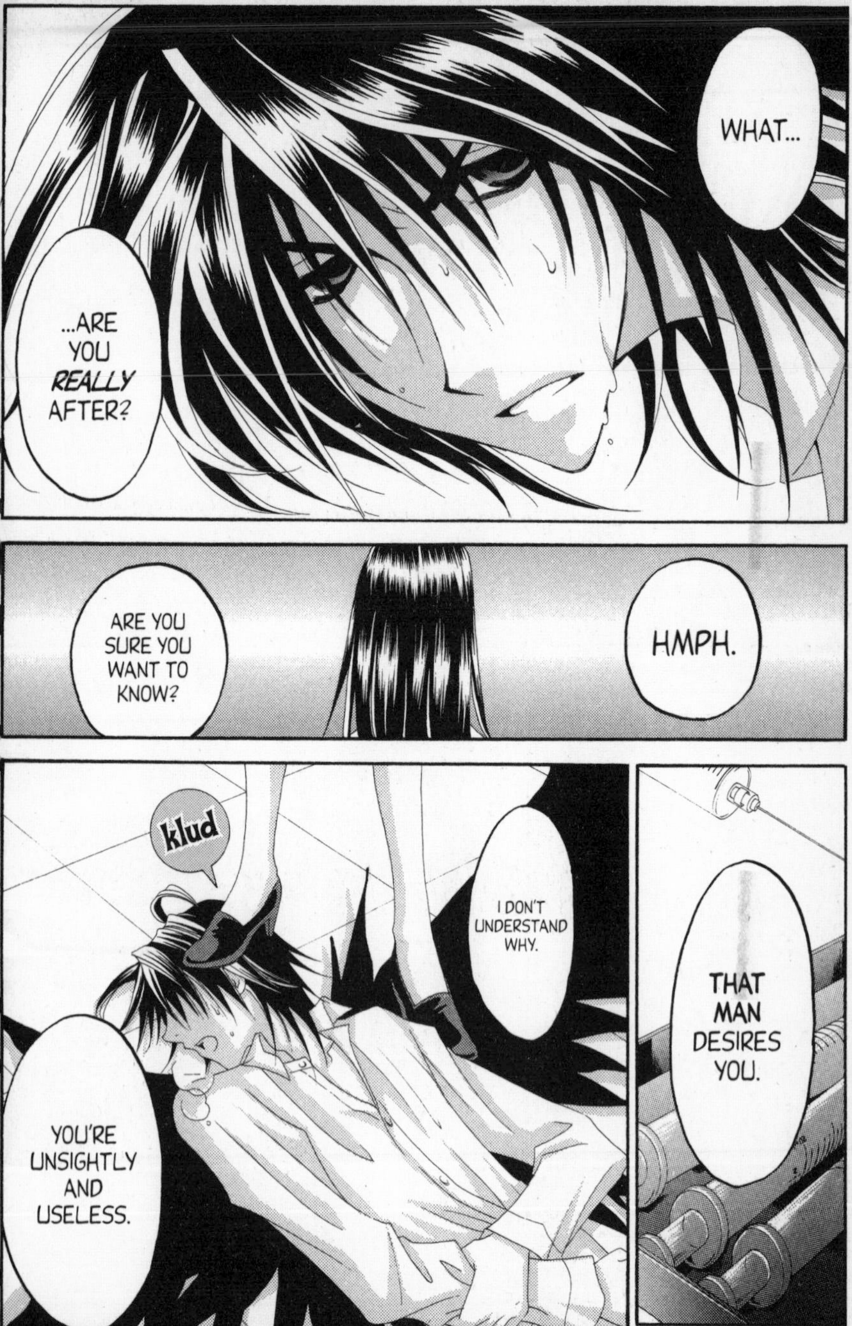
WHAT...
...ARE YOU *REALLY* AFTER?
HMPH.
ARE YOU SURE YOU WANT TO KNOW?
THAT MAN DESIRES YOU.
I DON'T UNDERSTAND WHY.
klud
YOU'RE UNSIGHTLY AND USELESS.

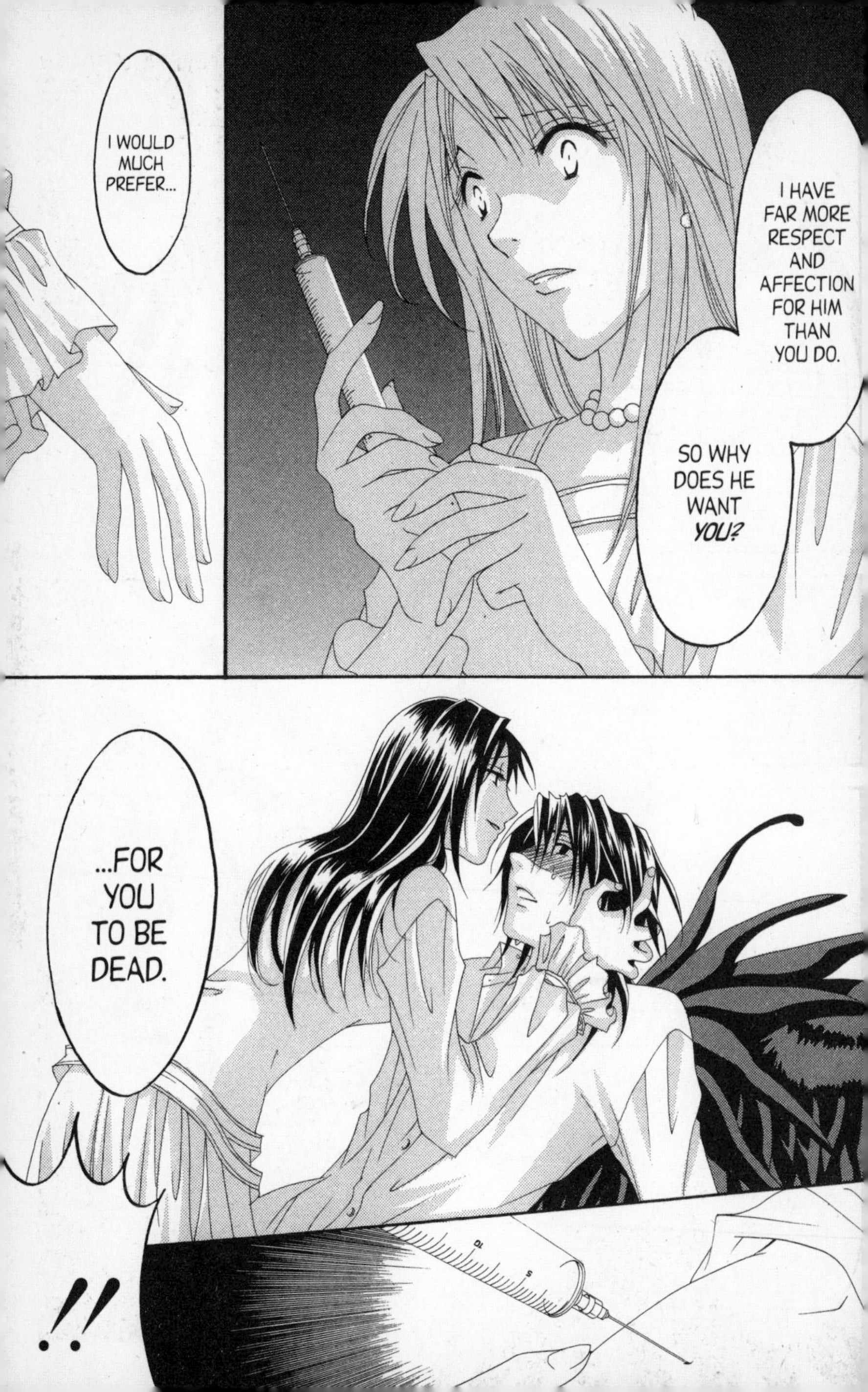
I HAVE FAR MORE RESPECT AND AFFECTION FOR HIM THAN YOU DO.
SO WHY DOES HE WANT *YOU?*
I WOULD MUCH PREFER...
...FOR YOU TO BE DEAD.
!!

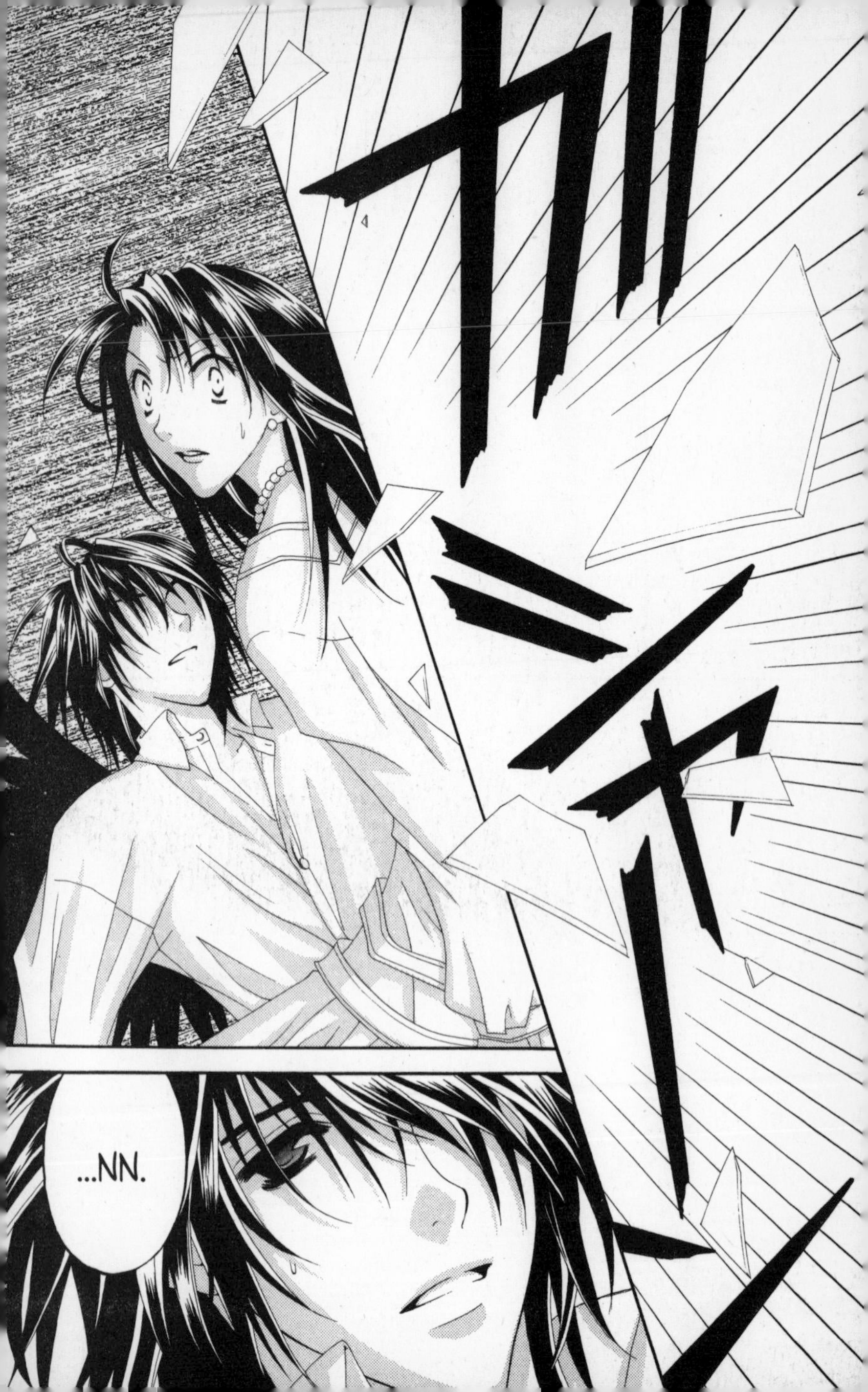
...NN.

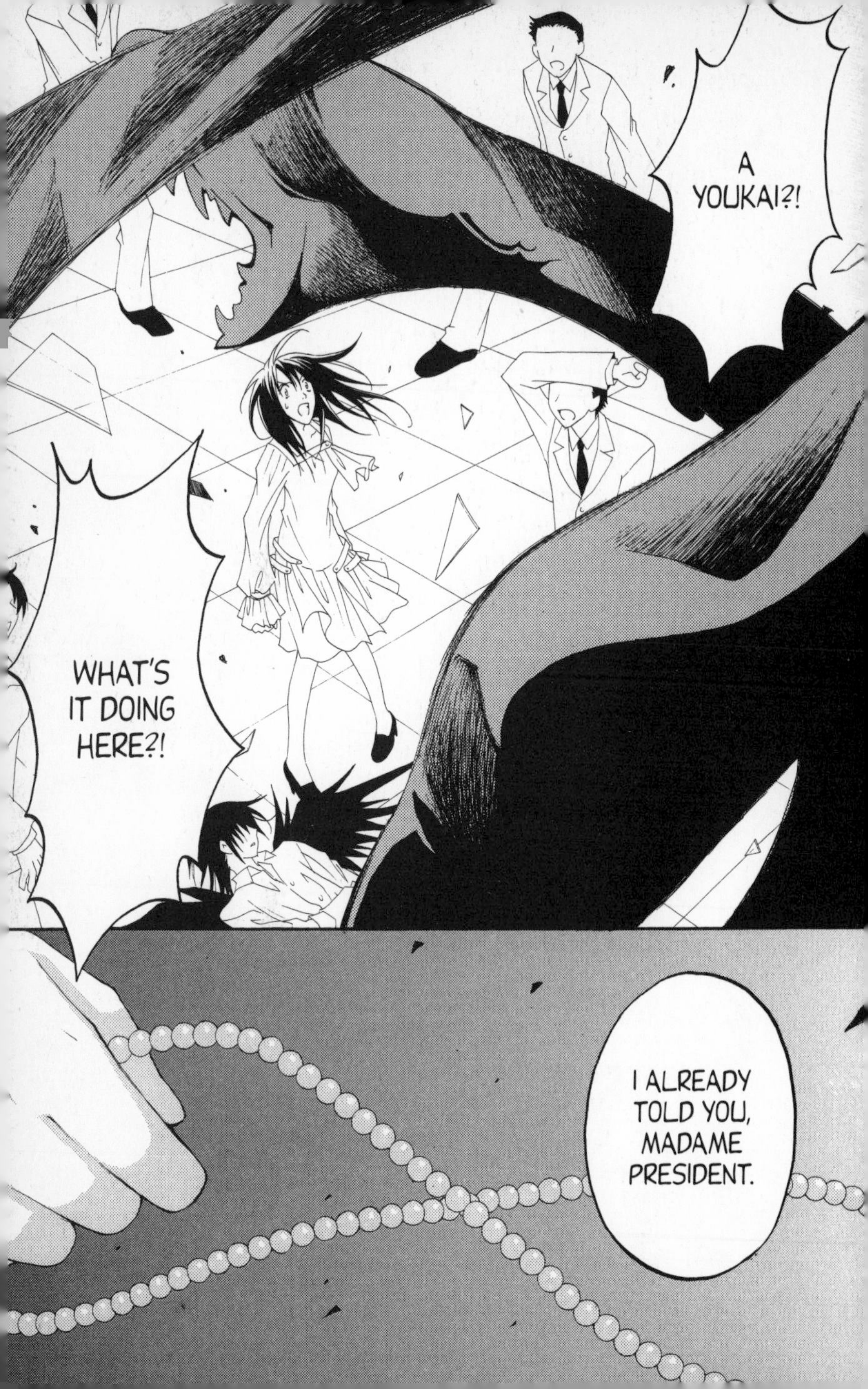
A YOUKAI?!
WHAT'S IT DOING HERE?!
I ALREADY TOLD YOU, MADAME PRESIDENT.

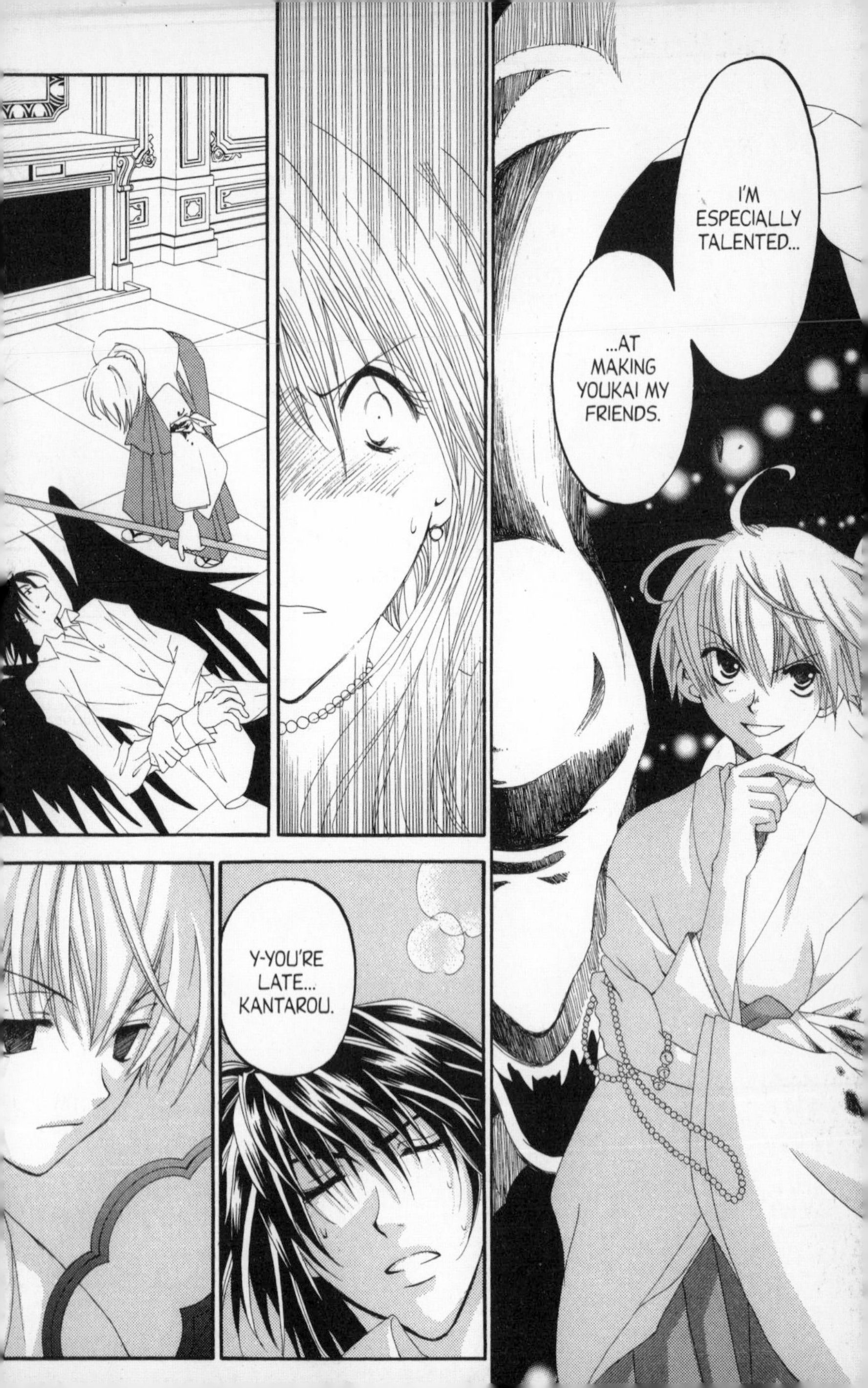
I'M ESPECIALLY TALENTED...
...AT MAKING YOUKAI MY FRIENDS.
Y-YOU'RE LATE... KANTAROU.

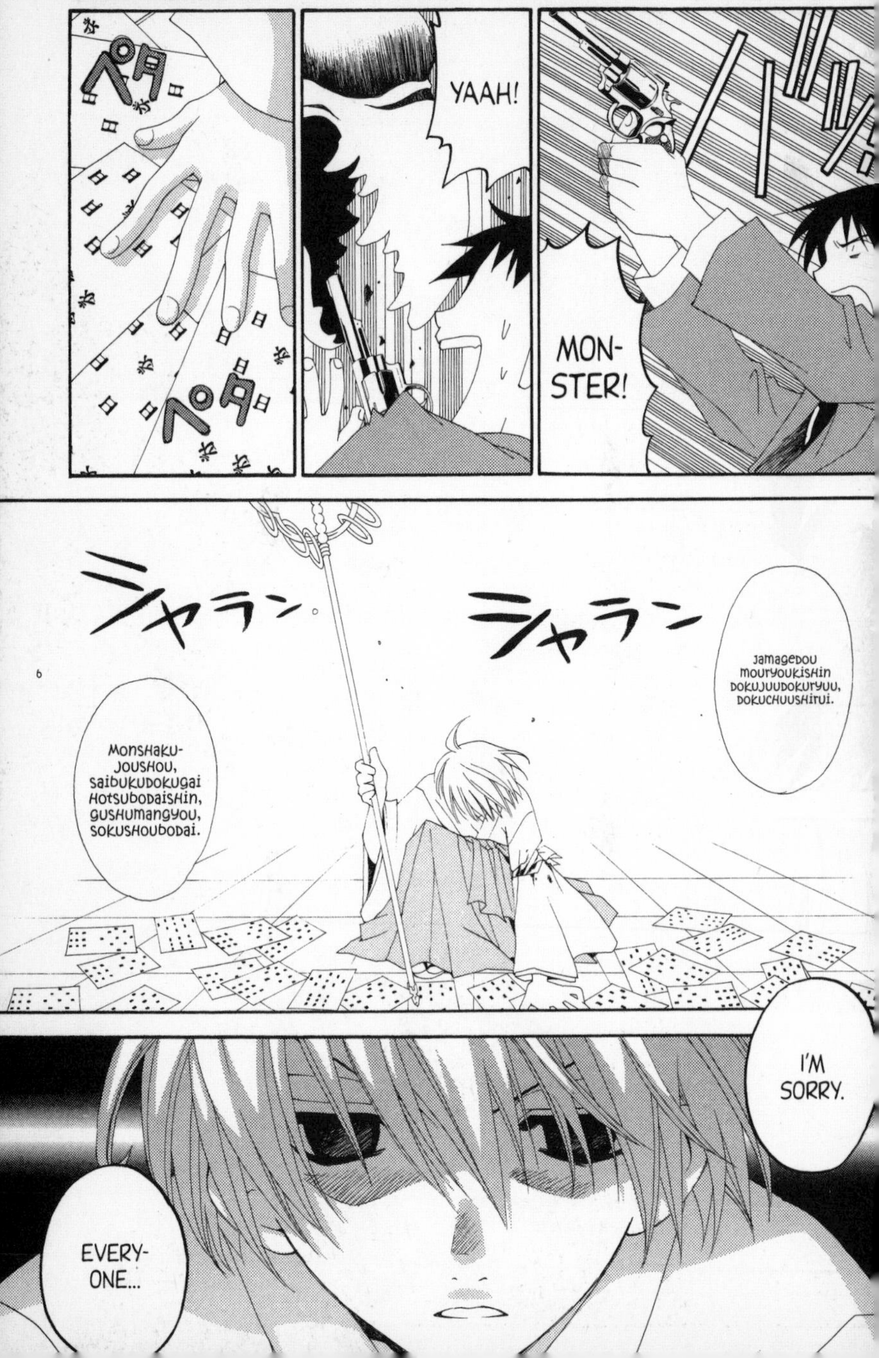
MON-
STER!
YAAH!
ペタ
ペタ
シャラン
シャラン
Jamagedou mouryoukishin dokujuudokuryuu, dokuchuushirui.
Monshaku-joushou, saibukudokugai hotsubodaishin, gushumangyou, sokushoubodai.
I'M SORRY.
EVERY-
ONE...

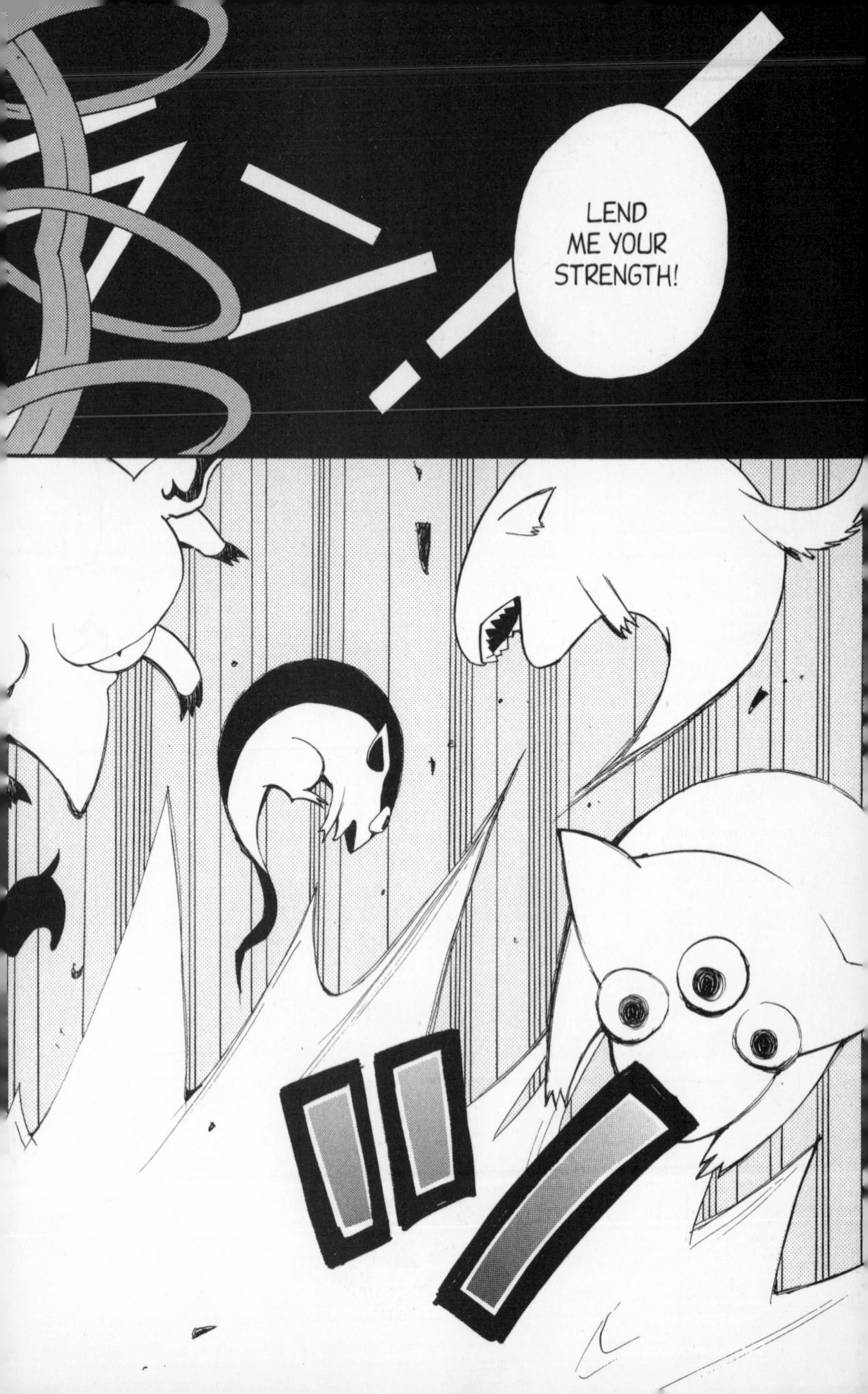
LEND ME YOUR STRENGTH!

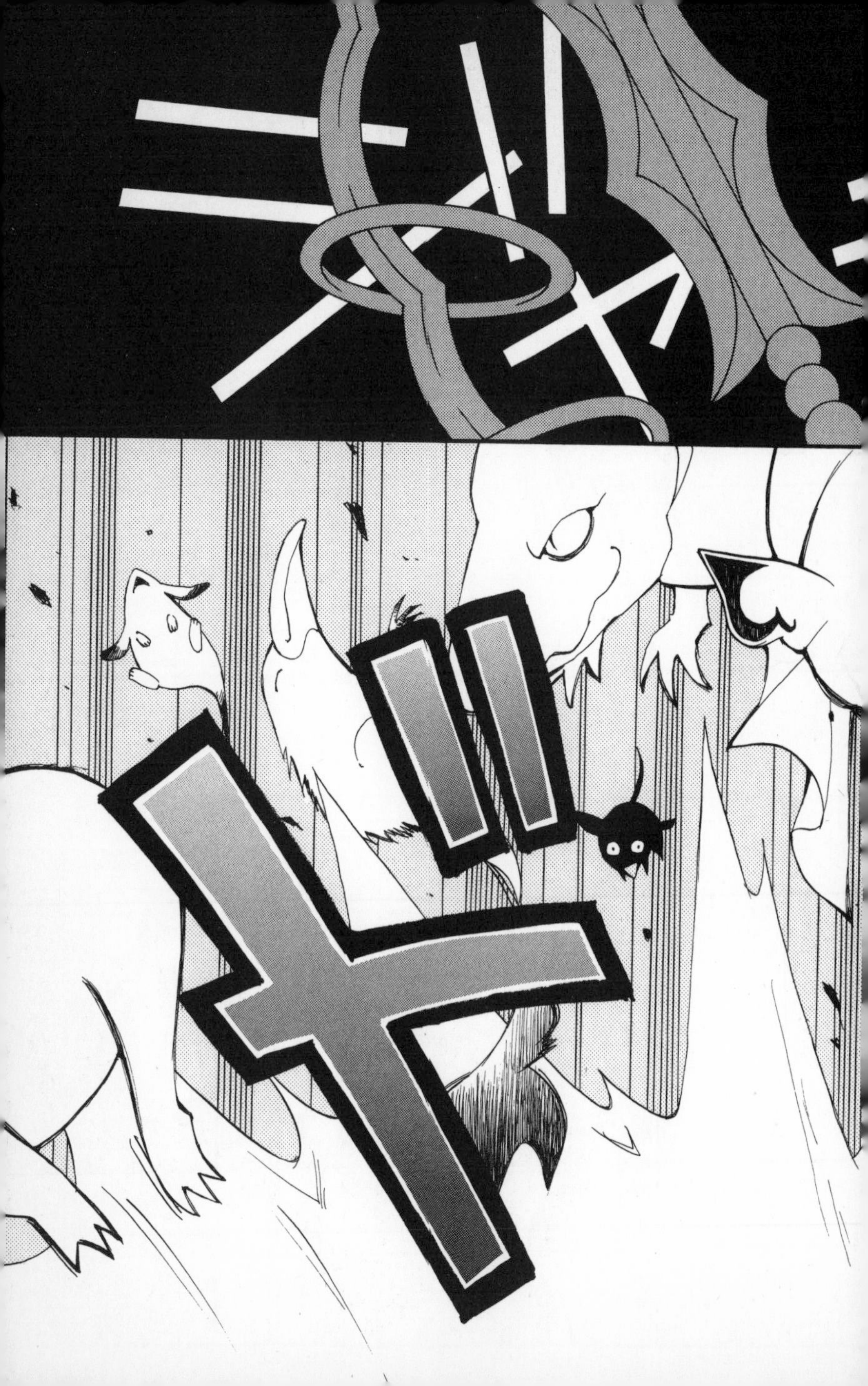

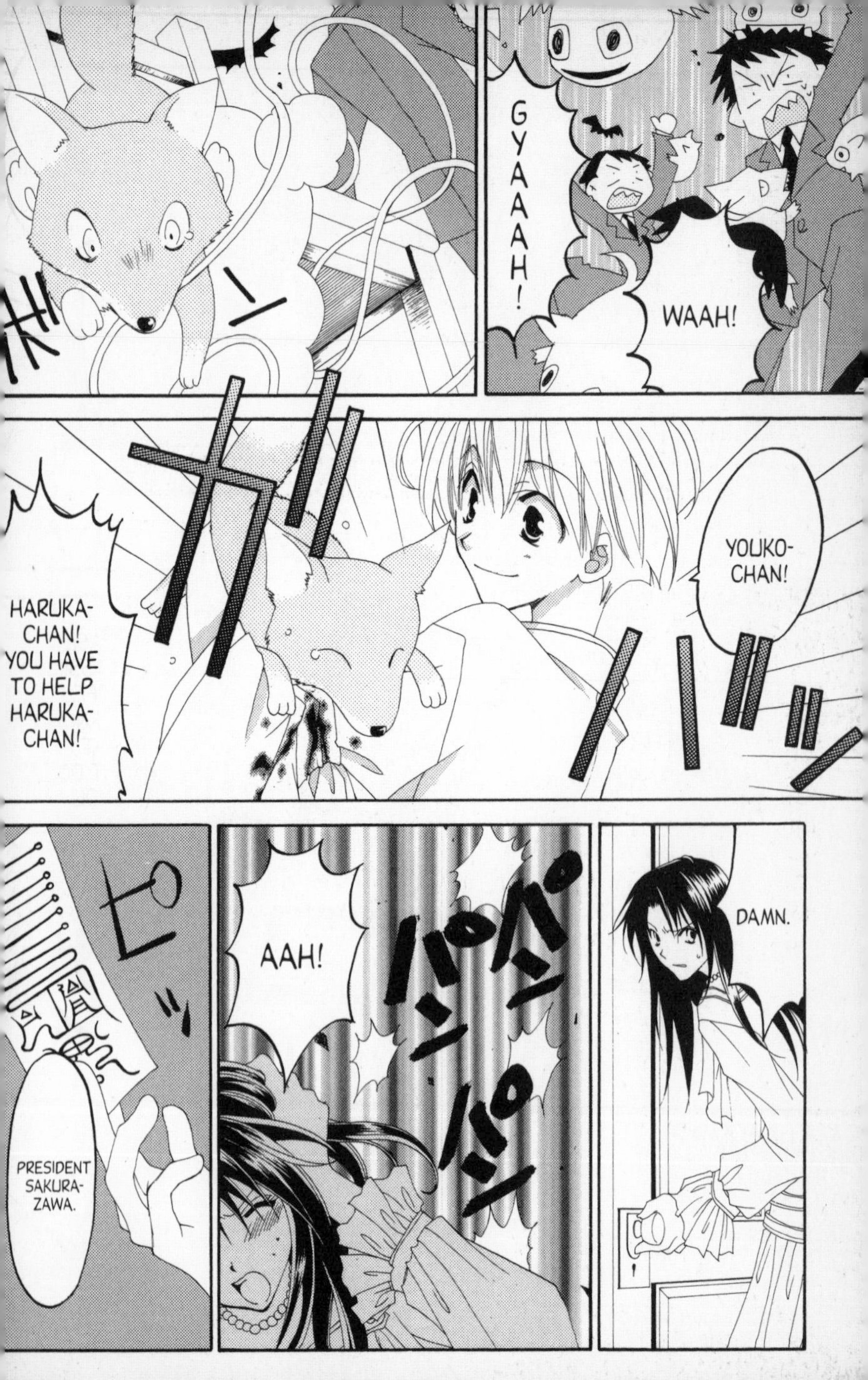
GYAAAAH!
WAAH!
YOUKO-CHAN!
HARUKA-CHAN! YOU HAVE TO HELP HARUKA-CHAN!
DAMN.
AAH!
PRESIDENT SAKURA-ZAWA.

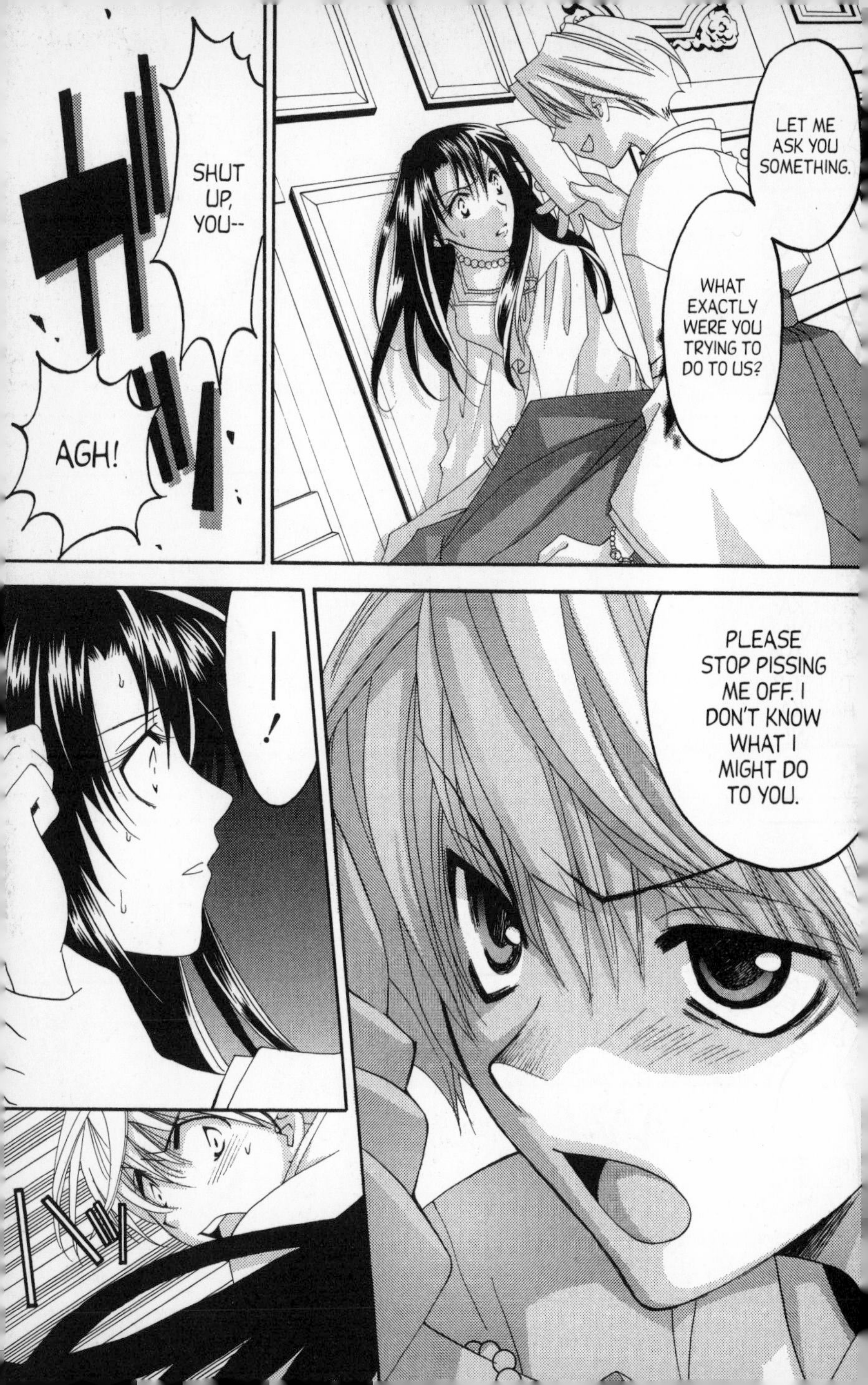
LET ME ASK YOU SOMETHING.
WHAT EXACTLY WERE YOU TRYING TO DO TO US?
SHUT UP, YOU--
AGH!
PLEASE STOP PISSING ME OFF. I DON'T KNOW WHAT I MIGHT DO TO YOU.
--!

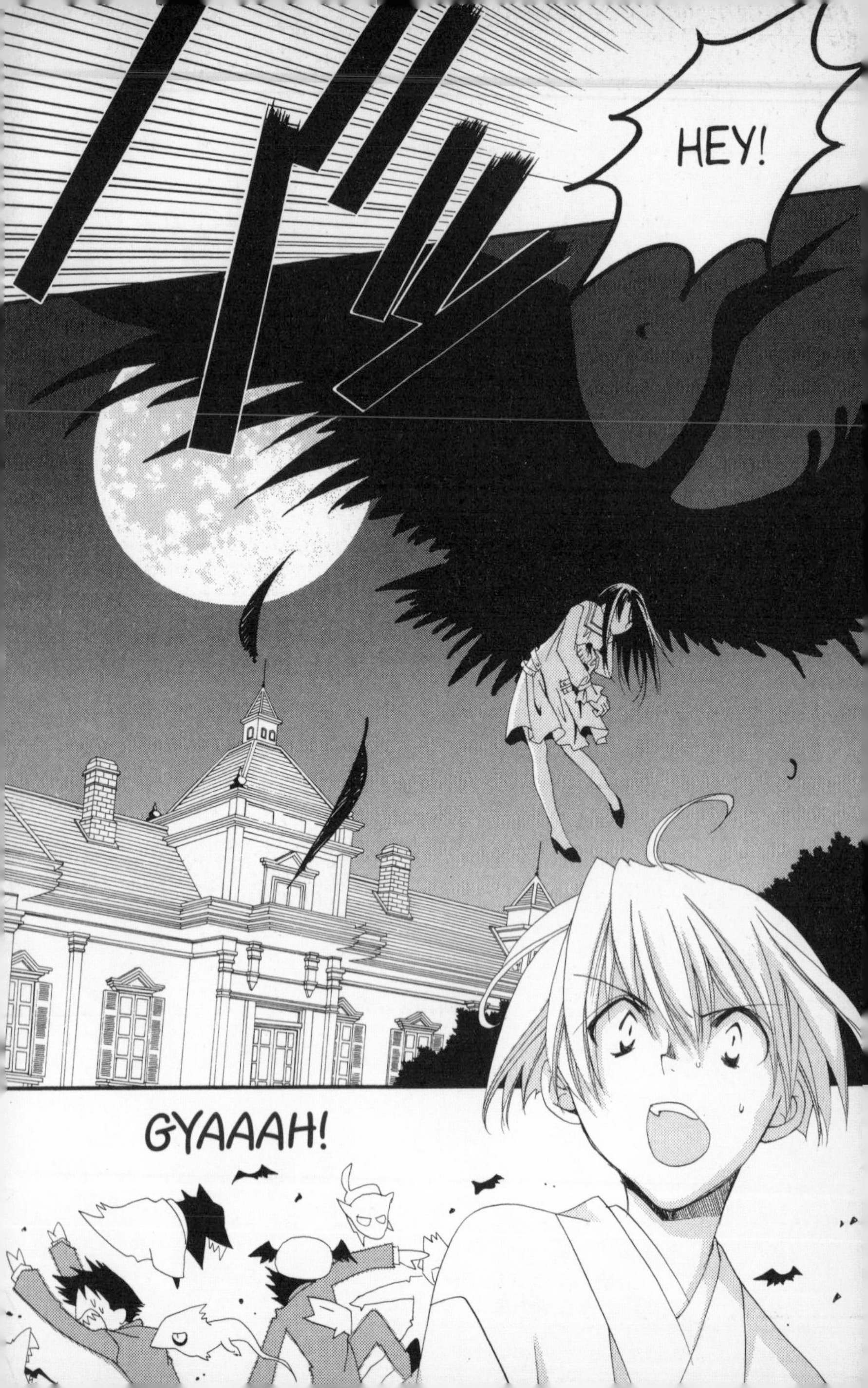
HEY!
GYAAAH!

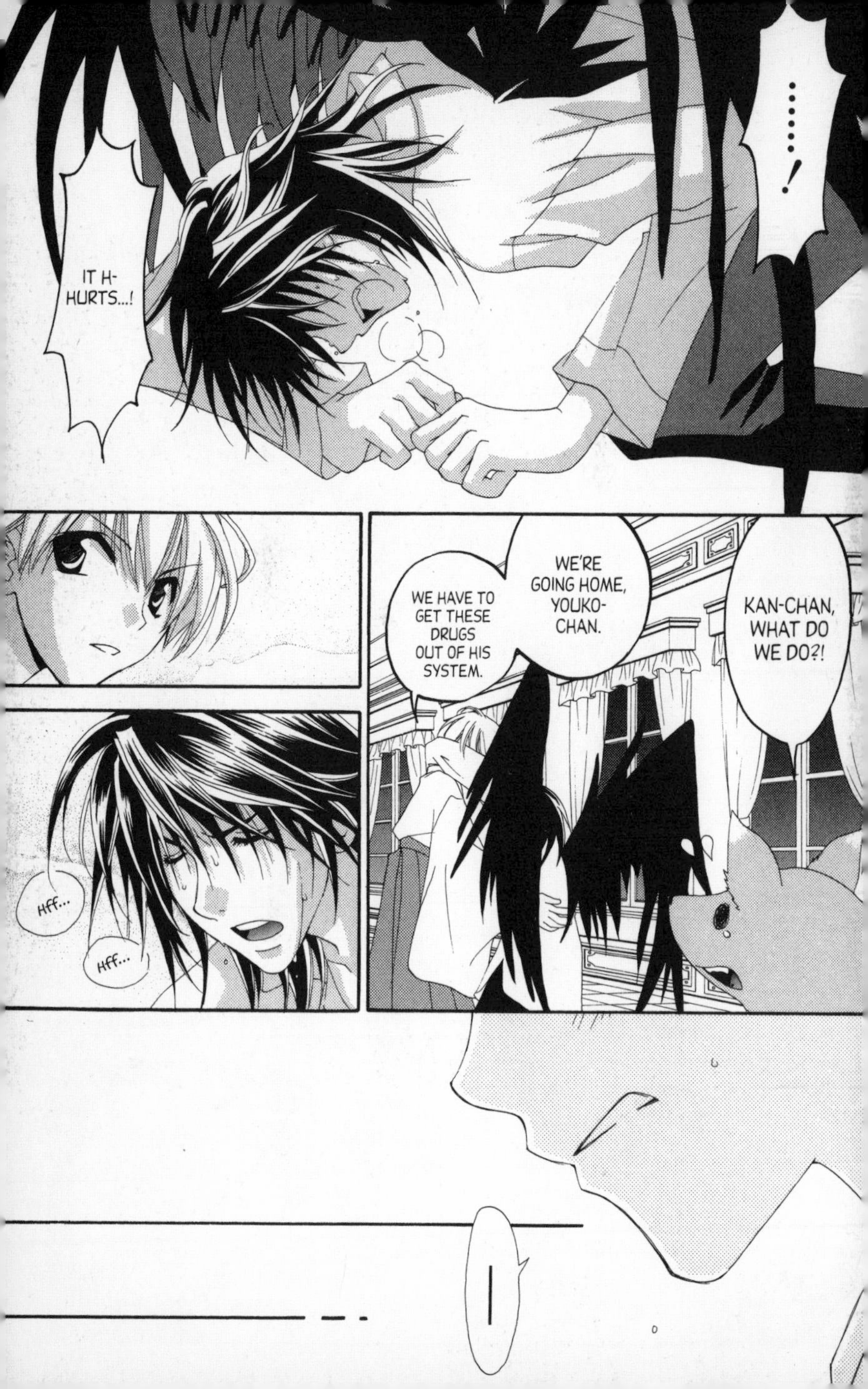
......!
IT H-HURTS...!
KAN-CHAN, WHAT DO WE DO?!
WE'RE GOING HOME, YOUKO-CHAN.
WE HAVE TO GET THESE DRUGS OUT OF HIS SYSTEM.
HFF...
HFF...

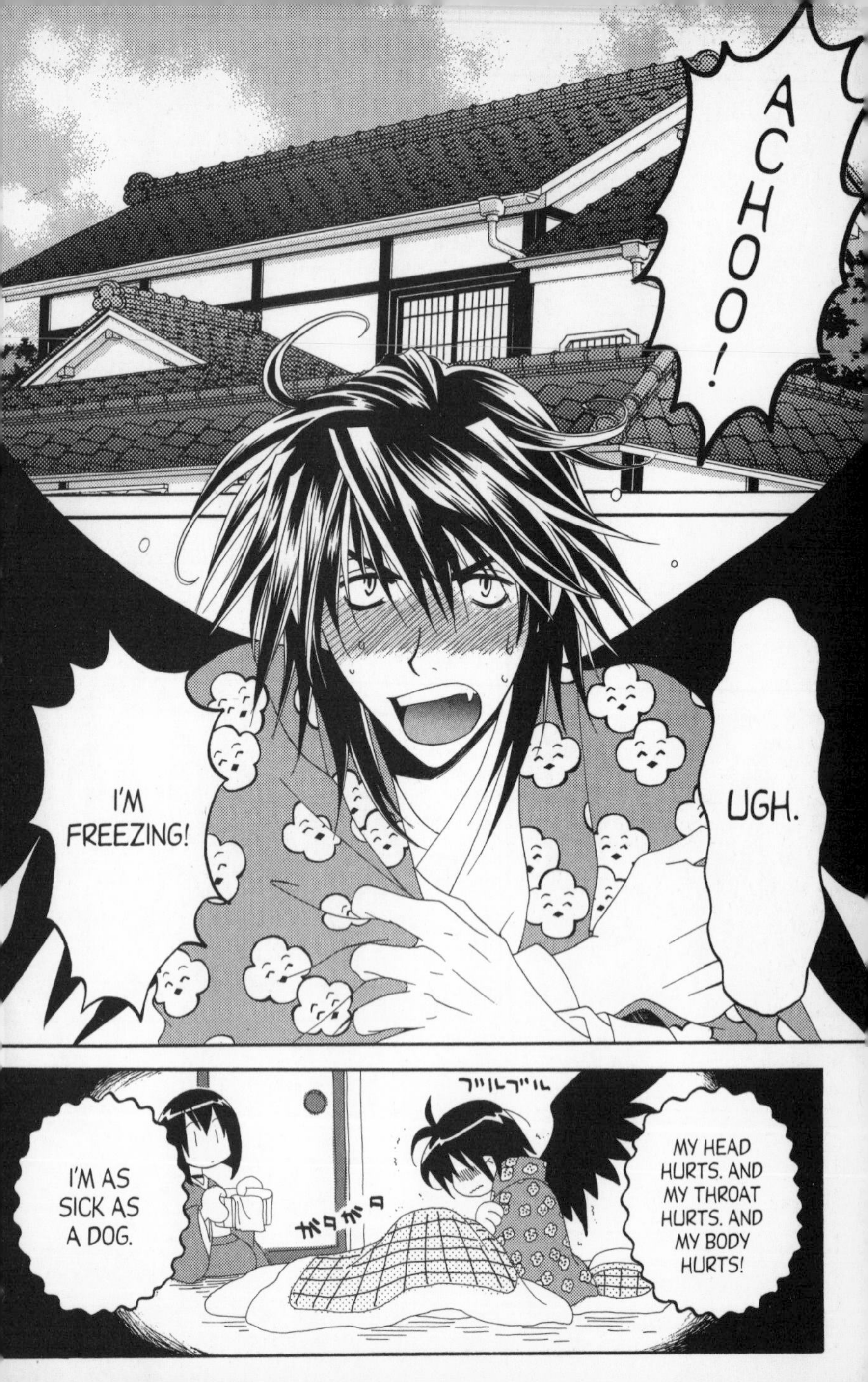
ACHOO!
UGH.
I'M FREEZING!
MY HEAD HURTS. AND MY THROAT HURTS. AND MY BODY HURTS!
ブルブル
ガタガタ
I'M AS SICK AS A DOG.

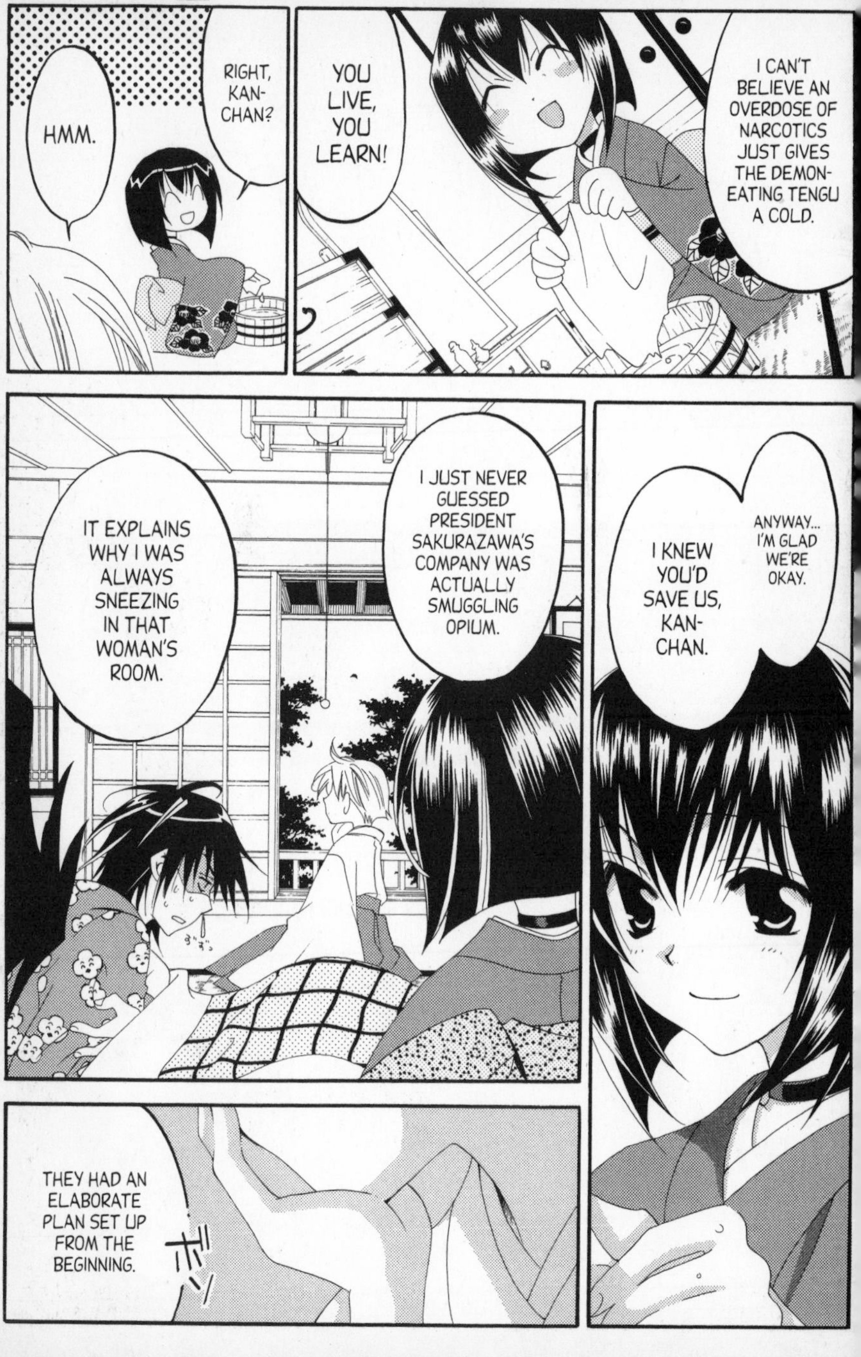
I CAN'T BELIEVE AN OVERDOSE OF NARCOTICS JUST GIVES THE DEMON-EATING TENGU A COLD.
YOU LIVE, YOU LEARN!
RIGHT, KAN-CHAN?
HMM.
ANYWAY... I'M GLAD WE'RE OKAY.
I KNEW YOU'D SAVE US, KAN-CHAN.
I JUST NEVER GUESSED PRESIDENT SAKURAZAWA'S COMPANY WAS ACTUALLY SMUGGLING OPIUM.
IT EXPLAINS WHY I WAS ALWAYS SNEEZING IN THAT WOMAN'S ROOM.
THEY HAD AN ELABORATE PLAN SET UP FROM THE BEGINNING.

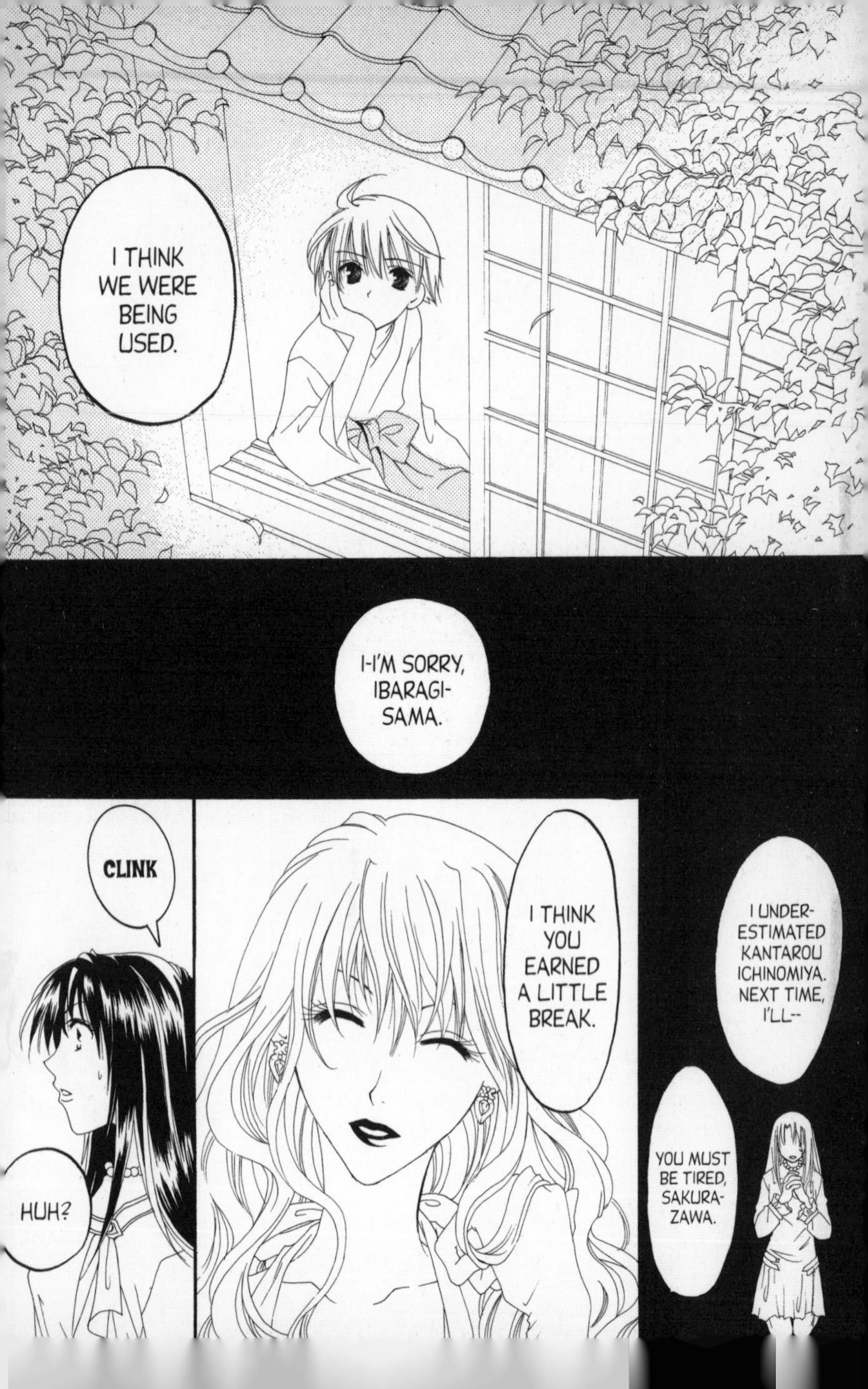

I THINK WE WERE BEING USED.
I-I'M SORRY, IBARAGI-SAMA.
I UNDER-ESTIMATED KANTAROU ICHINOMIYA. NEXT TIME, I'LL--
YOU MUST BE TIRED, SAKURA-ZAWA.
I THINK YOU EARNED A LITTLE BREAK.
CLINK
HUH?

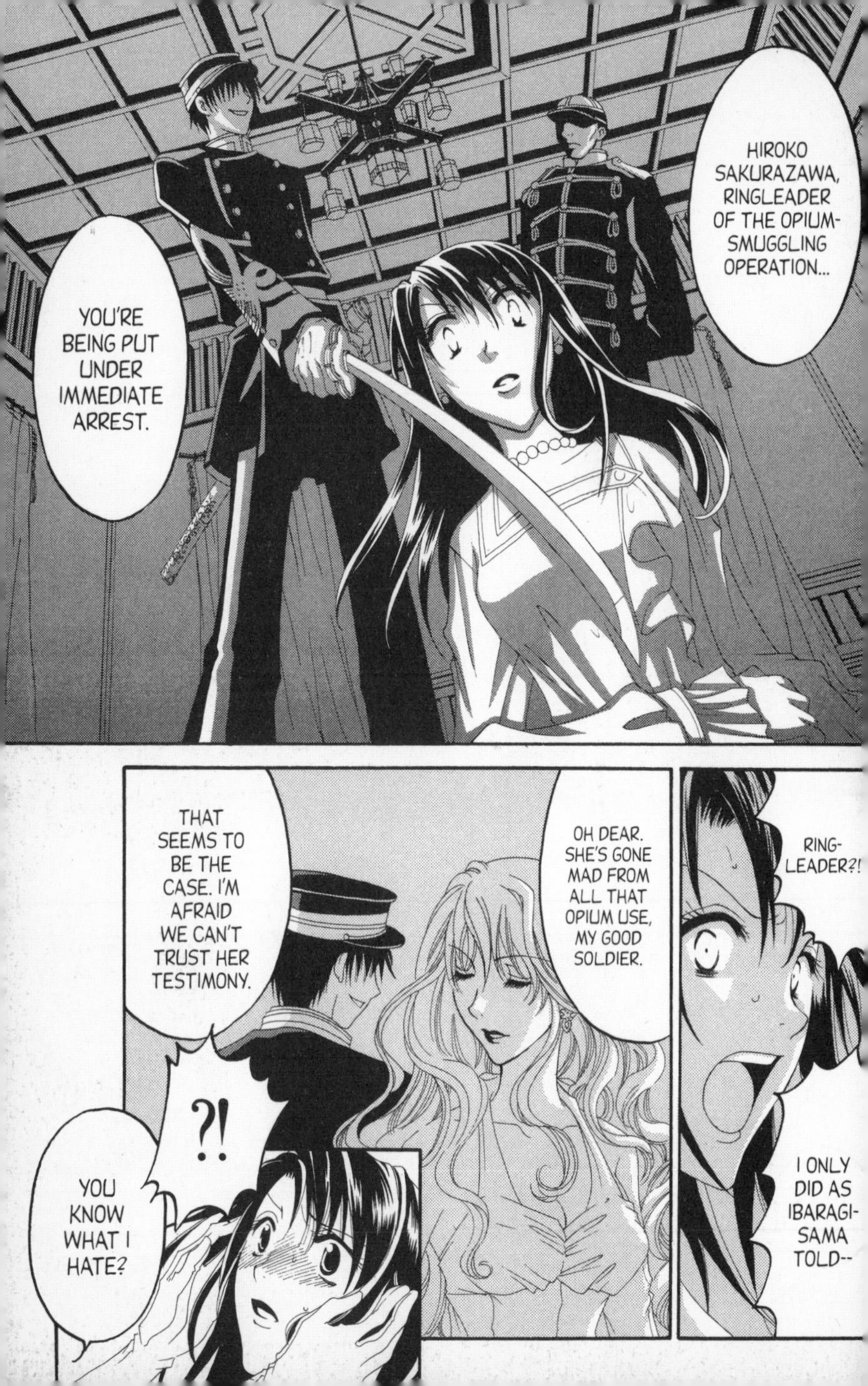
HIROKO SAKURAZAWA, RINGLEADER OF THE OPIUM-SMUGGLING OPERATION...
YOU'RE BEING PUT UNDER IMMEDIATE ARREST.
RING-LEADER?!
I ONLY DID AS IBARAGI-SAMA TOLD--
OH DEAR. SHE'S GONE MAD FROM ALL THAT OPIUM USE, MY GOOD SOLDIER.
THAT SEEMS TO BE THE CASE. I'M AFRAID WE CAN'T TRUST HER TESTIMONY.
?!
YOU KNOW WHAT I HATE?

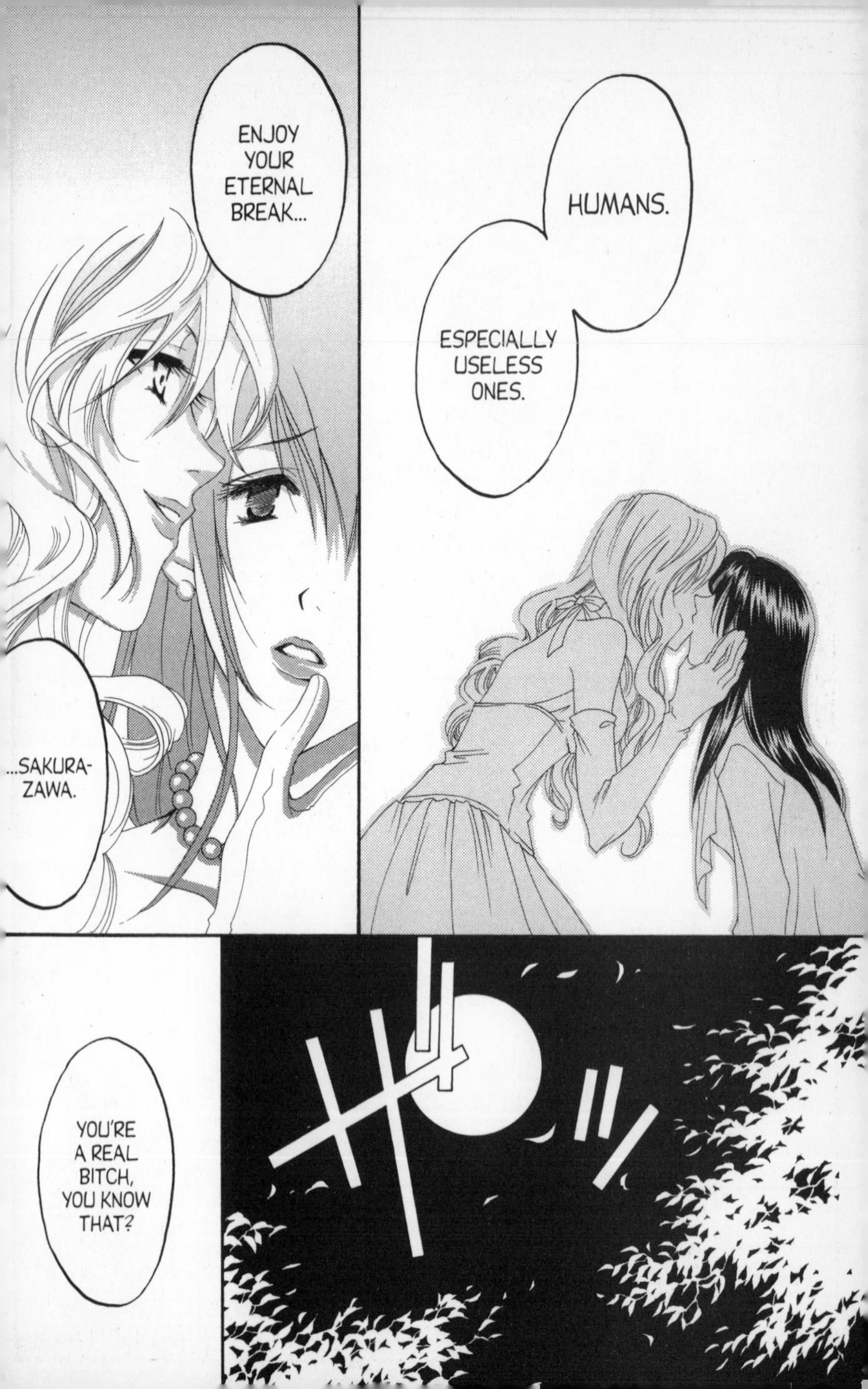
HUMANS.
ESPECIALLY USELESS ONES.
ENJOY YOUR ETERNAL BREAK...
...SAKURA-ZAWA.
YOU'RE A REAL BITCH, YOU KNOW THAT?

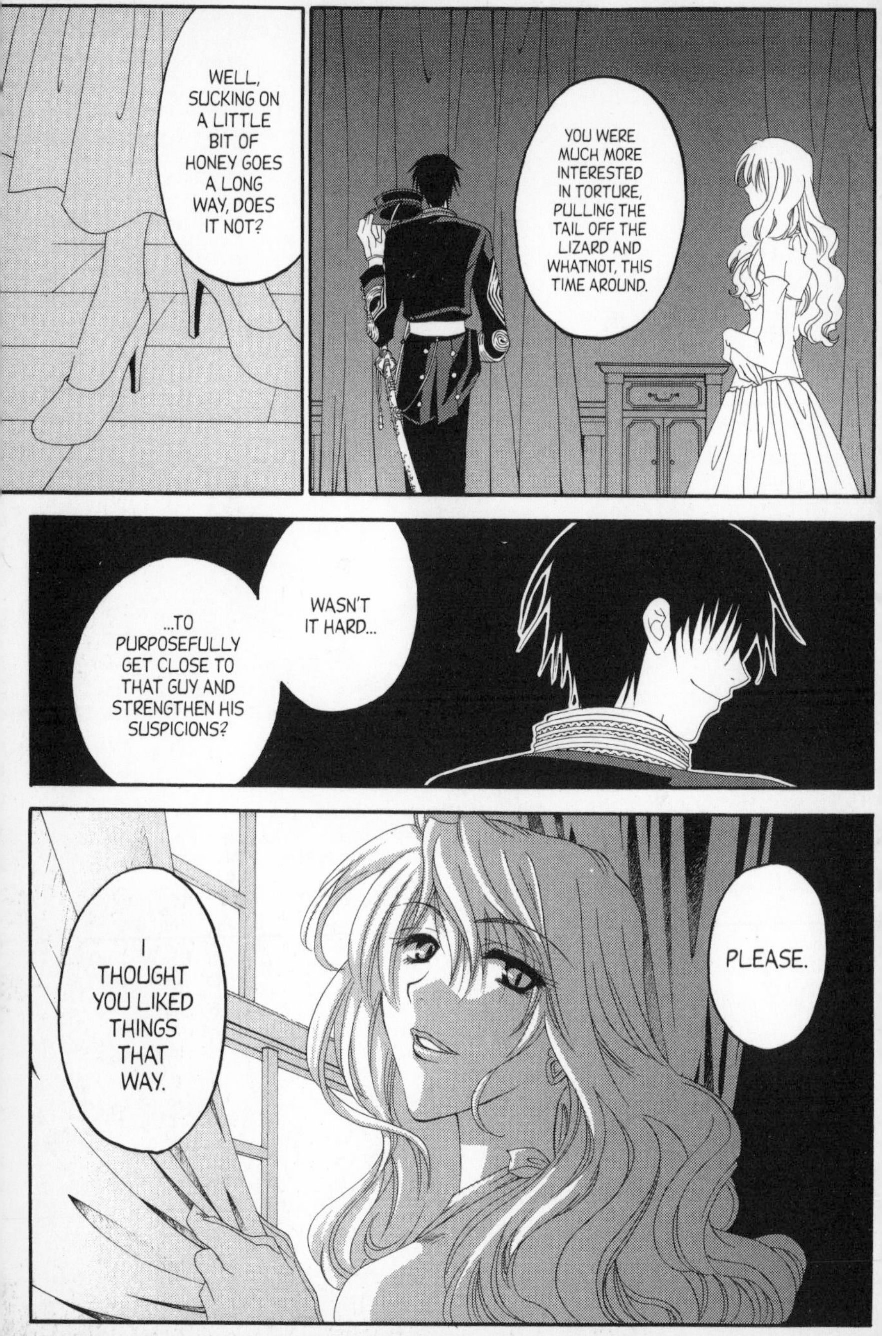
YOU WERE MUCH MORE INTERESTED IN TORTURE, PULLING THE TAIL OFF THE LIZARD AND WHATNOT, THIS TIME AROUND.
WELL, SUCKING ON A LITTLE BIT OF HONEY GOES A LONG WAY, DOES IT NOT?
WASN'T IT HARD...
...TO PURPOSEFULLY GET CLOSE TO THAT GUY AND STRENGTHEN HIS SUSPICIONS?
PLEASE.
I THOUGHT YOU LIKED THINGS THAT WAY.

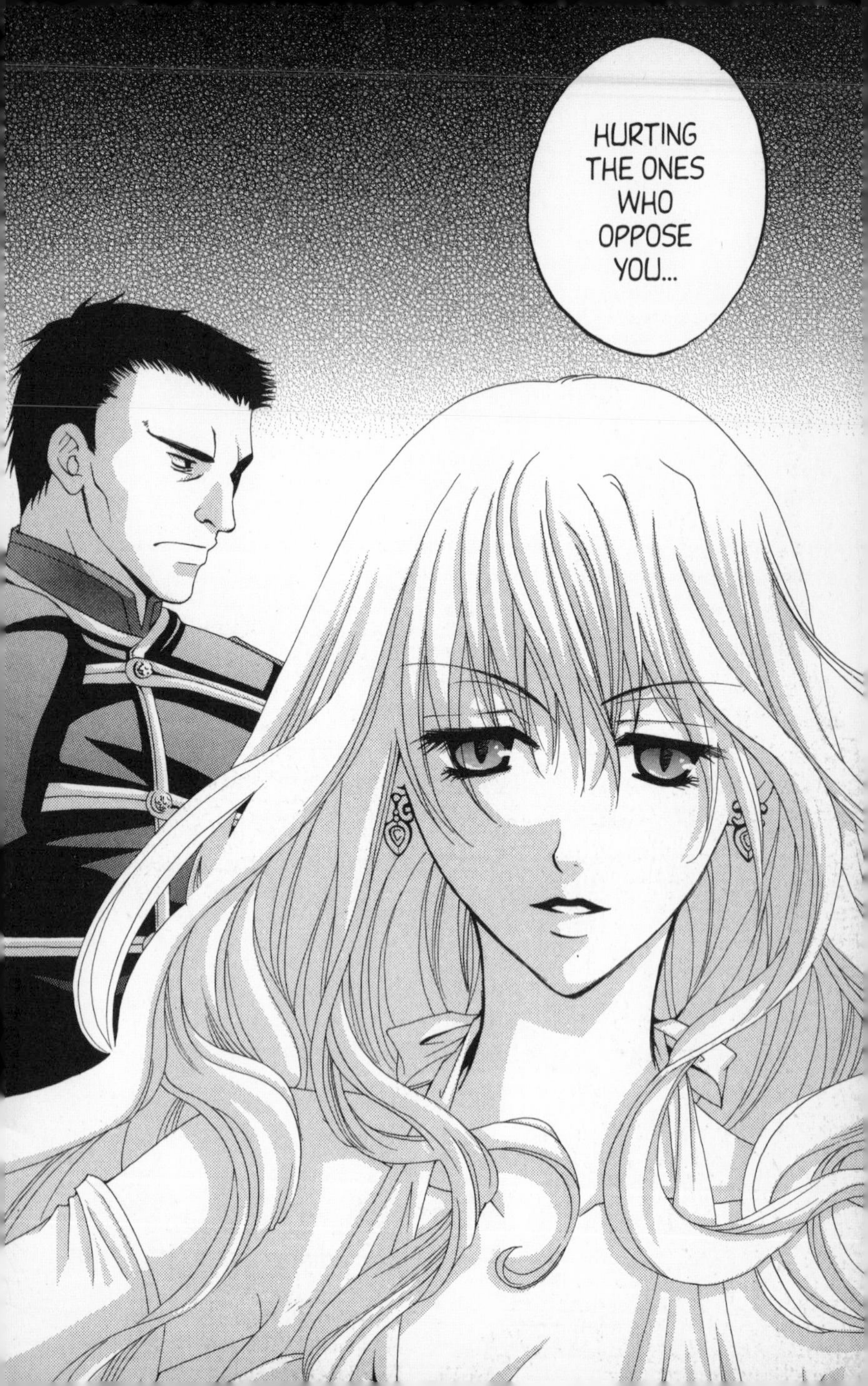
HURTING THE ONES WHO OPPOSE YOU...

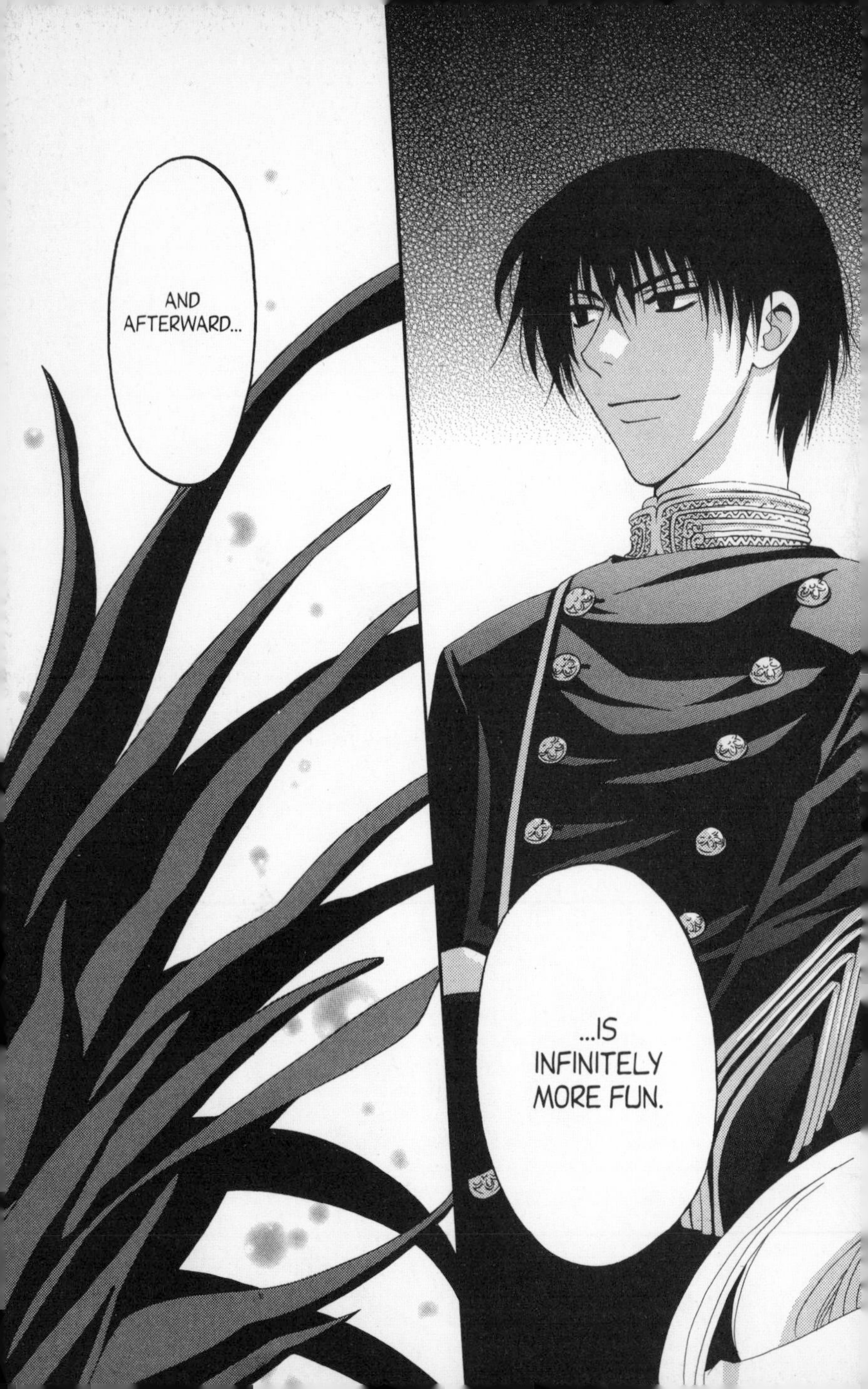
AND AFTERWARD...
...IS INFINITELY MORE FUN.

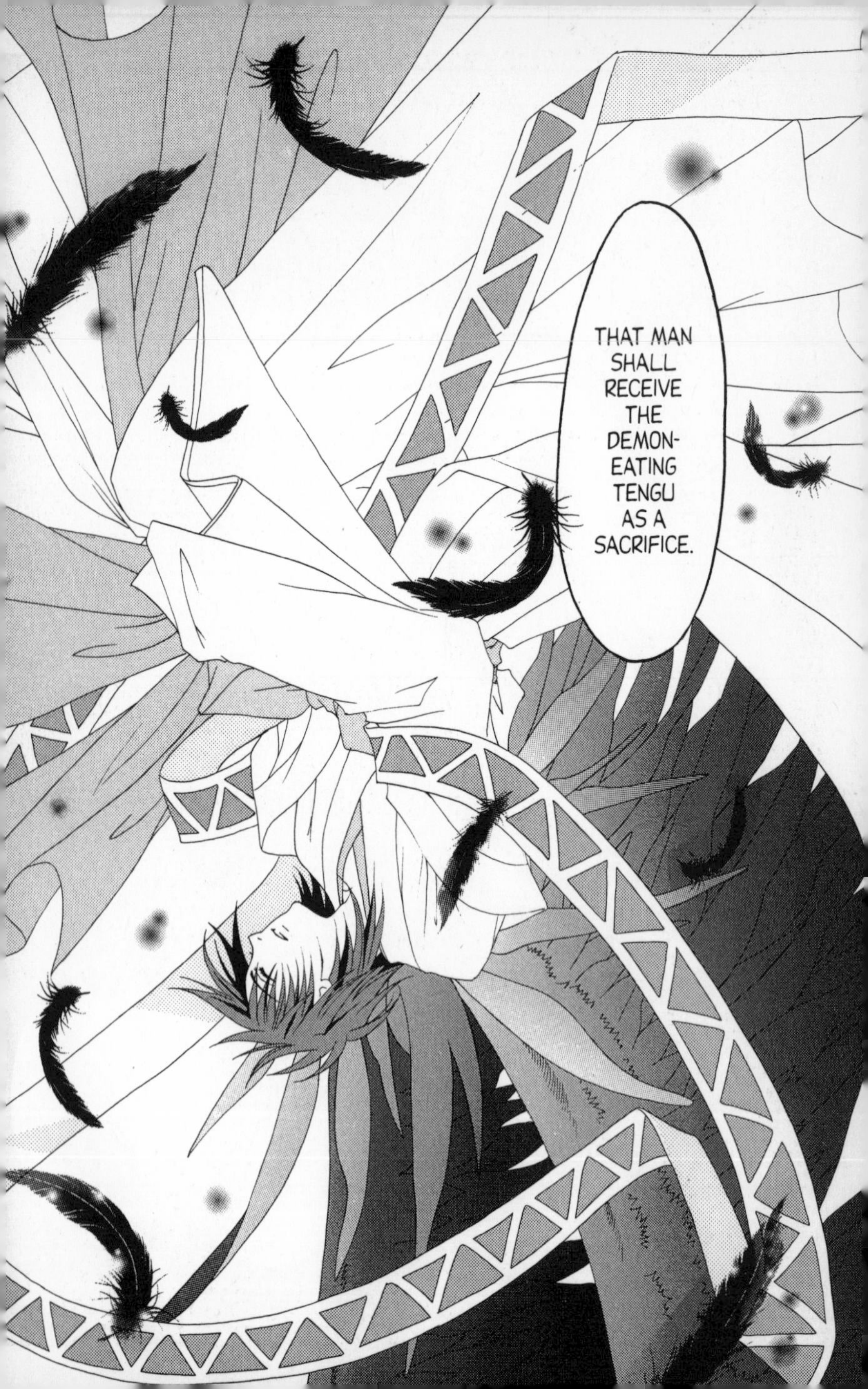
THAT MAN SHALL RECEIVE THE DEMON-EATING TENGU AS A SACRIFICE.

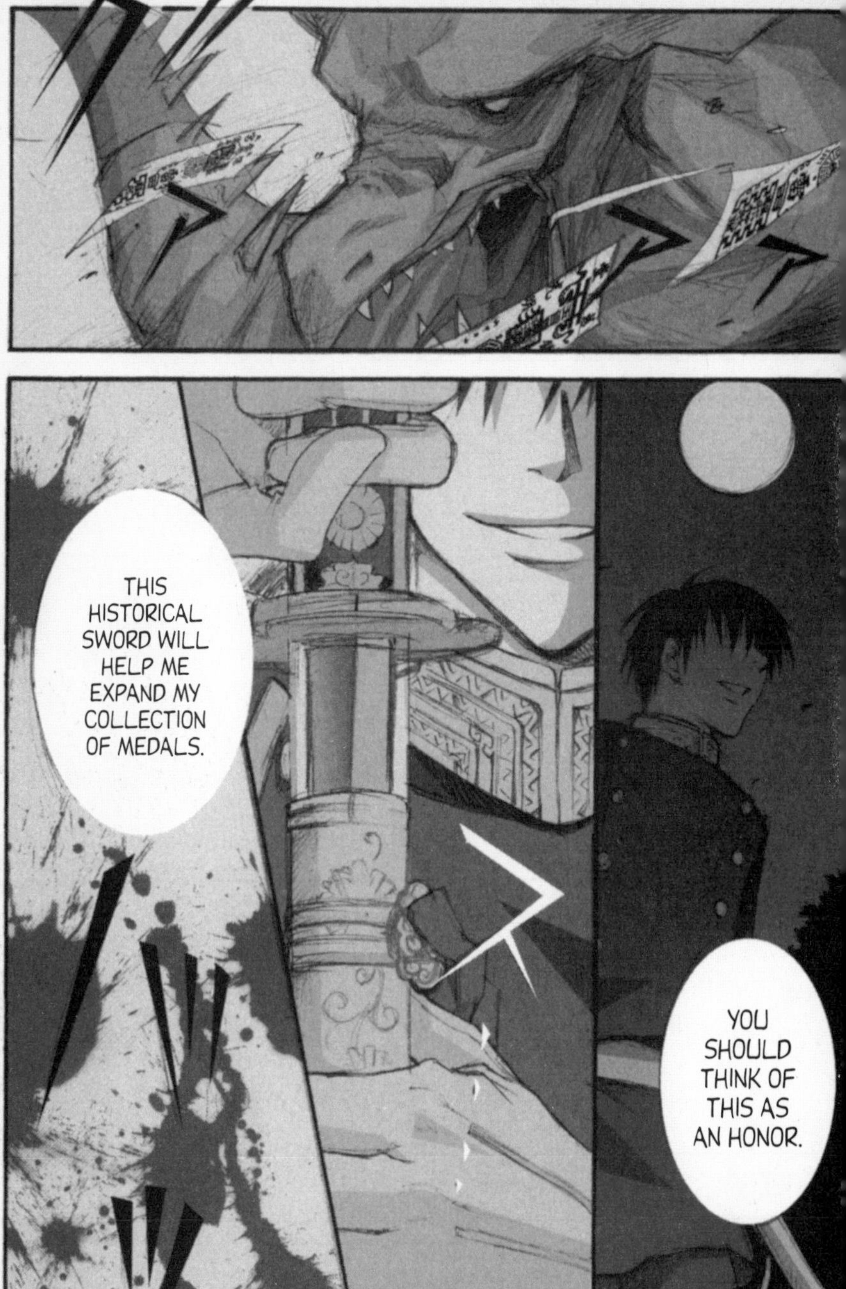
YOU SHOULD THINK OF THIS AS AN HONOR.
THIS HISTORICAL SWORD WILL HELP ME EXPAND MY COLLECTION OF MEDALS.

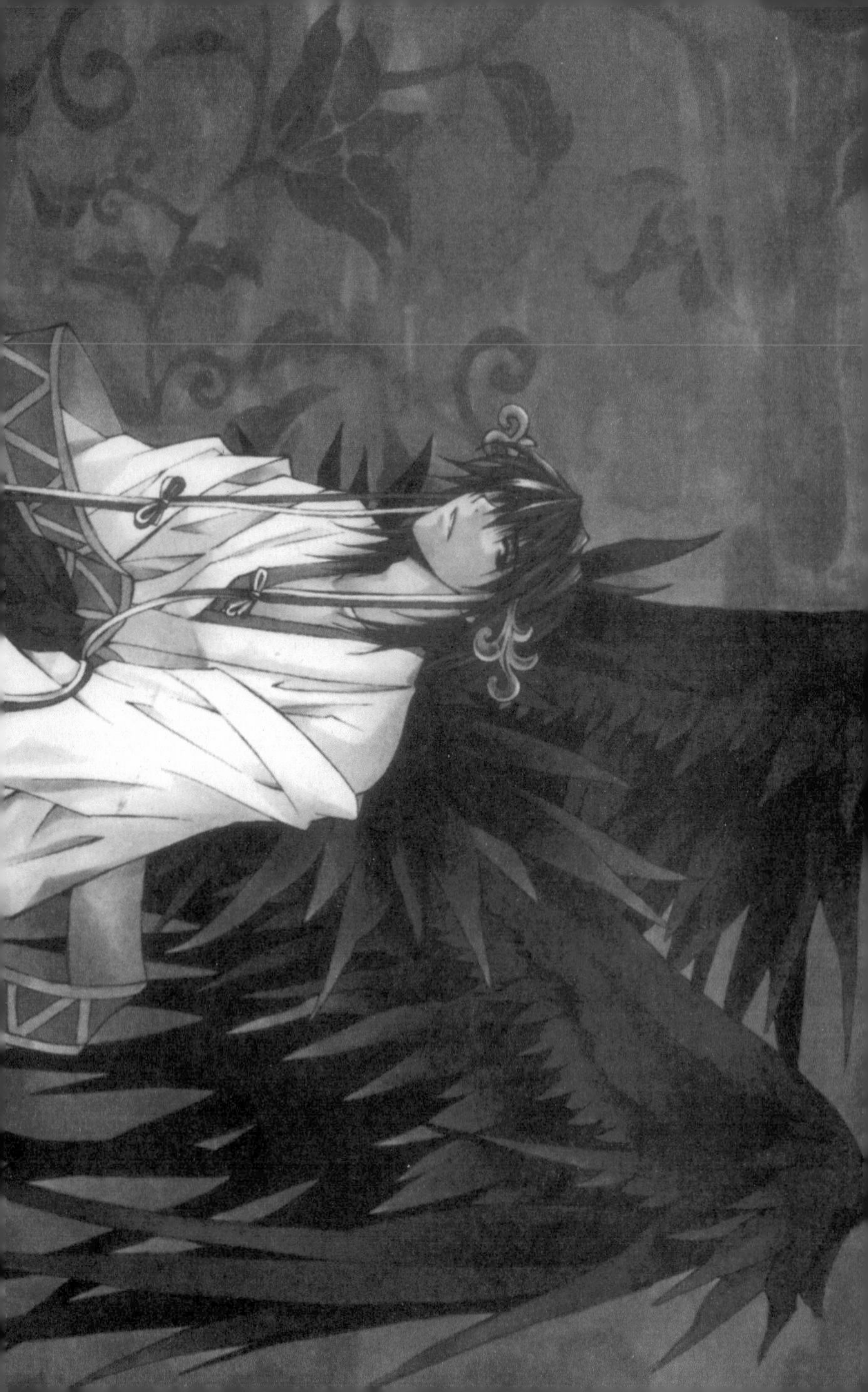

CHAPTER 10

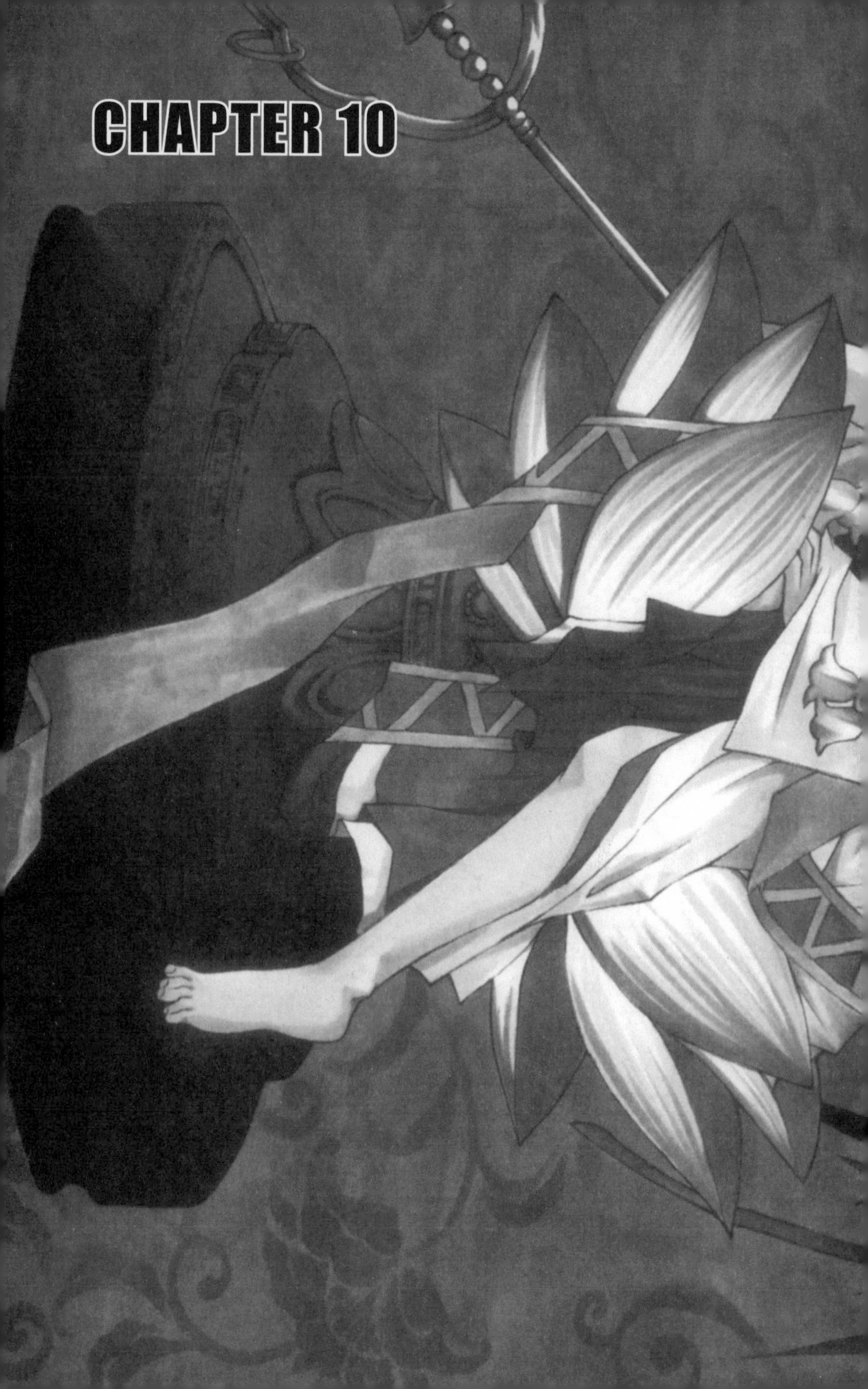

tactics Drama CD Off-Recording Report--Take 2!

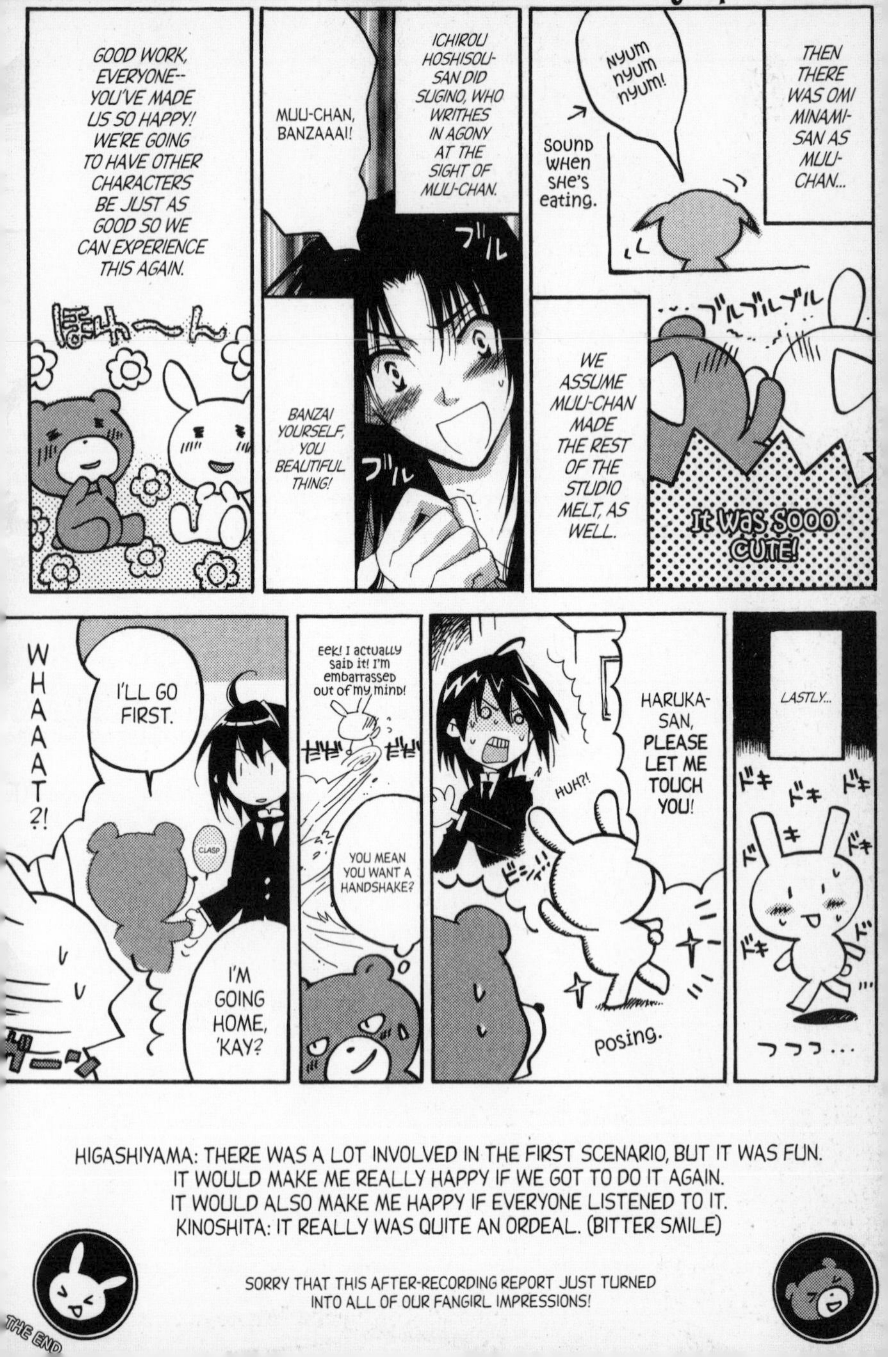
THEN THERE WAS OMI MINAMI-SAN AS MUU-CHAN...
NYUM NYUM NYUM!
SOUND WHEN SHE'S eating.
WE ASSUME MUU-CHAN MADE THE REST OF THE STUDIO MELT, AS WELL.
It was SOOO CUTE!
ICHIROU HOSHISOU-SAN DID SUGINO, WHO WRITHES IN AGONY AT THE SIGHT OF MUU-CHAN.
MUU-CHAN, BANZAAAI!
BANZAI YOURSELF, YOU BEAUTIFUL THING!
GOOD WORK, EVERYONE-- YOU'VE MADE US SO HAPPY! WE'RE GOING TO HAVE OTHER CHARACTERS BE JUST AS GOOD SO WE CAN EXPERIENCE THIS AGAIN.
LASTLY...
HARUKA-SAN, PLEASE LET ME TOUCH YOU!
HUH?!
posing.
Eek! I actually said it! I'm embarrassed out of my mind!
YOU MEAN YOU WANT A HANDSHAKE?
I'LL GO FIRST.
WHAAAAT?!
CLASP
I'M GOING HOME, 'KAY?

HIGASHIYAMA: THERE WAS A LOT INVOLVED IN THE FIRST SCENARIO, BUT IT WAS FUN. IT WOULD MAKE ME REALLY HAPPY IF WE GOT TO DO IT AGAIN. IT WOULD ALSO MAKE ME HAPPY IF EVERYONE LISTENED TO IT.

KINOSHITA: IT REALLY WAS QUITE AN ORDEAL. (BITTER SMILE)

SORRY THAT THIS AFTER-RECORDING REPORT JUST TURNED INTO ALL OF OUR FANGIRL IMPRESSIONS!

THE END

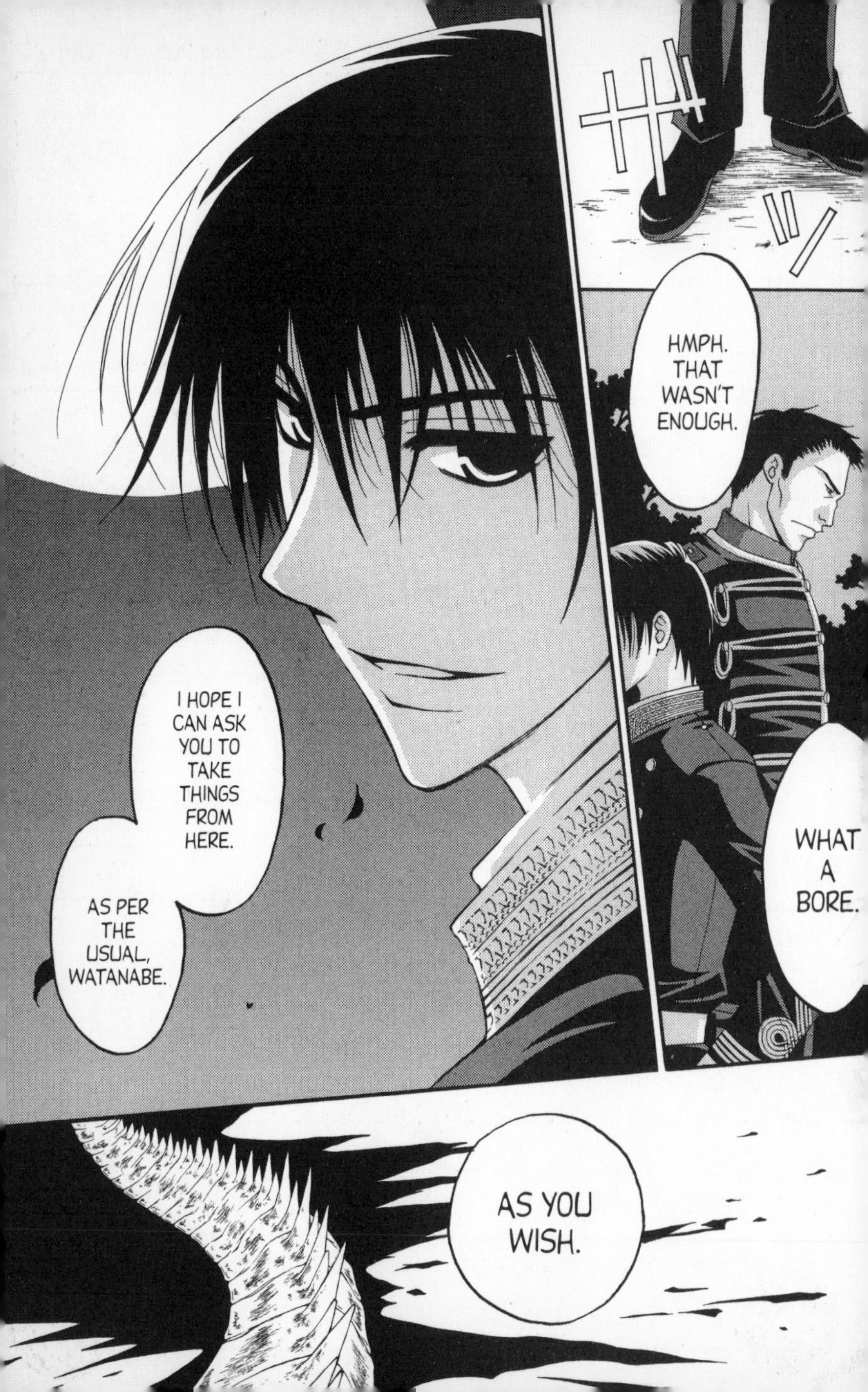
HMPH. THAT WASN'T ENOUGH.
WHAT A BORE.
I HOPE I CAN ASK YOU TO TAKE THINGS FROM HERE.
AS PER THE USUAL, WATANABE.
AS YOU WISH.

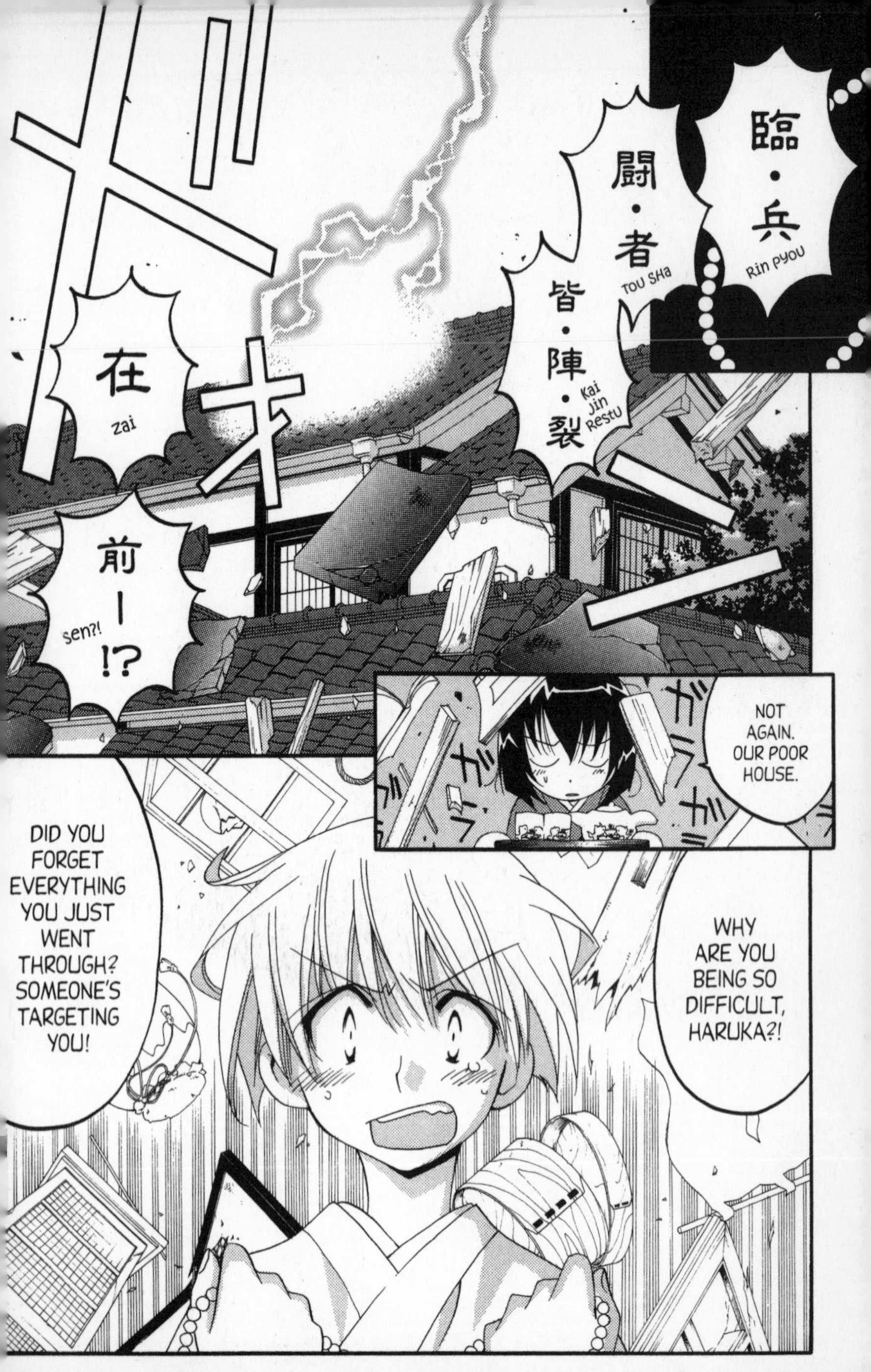
臨・兵
Rin pyou
闘・者
TOU SHa
皆・陣・裂
Kai Jin Restu
在
zai
前ー!?
sen?!
NOT AGAIN. OUR POOR HOUSE.
WHY ARE YOU BEING SO DIFFICULT, HARUKA?!
DID YOU FORGET EVERYTHING YOU JUST WENT THROUGH? SOMEONE'S TARGETING YOU!

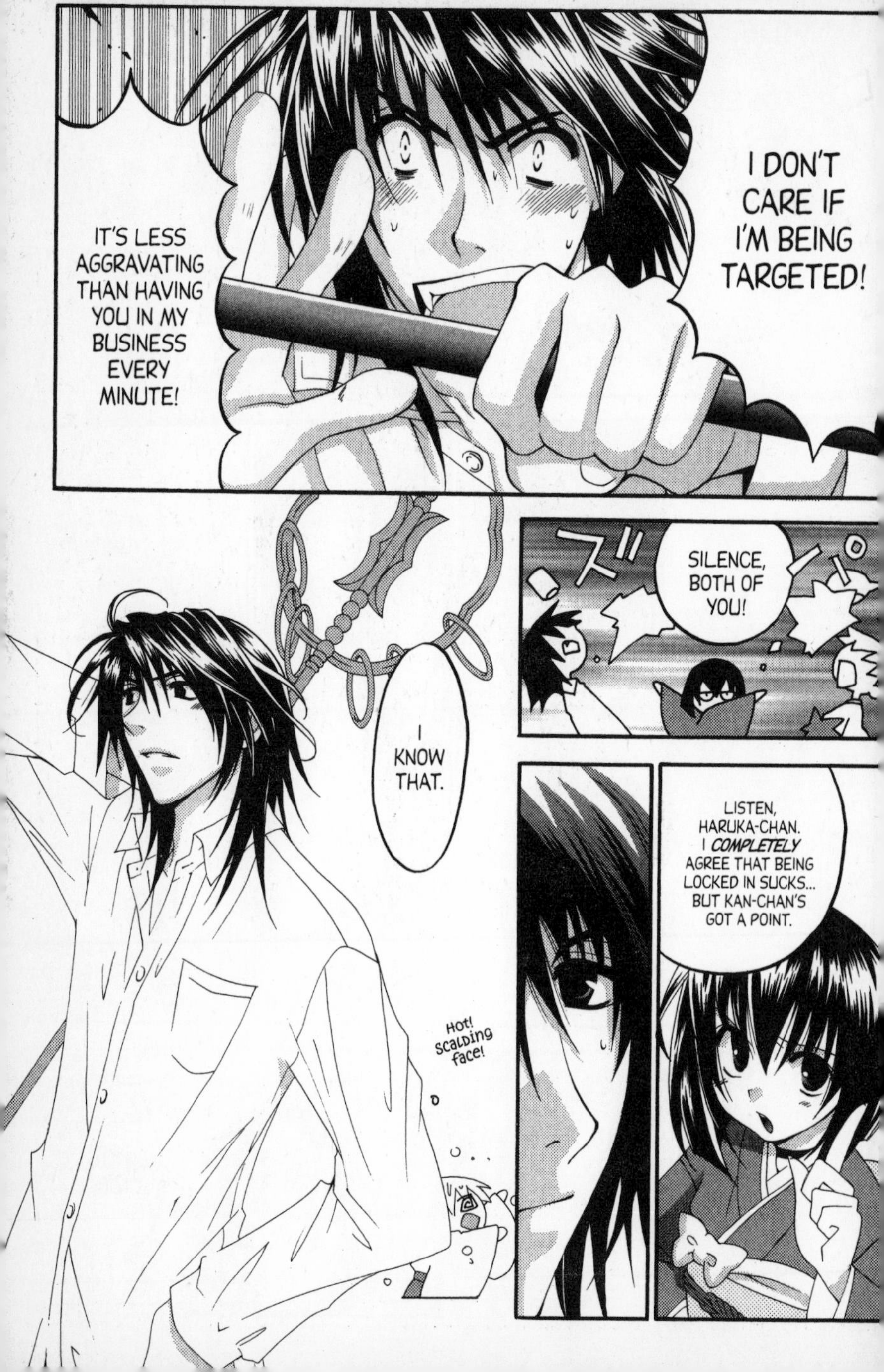
I DON'T CARE IF I'M BEING TARGETED!
IT'S LESS AGGRAVATING THAN HAVING YOU IN MY BUSINESS EVERY MINUTE!
SILENCE, BOTH OF YOU!
LISTEN, HARUKA-CHAN. I *COMPLETELY* AGREE THAT BEING LOCKED IN SUCKS... BUT KAN-CHAN'S GOT A POINT.
I KNOW THAT.
Hot! Scalding face!

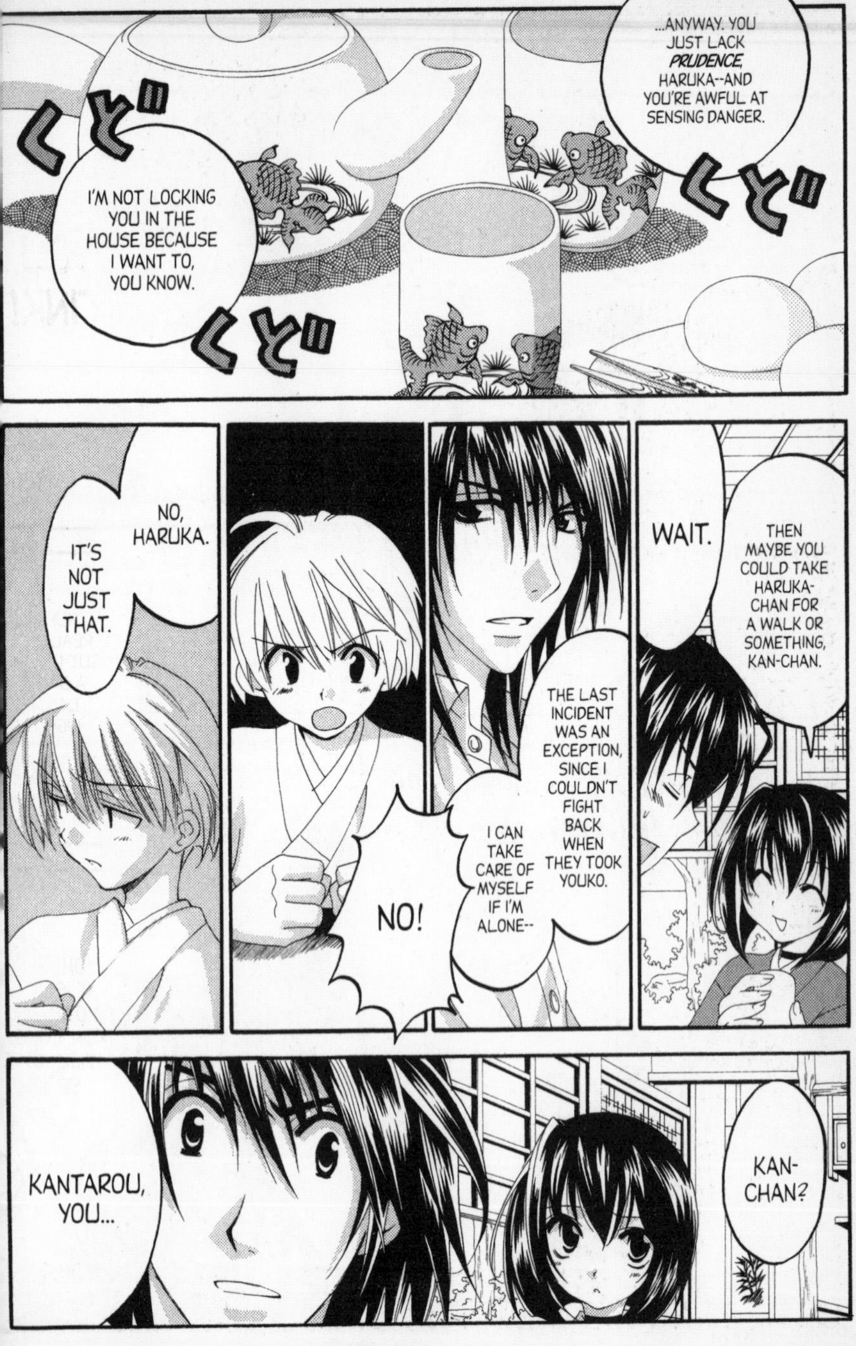
...ANYWAY. YOU JUST LACK *PRUDENCE*, HARUKA--AND YOU'RE AWFUL AT SENSING DANGER.
くど"
くど"
I'M NOT LOCKING YOU IN THE HOUSE BECAUSE I WANT TO, YOU KNOW.
くど"
THEN MAYBE YOU COULD TAKE HARUKA-CHAN FOR A WALK OR SOMETHING, KAN-CHAN.
WAIT.
THE LAST INCIDENT WAS AN EXCEPTION, SINCE I COULDN'T FIGHT BACK WHEN THEY TOOK YOUKO.
I CAN TAKE CARE OF MYSELF IF I'M ALONE--
NO!
NO, HARUKA.
IT'S NOT JUST THAT.
KAN-CHAN?
KANTAROU, YOU...

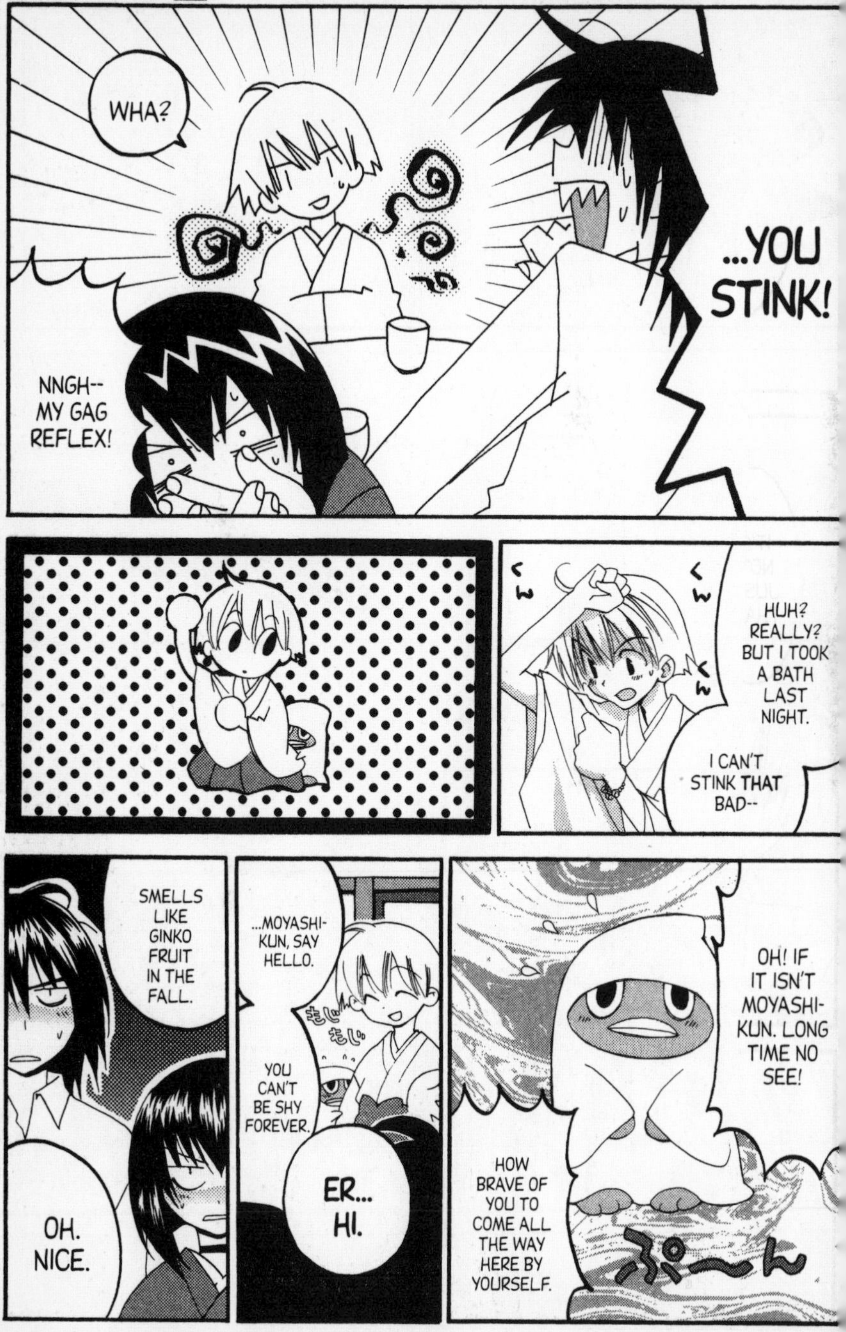
...YOU STINK!
WHA?
NNGH-- MY GAG REFLEX!
くんくん
HUH? REALLY? BUT I TOOK A BATH LAST NIGHT.
I CAN'T STINK **THAT** BAD--
OH! IF IT ISN'T MOYASHI-KUN. LONG TIME NO SEE!
HOW BRAVE OF YOU TO COME ALL THE WAY HERE BY YOURSELF.
ぷ〜ん
...MOYASHI-KUN, SAY HELLO.
もじもじ
YOU CAN'T BE SHY FOREVER.
ER... HI.
SMELLS LIKE GINKO FRUIT IN THE FALL.
OH. NICE.

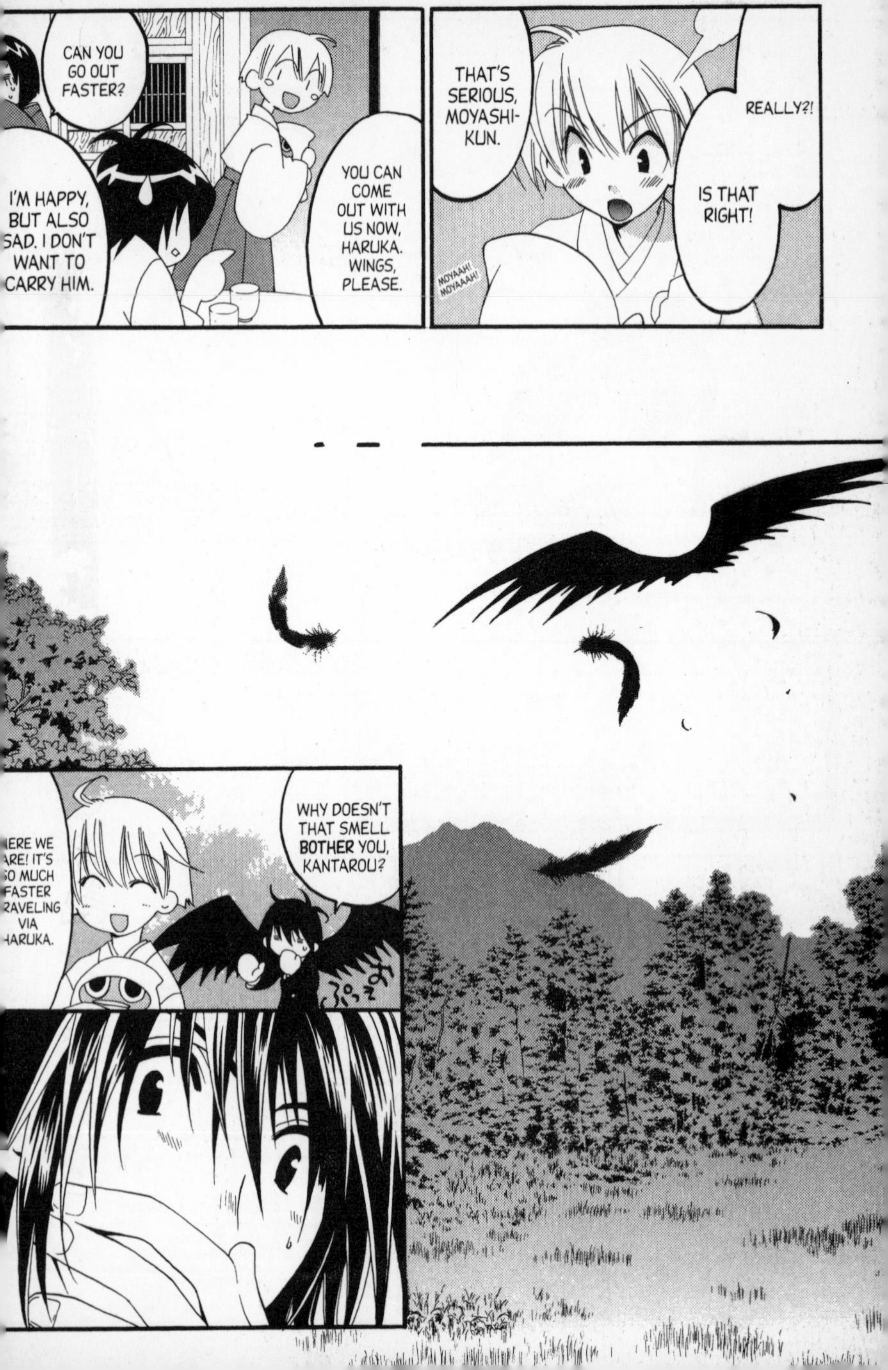
REALLY?!
IS THAT RIGHT!
THAT'S SERIOUS, MOYASHI-KUN.
MOYAAH! MOYAAAH!
YOU CAN COME OUT WITH US NOW, HARUKA. WINGS, PLEASE.
CAN YOU GO OUT FASTER?
I'M HAPPY, BUT ALSO SAD. I DON'T WANT TO CARRY HIM.
WHY DOESN'T THAT SMELL BOTHER YOU, KANTAROU?
ERE WE ARE! IT'S O MUCH FASTER RAVELING VIA ARUKA.

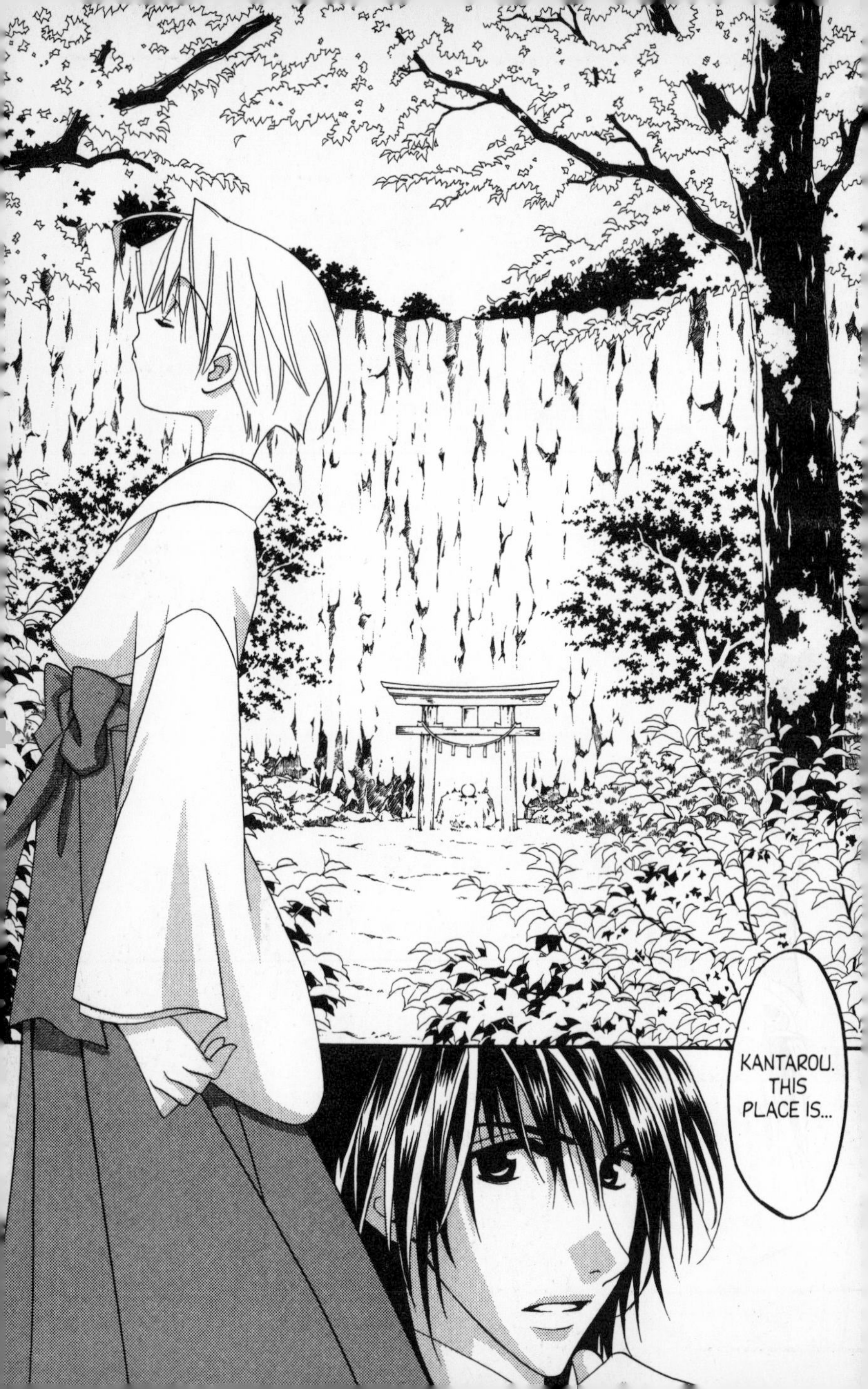
KANTAROU.
THIS
PLACE IS...

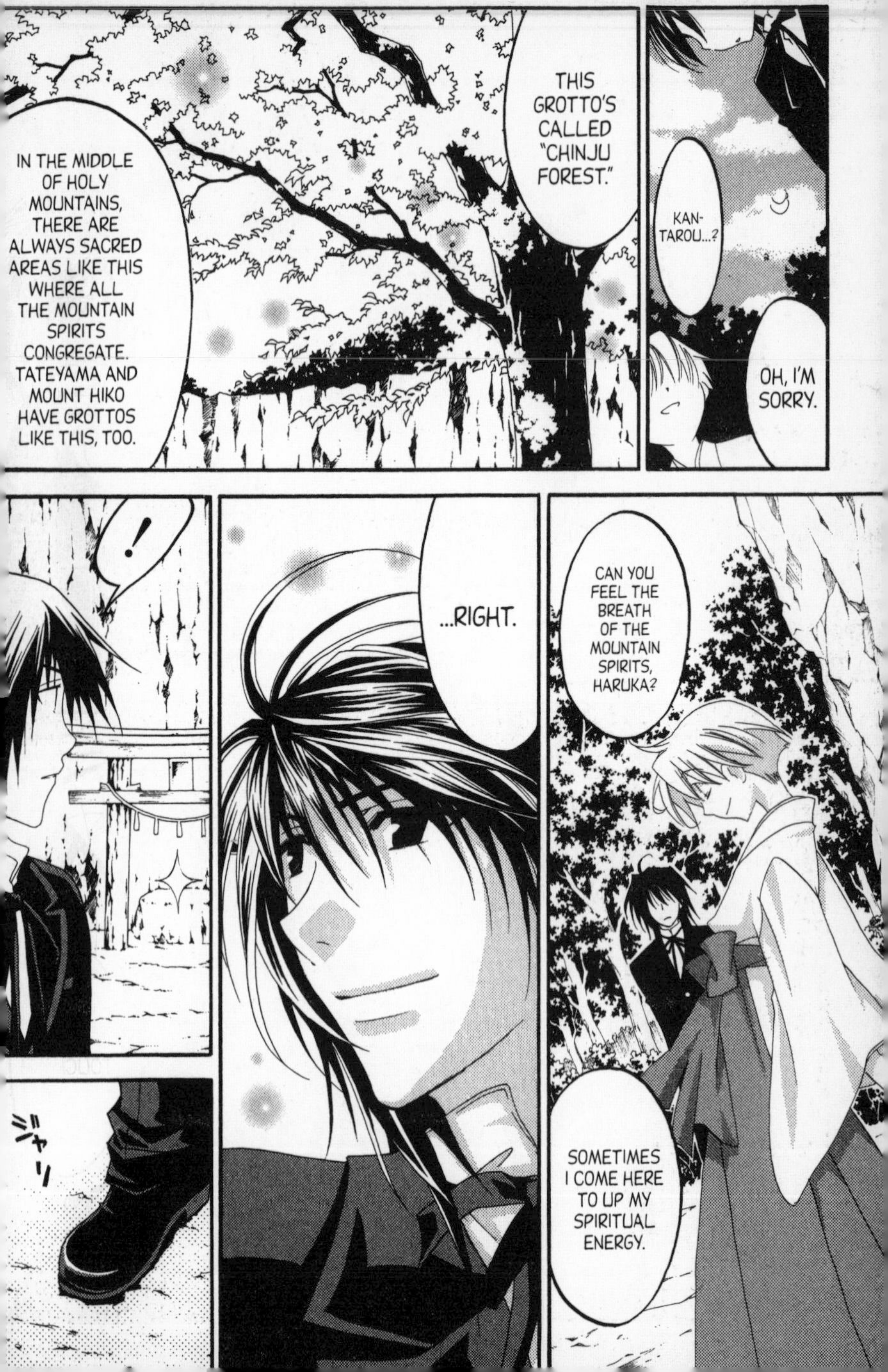
KAN-TAROU...?
OH, I'M SORRY.
THIS GROTTO'S CALLED "CHINJU FOREST."
IN THE MIDDLE OF HOLY MOUNTAINS, THERE ARE ALWAYS SACRED AREAS LIKE THIS WHERE ALL THE MOUNTAIN SPIRITS CONGREGATE. TATEYAMA AND MOUNT HIKO HAVE GROTTOS LIKE THIS, TOO.
CAN YOU FEEL THE BREATH OF THE MOUNTAIN SPIRITS, HARUKA?
SOMETIMES I COME HERE TO UP MY SPIRITUAL ENERGY.
...RIGHT.
!
ジャリ

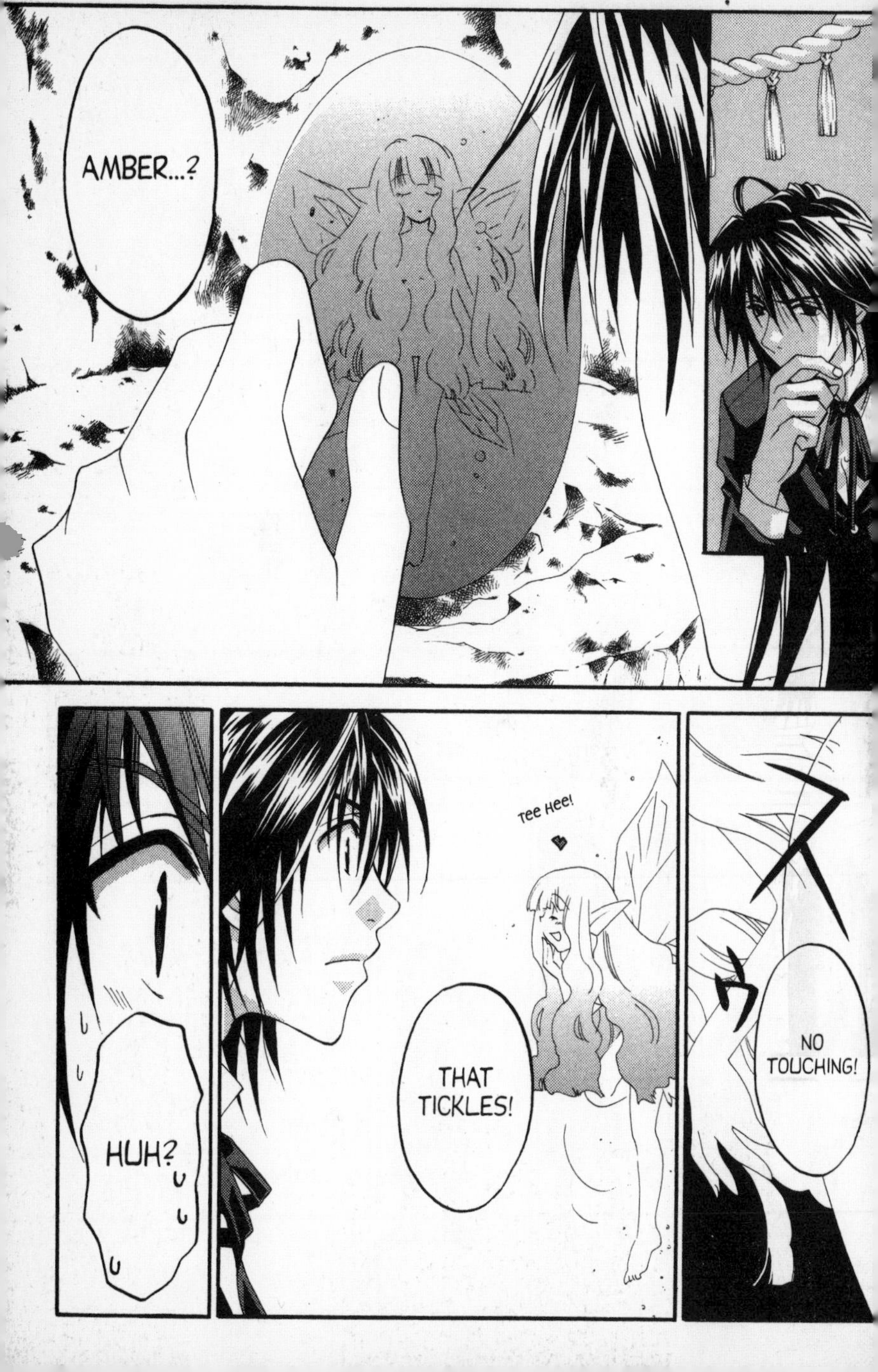
AMBER...?
NO TOUCHING!
TEE HEE!
THAT TICKLES!
HUH?

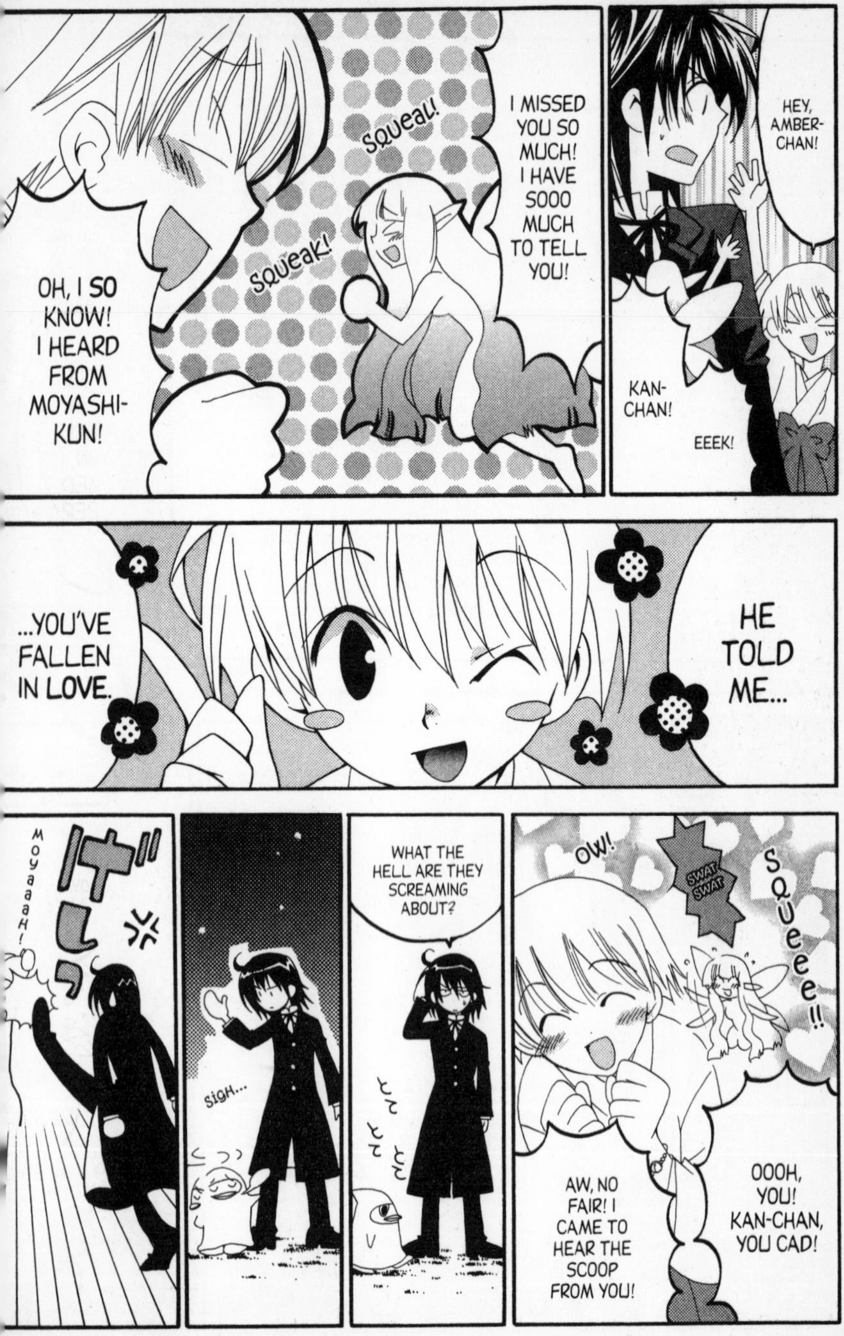
HEY, AMBER-CHAN!
KAN-CHAN!
EEEK!
I MISSED YOU SO MUCH! I HAVE SOOO MUCH TO TELL YOU!
SQUEAL!
SQUEAK!
OH, I SO KNOW! I HEARD FROM MOYASHI-KUN!
HE TOLD ME...
...YOU'VE FALLEN IN LOVE.
SQUEEE!!
OW!
SWAT SWAT
OOOH, YOU! KAN-CHAN, YOU CAD!
AW, NO FAIR! I CAME TO HEAR THE SCOOP FROM YOU!
WHAT THE HELL ARE THEY SCREAMING ABOUT?
とて とて とて
SIGH...
Moyaaaah!

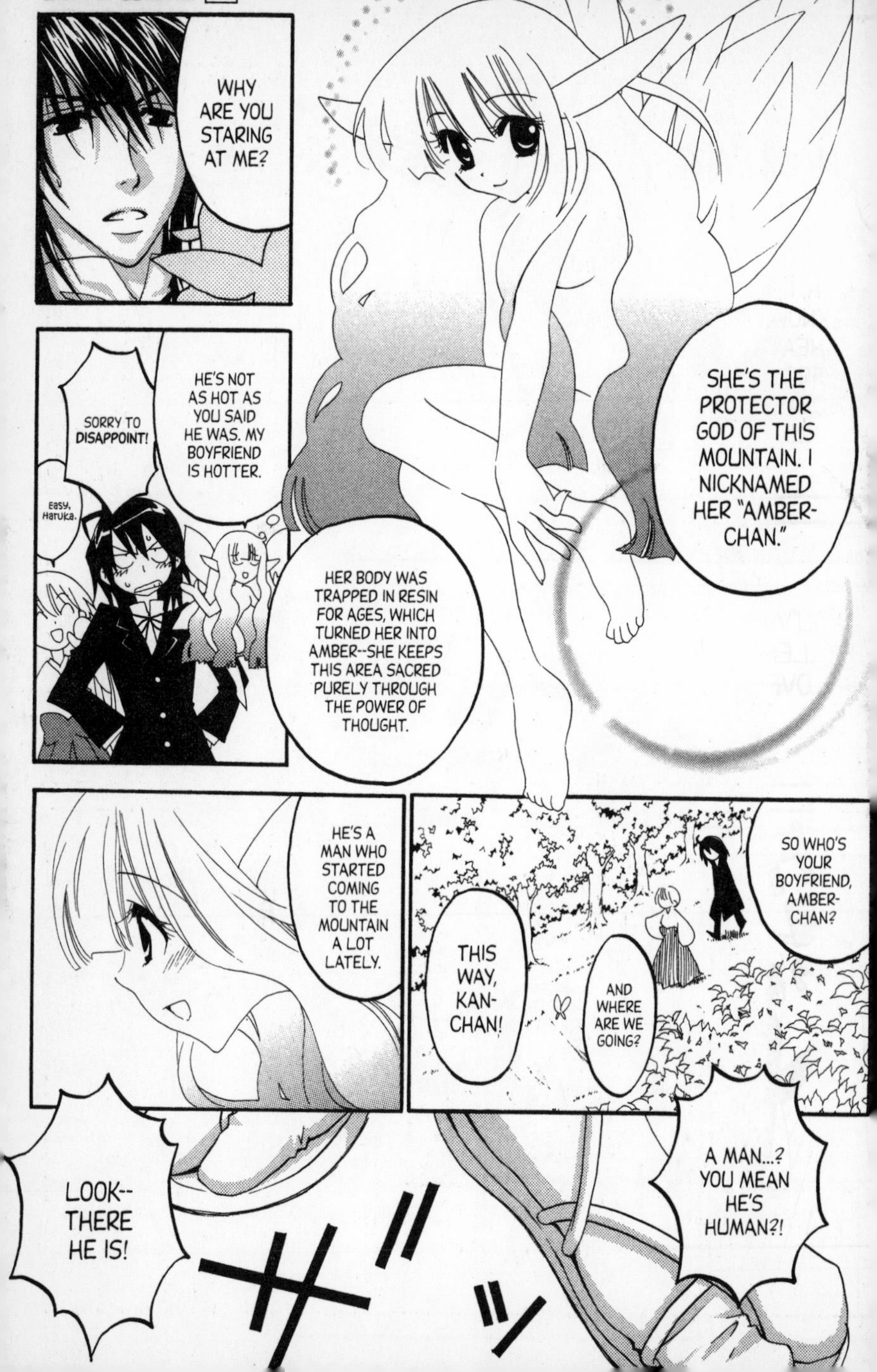
SHE'S THE PROTECTOR GOD OF THIS MOUNTAIN. I NICKNAMED HER "AMBER-CHAN."
HER BODY WAS TRAPPED IN RESIN FOR AGES, WHICH TURNED HER INTO AMBER--SHE KEEPS THIS AREA SACRED PURELY THROUGH THE POWER OF THOUGHT.
WHY ARE YOU STARING AT ME?
HE'S NOT AS HOT AS YOU SAID HE WAS. MY BOYFRIEND IS HOTTER.
SORRY TO DISAPPOINT!
Easy, Haruka.
SO WHO'S YOUR BOYFRIEND, AMBER-CHAN?
AND WHERE ARE WE GOING?
THIS WAY, KAN-CHAN!
HE'S A MAN WHO STARTED COMING TO THE MOUNTAIN A LOT LATELY.
A MAN...? YOU MEAN HE'S HUMAN?!
LOOK--THERE HE IS!

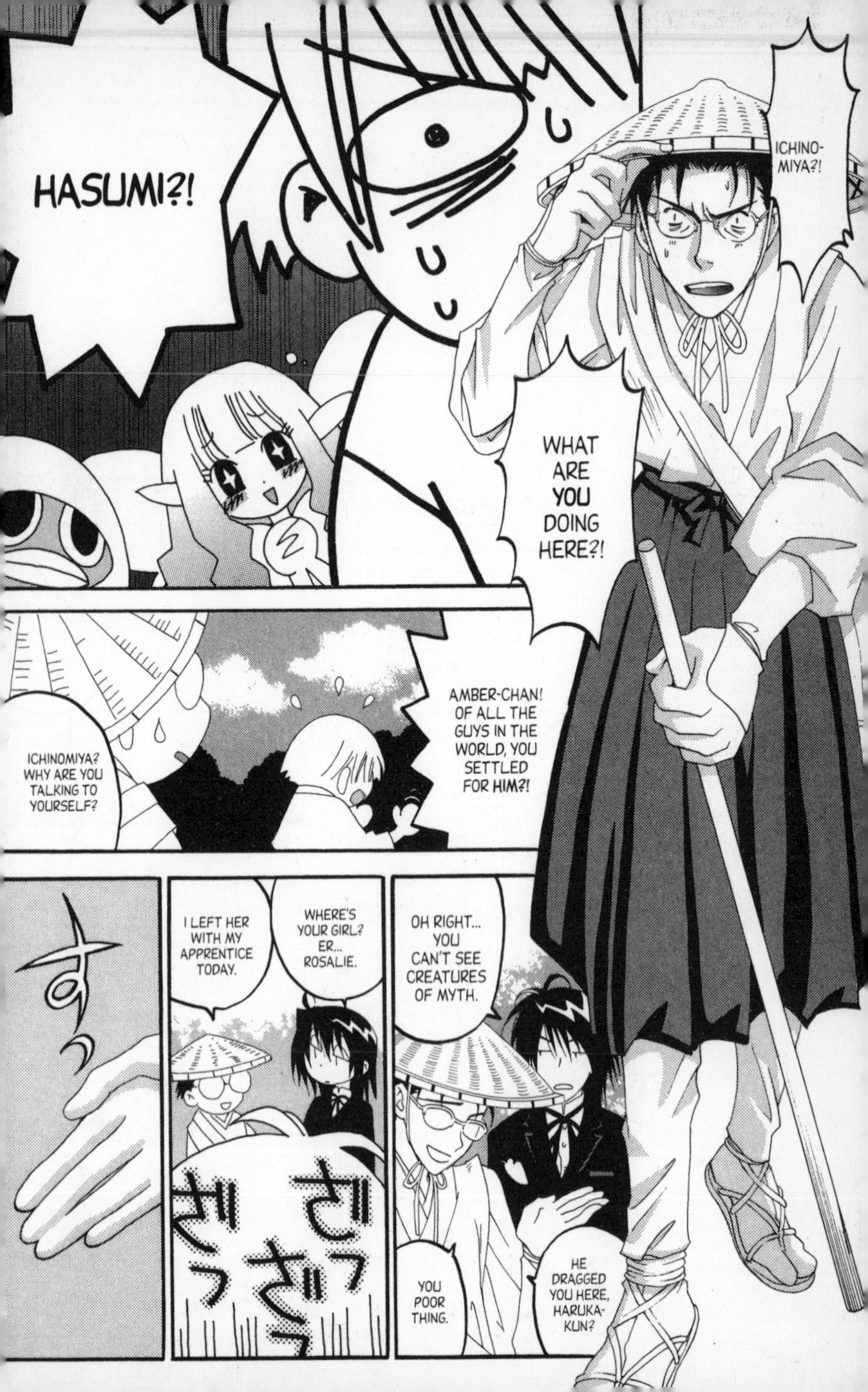
ICHINO-MIYA?!
WHAT ARE YOU DOING HERE?!
AMBER-CHAN! OF ALL THE GUYS IN THE WORLD, YOU SETTLED FOR HIM?!
HASUMI?!
ICHINOMIYA? WHY ARE YOU TALKING TO YOURSELF?
OH RIGHT... YOU CAN'T SEE CREATURES OF MYTH.
HE DRAGGED YOU HERE, HARUKA-KUN?
YOU POOR THING.
WHERE'S YOUR GIRL? ER... ROSALIE.
I LEFT HER WITH MY APPRENTICE TODAY.
ざわっ ざわっ
すっ

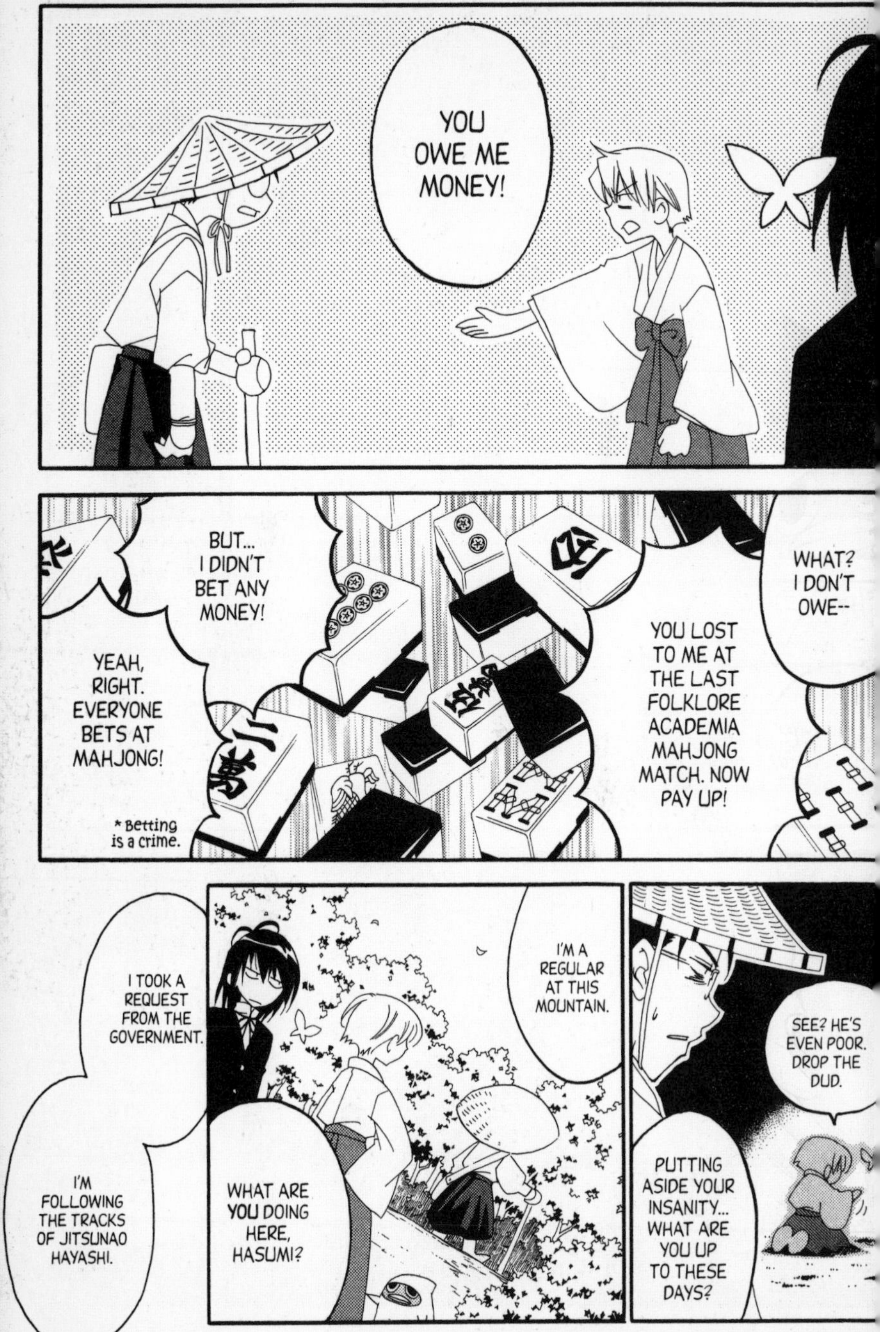
YOU OWE ME MONEY!
WHAT? I DON'T OWE--
YOU LOST TO ME AT THE LAST FOLKLORE ACADEMIA MAHJONG MATCH. NOW PAY UP!
BUT... I DIDN'T BET ANY MONEY!
YEAH, RIGHT. EVERYONE BETS AT MAHJONG!
* Betting is a crime.
SEE? HE'S EVEN POOR. DROP THE DUD.
PUTTING ASIDE YOUR INSANITY... WHAT ARE YOU UP TO THESE DAYS?
I'M A REGULAR AT THIS MOUNTAIN.
WHAT ARE YOU DOING HERE, HASUMI?
I TOOK A REQUEST FROM THE GOVERNMENT.
I'M FOLLOWING THE TRACKS OF JITSUNAO HAYASHI.

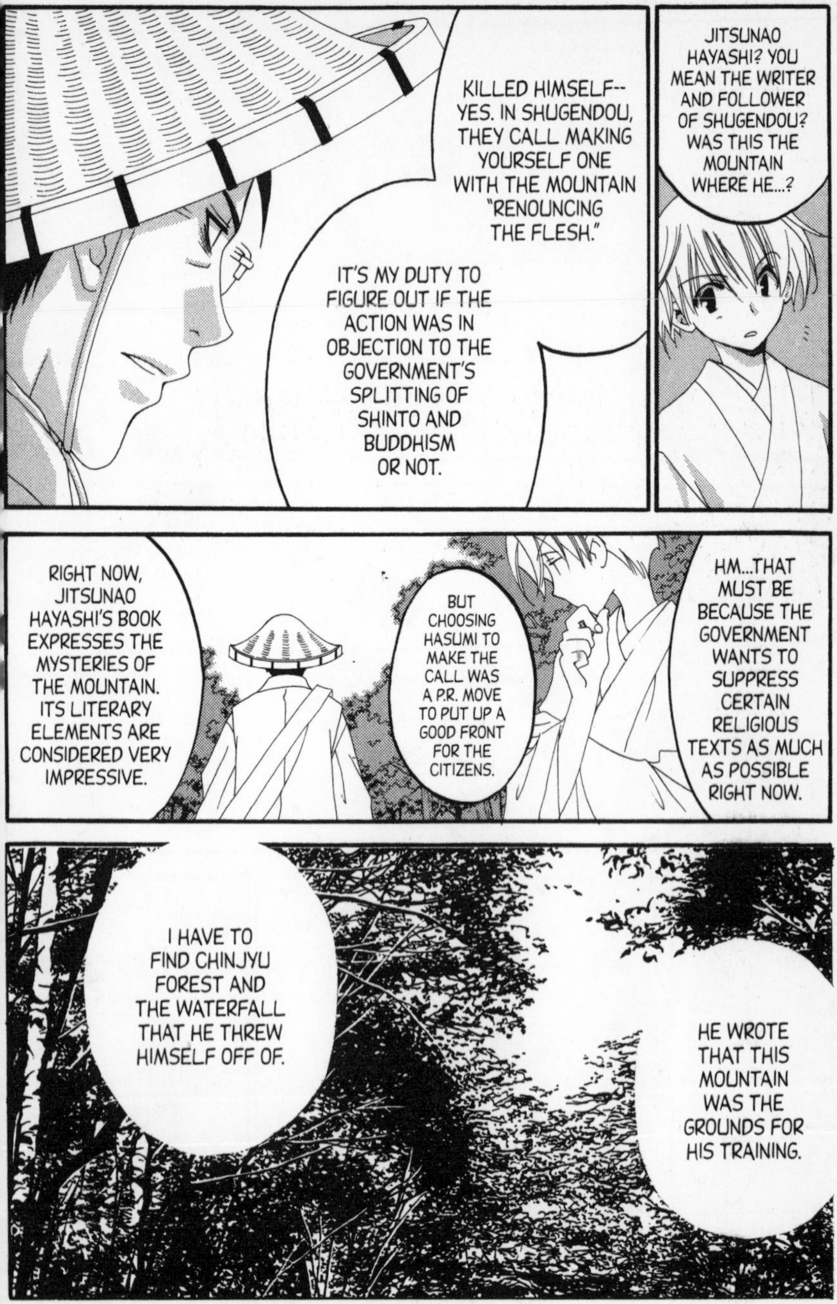
JITSUNAO HAYASHI? YOU MEAN THE WRITER AND FOLLOWER OF SHUGENDOU? WAS THIS THE MOUNTAIN WHERE HE...?
KILLED HIMSELF-- YES. IN SHUGENDOU, THEY CALL MAKING YOURSELF ONE WITH THE MOUNTAIN "RENOUNCING THE FLESH."
IT'S MY DUTY TO FIGURE OUT IF THE ACTION WAS IN OBJECTION TO THE GOVERNMENT'S SPLITTING OF SHINTO AND BUDDHISM OR NOT.
HM...THAT MUST BE BECAUSE THE GOVERNMENT WANTS TO SUPPRESS CERTAIN RELIGIOUS TEXTS AS MUCH AS POSSIBLE RIGHT NOW.
BUT CHOOSING HASUMI TO MAKE THE CALL WAS A P.R. MOVE TO PUT UP A GOOD FRONT FOR THE CITIZENS.
RIGHT NOW, JITSUNAO HAYASHI'S BOOK EXPRESSES THE MYSTERIES OF THE MOUNTAIN. ITS LITERARY ELEMENTS ARE CONSIDERED VERY IMPRESSIVE.
HE WROTE THAT THIS MOUNTAIN WAS THE GROUNDS FOR HIS TRAINING.
I HAVE TO FIND CHINJYU FOREST AND THE WATERFALL THAT HE THREW HIMSELF OFF OF.

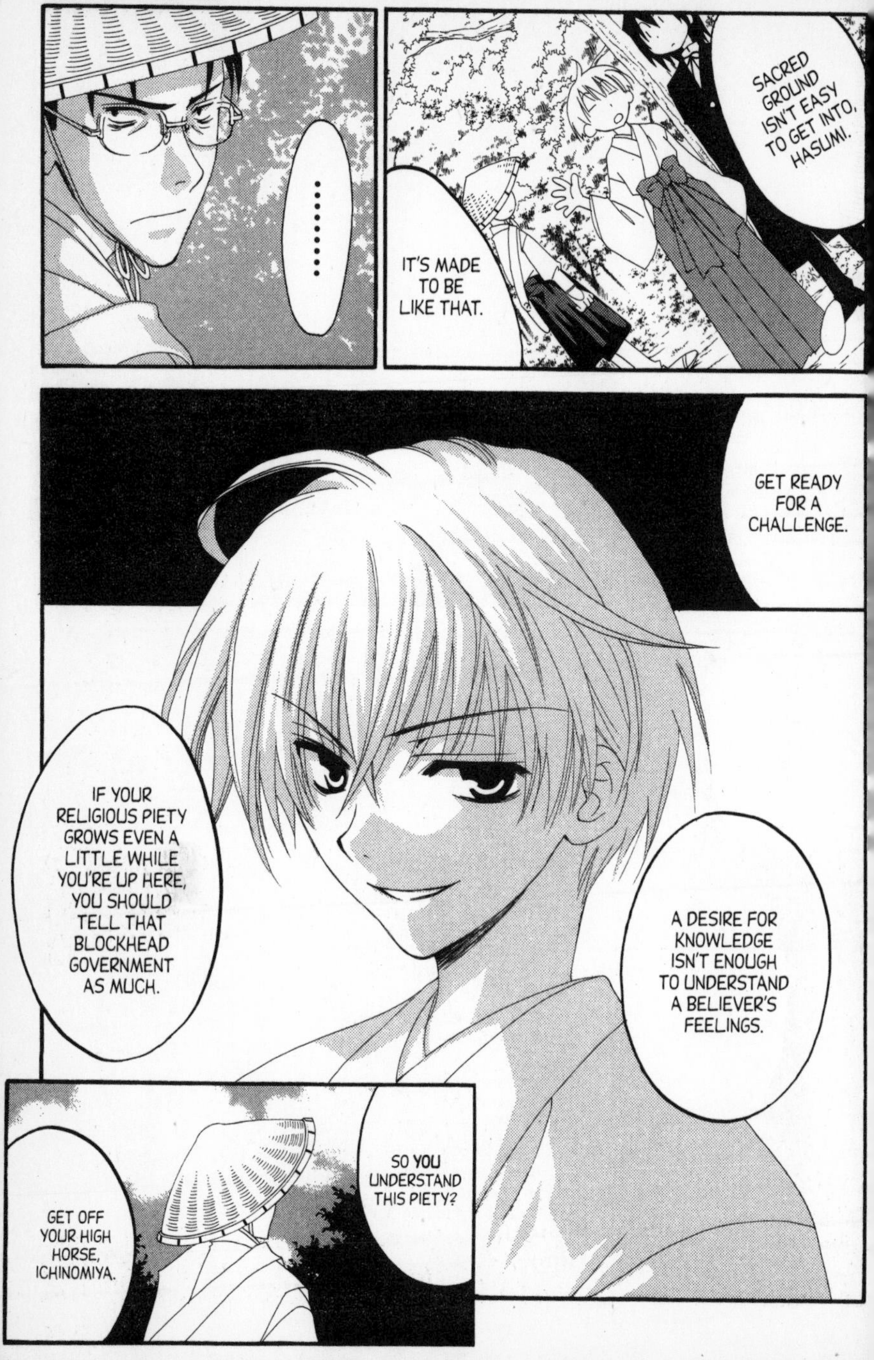
SACRED GROUND ISN'T EASY TO GET INTO, HASUMI.
IT'S MADE TO BE LIKE THAT.
....
GET READY FOR A CHALLENGE.
A DESIRE FOR KNOWLEDGE ISN'T ENOUGH TO UNDERSTAND A BELIEVER'S FEELINGS.
IF YOUR RELIGIOUS PIETY GROWS EVEN A LITTLE WHILE YOU'RE UP HERE, YOU SHOULD TELL THAT BLOCKHEAD GOVERNMENT AS MUCH.
SO YOU UNDERSTAND THIS PIETY?
GET OFF YOUR HIGH HORSE, ICHINOMIYA.

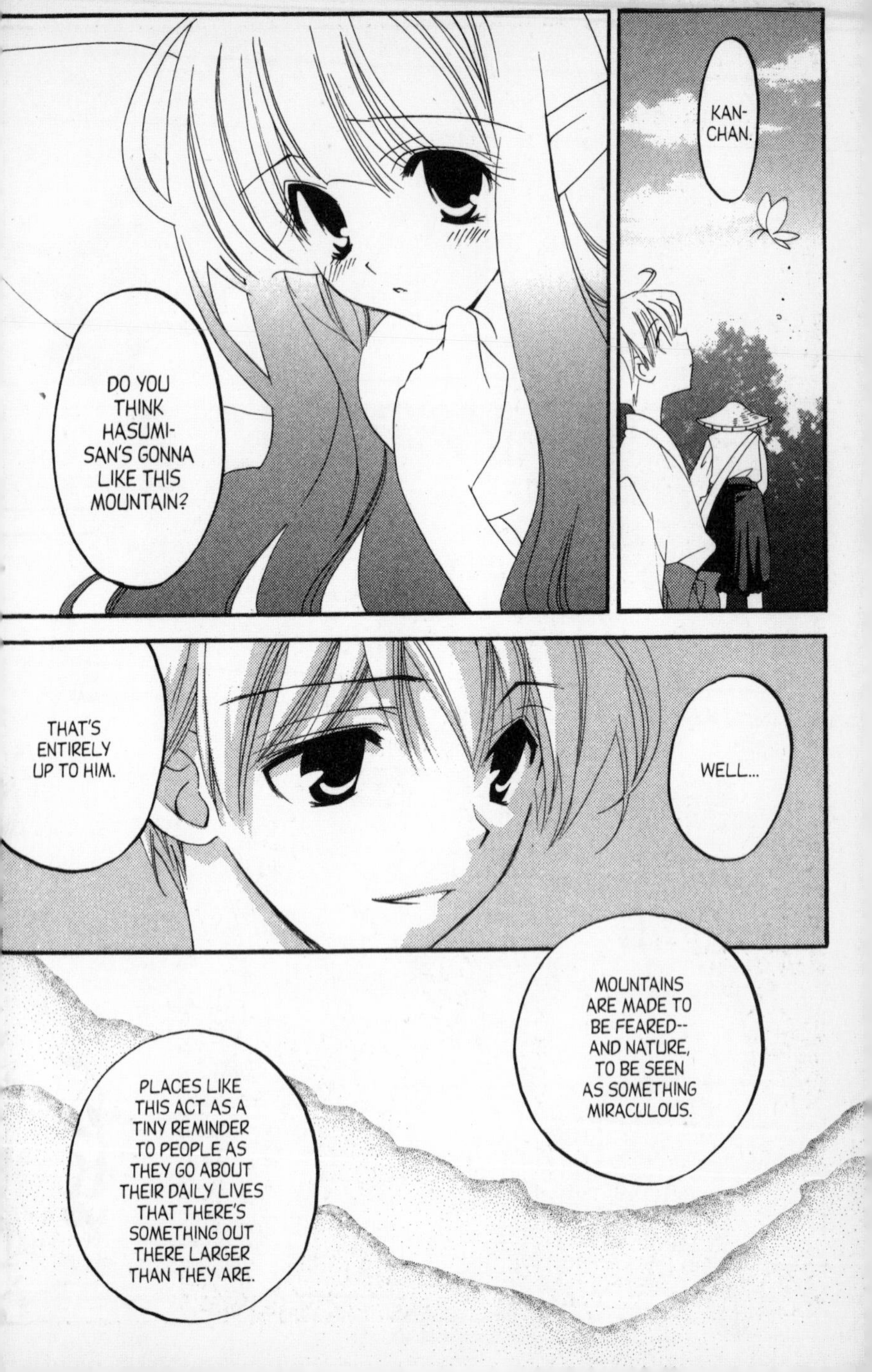
KAN-CHAN.
DO YOU THINK HASUMI-SAN'S GONNA LIKE THIS MOUNTAIN?
WELL...
THAT'S ENTIRELY UP TO HIM.
MOUNTAINS ARE MADE TO BE FEARED--AND NATURE, TO BE SEEN AS SOMETHING MIRACULOUS.
PLACES LIKE THIS ACT AS A TINY REMINDER TO PEOPLE AS THEY GO ABOUT THEIR DAILY LIVES THAT THERE'S SOMETHING OUT THERE LARGER THAN THEY ARE.

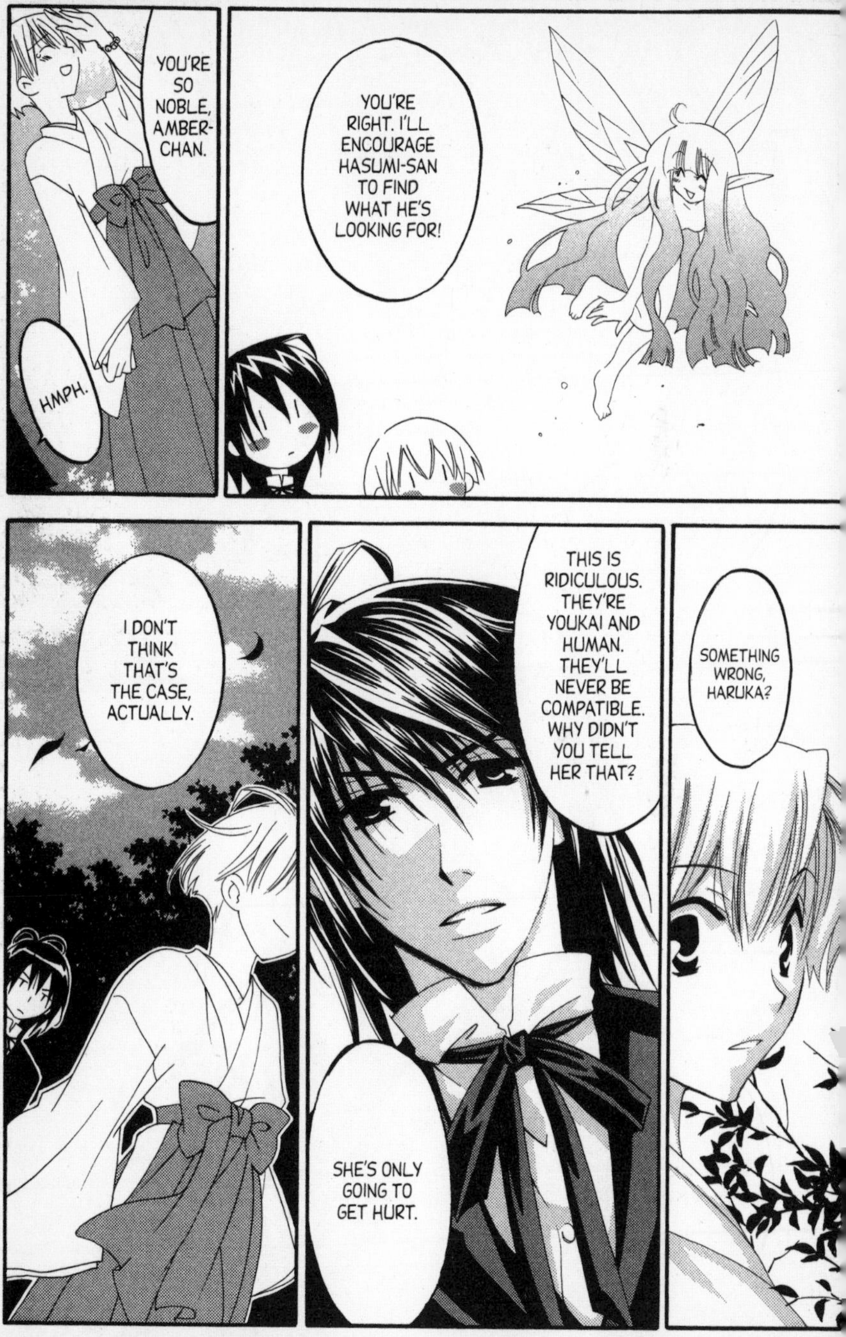
YOU'RE RIGHT. I'LL ENCOURAGE HASUMI-SAN TO FIND WHAT HE'S LOOKING FOR!
YOU'RE SO NOBLE, AMBER-CHAN.
HMPH.
SOMETHING WRONG, HARUKA?
THIS IS RIDICULOUS. THEY'RE YOUKAI AND HUMAN. THEY'LL NEVER BE COMPATIBLE. WHY DIDN'T YOU TELL HER THAT?
SHE'S ONLY GOING TO GET HURT.
I DON'T THINK THAT'S THE CASE, ACTUALLY.

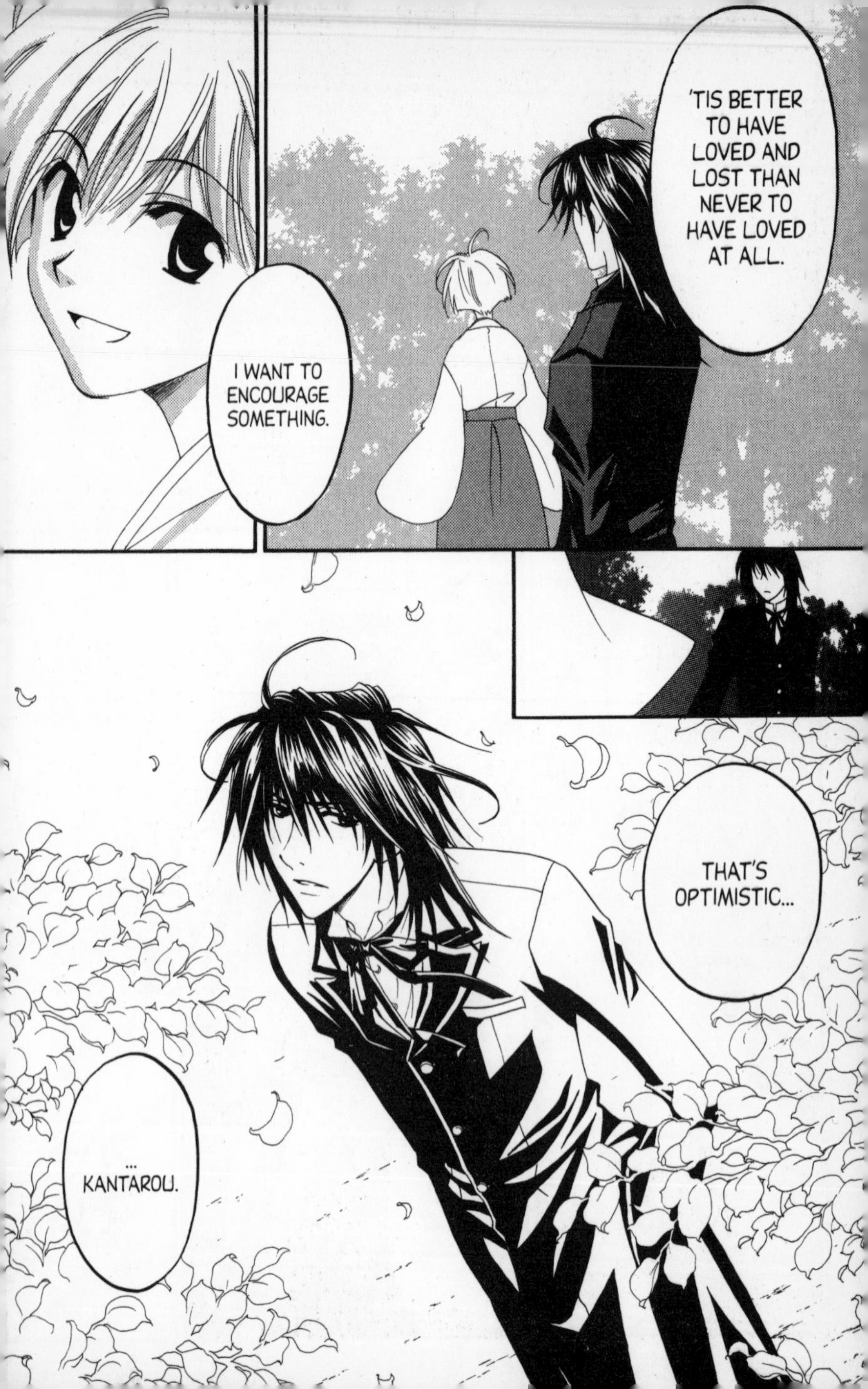
'TIS BETTER TO HAVE LOVED AND LOST THAN NEVER TO HAVE LOVED AT ALL.
I WANT TO ENCOURAGE SOMETHING.
THAT'S OPTIMISTIC...
... KANTAROU.

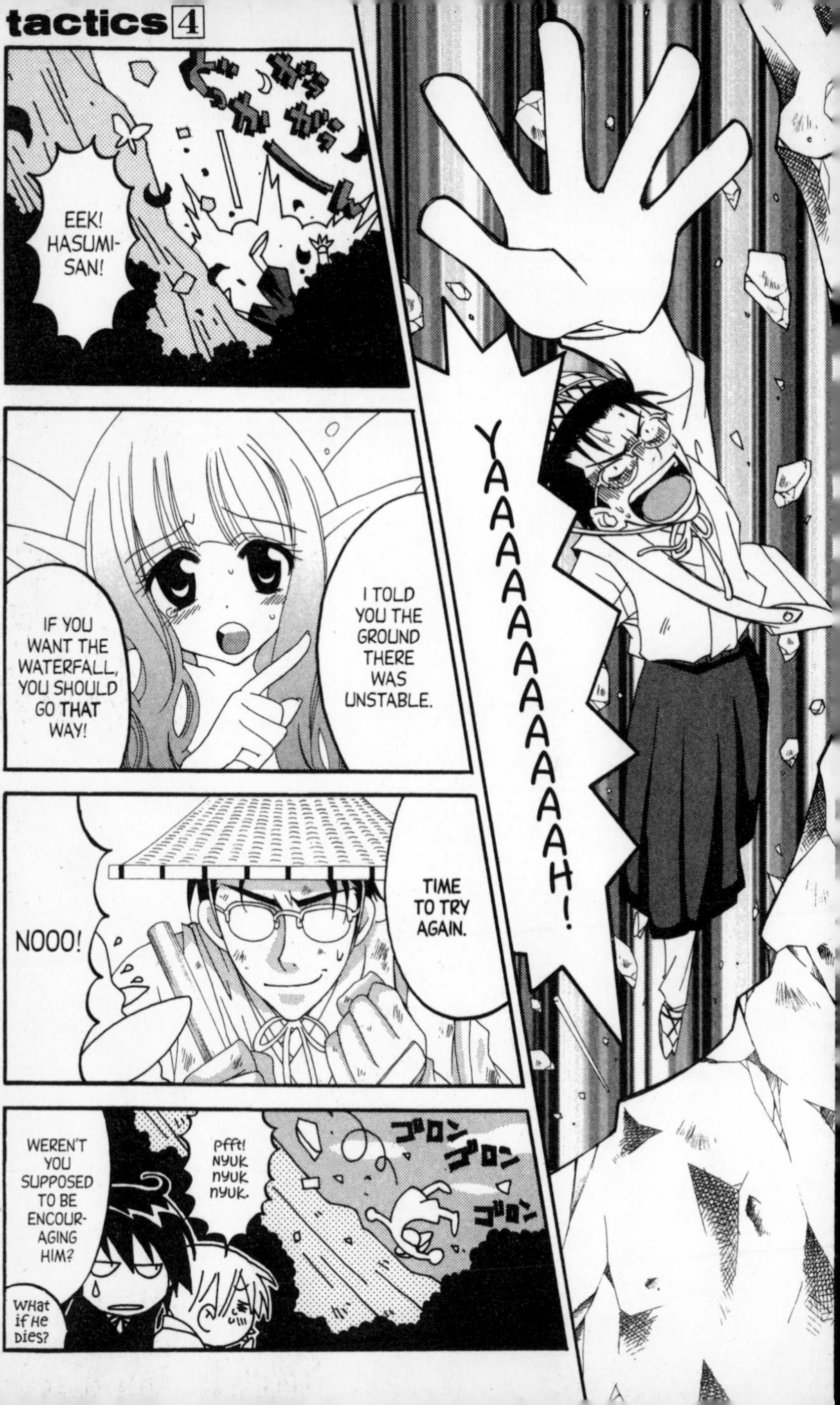
YAAAAAAAAAAAAH!
EEK! HASUMI-SAN!
I TOLD YOU THE GROUND THERE WAS UNSTABLE.
IF YOU WANT THE WATERFALL, YOU SHOULD GO THAT WAY!
TIME TO TRY AGAIN.
NOOO!
ゴロン ゴロン
ゴロン
pfft! nyuk nyuk nyuk.
WEREN'T YOU SUPPOSED TO BE ENCOURAGING HIM?
What if he dies?

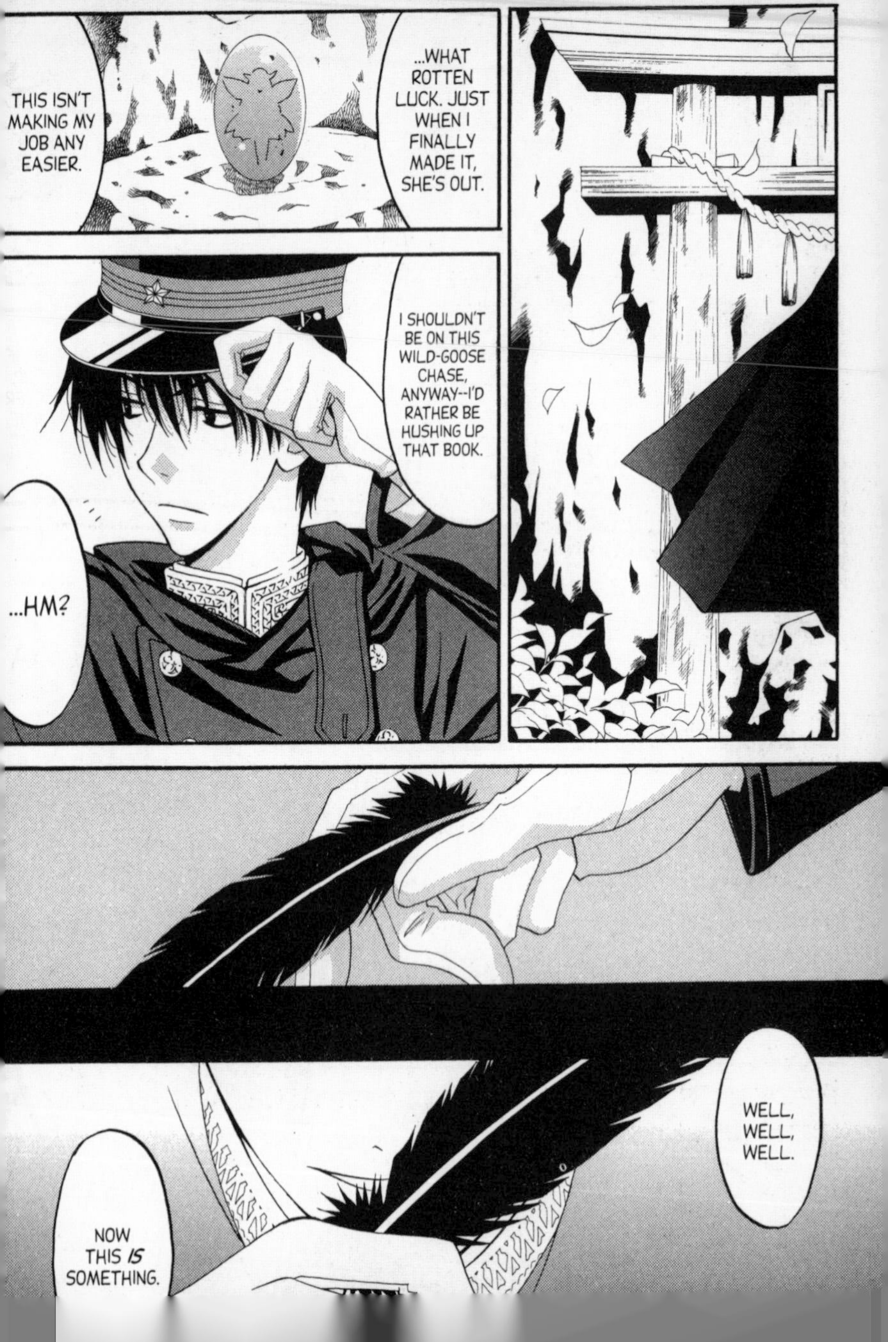
...WHAT ROTTEN LUCK. JUST WHEN I FINALLY MADE IT, SHE'S OUT.
THIS ISN'T MAKING MY JOB ANY EASIER.
I SHOULDN'T BE ON THIS WILD-GOOSE CHASE, ANYWAY--I'D RATHER BE HUSHING UP THAT BOOK.
...HM?
WELL, WELL, WELL.
NOW THIS *IS* SOMETHING.

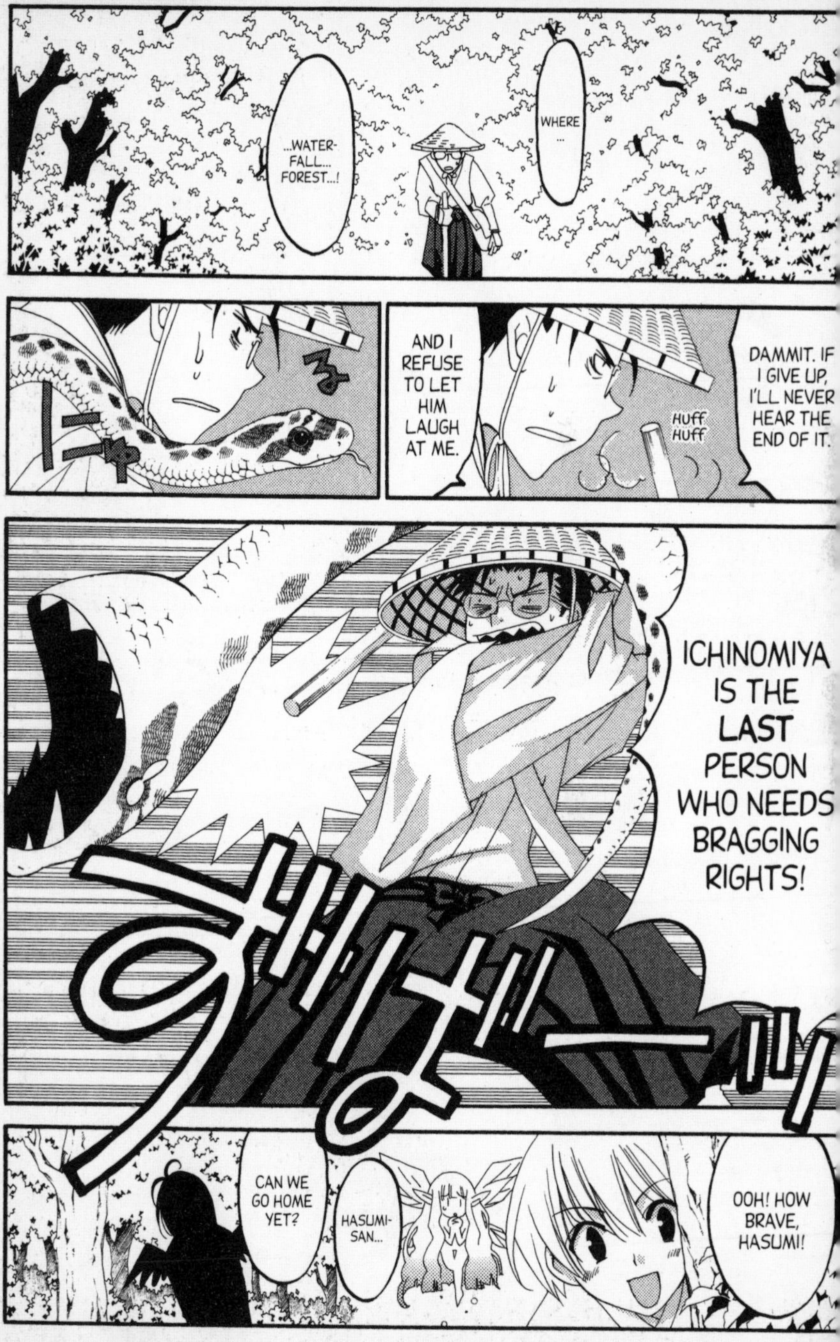
WHERE ...
...WATER-FALL... FOREST...!
DAMMIT. IF I GIVE UP, I'LL NEVER HEAR THE END OF IT.
HUFF HUFF
AND I REFUSE TO LET HIM LAUGH AT ME.
ICHINOMIYA IS THE LAST PERSON WHO NEEDS BRAGGING RIGHTS!
OOH! HOW BRAVE, HASUMI!
HASUMI-SAN...
CAN WE GO HOME YET?

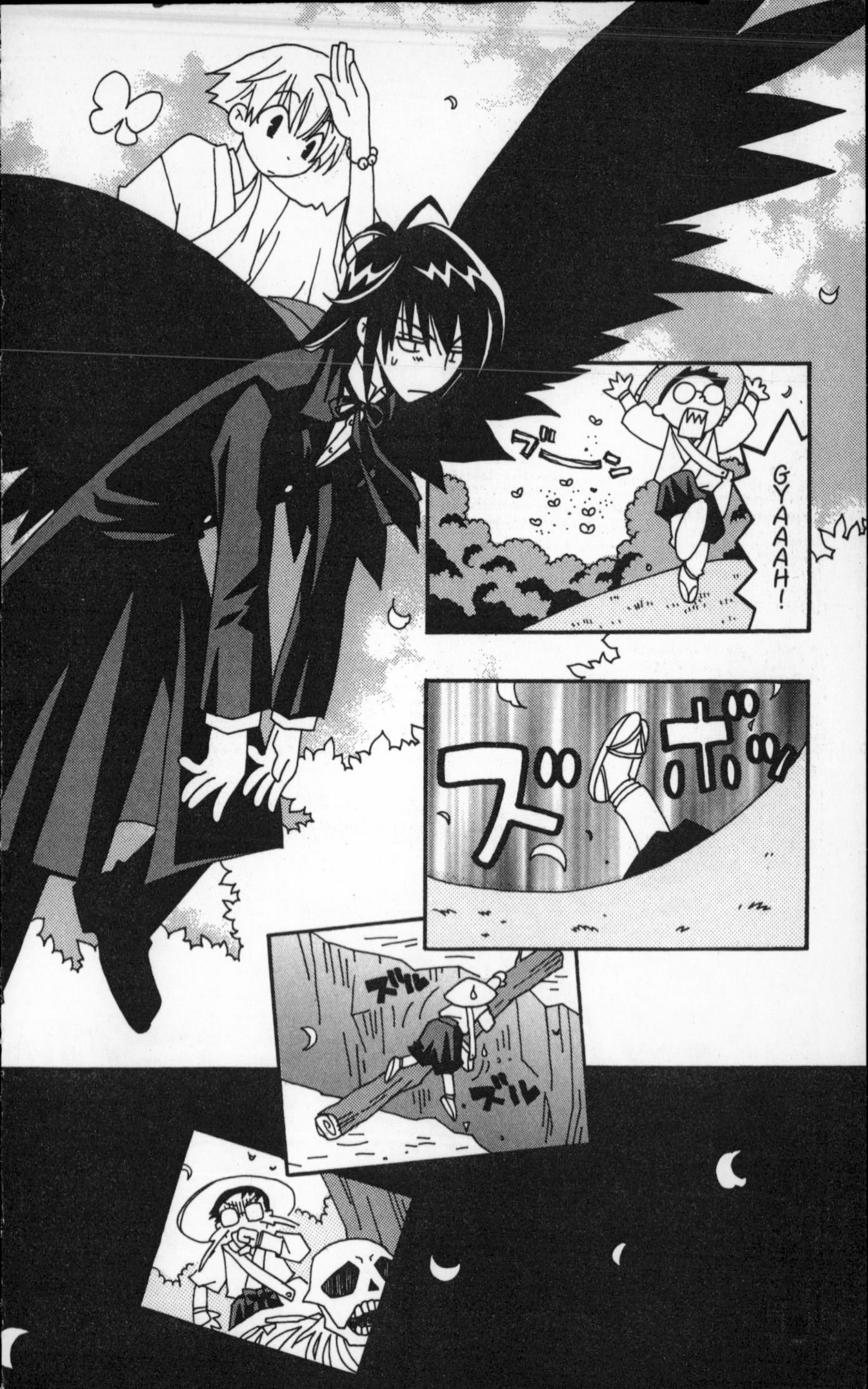
GYAAAAH!
ブーン
ズボッ
ズル
ズル

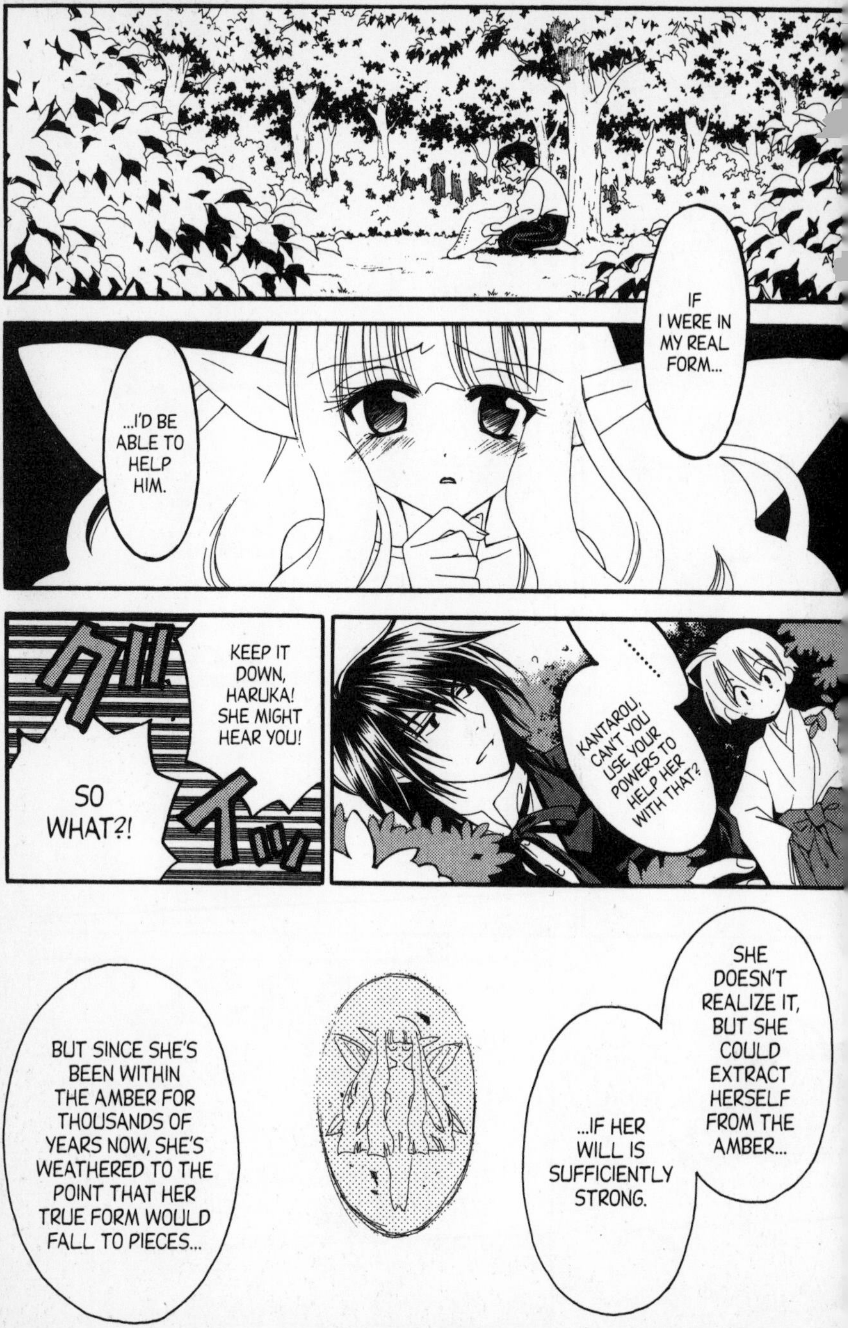
IF I WERE IN MY REAL FORM...
...I'D BE ABLE TO HELP HIM.
......
KANTAROU, CAN'T YOU USE YOUR POWERS TO HELP HER WITH THAT?
KEEP IT DOWN, HARUKA! SHE MIGHT HEAR YOU!
SO WHAT?!
SHE DOESN'T REALIZE IT, BUT SHE COULD EXTRACT HERSELF FROM THE AMBER...
...IF HER WILL IS SUFFICIENTLY STRONG.
BUT SINCE SHE'S BEEN WITHIN THE AMBER FOR THOUSANDS OF YEARS NOW, SHE'S WEATHERED TO THE POINT THAT HER TRUE FORM WOULD FALL TO PIECES...

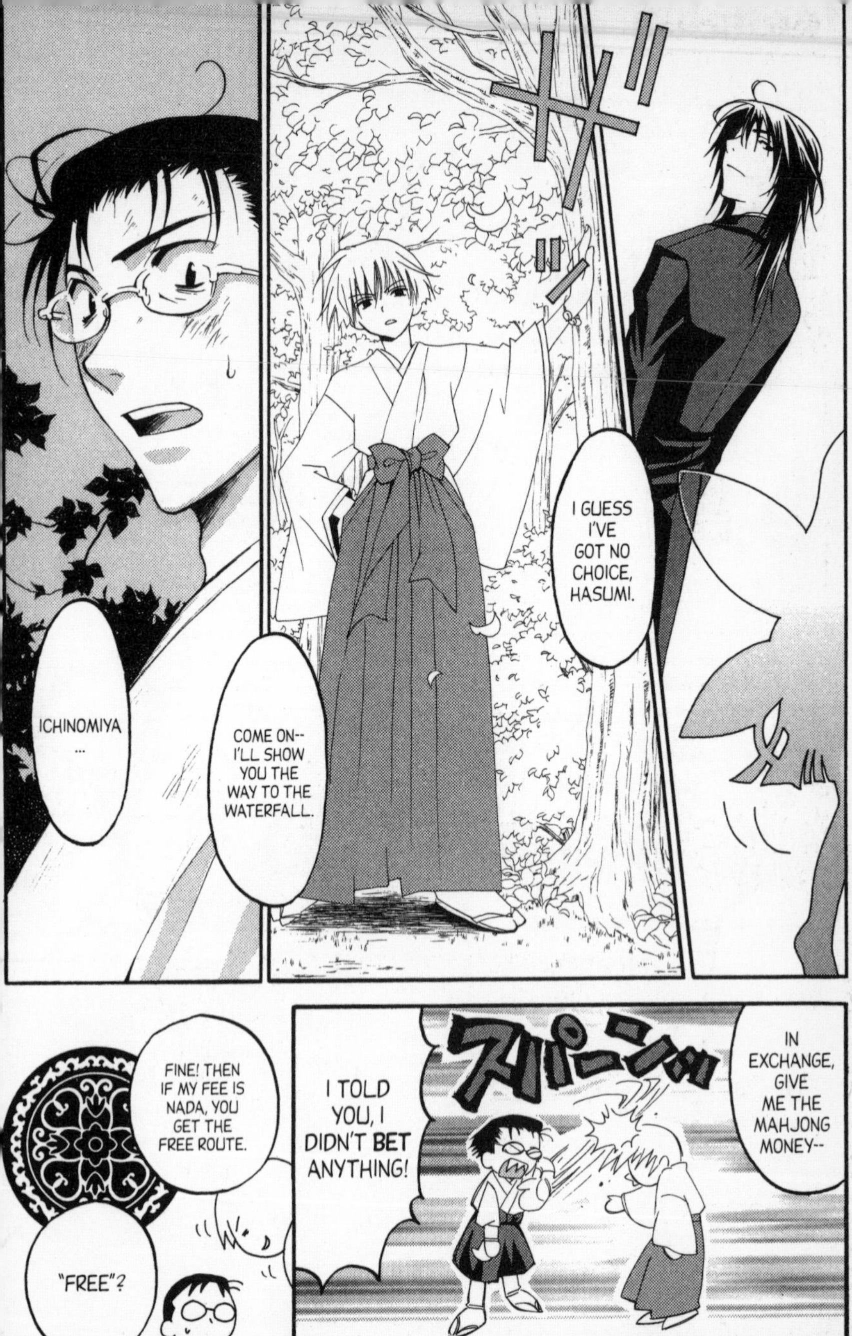
I GUESS I'VE GOT NO CHOICE, HASUMI.
COME ON-- I'LL SHOW YOU THE WAY TO THE WATERFALL.
ICHINOMIYA ...
IN EXCHANGE, GIVE ME THE MAHJONG MONEY--
スパーン!!
I TOLD YOU, I DIDN'T **BET** ANYTHING!
FINE! THEN IF MY FEE IS NADA, YOU GET THE FREE ROUTE.
"FREE"?

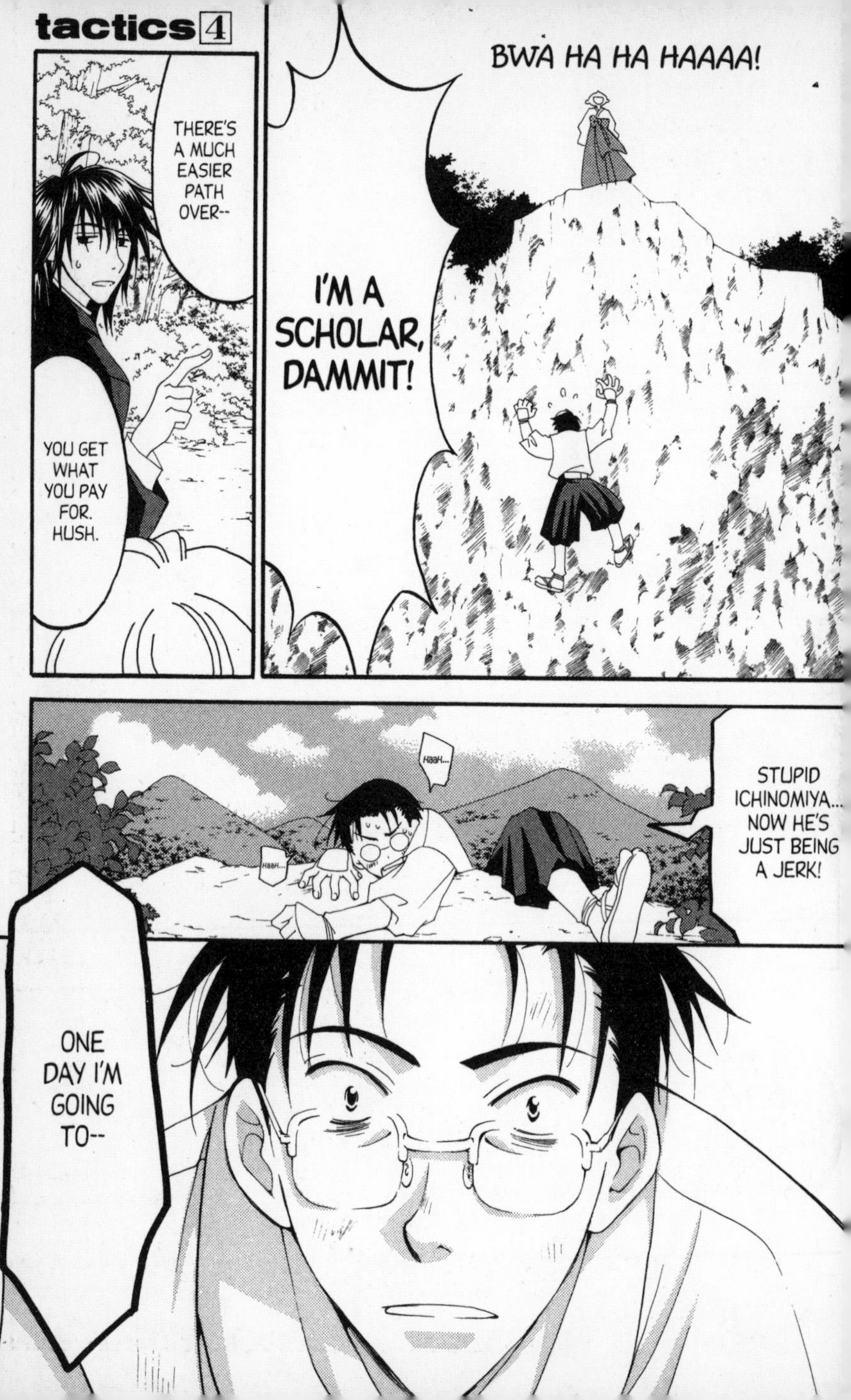
BWA HA HA HAAAA!
I'M A SCHOLAR, DAMMIT!
THERE'S A MUCH EASIER PATH OVER--
YOU GET WHAT YOU PAY FOR. HUSH.
STUPID ICHINOMIYA... NOW HE'S JUST BEING A JERK!
ONE DAY I'M GOING TO--

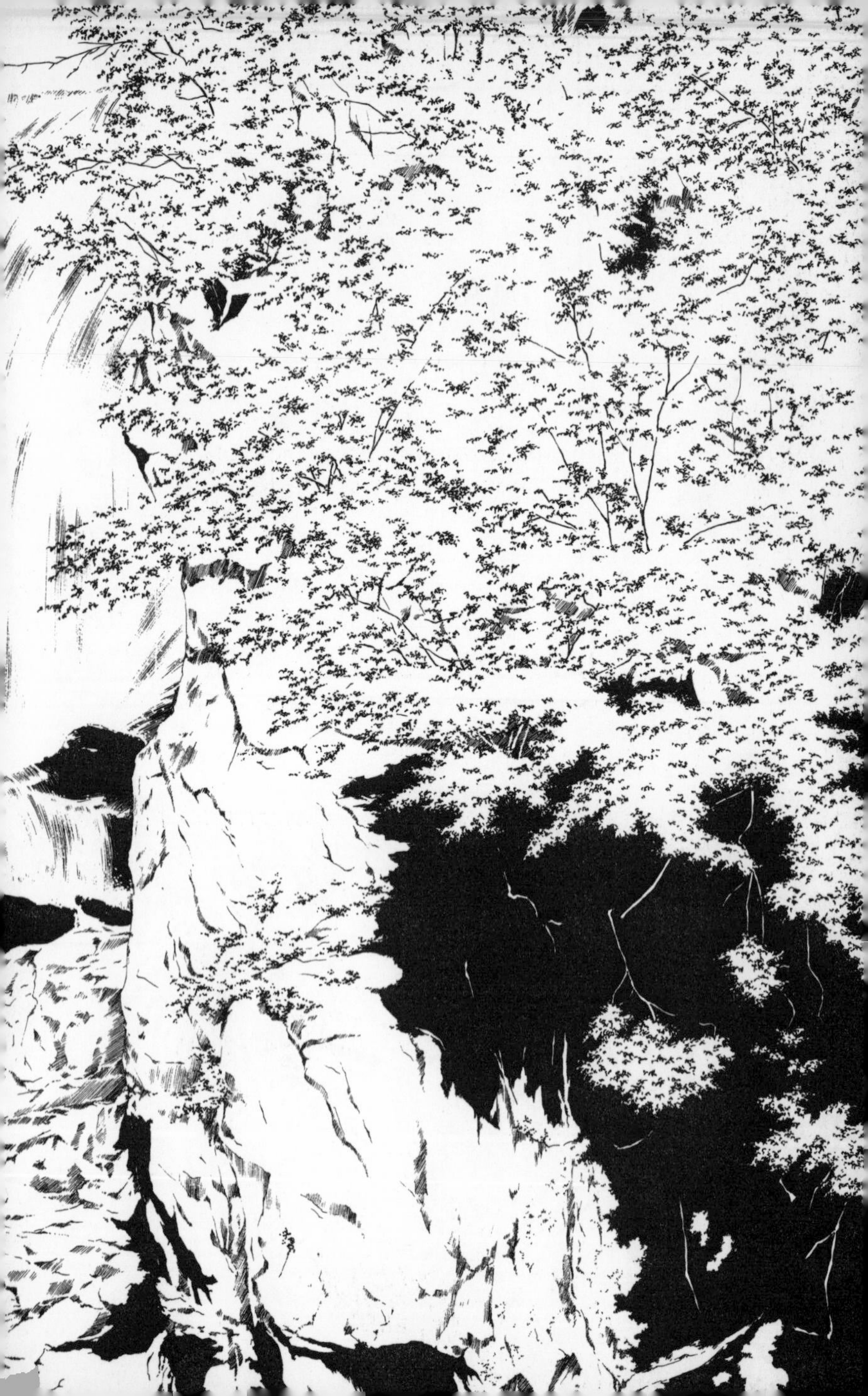

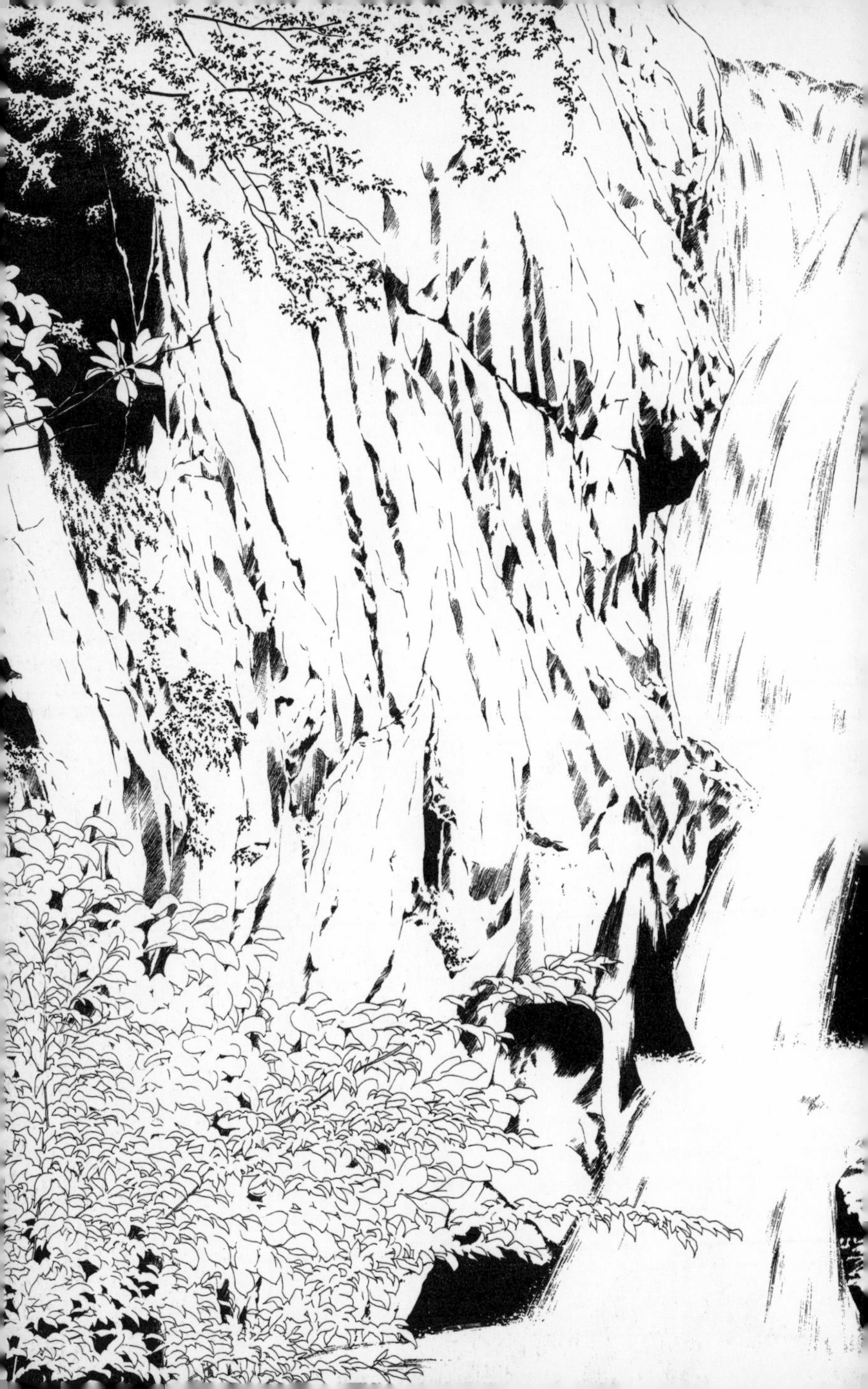

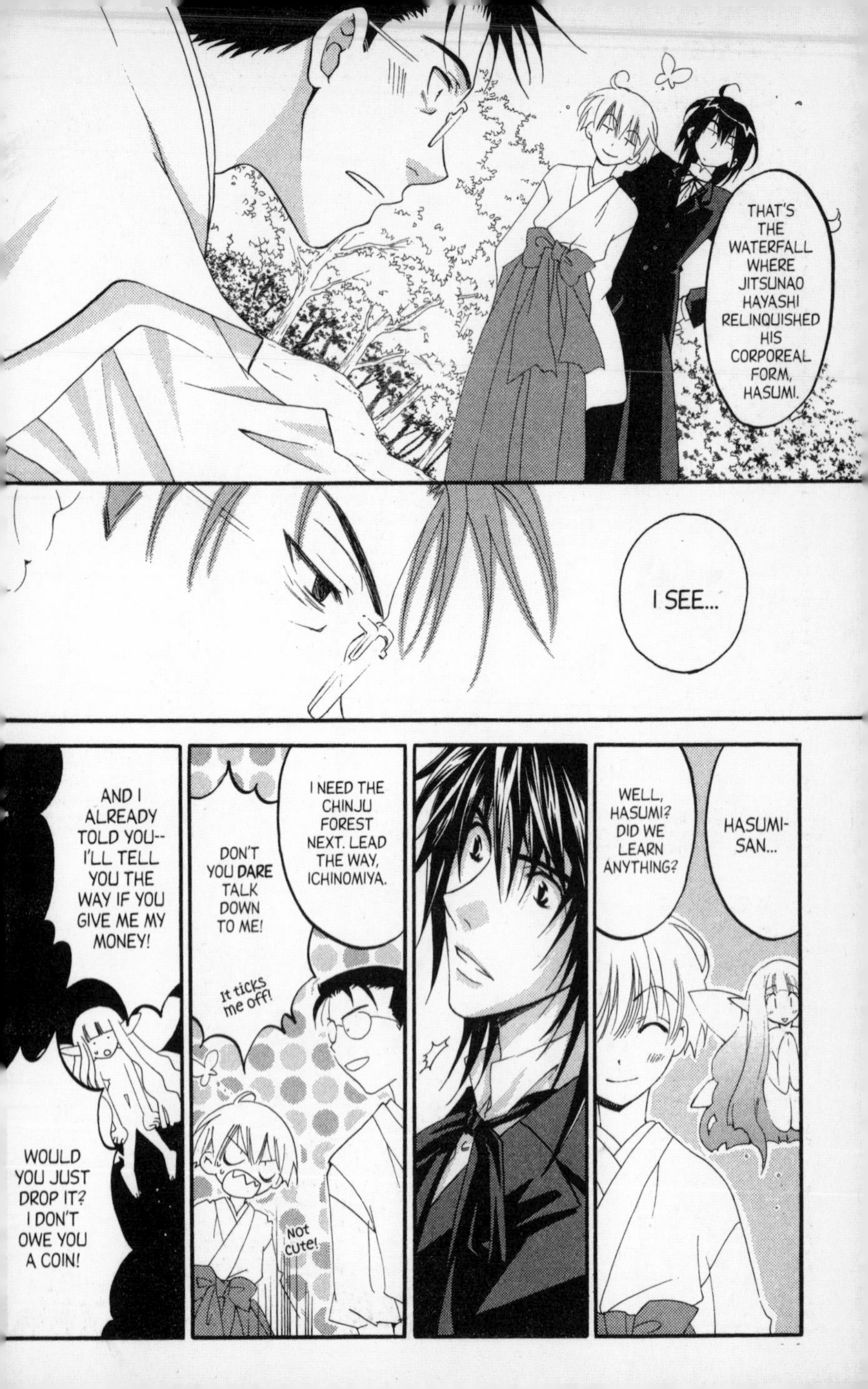
THAT'S THE WATERFALL WHERE JITSUNAO HAYASHI RELINQUISHED HIS CORPOREAL FORM, HASUMI.
I SEE...
HASUMI-SAN...
WELL, HASUMI? DID WE LEARN ANYTHING?
I NEED THE CHINJU FOREST NEXT. LEAD THE WAY, ICHINOMIYA.
DON'T YOU DARE TALK DOWN TO ME!
It ticks me off!
Not cute!
AND I ALREADY TOLD YOU-- I'LL TELL YOU THE WAY IF YOU GIVE ME MY MONEY!
WOULD YOU JUST DROP IT? I DON'T OWE YOU A COIN!

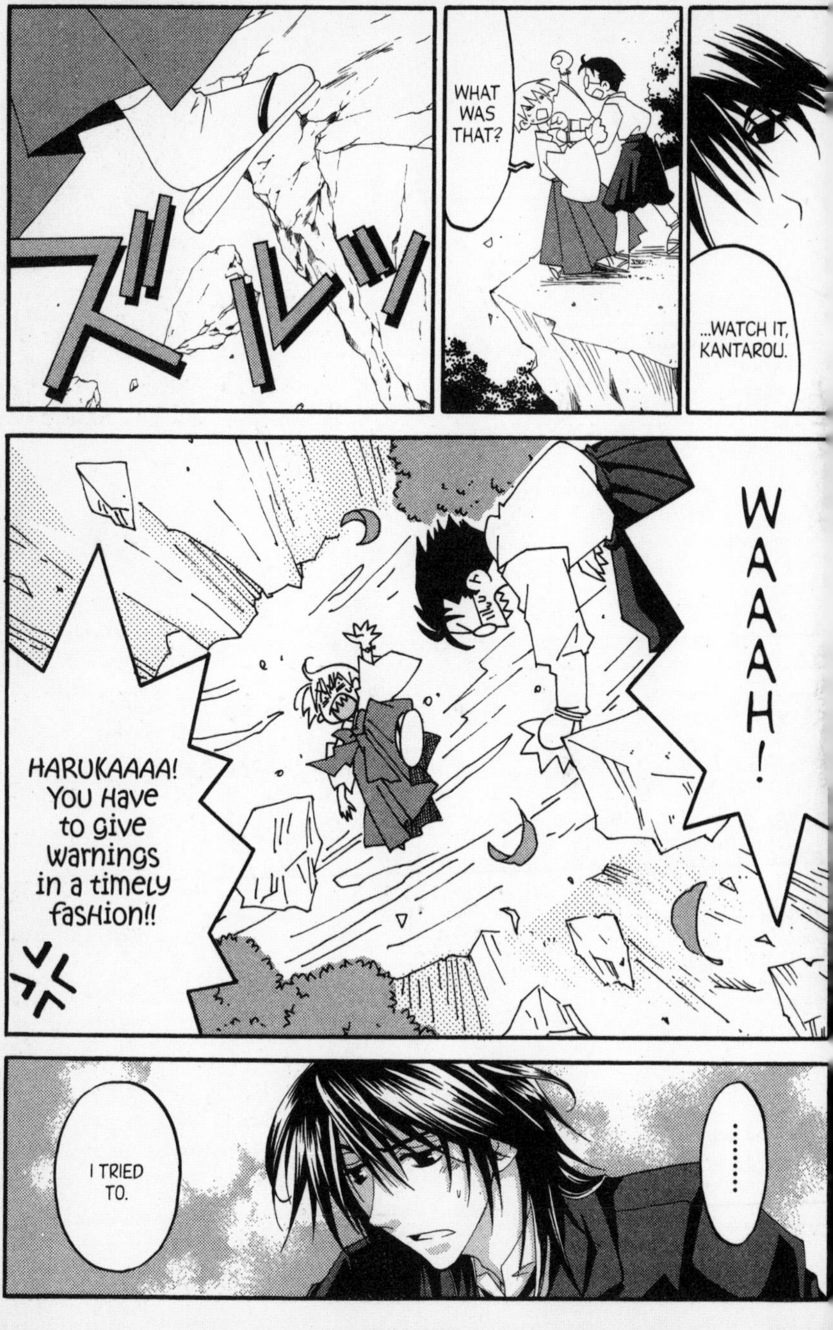
...WATCH IT, KANTAROU.
WHAT WAS THAT?
ズルッ
WAAAAH!
HARUKAAAA! You Have to give warnings in a timely fashion!!
......
I TRIED TO.

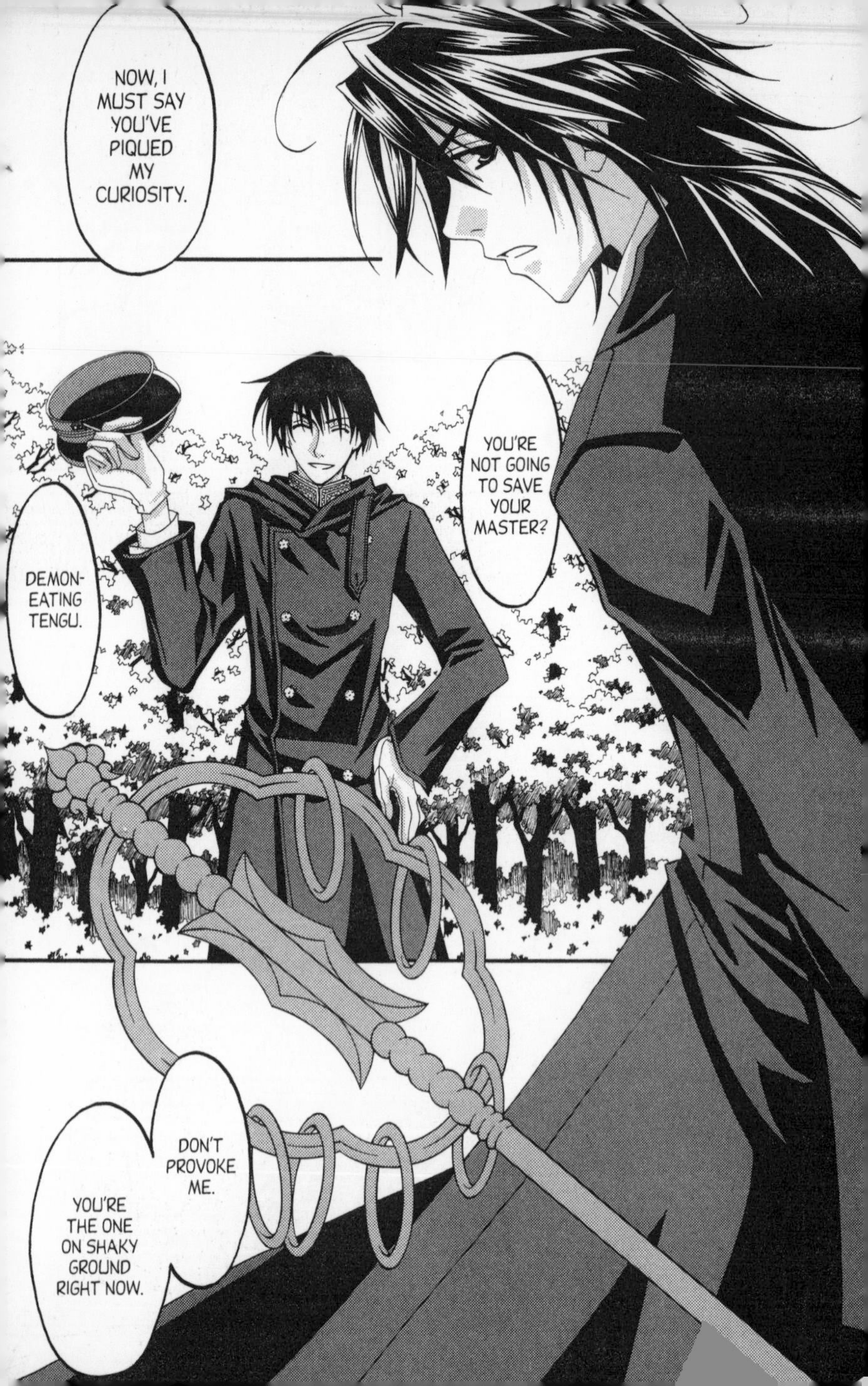
NOW, I MUST SAY YOU'VE PIQUED MY CURIOSITY.
YOU'RE NOT GOING TO SAVE YOUR MASTER?
DEMON-EATING TENGU.
DON'T PROVOKE ME.
YOU'RE THE ONE ON SHAKY GROUND RIGHT NOW.

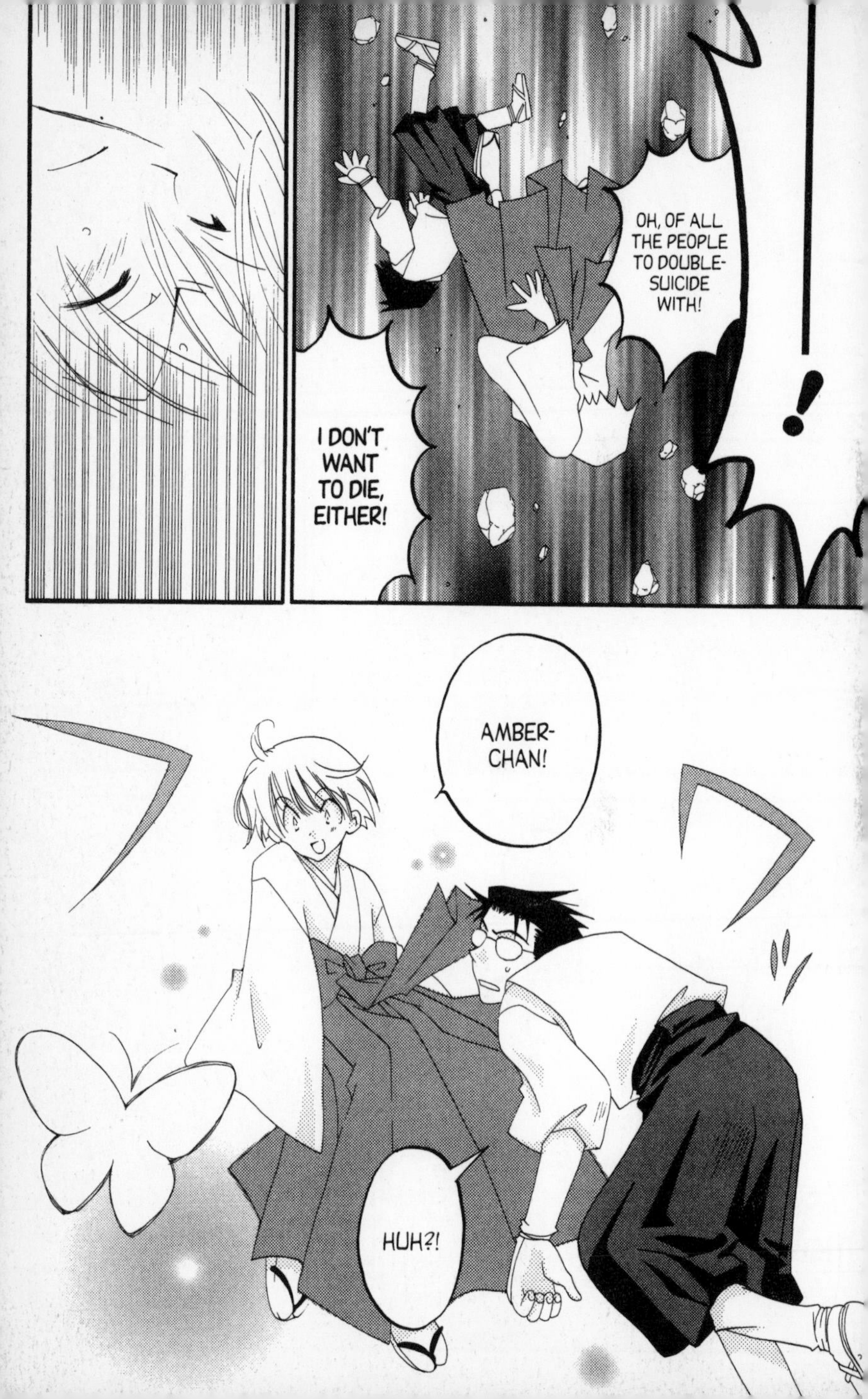
OH, OF ALL THE PEOPLE TO DOUBLE-SUICIDE WITH!
!
I DON'T WANT TO DIE, EITHER!
AMBER-CHAN!
HUH?!

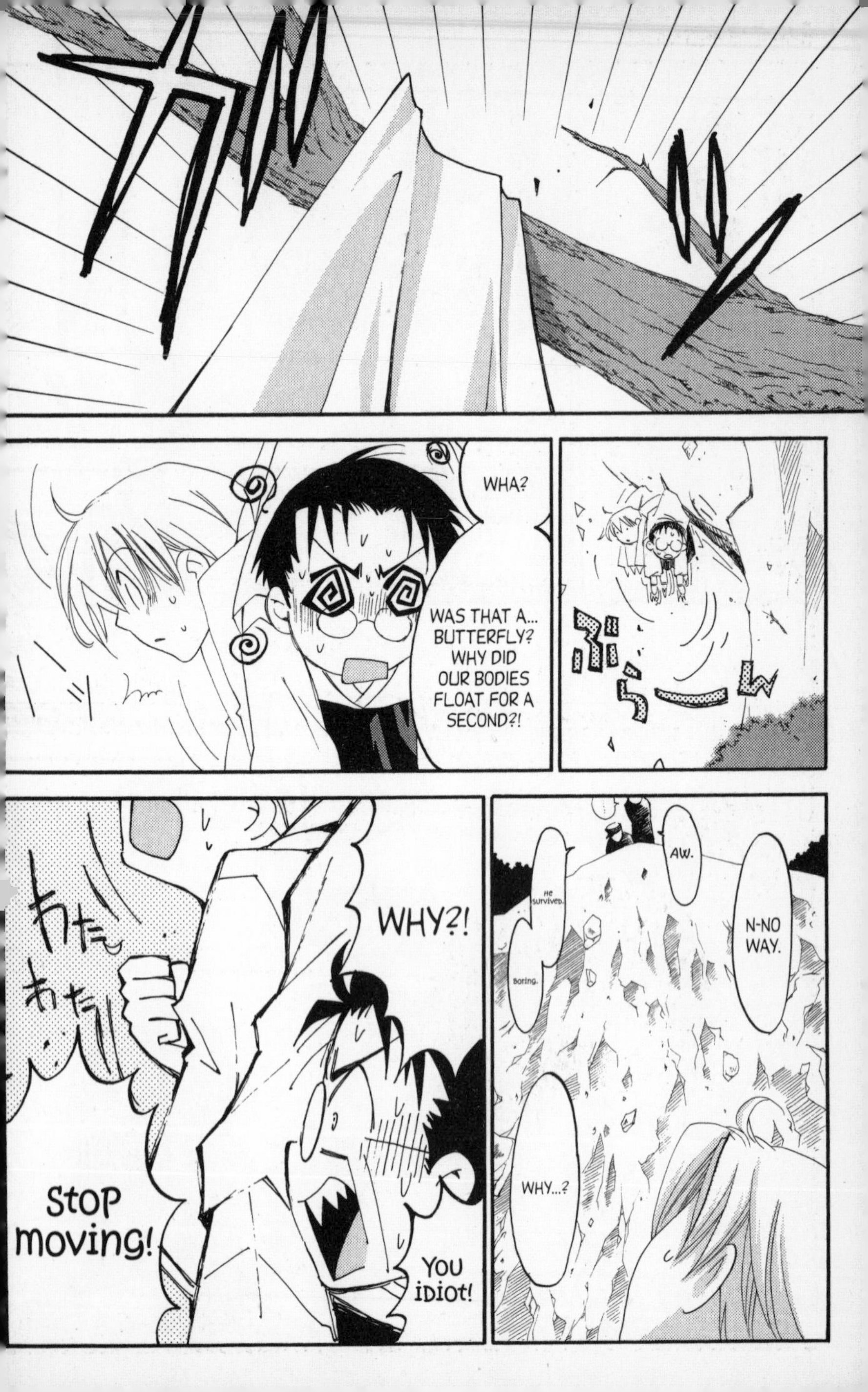

ぶらーん
WHA?
WAS THAT A... BUTTERFLY? WHY DID OUR BODIES FLOAT FOR A SECOND?!
N-NO WAY.
AW.
He survived.
Boring.
WHY...?
WHY?!
You idiot!
Stop moving!
わたわた

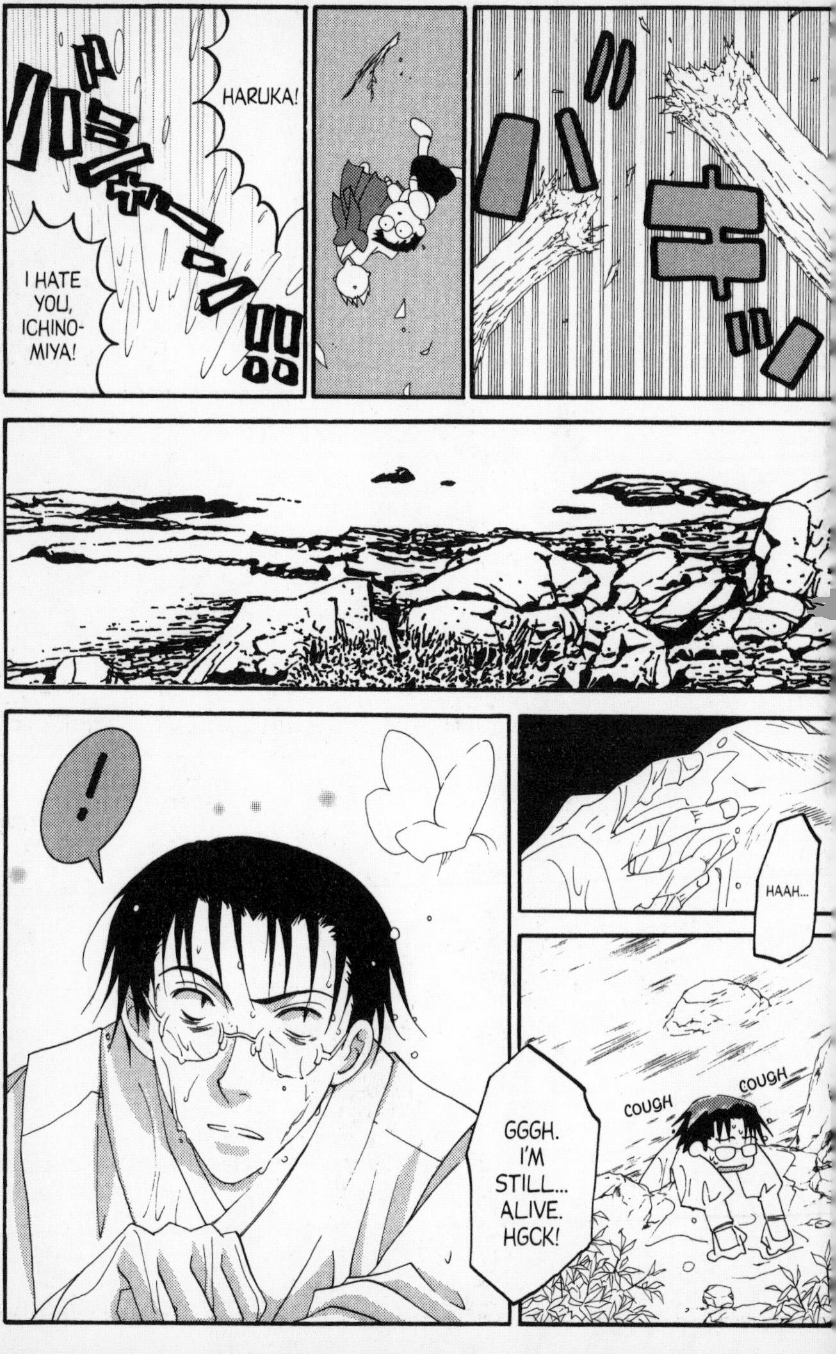
HARUKA!
I HATE YOU, ICHINO-MIYA!
HAAH...
COUGH
COUGH
GGGH. I'M STILL... ALIVE. HGCK!
!

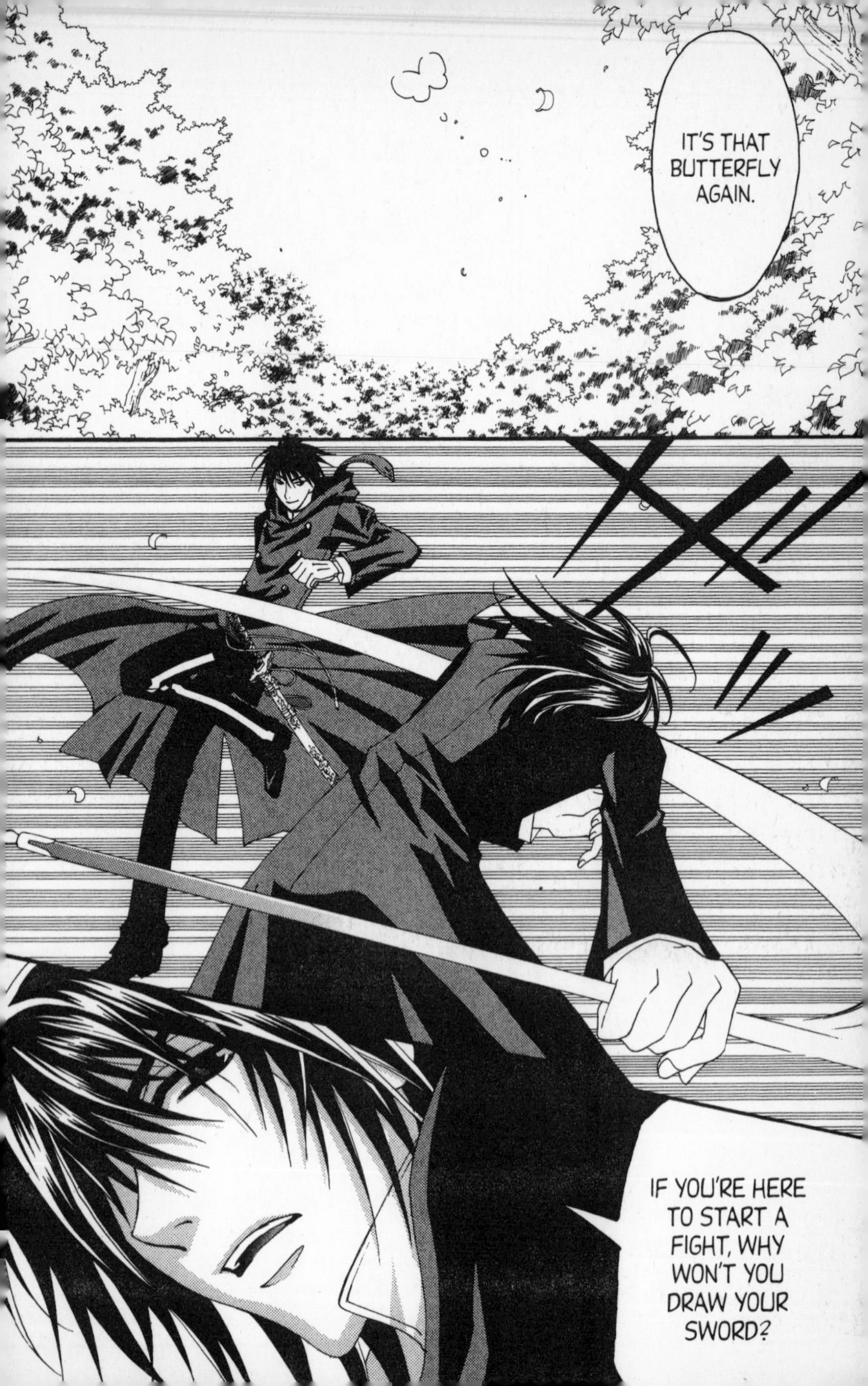
IT'S THAT BUTTERFLY AGAIN.
IF YOU'RE HERE TO START A FIGHT, WHY WON'T YOU DRAW YOUR SWORD?

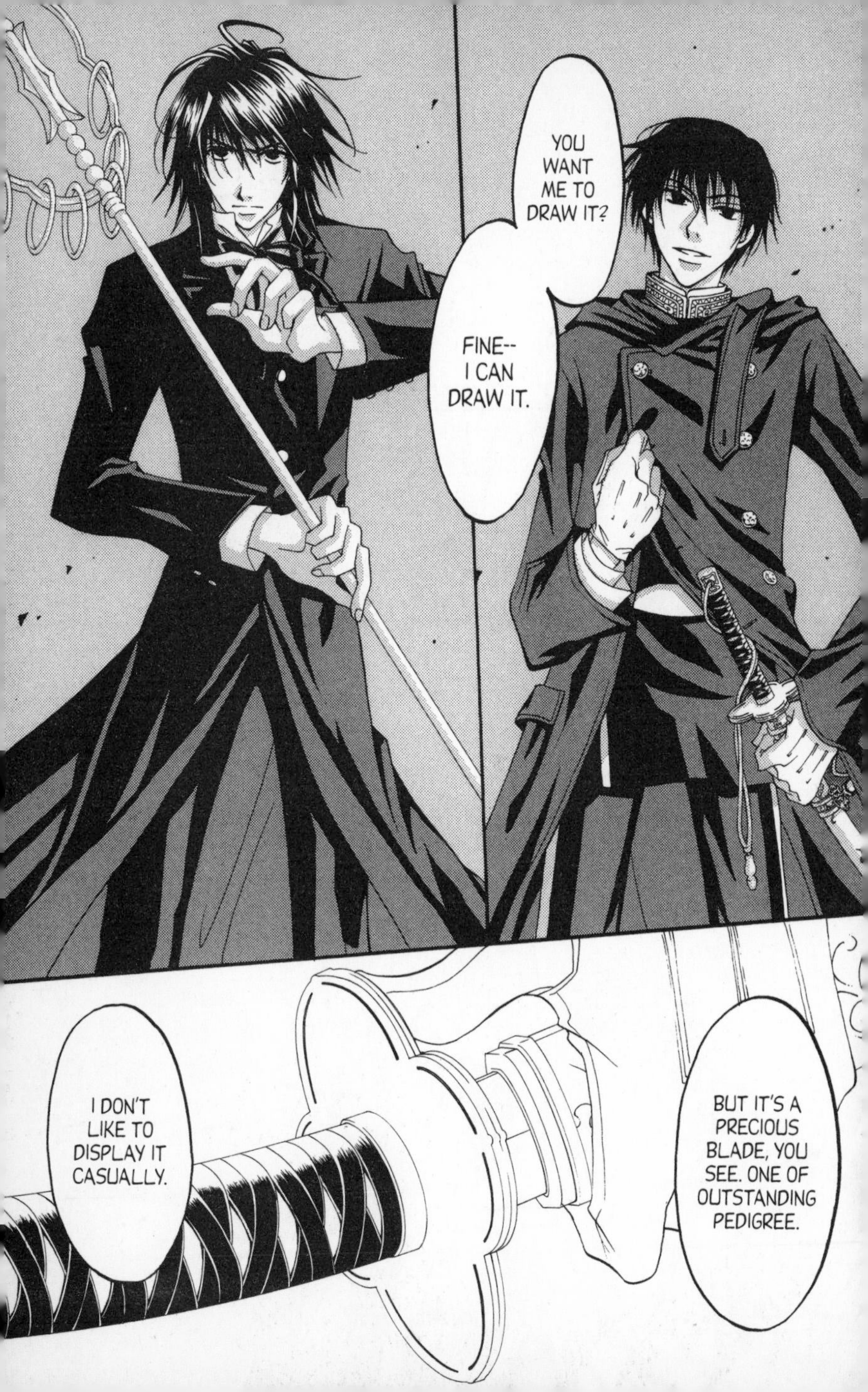
YOU WANT ME TO DRAW IT?
FINE-- I CAN DRAW IT.
BUT IT'S A PRECIOUS BLADE, YOU SEE. ONE OF OUTSTANDING PEDIGREE.
I DON'T LIKE TO DISPLAY IT CASUALLY.

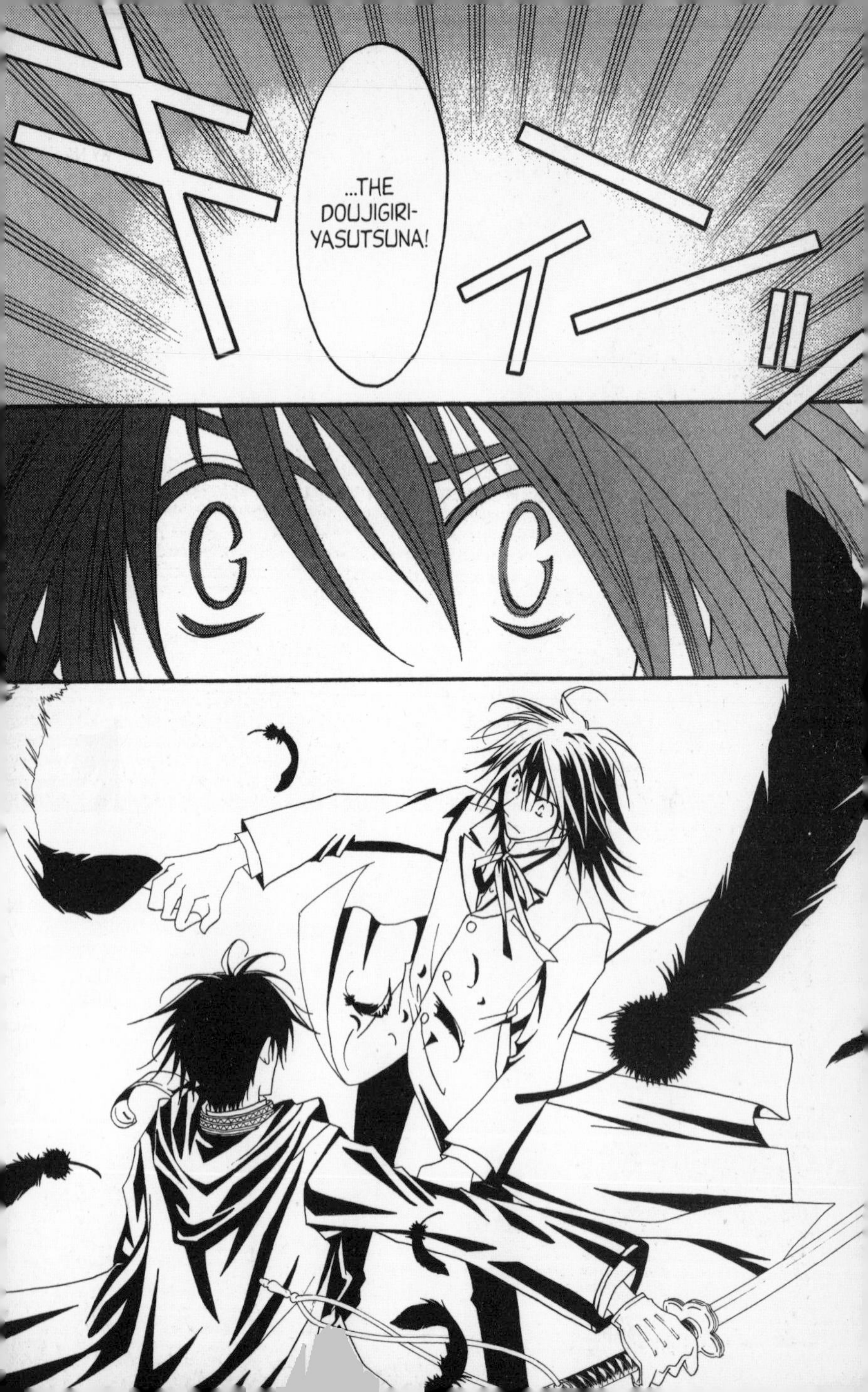
...THE DOUJIGIRI-YASUTSUNA!

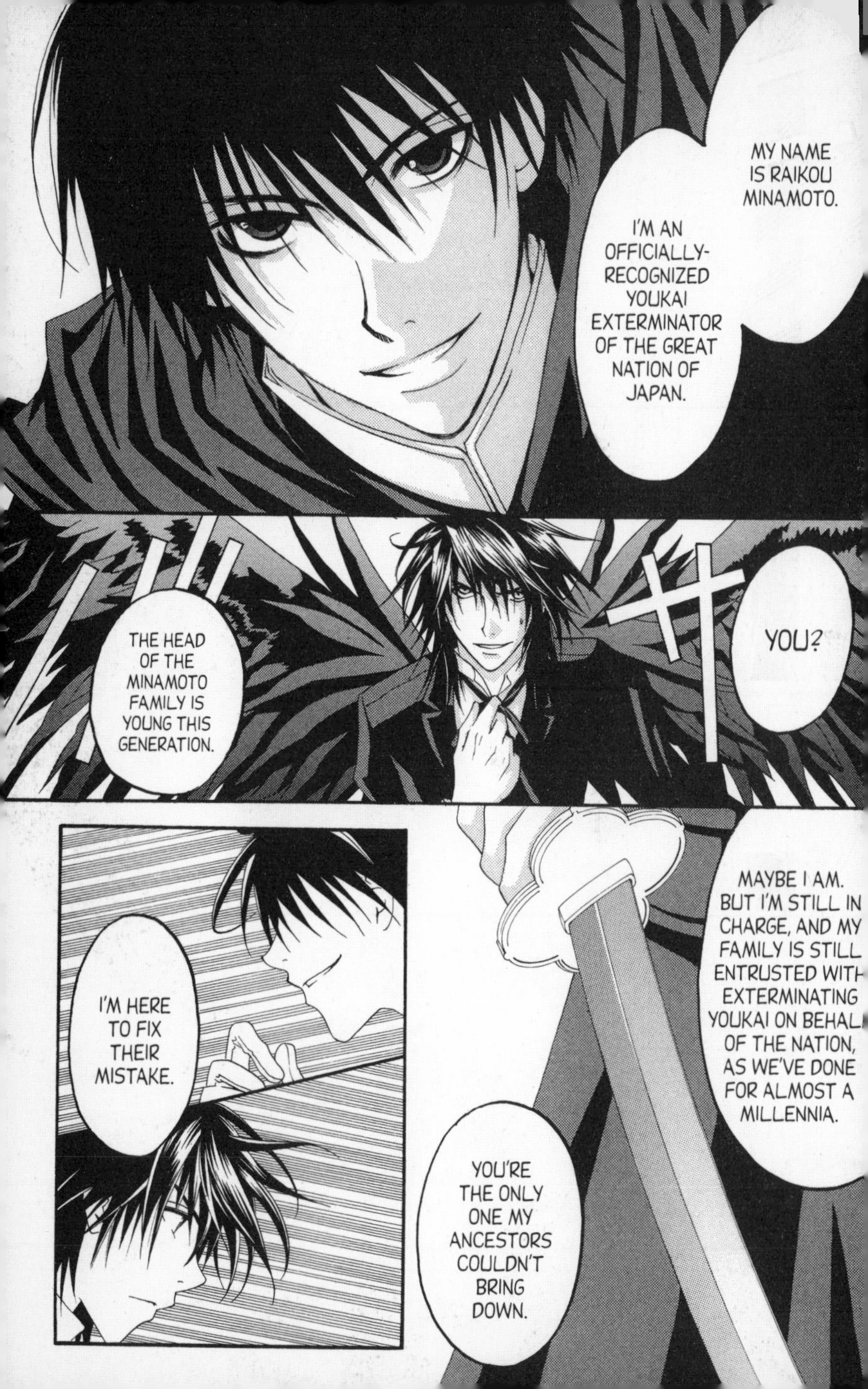
MY NAME IS RAIKOU MINAMOTO.
I'M AN OFFICIALLY-RECOGNIZED YOUKAI EXTERMINATOR OF THE GREAT NATION OF JAPAN.
YOU?
THE HEAD OF THE MINAMOTO FAMILY IS YOUNG THIS GENERATION.
MAYBE I AM. BUT I'M STILL IN CHARGE, AND MY FAMILY IS STILL ENTRUSTED WITH EXTERMINATING YOUKAI ON BEHAL OF THE NATION, AS WE'VE DONE FOR ALMOST A MILLENNIA.
YOU'RE THE ONLY ONE MY ANCESTORS COULDN'T BRING DOWN.
I'M HERE TO FIX THEIR MISTAKE.

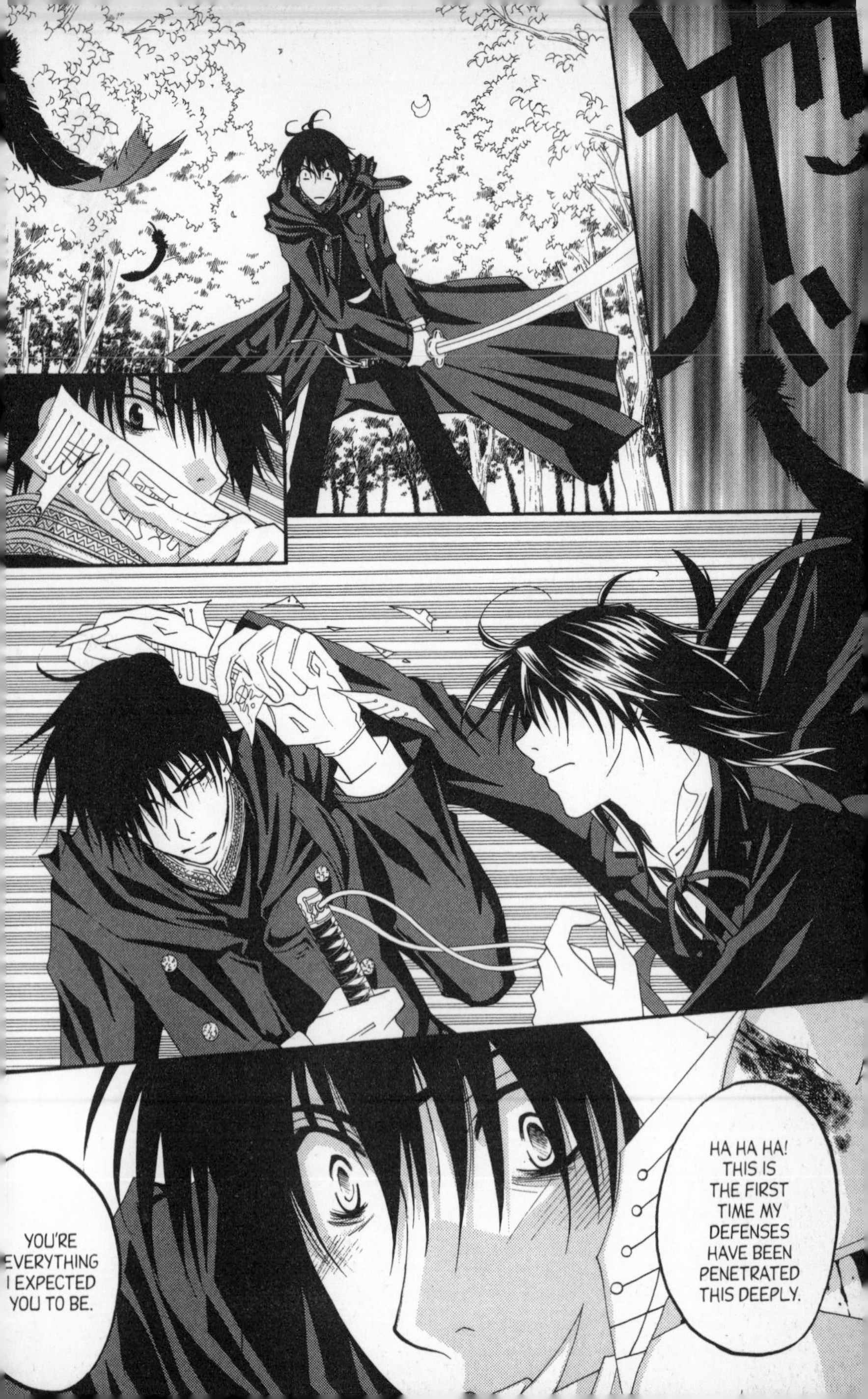
HA HA HA! THIS IS THE FIRST TIME MY DEFENSES HAVE BEEN PENETRATED THIS DEEPLY.
YOU'RE EVERYTHING I EXPECTED YOU TO BE.

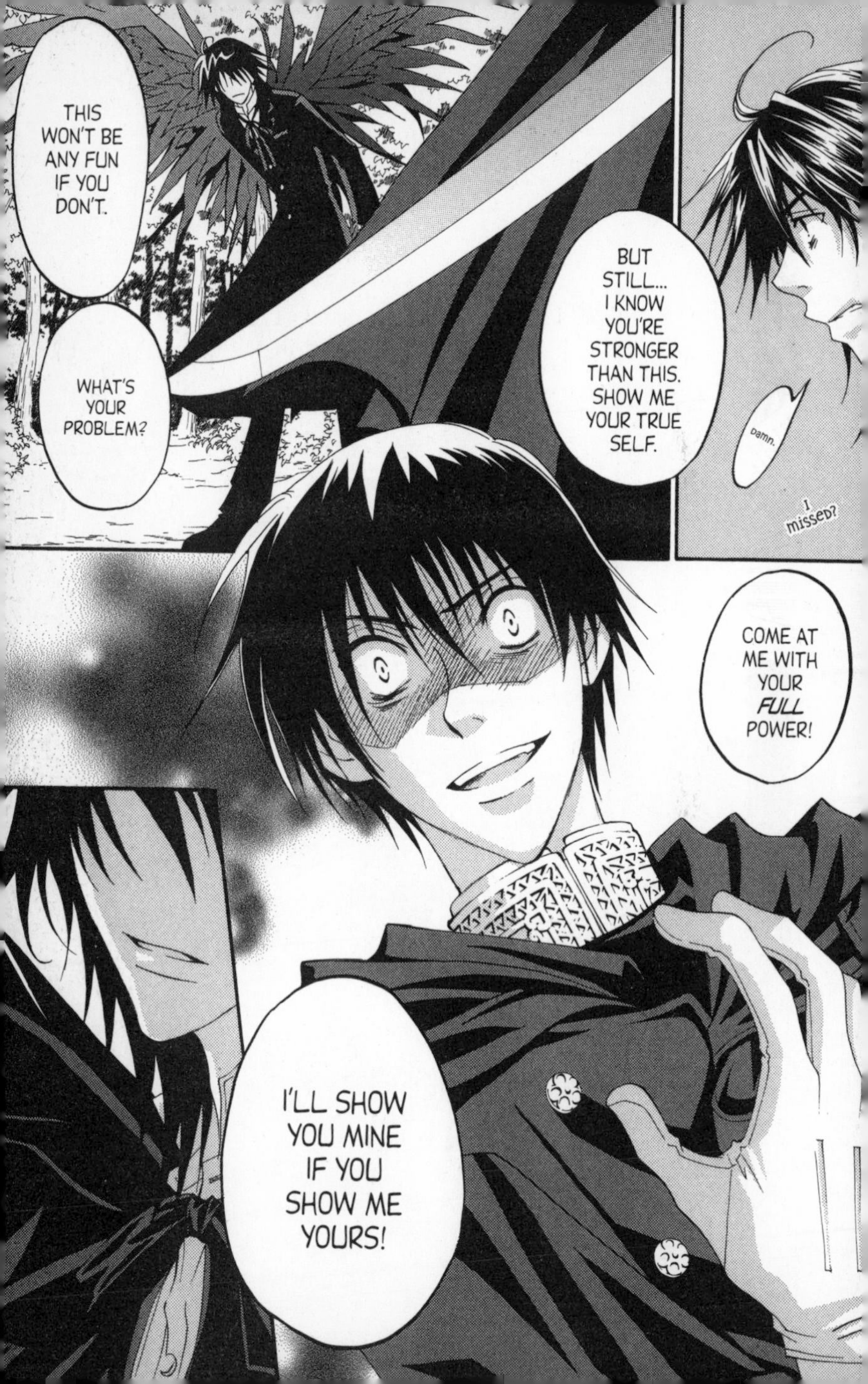

Damn.
I missed?
THIS WON'T BE ANY FUN IF YOU DON'T.
WHAT'S YOUR PROBLEM?
BUT STILL... I KNOW YOU'RE STRONGER THAN THIS. SHOW ME YOUR TRUE SELF.
COME AT ME WITH YOUR *FULL* POWER!
I'LL SHOW YOU MINE IF YOU SHOW ME YOURS!

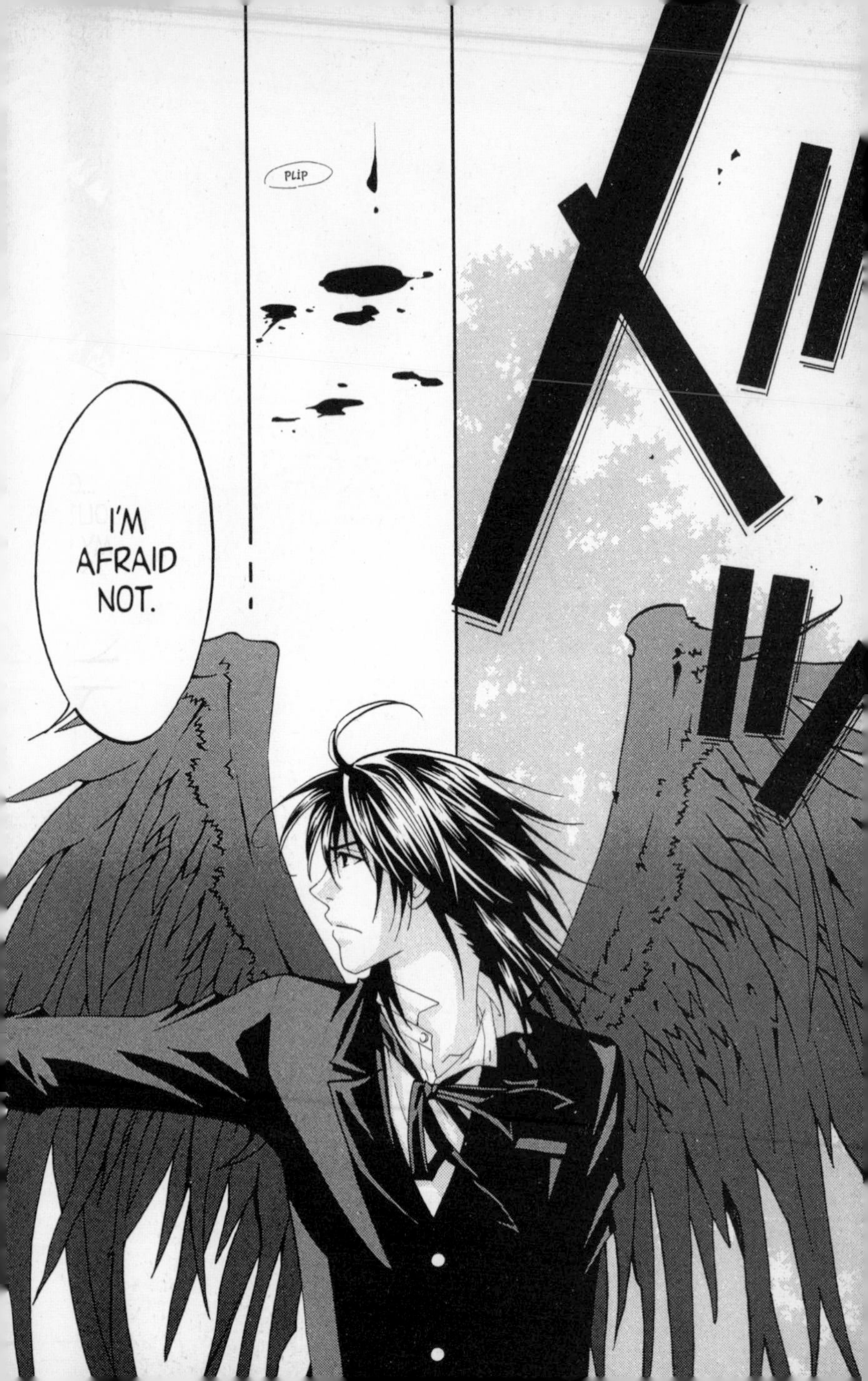
PLIP
I'M AFRAID NOT.

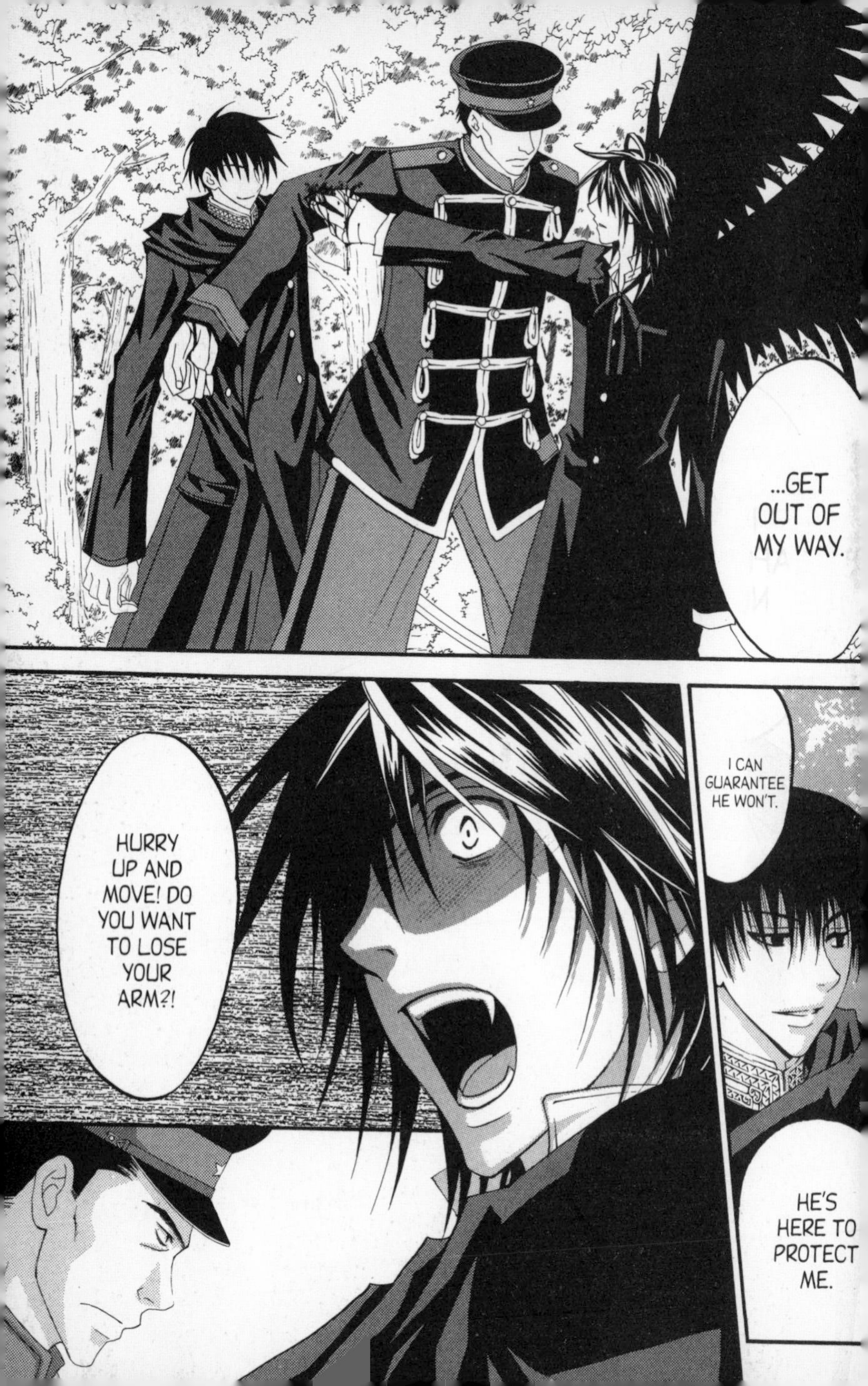
...GET OUT OF MY WAY.
HURRY UP AND MOVE! DO YOU WANT TO LOSE YOUR ARM?!
I CAN GUARANTEE HE WON'T.
HE'S HERE TO PROTECT ME.

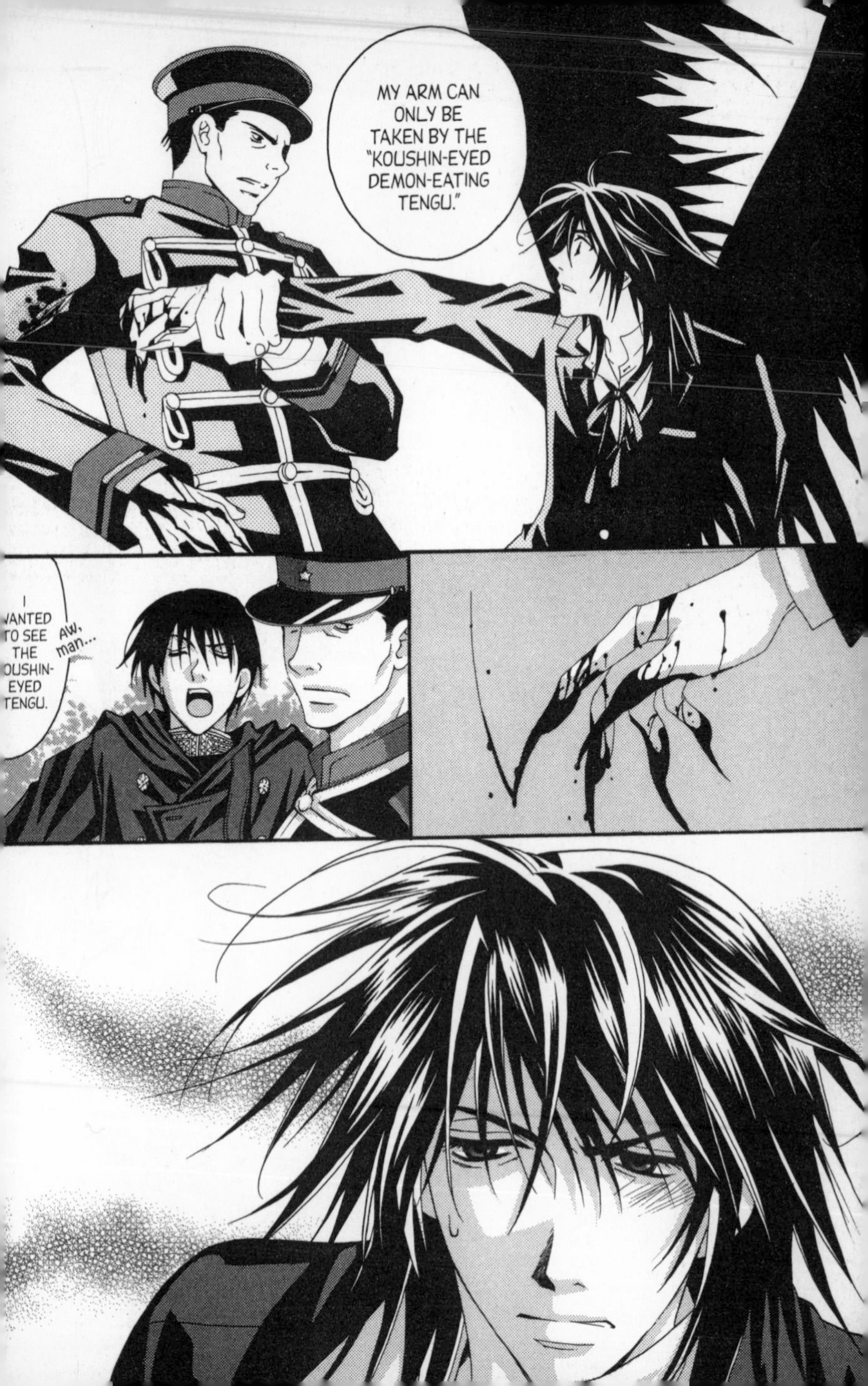
MY ARM CAN ONLY BE TAKEN BY THE "KOUSHIN-EYED DEMON-EATING TENGU."
AW, man...
I WANTED TO SEE THE KOUSHIN-EYED TENGU.

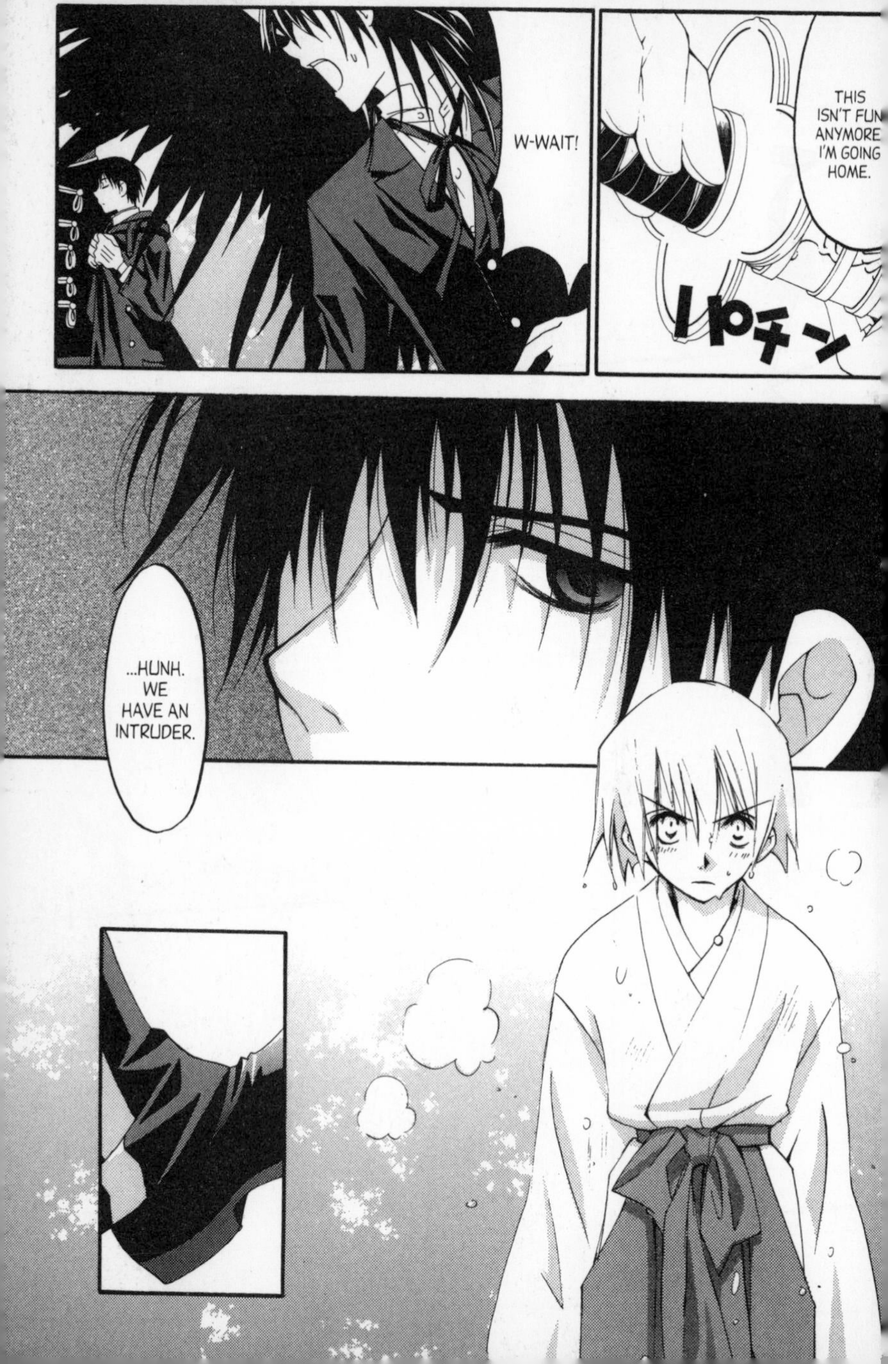
THIS ISN'T FUN ANYMORE I'M GOING HOME.
W-WAIT!
...HUNH. WE HAVE AN INTRUDER.

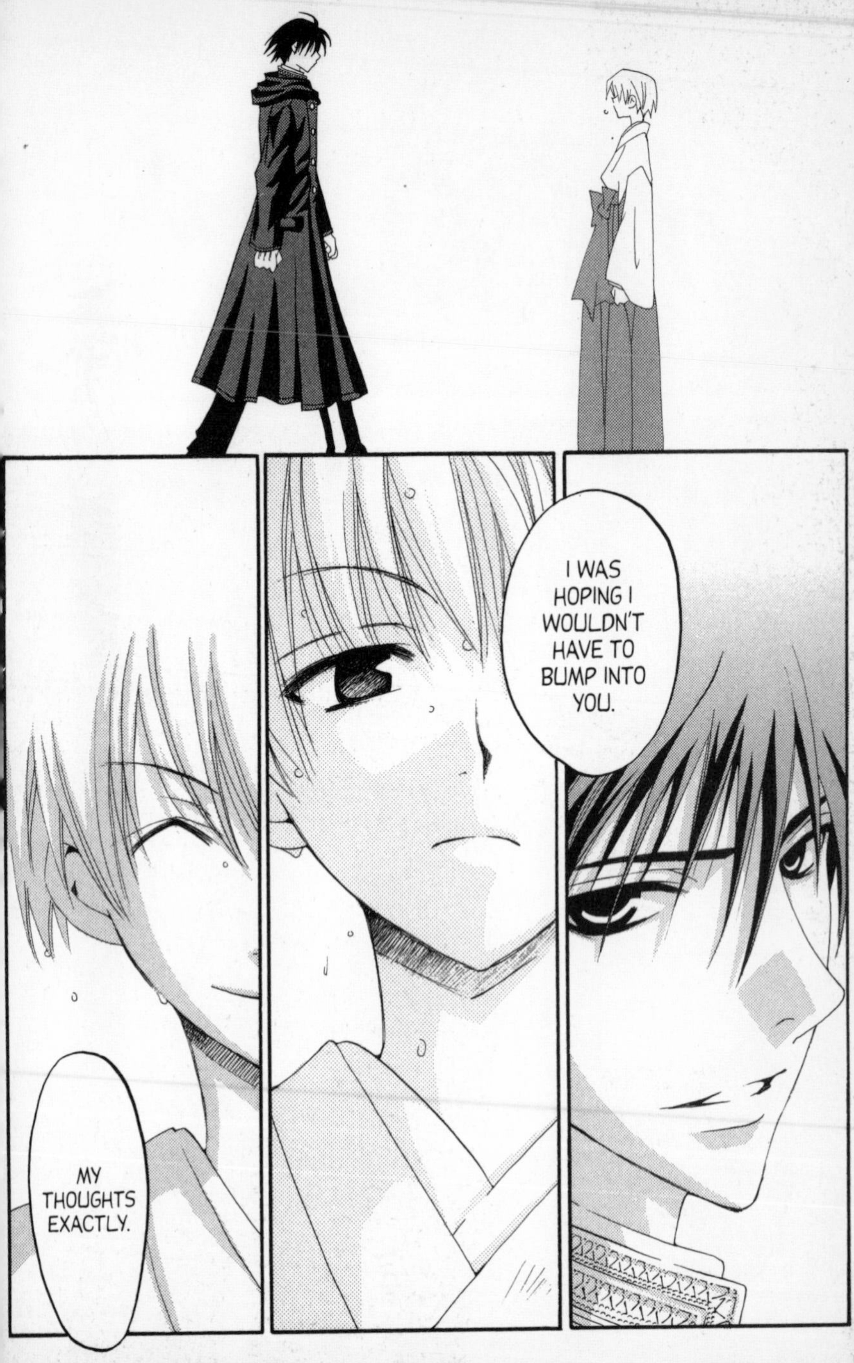
I WAS HOPING I WOULDN'T HAVE TO BUMP INTO YOU.
MY THOUGHTS EXACTLY.

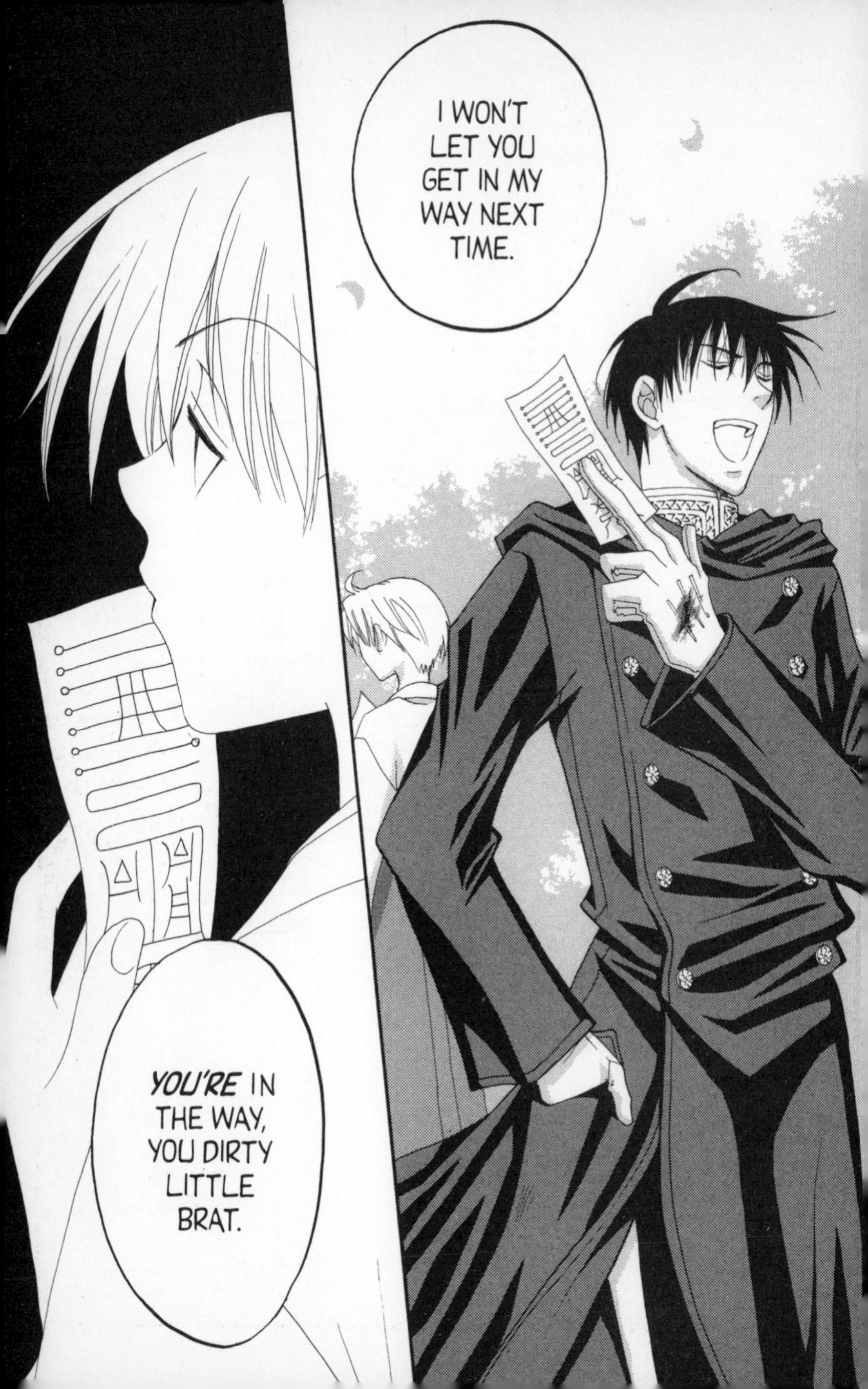
I WON'T LET YOU GET IN MY WAY NEXT TIME.
YOU'RE IN THE WAY, YOU DIRTY LITTLE BRAT.

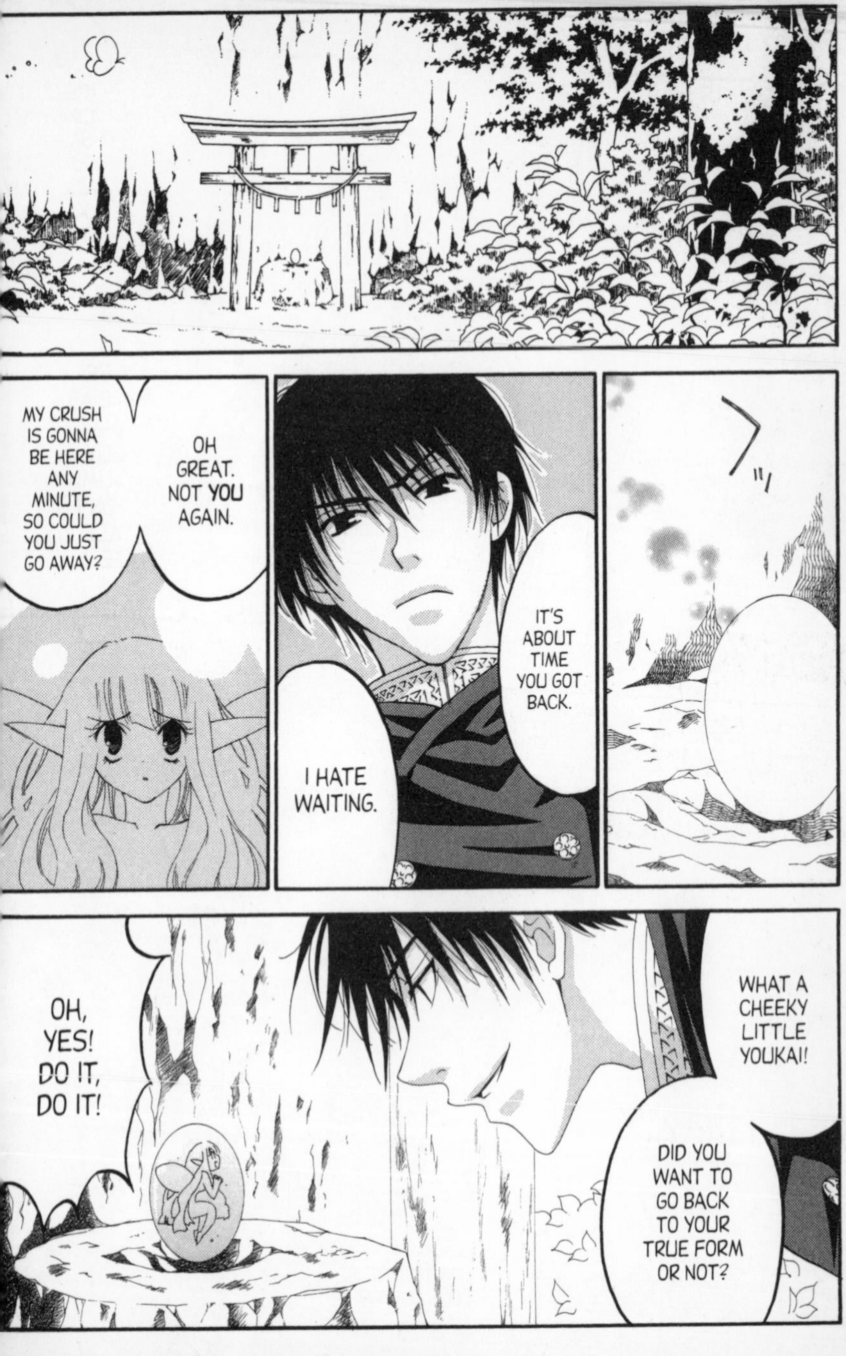
IT'S ABOUT TIME YOU GOT BACK.
I HATE WAITING.
OH GREAT. NOT YOU AGAIN.
MY CRUSH IS GONNA BE HERE ANY MINUTE, SO COULD YOU JUST GO AWAY?
WHAT A CHEEKY LITTLE YOUKAI!
DID YOU WANT TO GO BACK TO YOUR TRUE FORM OR NOT?
OH, YES! DO IT, DO IT!

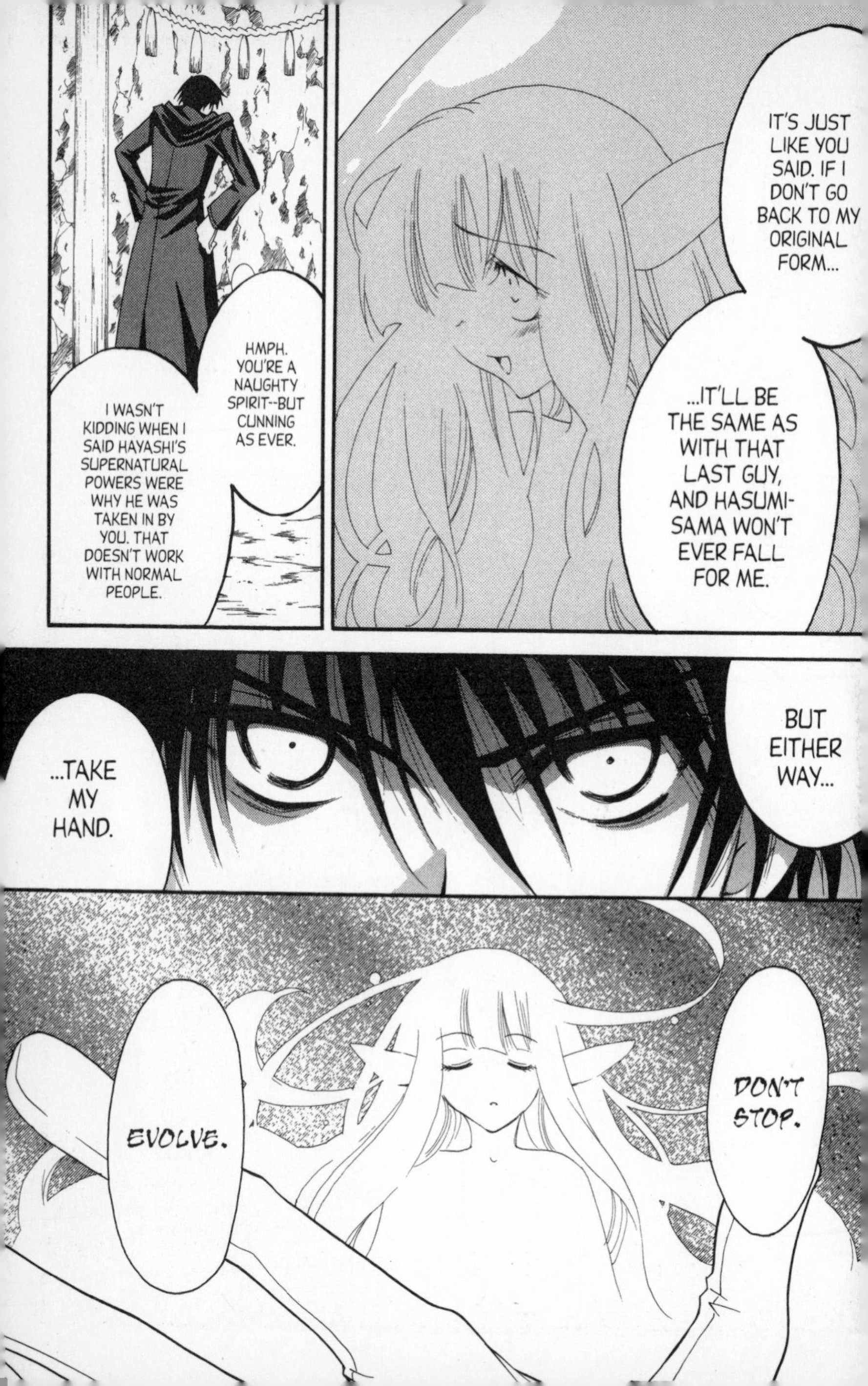
IT'S JUST LIKE YOU SAID. IF I DON'T GO BACK TO MY ORIGINAL FORM...
...IT'LL BE THE SAME AS WITH THAT LAST GUY, AND HASUMI-SAMA WON'T EVER FALL FOR ME.
HMPH. YOU'RE A NAUGHTY SPIRIT--BUT CUNNING AS EVER.
I WASN'T KIDDING WHEN I SAID HAYASHI'S SUPERNATURAL POWERS WERE WHY HE WAS TAKEN IN BY YOU. THAT DOESN'T WORK WITH NORMAL PEOPLE.
BUT EITHER WAY...
...TAKE MY HAND.
DON'T STOP.
EVOLVE.

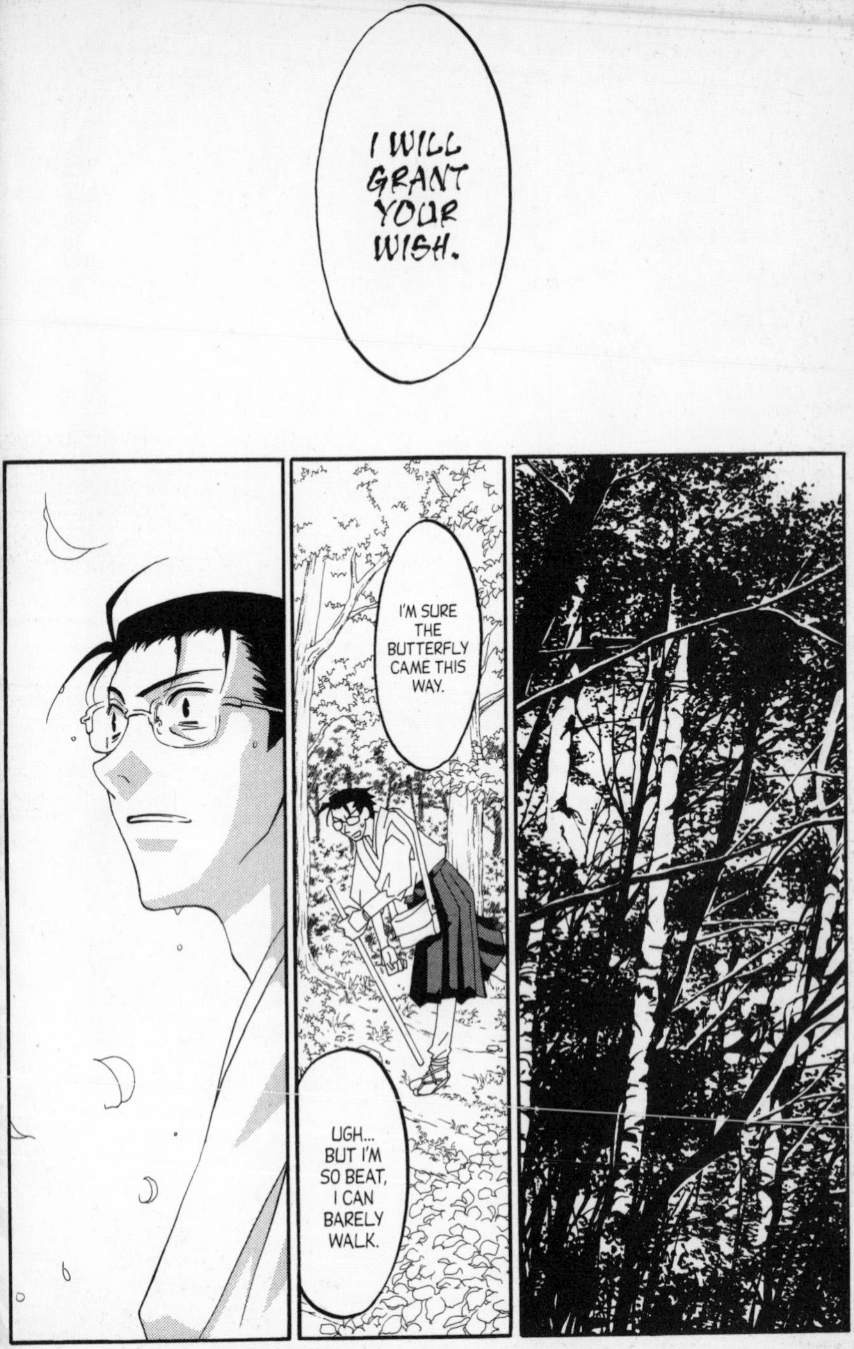
I WILL GRANT YOUR WISH.
I'M SURE THE BUTTERFLY CAME THIS WAY.
UGH... BUT I'M SO BEAT, I CAN BARELY WALK.

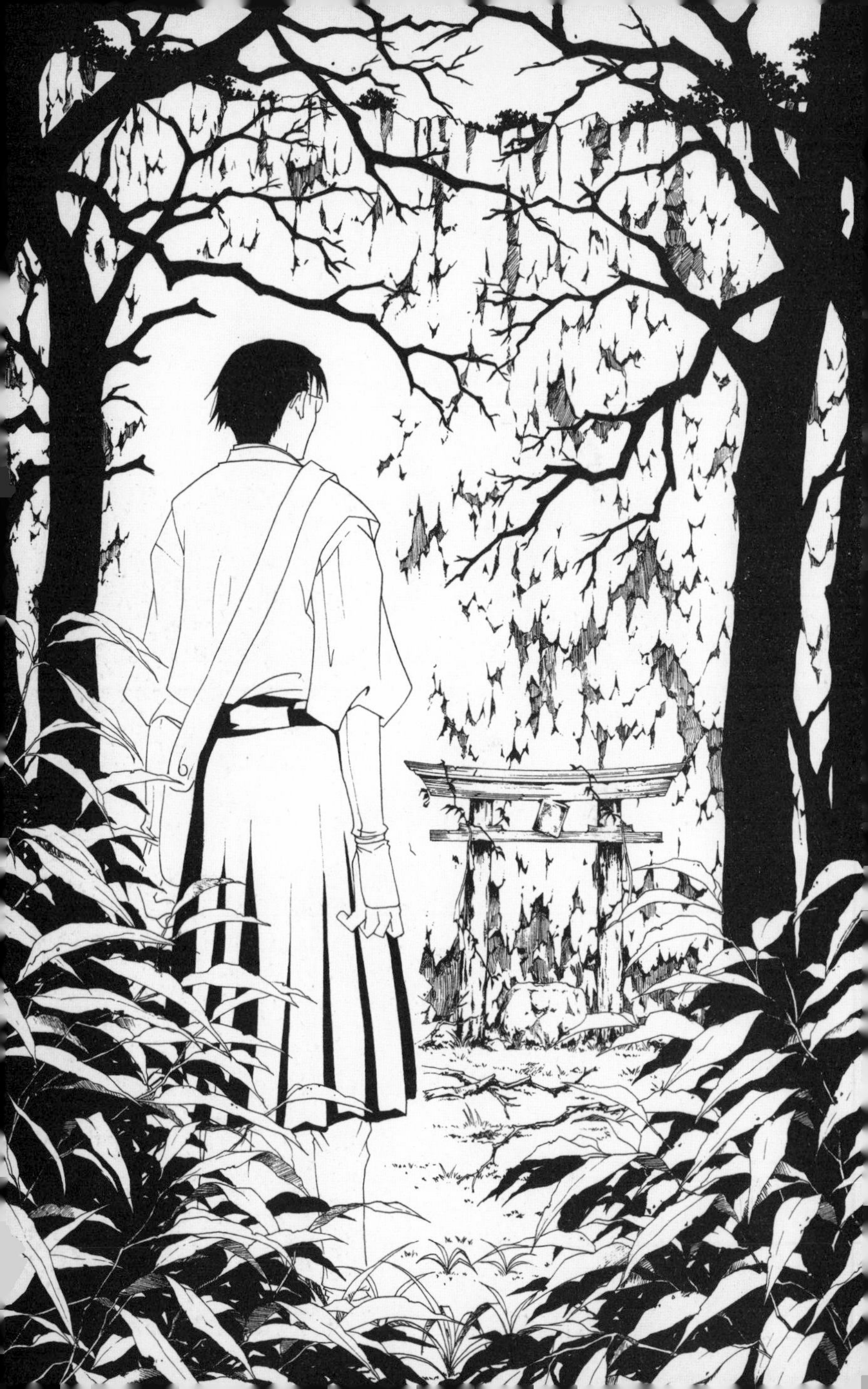

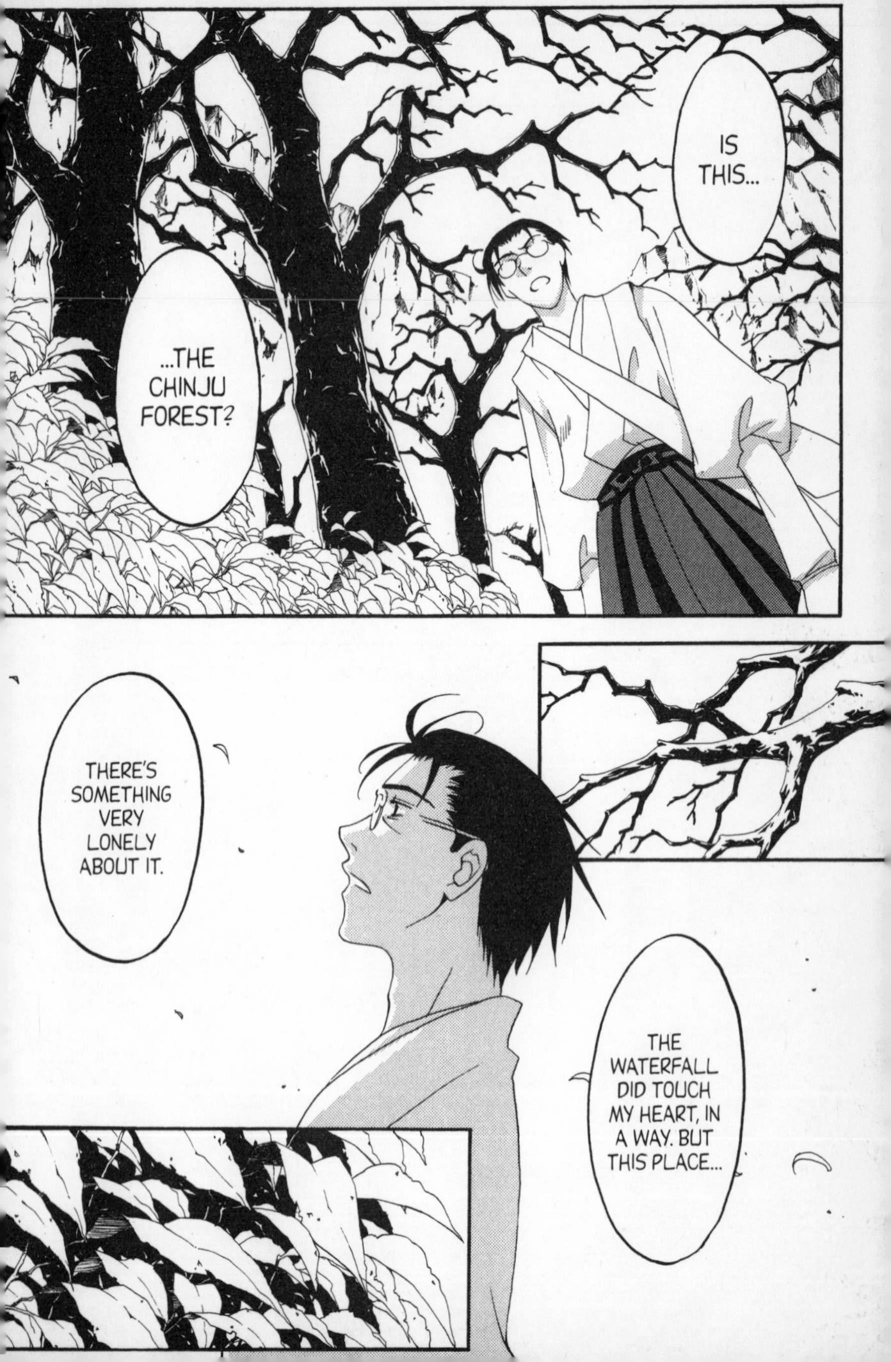
IS THIS...
...THE CHINJU FOREST?
THERE'S SOMETHING VERY LONELY ABOUT IT.
THE WATERFALL DID TOUCH MY HEART, IN A WAY. BUT THIS PLACE...

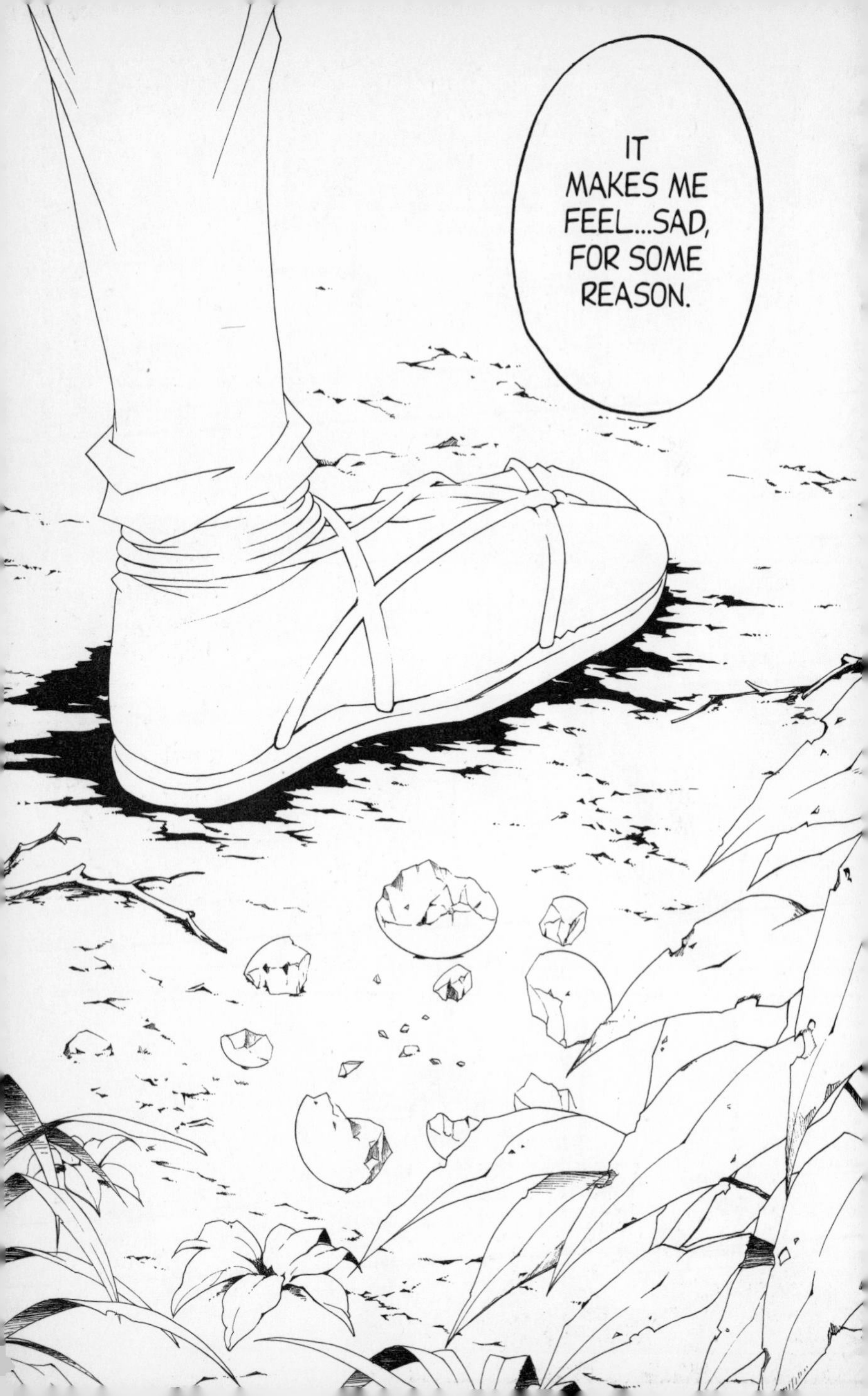
IT MAKES ME FEEL...SAD, FOR SOME REASON.

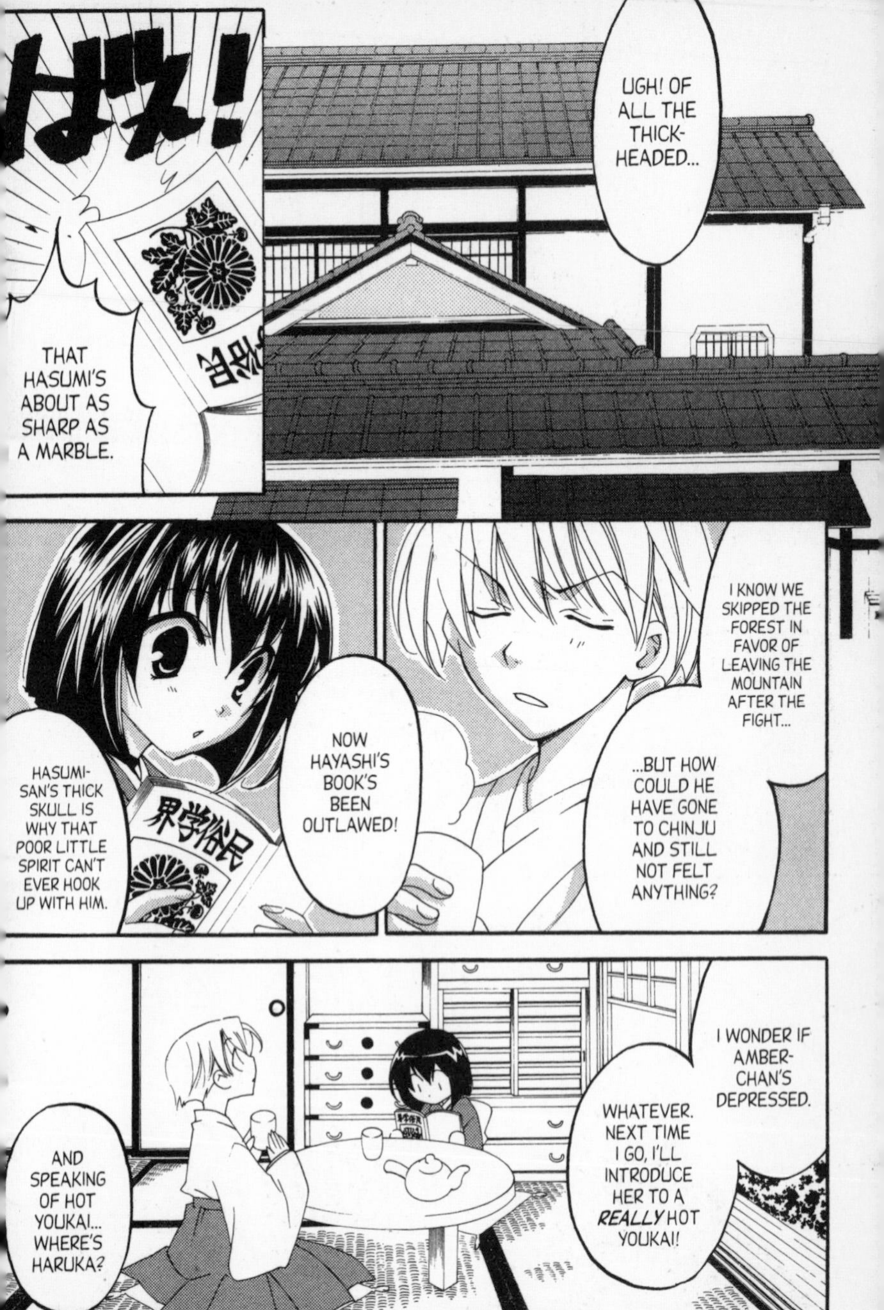
UGH! OF ALL THE THICK-HEADED...
THAT HASUMI'S ABOUT AS SHARP AS A MARBLE.
I KNOW WE SKIPPED THE FOREST IN FAVOR OF LEAVING THE MOUNTAIN AFTER THE FIGHT...
...BUT HOW COULD HE HAVE GONE TO CHINJU AND STILL NOT FELT ANYTHING?
NOW HAYASHI'S BOOK'S BEEN OUTLAWED!
HASUMI-SAN'S THICK SKULL IS WHY THAT POOR LITTLE SPIRIT CAN'T EVER HOOK UP WITH HIM.
I WONDER IF AMBER-CHAN'S DEPRESSED.
WHATEVER. NEXT TIME I GO, I'LL INTRODUCE HER TO A *REALLY* HOT YOUKAI!
AND SPEAKING OF HOT YOUKAI... WHERE'S HARUKA?

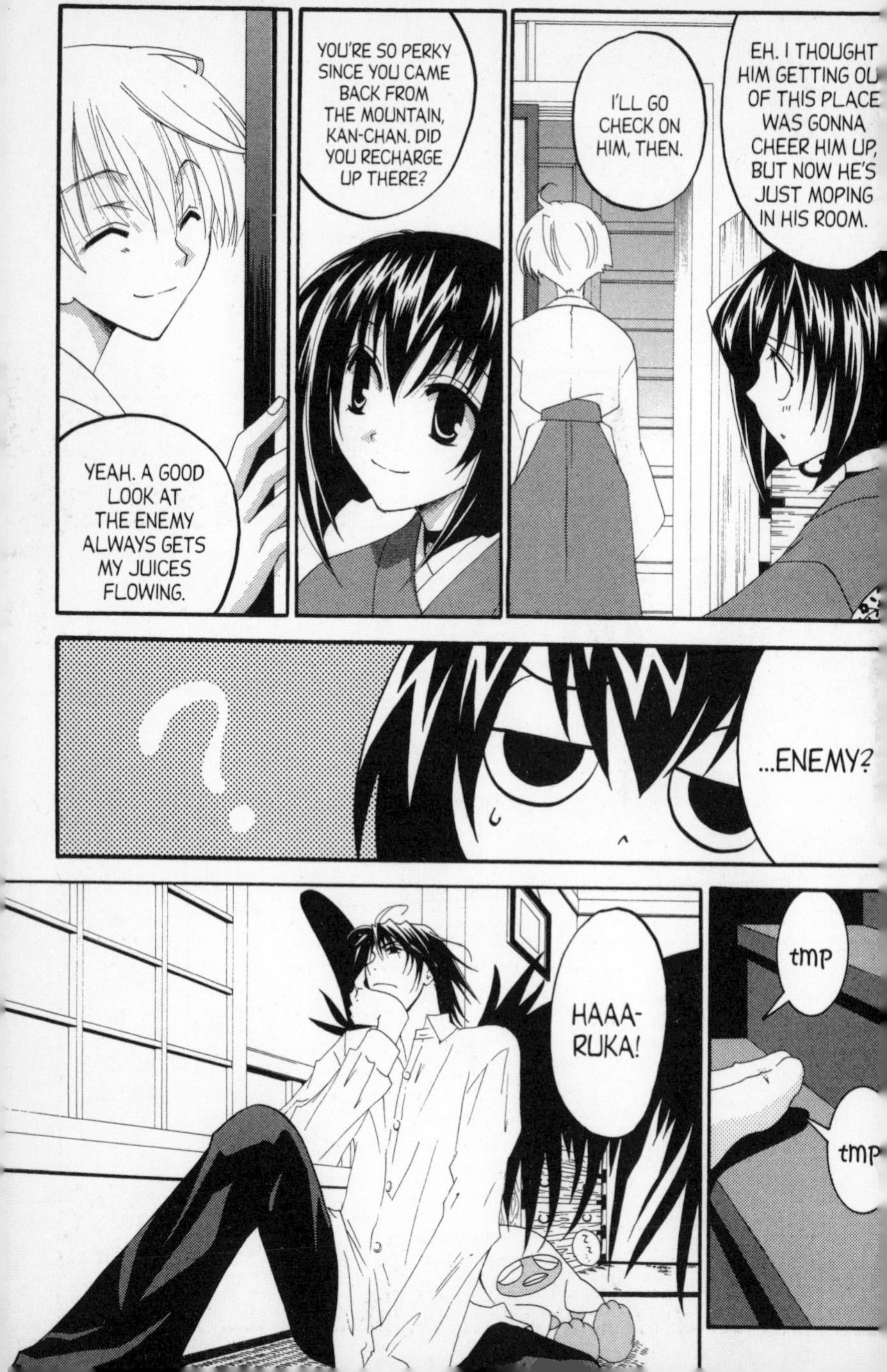
EH. I THOUGHT HIM GETTING OU OF THIS PLACE WAS GONNA CHEER HIM UP, BUT NOW HE'S JUST MOPING IN HIS ROOM.
I'LL GO CHECK ON HIM, THEN.
YOU'RE SO PERKY SINCE YOU CAME BACK FROM THE MOUNTAIN, KAN-CHAN. DID YOU RECHARGE UP THERE?
YEAH. A GOOD LOOK AT THE ENEMY ALWAYS GETS MY JUICES FLOWING.
...ENEMY?
tmp
tmp
HAAA-RUKA!

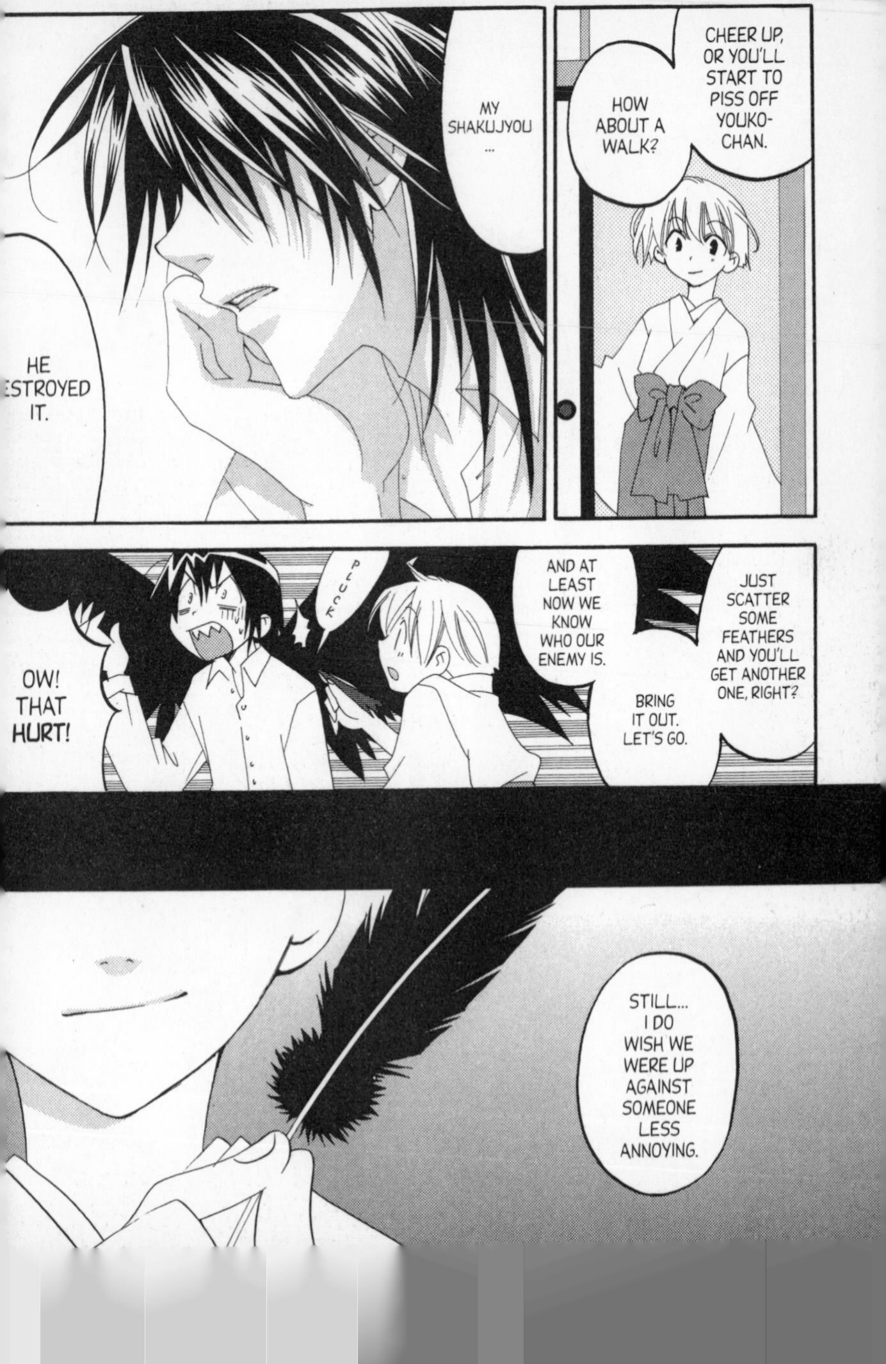
CHEER UP, OR YOU'LL START TO PISS OFF YOUKO-CHAN.
HOW ABOUT A WALK?
MY SHAKUJYOU ...
HE ESTROYED IT.
JUST SCATTER SOME FEATHERS AND YOU'LL GET ANOTHER ONE, RIGHT?
AND AT LEAST NOW WE KNOW WHO OUR ENEMY IS.
BRING IT OUT. LET'S GO.
PLUCK
OW! THAT HURT!
STILL... I DO WISH WE WERE UP AGAINST SOMEONE LESS ANNOYING.

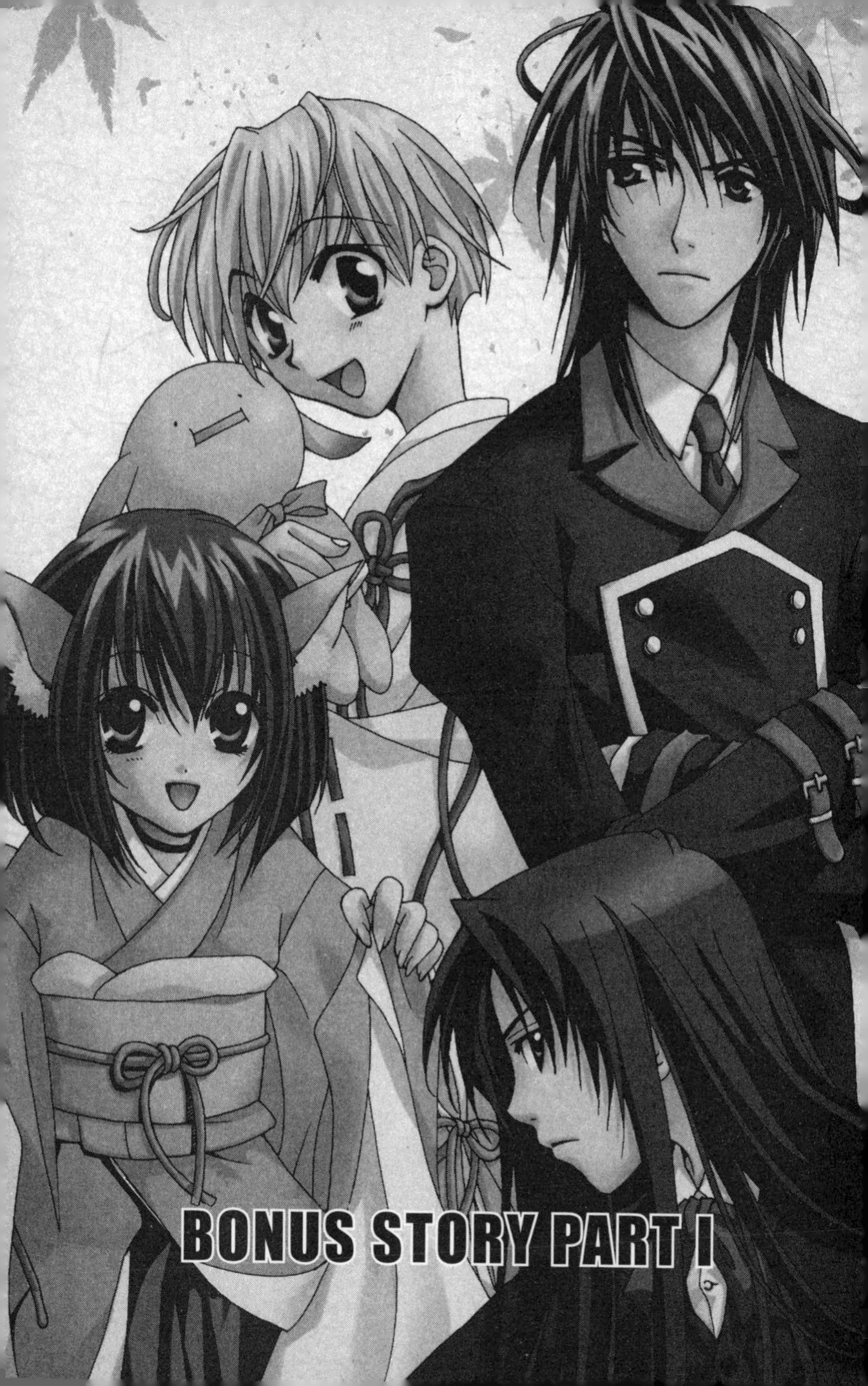
BONUS STORY PART I

tactics

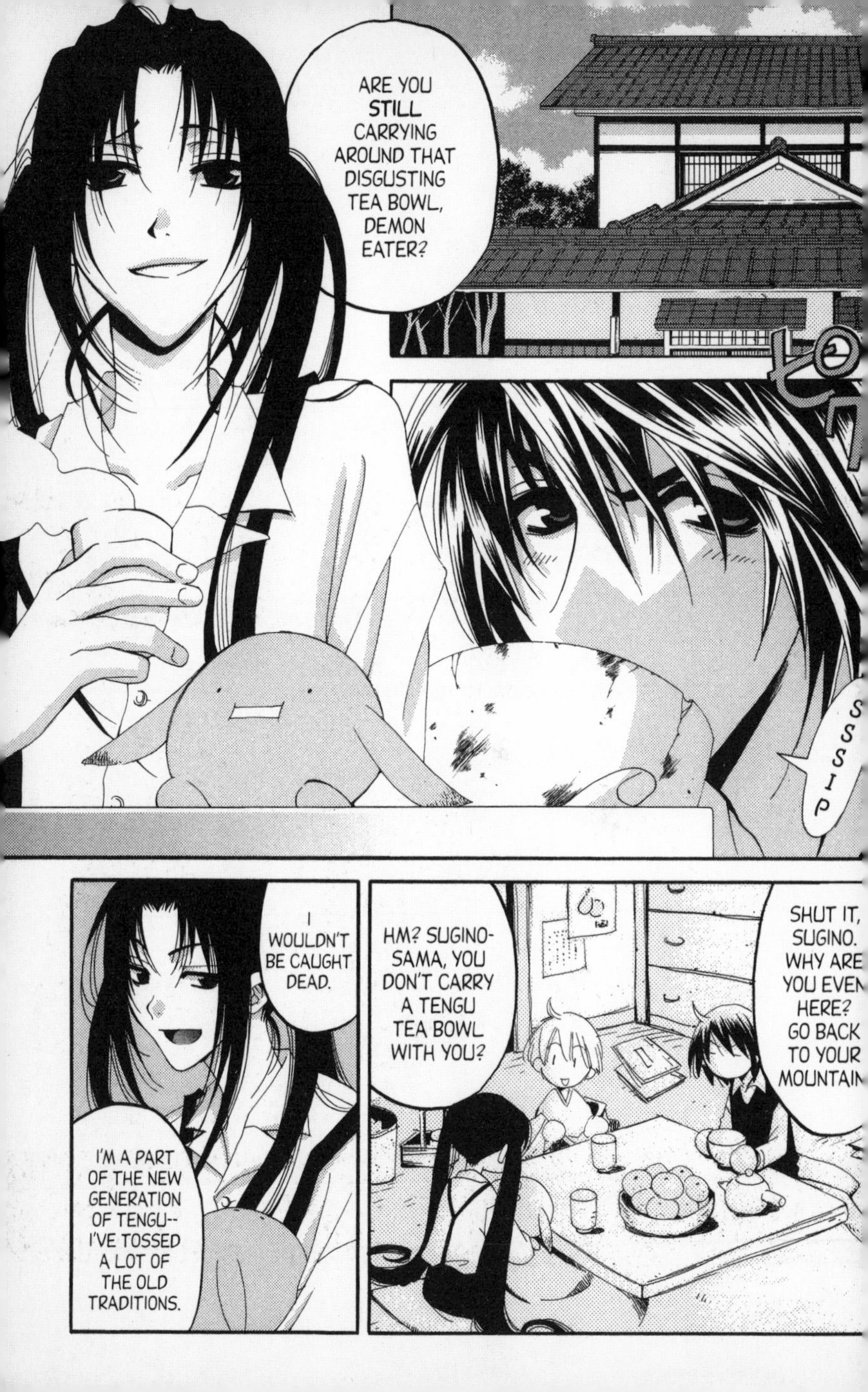
ARE YOU STILL CARRYING AROUND THAT DISGUSTING TEA BOWL, DEMON EATER?
SSSIP
SHUT IT, SUGINO. WHY ARE YOU EVEN HERE? GO BACK TO YOUR MOUNTAIN
HM? SUGINO-SAMA, YOU DON'T CARRY A TENGU TEA BOWL WITH YOU?
I WOULDN'T BE CAUGHT DEAD.
I'M A PART OF THE NEW GENERATION OF TENGU-- I'VE TOSSED A LOT OF THE OLD TRADITIONS.

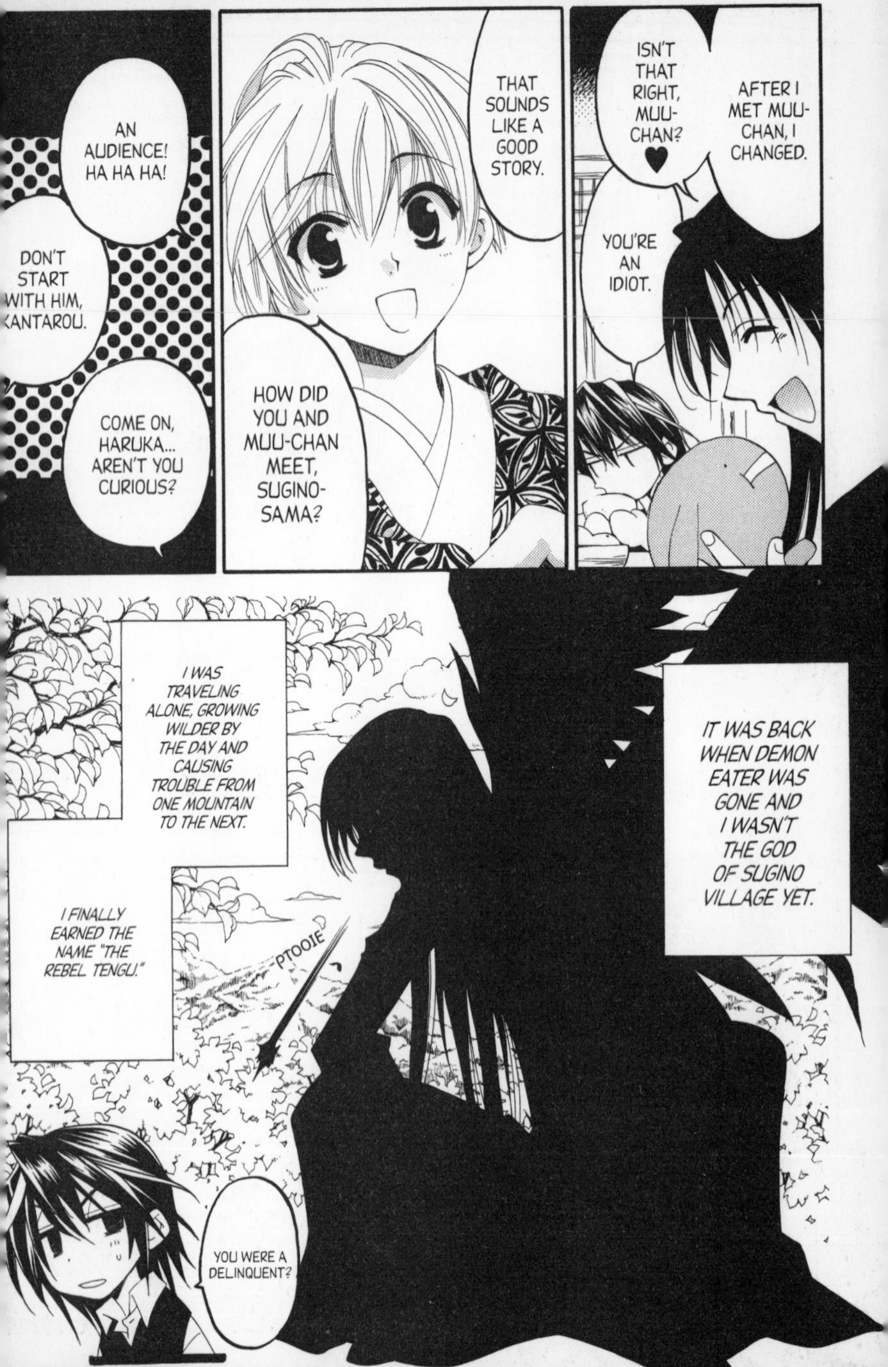
AFTER I MET MUU-CHAN, I CHANGED.
ISN'T THAT RIGHT, MUU-CHAN? ♥
YOU'RE AN IDIOT.
THAT SOUNDS LIKE A GOOD STORY.
HOW DID YOU AND MUU-CHAN MEET, SUGINO-SAMA?
AN AUDIENCE! HA HA HA!
DON'T START WITH HIM, KANTAROU.
COME ON, HARUKA... AREN'T YOU CURIOUS?
IT WAS BACK WHEN DEMON EATER WAS GONE AND I WASN'T THE GOD OF SUGINO VILLAGE YET.
I WAS TRAVELING ALONE, GROWING WILDER BY THE DAY AND CAUSING TROUBLE FROM ONE MOUNTAIN TO THE NEXT.
I FINALLY EARNED THE NAME "THE REBEL TENGU."
PTOOIE
YOU WERE A DELINQUENT?

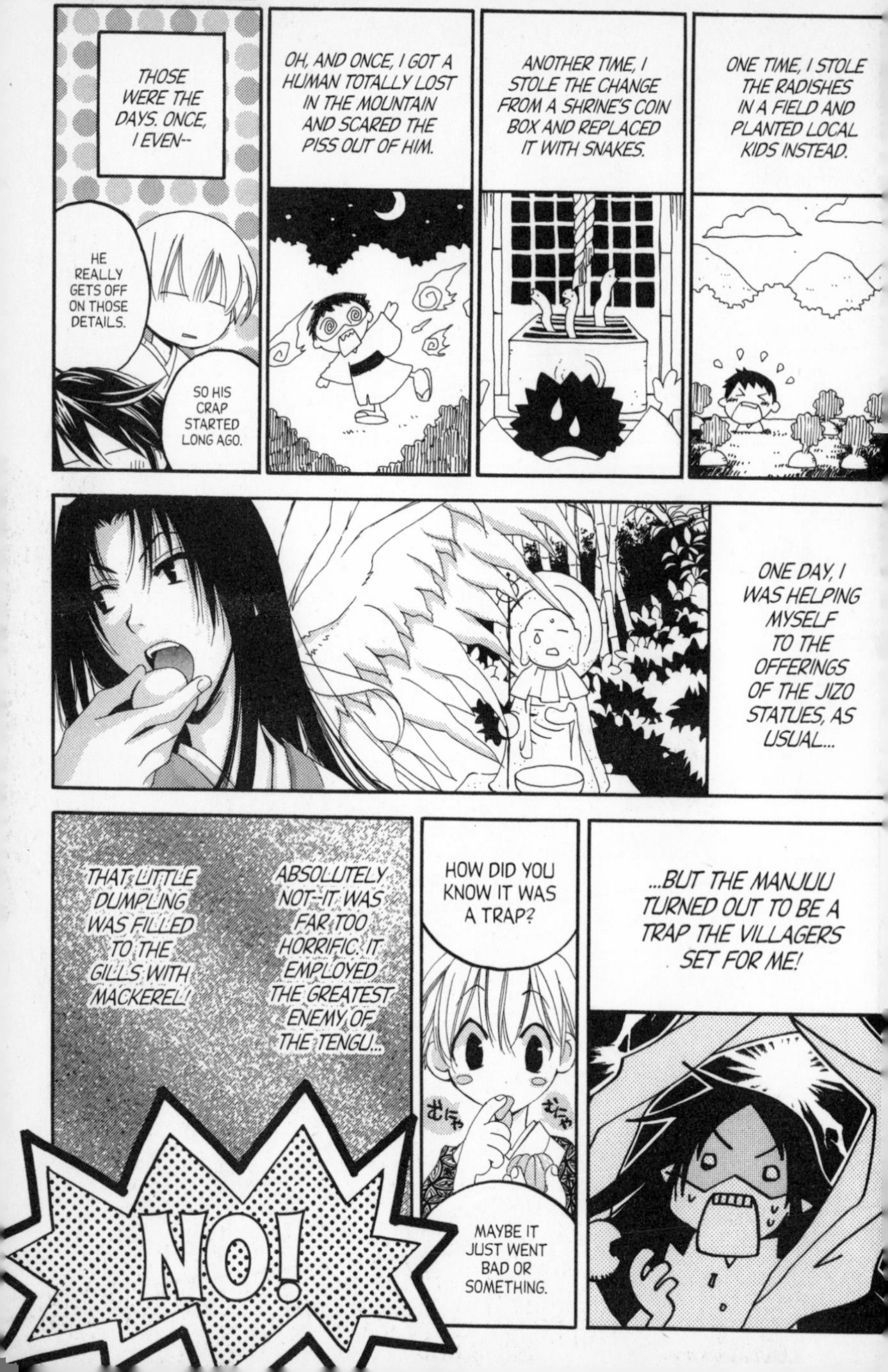
ONE TIME, I STOLE THE RADISHES IN A FIELD AND PLANTED LOCAL KIDS INSTEAD.
ANOTHER TIME, I STOLE THE CHANGE FROM A SHRINE'S COIN BOX AND REPLACED IT WITH SNAKES.
OH, AND ONCE, I GOT A HUMAN TOTALLY LOST IN THE MOUNTAIN AND SCARED THE PISS OUT OF HIM.
THOSE WERE THE DAYS. ONCE, I EVEN--
HE REALLY GETS OFF ON THOSE DETAILS.
SO HIS CRAP STARTED LONG AGO.
ONE DAY, I WAS HELPING MYSELF TO THE OFFERINGS OF THE JIZO STATUES, AS USUAL...
...BUT THE MANJUU TURNED OUT TO BE A TRAP THE VILLAGERS SET FOR ME!
HOW DID YOU KNOW IT WAS A TRAP?
むにゃ
むにゃ
MAYBE IT JUST WENT BAD OR SOMETHING.
ABSOLUTELY NOT--IT WAS FAR TOO HORRIFIC. IT EMPLOYED THE GREATEST ENEMY OF THE TENGU...
THAT LITTLE DUMPLING WAS FILLED TO THE GILLS WITH MACKEREL!
NO!

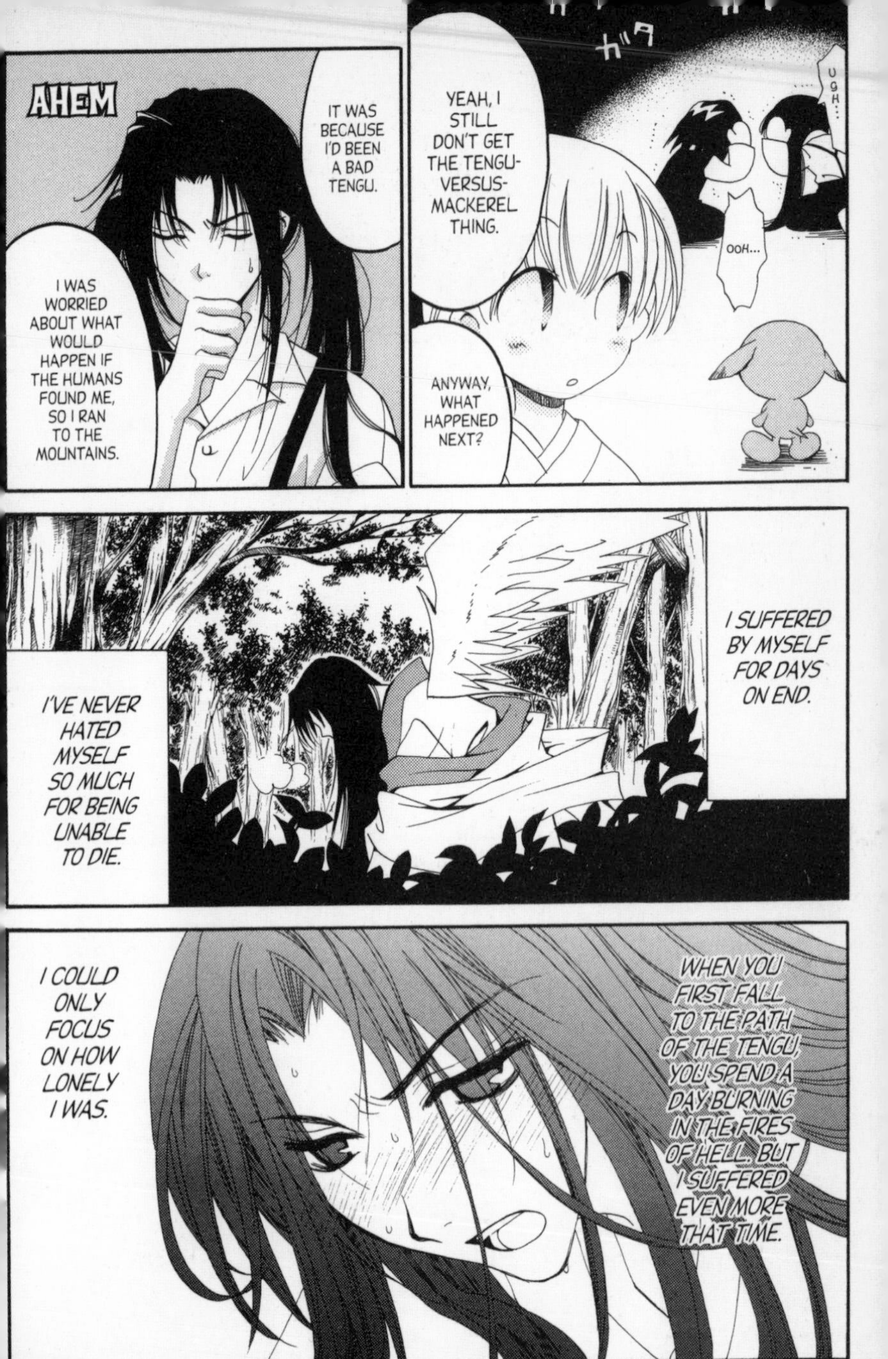
ガタ
UGH...
OOH...
YEAH, I STILL DON'T GET THE TENGU-VERSUS-MACKEREL THING.
ANYWAY, WHAT HAPPENED NEXT?
AHEM
IT WAS BECAUSE I'D BEEN A BAD TENGU.
I WAS WORRIED ABOUT WHAT WOULD HAPPEN IF THE HUMANS FOUND ME, SO I RAN TO THE MOUNTAINS.
I SUFFERED BY MYSELF FOR DAYS ON END.
I'VE NEVER HATED MYSELF SO MUCH FOR BEING UNABLE TO DIE.
WHEN YOU FIRST FALL TO THE PATH OF THE TENGU, YOU SPEND A DAY BURNING IN THE FIRES OF HELL. BUT I SUFFERED EVEN MORE THAT TIME.
I COULD ONLY FOCUS ON HOW LONELY I WAS.

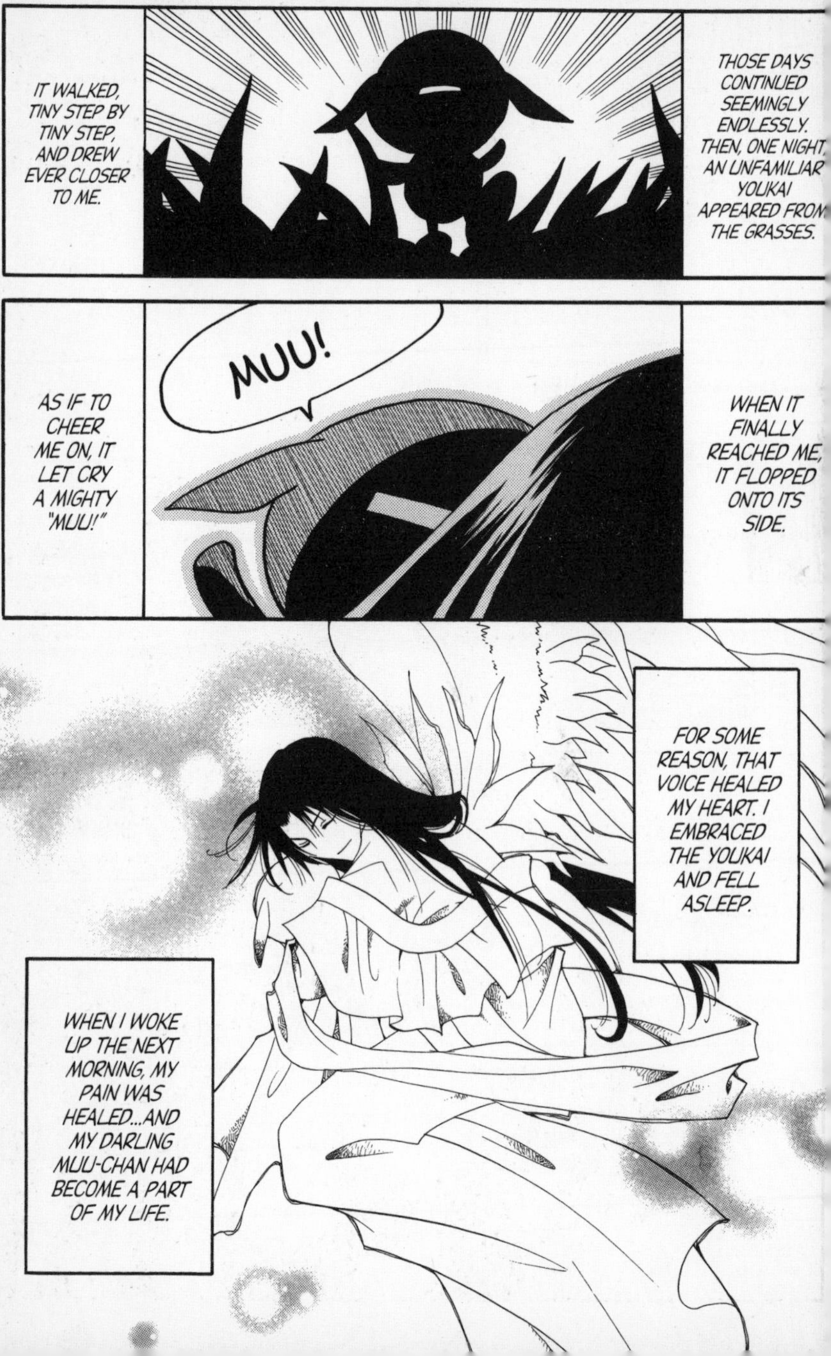
THOSE DAYS CONTINUED SEEMINGLY ENDLESSLY. THEN, ONE NIGHT, AN UNFAMILIAR YOUKAI APPEARED FROM THE GRASSES.
IT WALKED, TINY STEP BY TINY STEP, AND DREW EVER CLOSER TO ME.
WHEN IT FINALLY REACHED ME, IT FLOPPED ONTO ITS SIDE.
MUU!
AS IF TO CHEER ME ON, IT LET CRY A MIGHTY "MUU!"
FOR SOME REASON, THAT VOICE HEALED MY HEART. I EMBRACED THE YOUKAI AND FELL ASLEEP.
WHEN I WOKE UP THE NEXT MORNING, MY PAIN WAS HEALED...AND MY DARLING MUU-CHAN HAD BECOME A PART OF MY LIFE.

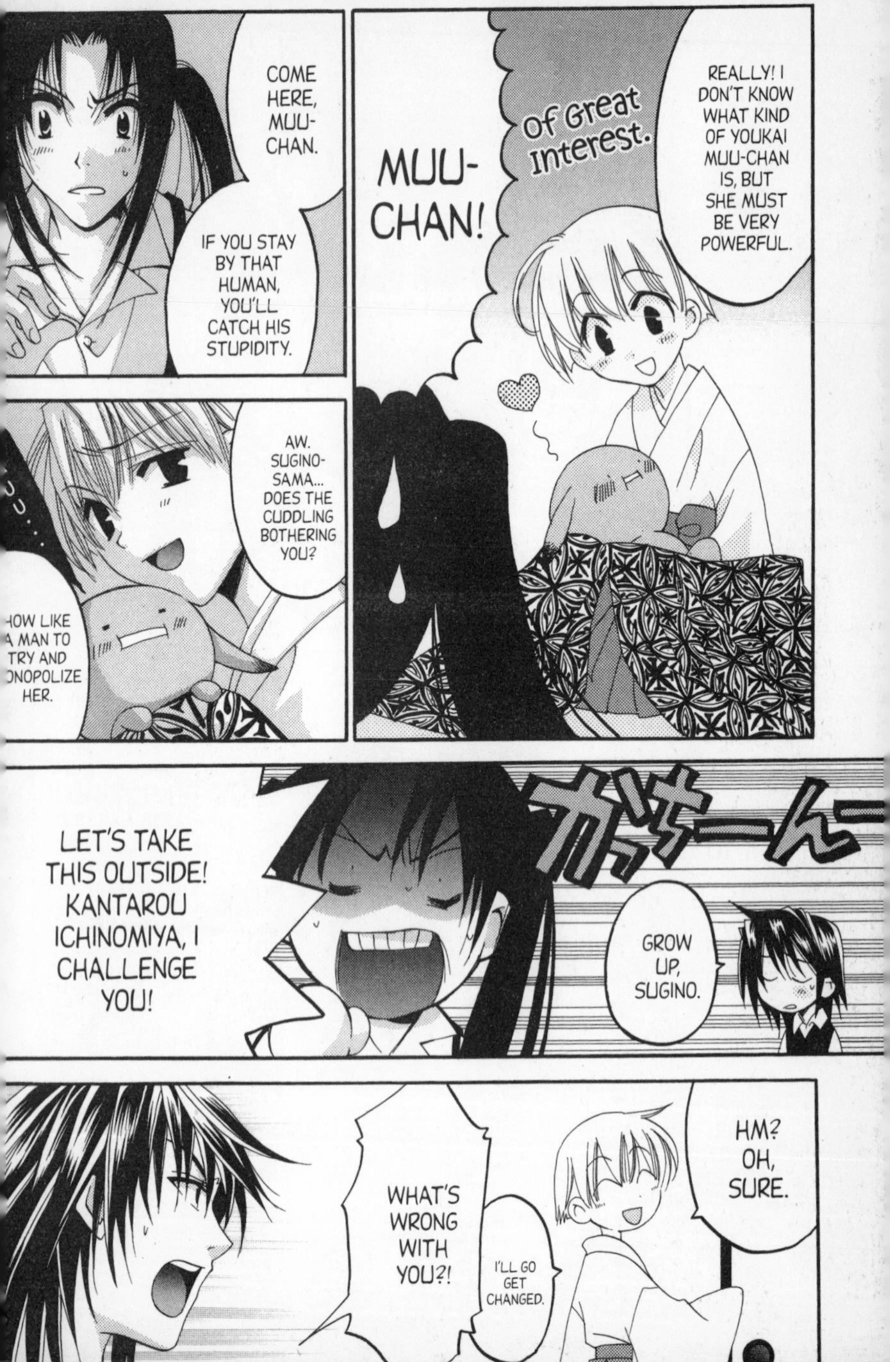

REALLY! I DON'T KNOW WHAT KIND OF YOUKAI MUU-CHAN IS, BUT SHE MUST BE VERY POWERFUL.
Of Great Interest.
MUU-CHAN!
COME HERE, MUU-CHAN.
IF YOU STAY BY THAT HUMAN, YOU'LL CATCH HIS STUPIDITY.
AW. SUGINO-SAMA... DOES THE CUDDLING BOTHERING YOU?
HOW LIKE A MAN TO TRY AND ONOPOLIZE HER.
GROW UP, SUGINO.
LET'S TAKE THIS OUTSIDE! KANTAROU ICHINOMIYA, I CHALLENGE YOU!
HM? OH, SURE.
I'LL GO GET CHANGED.
WHAT'S WRONG WITH YOU?!

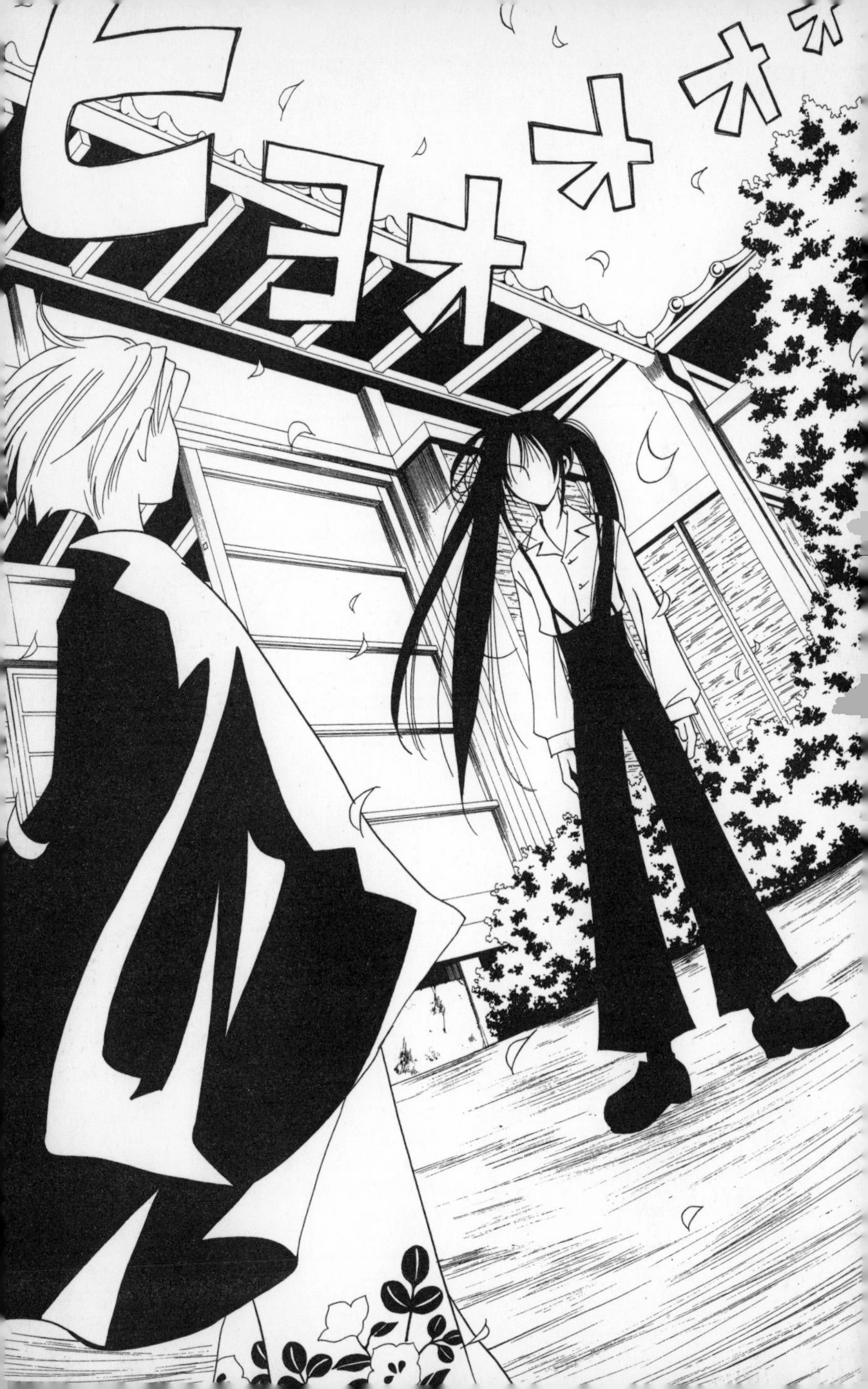
ヒョオオオォ

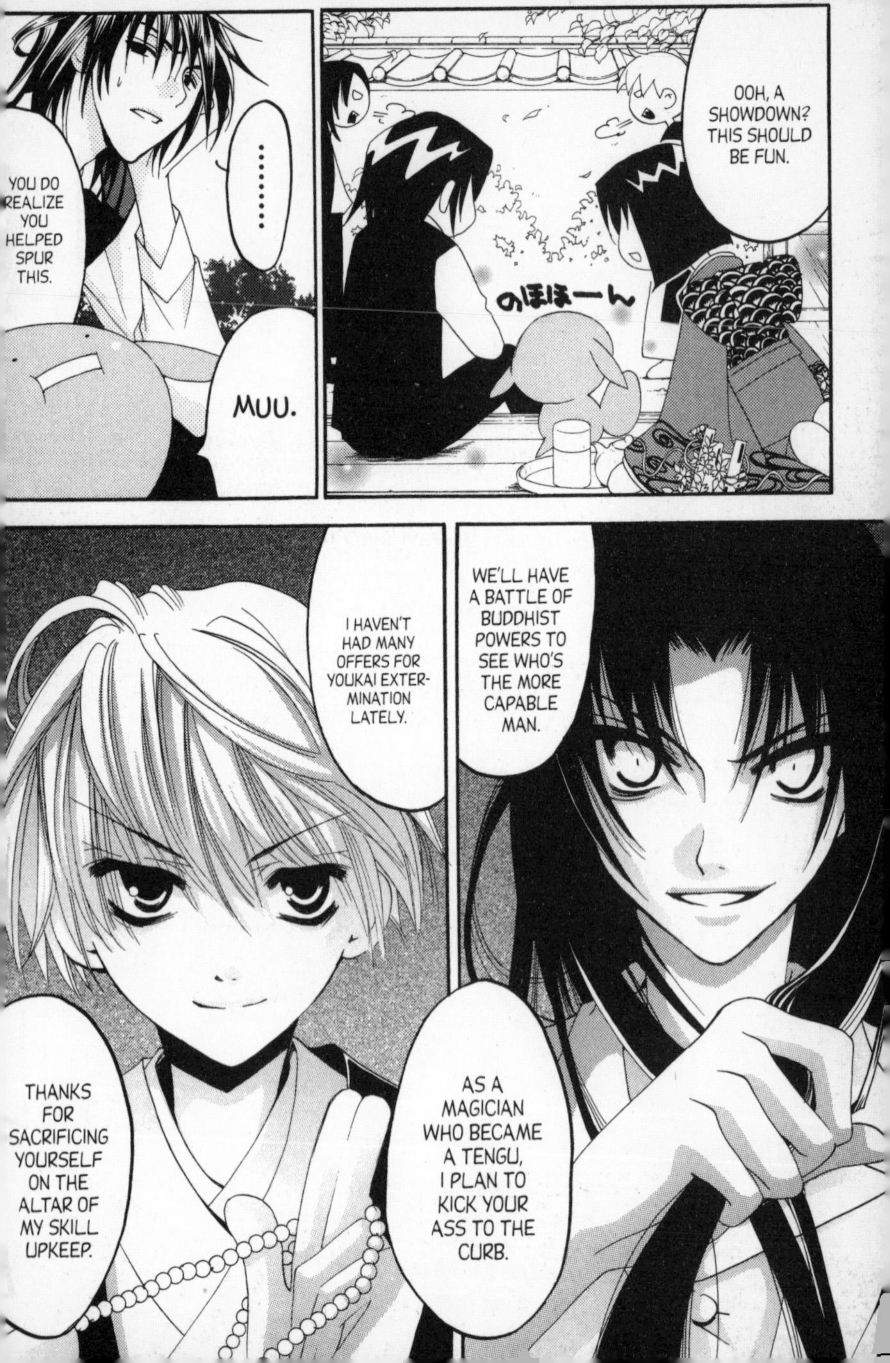
OOH, A SHOWDOWN? THIS SHOULD BE FUN.
のほほーん
......
YOU DO REALIZE YOU HELPED SPUR THIS.
MUU.
WE'LL HAVE A BATTLE OF BUDDHIST POWERS TO SEE WHO'S THE MORE CAPABLE MAN.
AS A MAGICIAN WHO BECAME A TENGU, I PLAN TO KICK YOUR ASS TO THE CURB.
I HAVEN'T HAD MANY OFFERS FOR YOUKAI EXTERMINATION LATELY.
THANKS FOR SACRIFICING YOURSELF ON THE ALTAR OF MY SKILL UPKEEP.

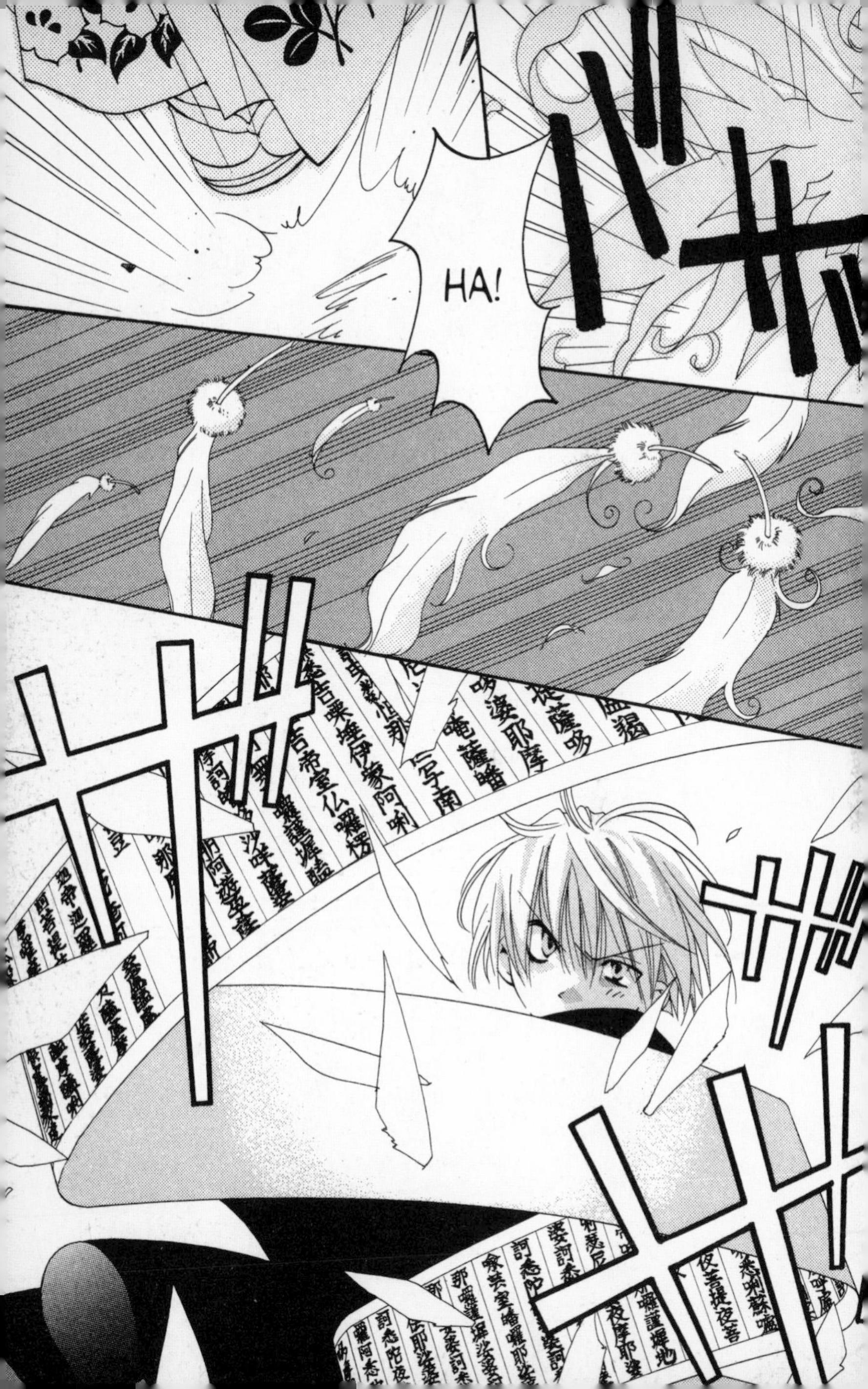
HA!

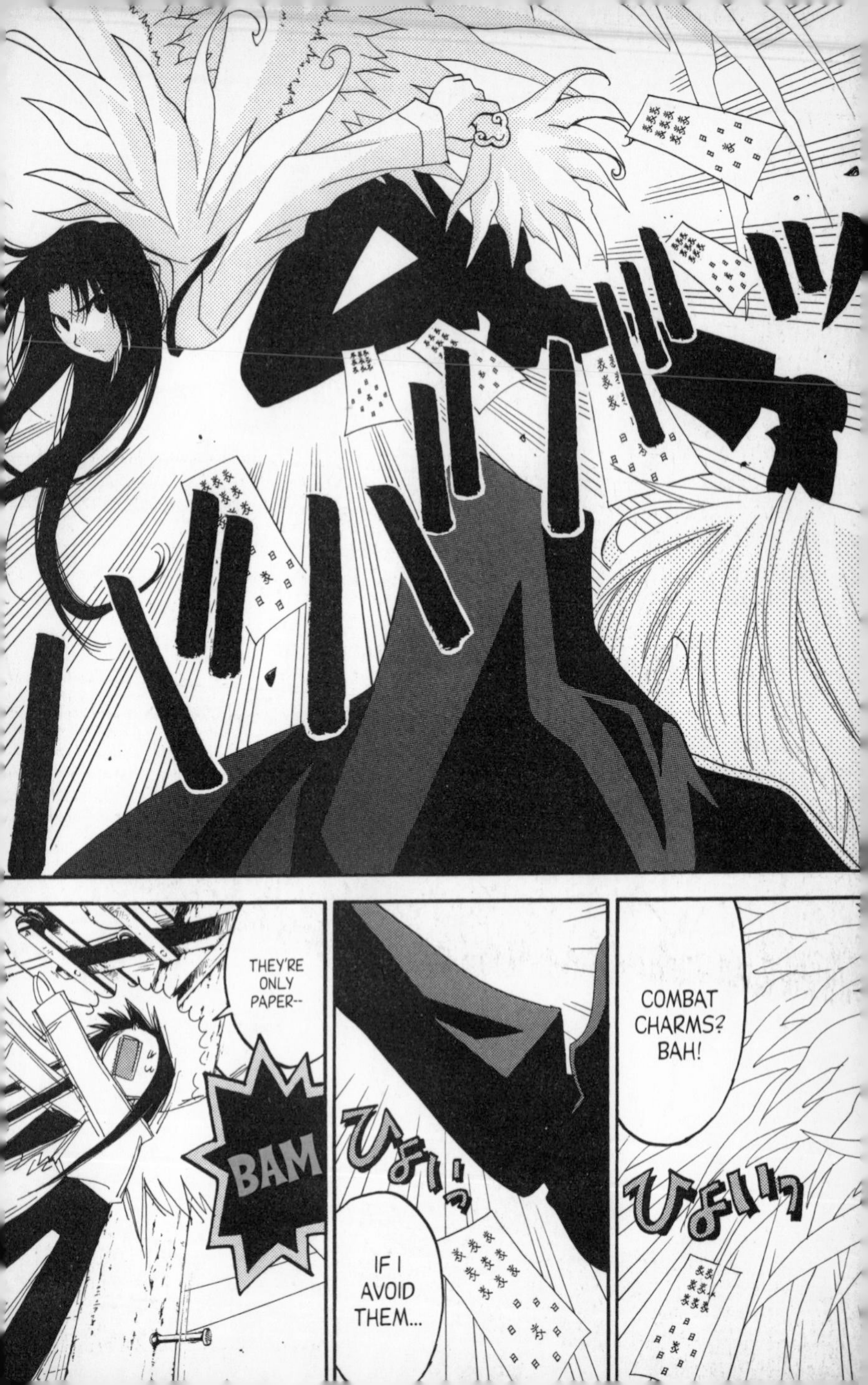
COMBAT CHARMS? BAH!
ひょいっ
ひょいっ
IF I AVOID THEM...
THEY'RE ONLY PAPER--
BAM

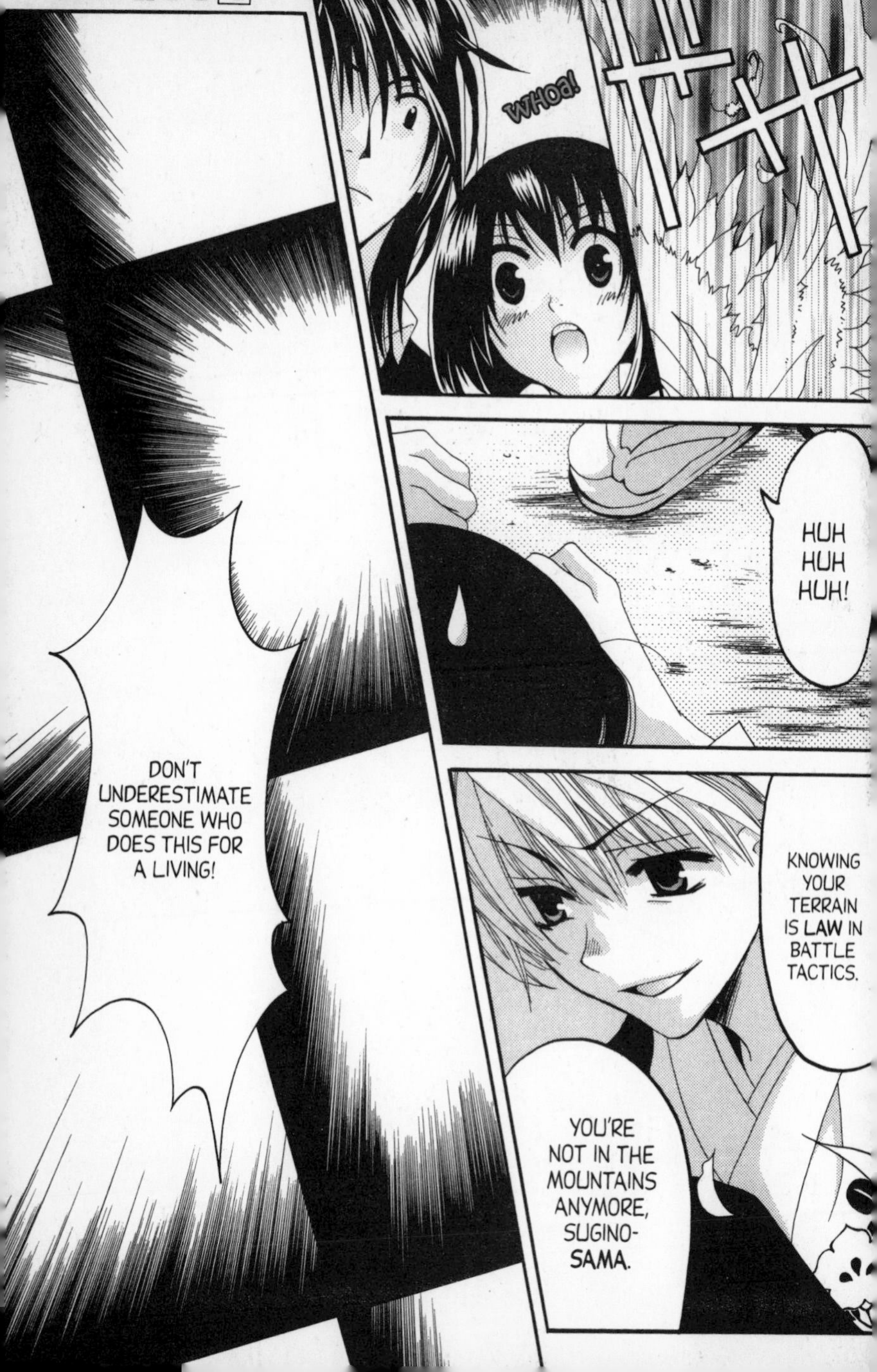
WHOA!
HUH HUH HUH!
KNOWING YOUR TERRAIN IS LAW IN BATTLE TACTICS.
YOU'RE NOT IN THE MOUNTAINS ANYMORE, SUGINO-SAMA.
DON'T UNDERESTIMATE SOMEONE WHO DOES THIS FOR A LIVING!

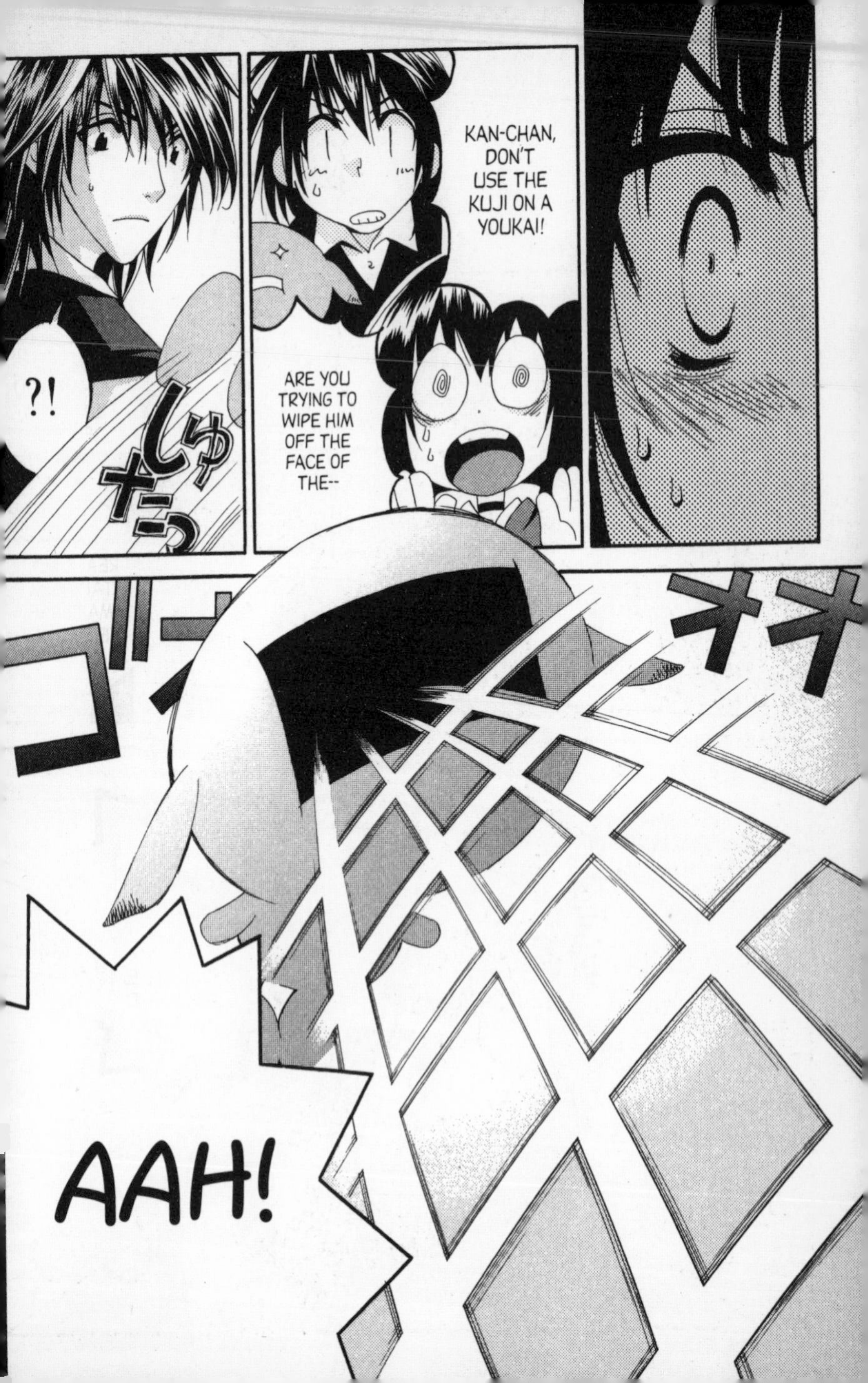
KAN-CHAN, DON'T USE THE KUJI ON A YOUKAI!
ARE YOU TRYING TO WIPE HIM OFF THE FACE OF THE--
?!
AAH!

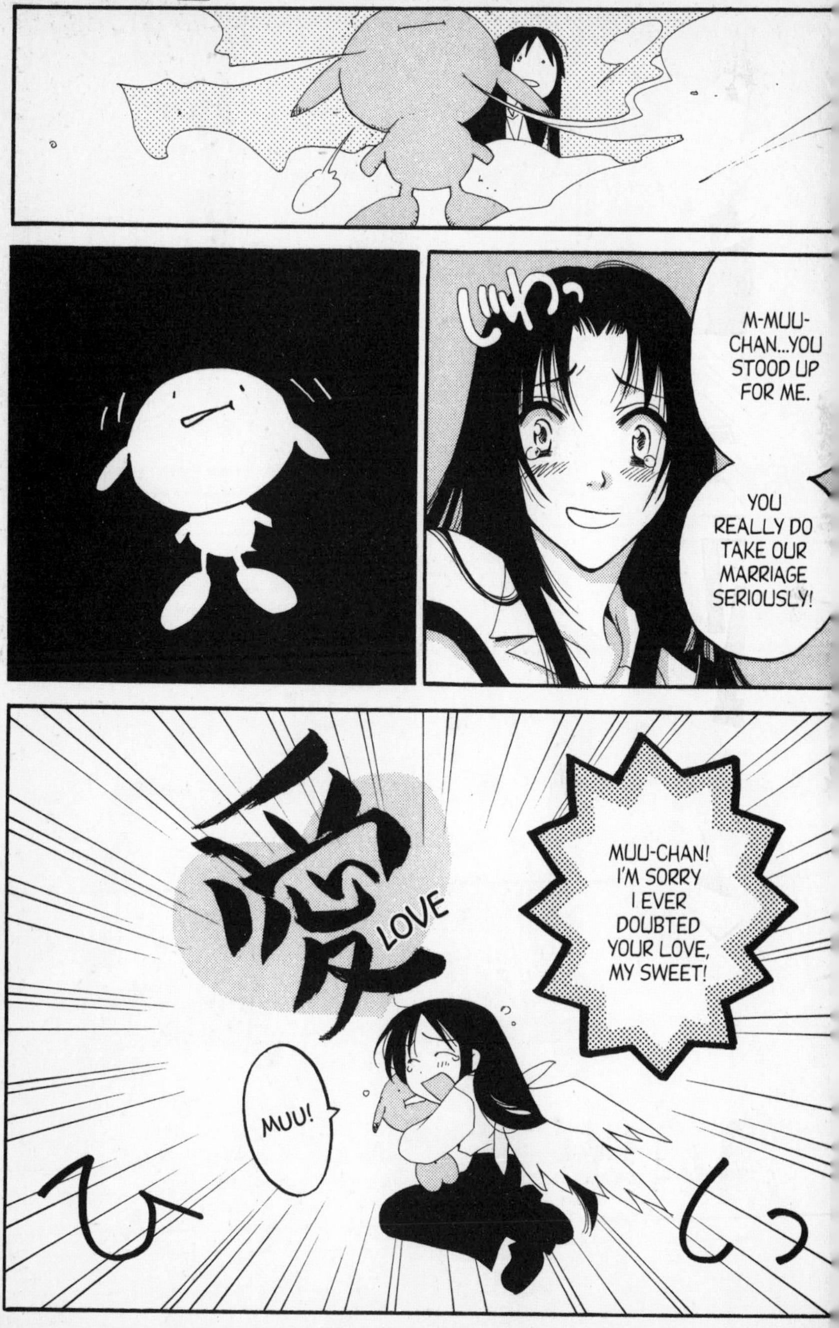
M-MUU-CHAN...YOU STOOD UP FOR ME.
YOU REALLY DO TAKE OUR MARRIAGE SERIOUSLY!
MUU-CHAN! I'M SORRY I EVER DOUBTED YOUR LOVE, MY SWEET!
愛
LOVE
MUU!

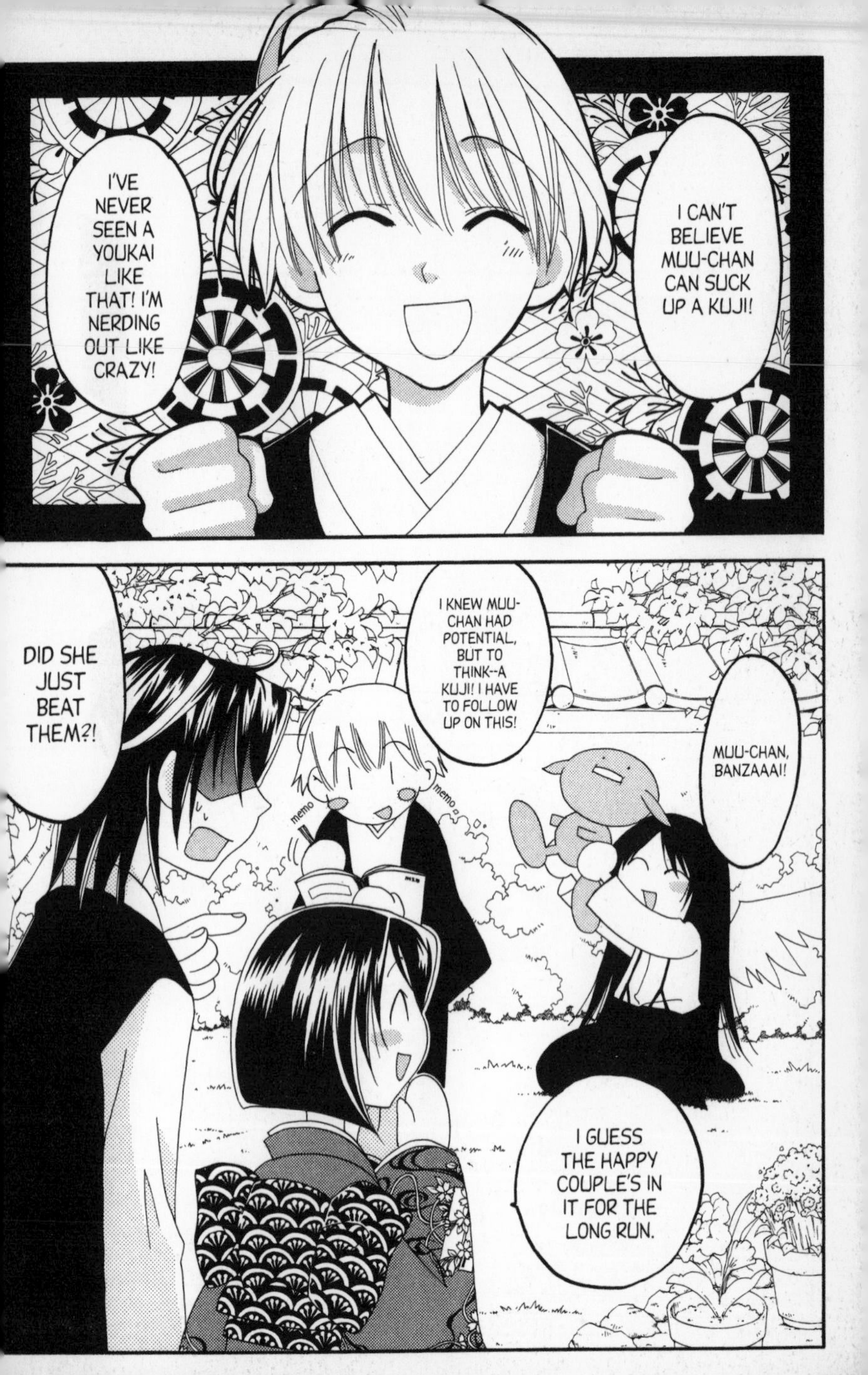
I CAN'T BELIEVE MUU-CHAN CAN SUCK UP A KUJI!
I'VE NEVER SEEN A YOUKAI LIKE THAT! I'M NERDING OUT LIKE CRAZY!
MUU-CHAN, BANZAAAI!
I KNEW MUU-CHAN HAD POTENTIAL, BUT TO THINK--A KUJI! I HAVE TO FOLLOW UP ON THIS!
memo memo
DID SHE JUST BEAT THEM?!
I GUESS THE HAPPY COUPLE'S IN IT FOR THE LONG RUN.

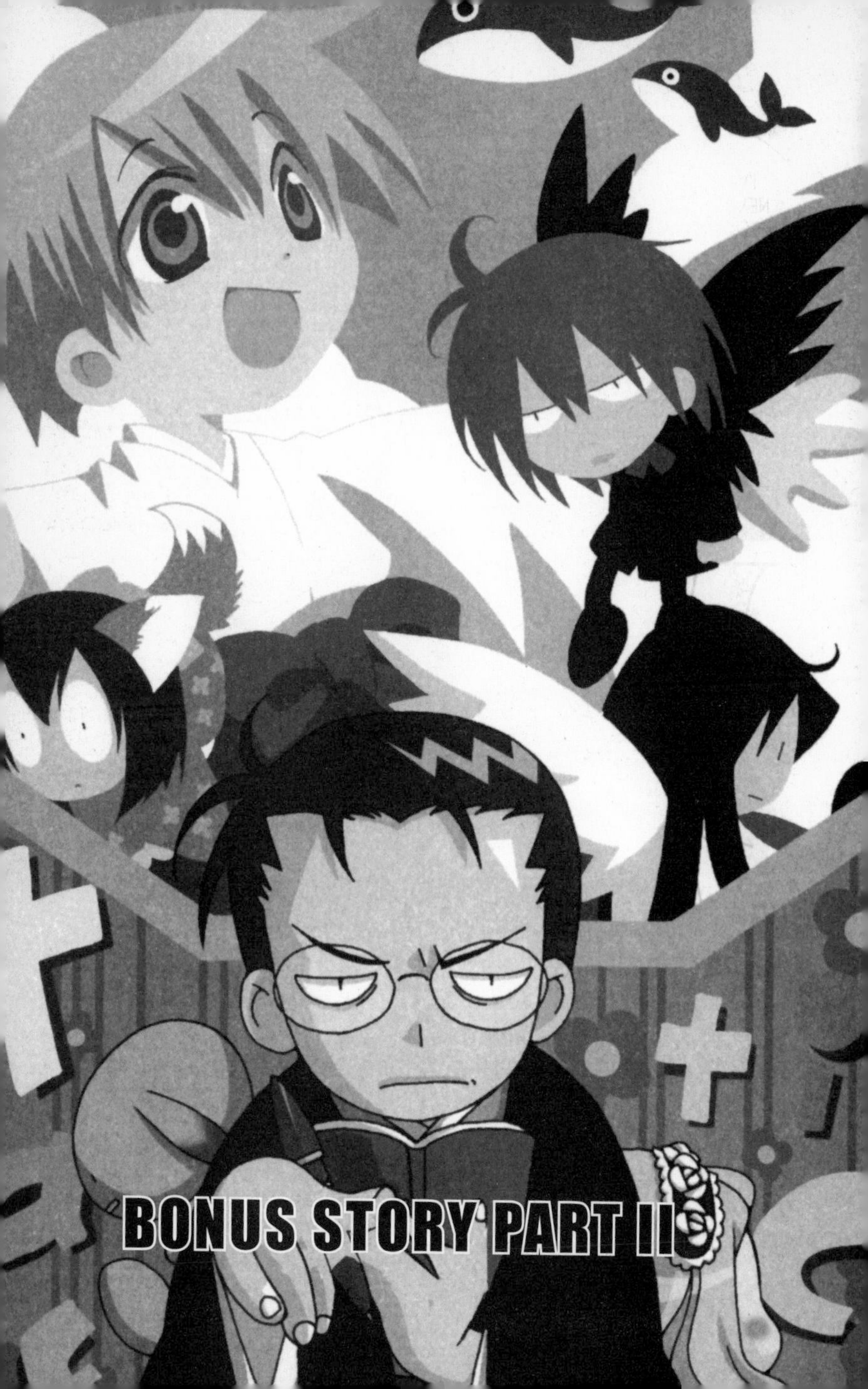
BONUS STORY PART II

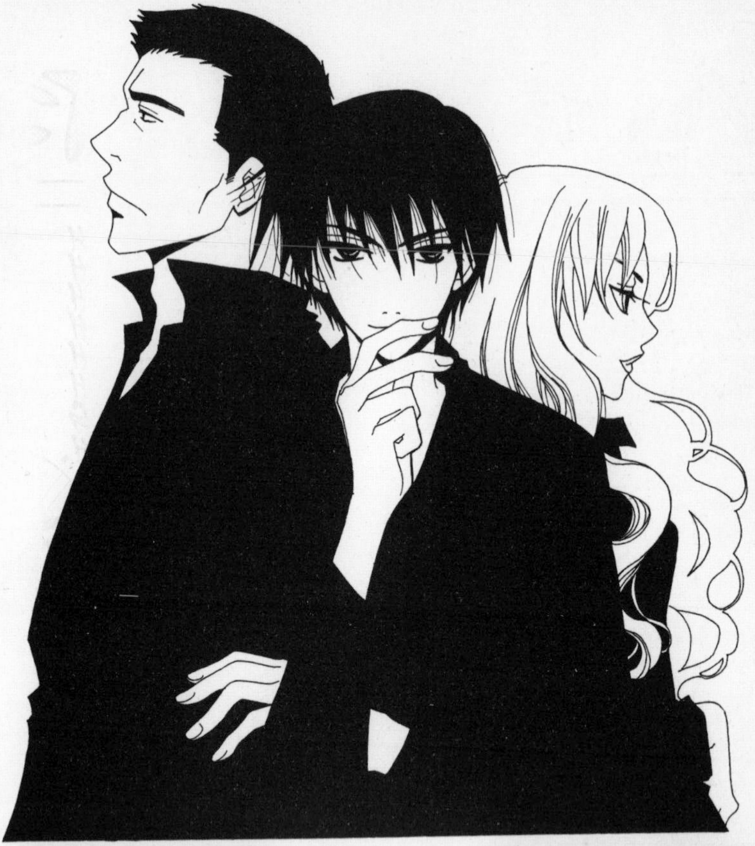

Raikou Minamoto Troup-sama

It's *tactics* Volume 4! Thank you so much!
Congrats! Hi--this is Kazuko Higashiyama, by the way.

Wow, I can't believe it's Volume 4 already...
my heart's pounding like a jackhammer!
I'm as happy as can be that we get to do this many volumes pretty safely (?). I hope for the best possible response from here on out, too.

Minamoto and company are important characters I wanted to have appear right along with Sugino-sama back in the day (right now he's almost completely that kind of god...but he'll be showing up again...I think), so I'm happy. Such fun. I love (?) this.
It was a blast devising characters so unlike Kantarou, Haruka and Youko.

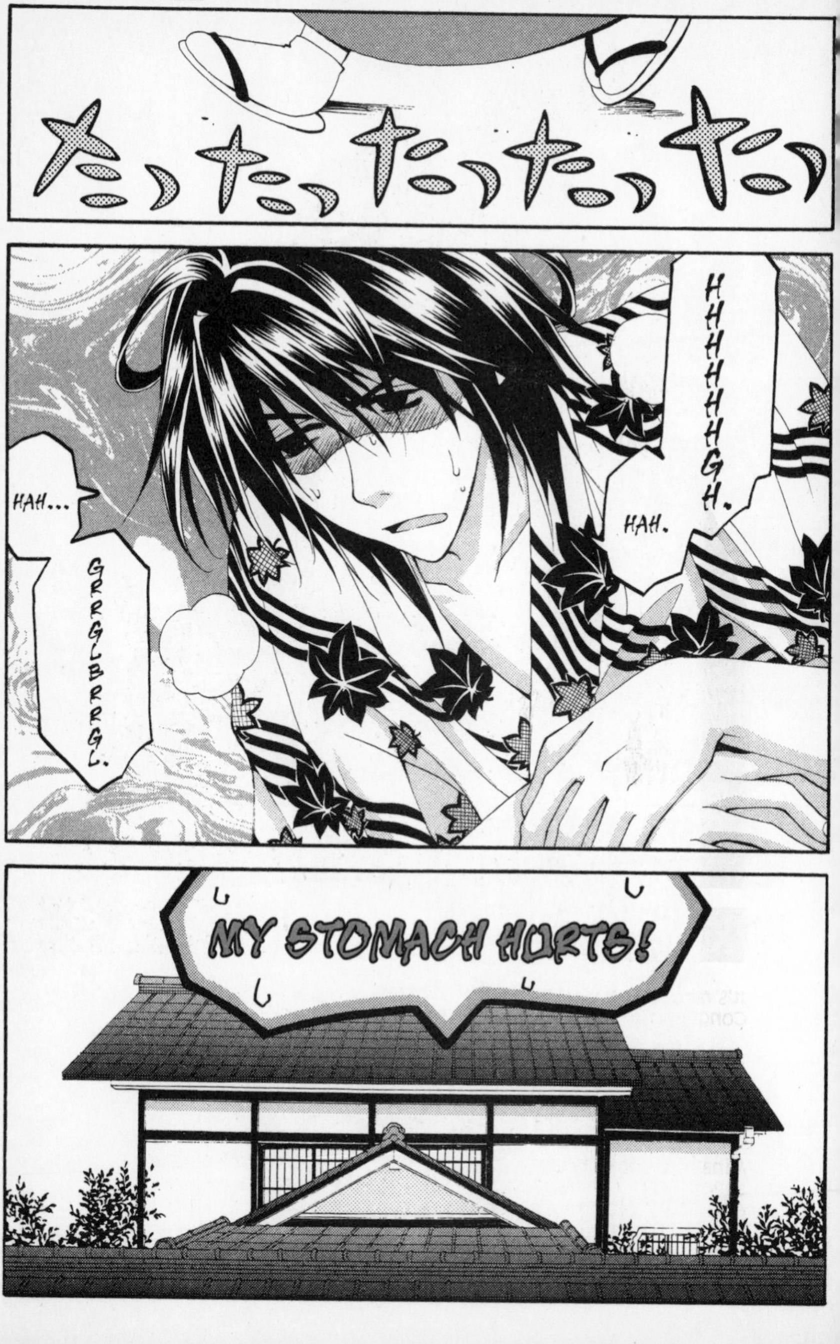
たっ たっ たっ たっ たっ
HHHHHHGH.
HAH.
HAH...
GRRGLBRRGL.
MY STOMACH HURTS!

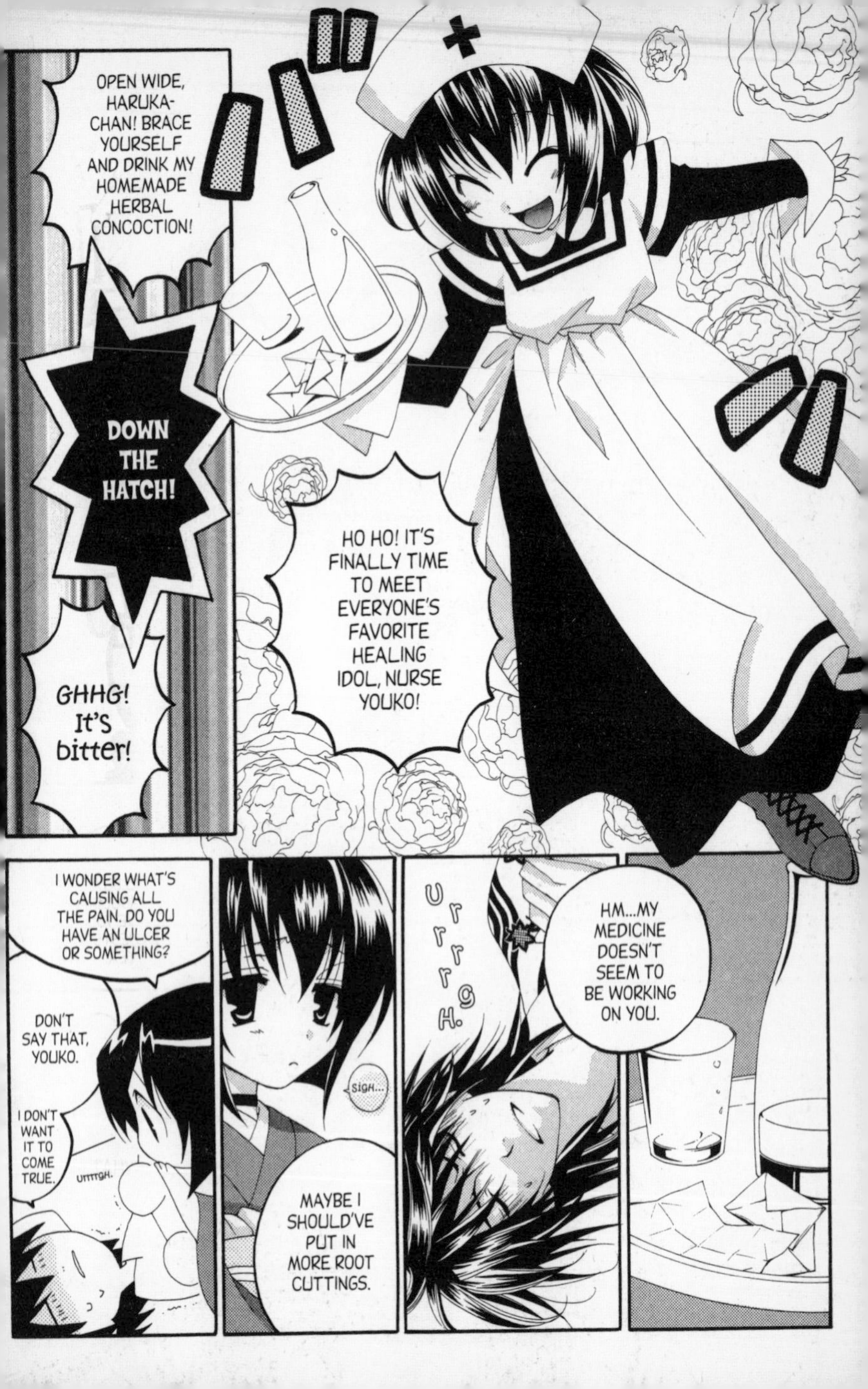
HO HO! IT'S FINALLY TIME TO MEET EVERYONE'S FAVORITE HEALING IDOL, NURSE YOUKO!
OPEN WIDE, HARUKA-CHAN! BRACE YOURSELF AND DRINK MY HOMEMADE HERBAL CONCOCTION!
DOWN THE HATCH!
GHHG! It's bitter!
HM...MY MEDICINE DOESN'T SEEM TO BE WORKING ON YOU.
Urrrrgh.
SIGH...
MAYBE I SHOULD'VE PUT IN MORE ROOT CUTTINGS.
I WONDER WHAT'S CAUSING ALL THE PAIN. DO YOU HAVE AN ULCER OR SOMETHING?
DON'T SAY THAT, YOUKO.
I DON'T WANT IT TO COME TRUE.
UHHGH.

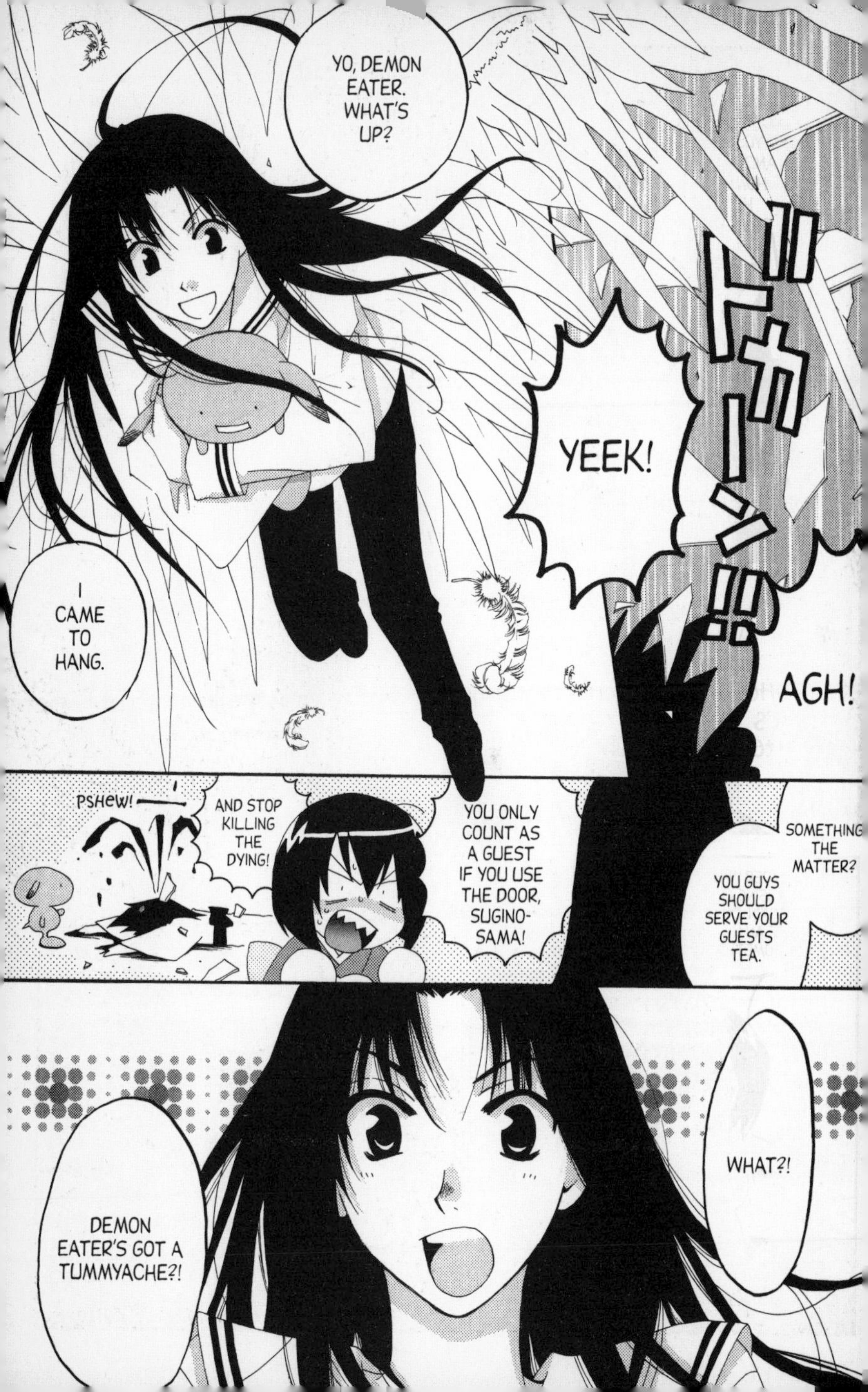

ドカーン!!
YEEK!
AGH!
YO, DEMON EATER. WHAT'S UP?
I CAME TO HANG.
SOMETHING THE MATTER?
YOU GUYS SHOULD SERVE YOUR GUESTS TEA.
YOU ONLY COUNT AS A GUEST IF YOU USE THE DOOR, SUGINO-SAMA!
AND STOP KILLING THE DYING!
PSHEW!
WHAT?!
DEMON EATER'S GOT A TUMMYACHE?!

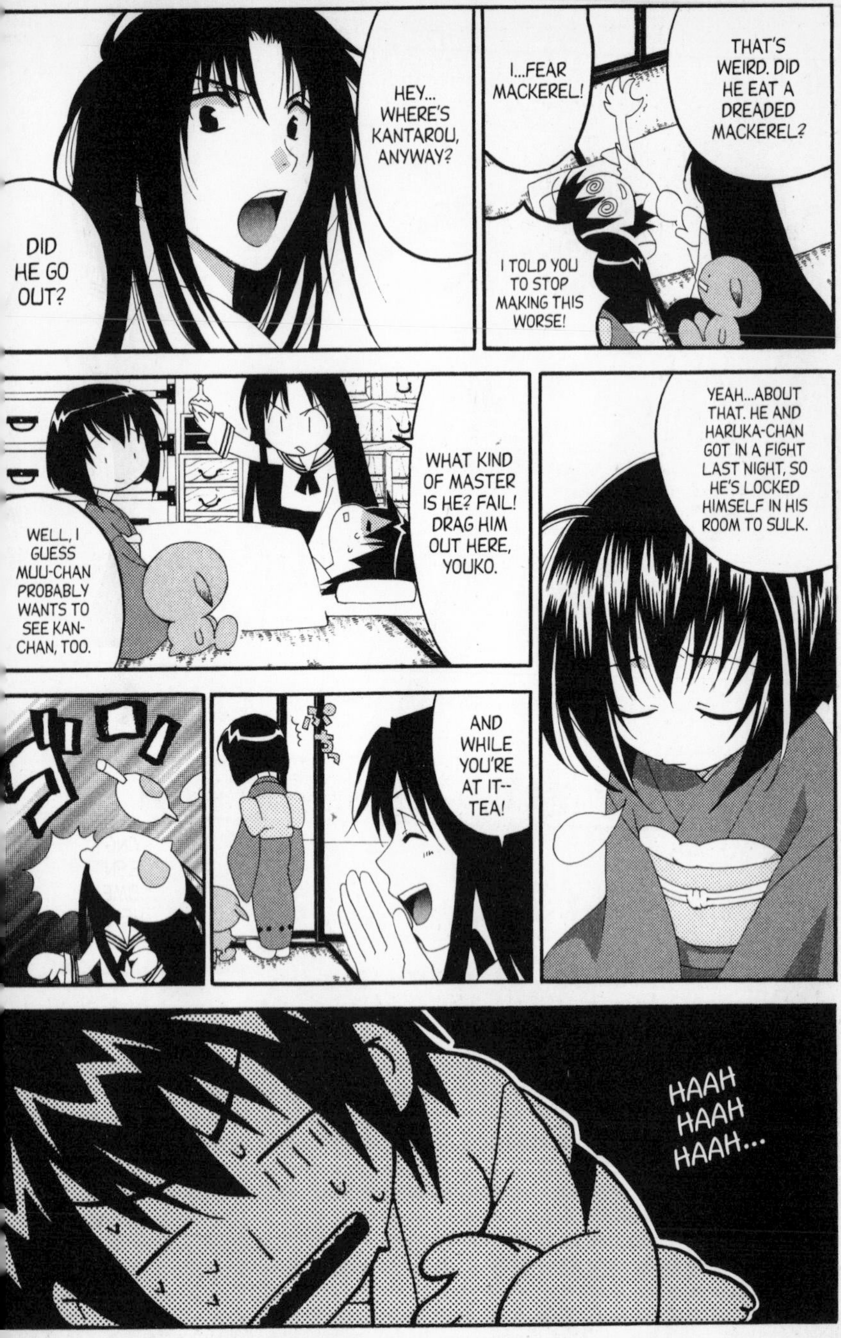
THAT'S WEIRD. DID HE EAT A DREADED MACKEREL?
I...FEAR MACKEREL!
I TOLD YOU TO STOP MAKING THIS WORSE!
HEY... WHERE'S KANTAROU, ANYWAY?
DID HE GO OUT?
YEAH...ABOUT THAT. HE AND HARUKA-CHAN GOT IN A FIGHT LAST NIGHT, SO HE'S LOCKED HIMSELF IN HIS ROOM TO SULK.
WHAT KIND OF MASTER IS HE? FAIL! DRAG HIM OUT HERE, YOUKO.
WELL, I GUESS MUU-CHAN PROBABLY WANTS TO SEE KAN-CHAN, TOO.
AND WHILE YOU'RE AT IT-- TEA!
HAAH HAAH HAAH...

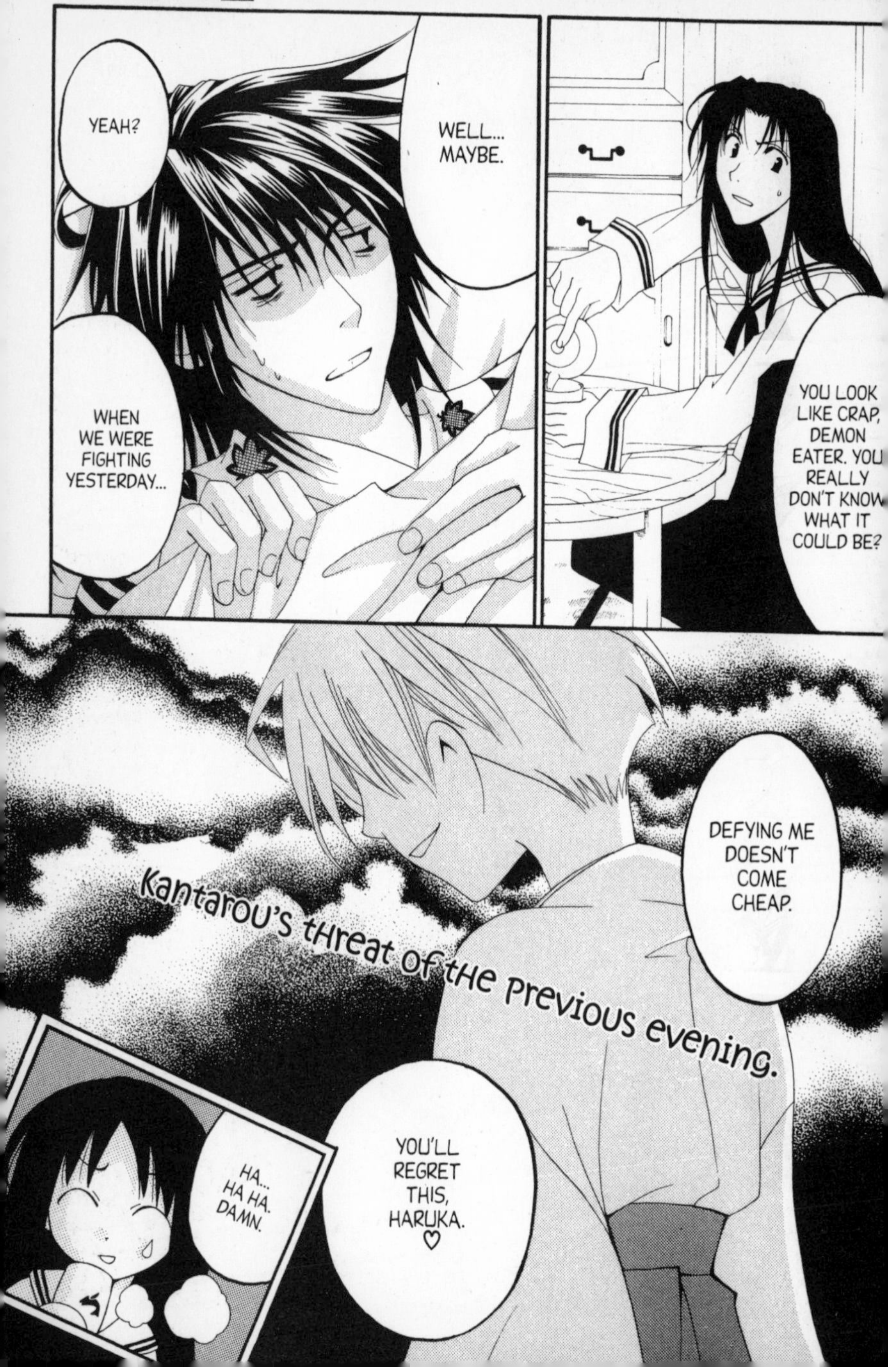
YOU LOOK LIKE CRAP, DEMON EATER. YOU REALLY DON'T KNOW WHAT IT COULD BE?
WELL... MAYBE.
YEAH?
WHEN WE WERE FIGHTING YESTERDAY...
DEFYING ME DOESN'T COME CHEAP.
Kantarou's threat of the previous evening.
YOU'LL REGRET THIS, HARUKA. ♡
HA... HA HA. DAMN.

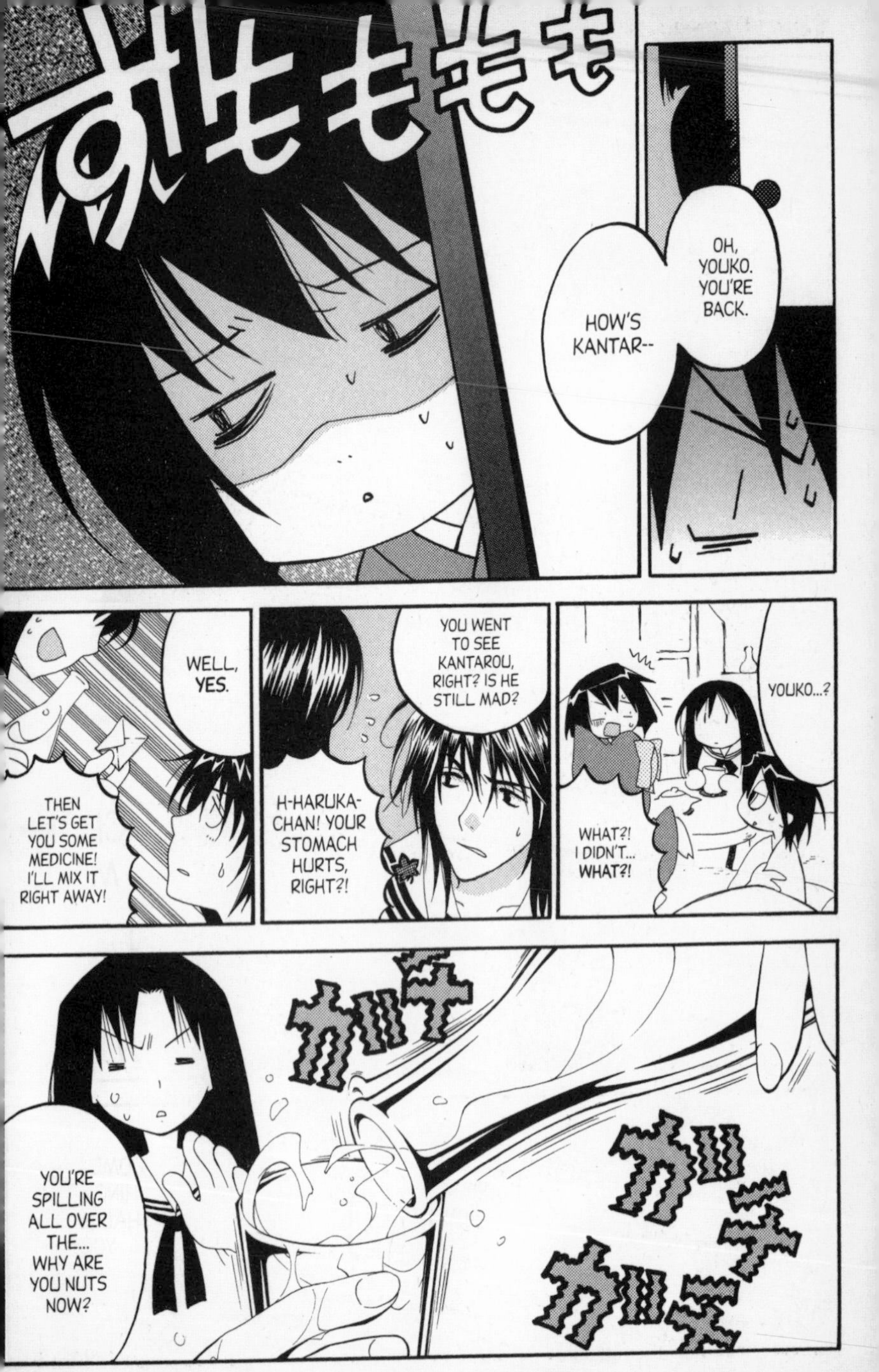

OH, YOUKO. YOU'RE BACK.
HOW'S KANTAR--
YOUKO...?
WHAT?! I DIDN'T... WHAT?!
YOU WENT TO SEE KANTAROU, RIGHT? IS HE STILL MAD?
H-HARUKA-CHAN! YOUR STOMACH HURTS, RIGHT?!
WELL, YES.
THEN LET'S GET YOU SOME MEDICINE! I'LL MIX IT RIGHT AWAY!
YOU'RE SPILLING ALL OVER THE... WHY ARE YOU NUTS NOW?

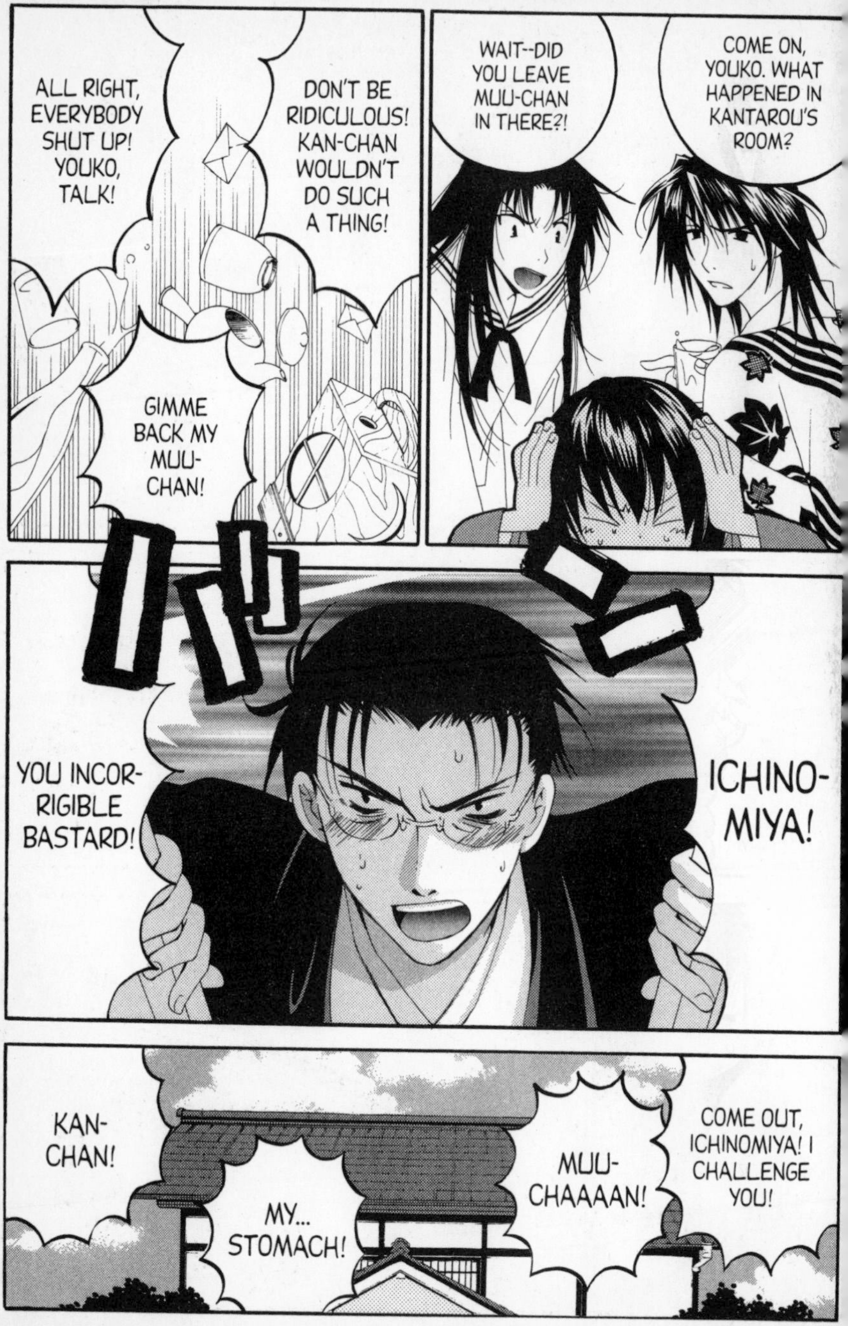
COME ON, YOUKO. WHAT HAPPENED IN KANTAROU'S ROOM?
WAIT--DID YOU LEAVE MUU-CHAN IN THERE?!
DON'T BE RIDICULOUS! KAN-CHAN WOULDN'T DO SUCH A THING!
ALL RIGHT, EVERYBODY SHUT UP! YOUKO, TALK!
GIMME BACK MY MUU-CHAN!
ICHINO-MIYA!
YOU INCOR-RIGIBLE BASTARD!
COME OUT, ICHINOMIYA! I CHALLENGE YOU!
MUU-CHAAAAN!
MY... STOMACH!
KAN-CHAN!

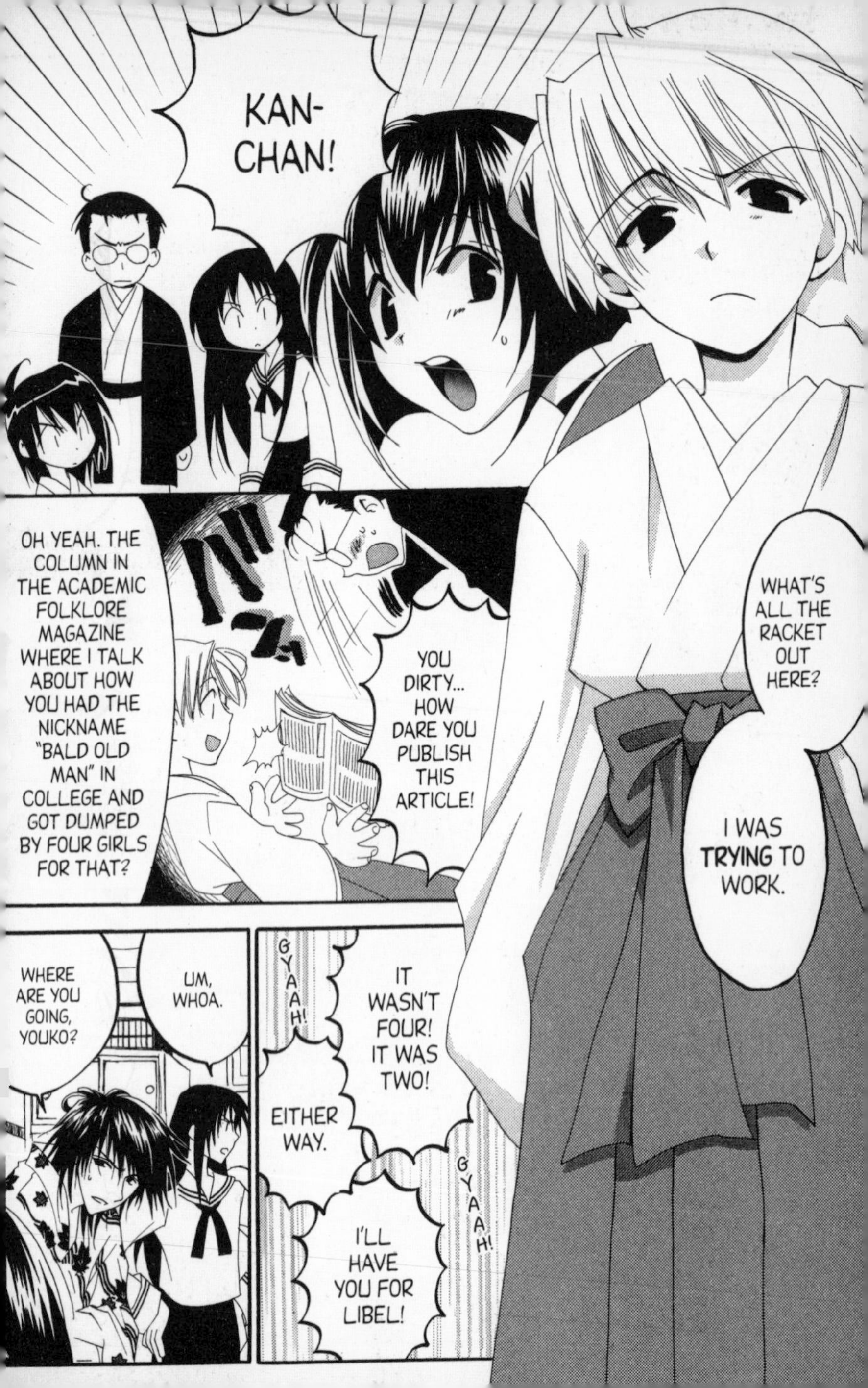
KAN-CHAN!
WHAT'S ALL THE RACKET OUT HERE?
I WAS **TRYING** TO WORK.
YOU DIRTY... HOW DARE YOU PUBLISH THIS ARTICLE!
OH YEAH. THE COLUMN IN THE ACADEMIC FOLKLORE MAGAZINE WHERE I TALK ABOUT HOW YOU HAD THE NICKNAME "BALD OLD MAN" IN COLLEGE AND GOT DUMPED BY FOUR GIRLS FOR THAT?
GYAAH!
IT WASN'T FOUR! IT WAS TWO!
EITHER WAY.
I'LL HAVE YOU FOR LIBEL!
GYAAH!
UM, WHOA.
WHERE ARE YOU GOING, YOUKO?

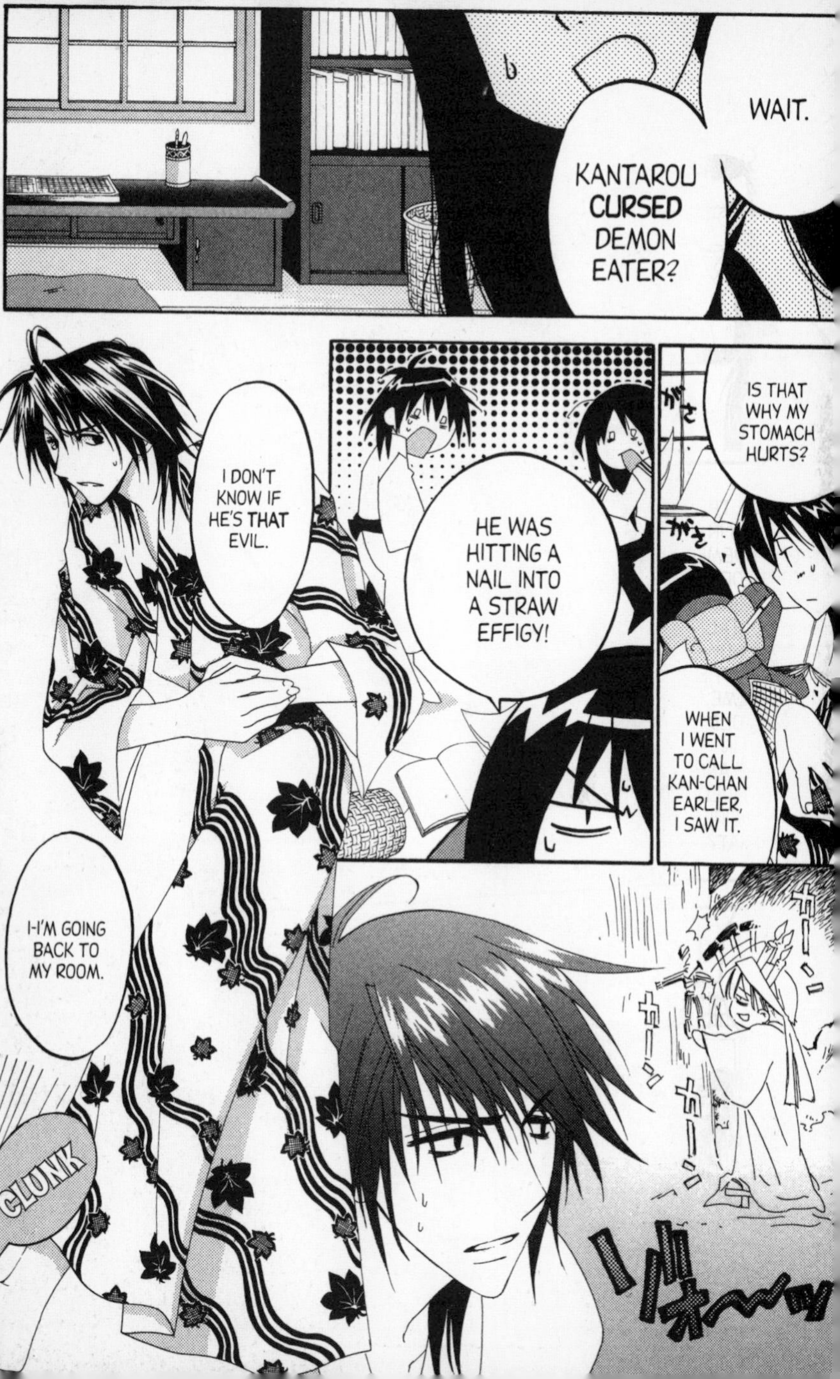
WAIT.
KANTAROU CURSED DEMON EATER?
IS THAT WHY MY STOMACH HURTS?
WHEN I WENT TO CALL KAN-CHAN EARLIER, I SAW IT.
HE WAS HITTING A NAIL INTO A STRAW EFFIGY!
I DON'T KNOW IF HE'S THAT EVIL.
I-I'M GOING BACK TO MY ROOM.
CLUNK

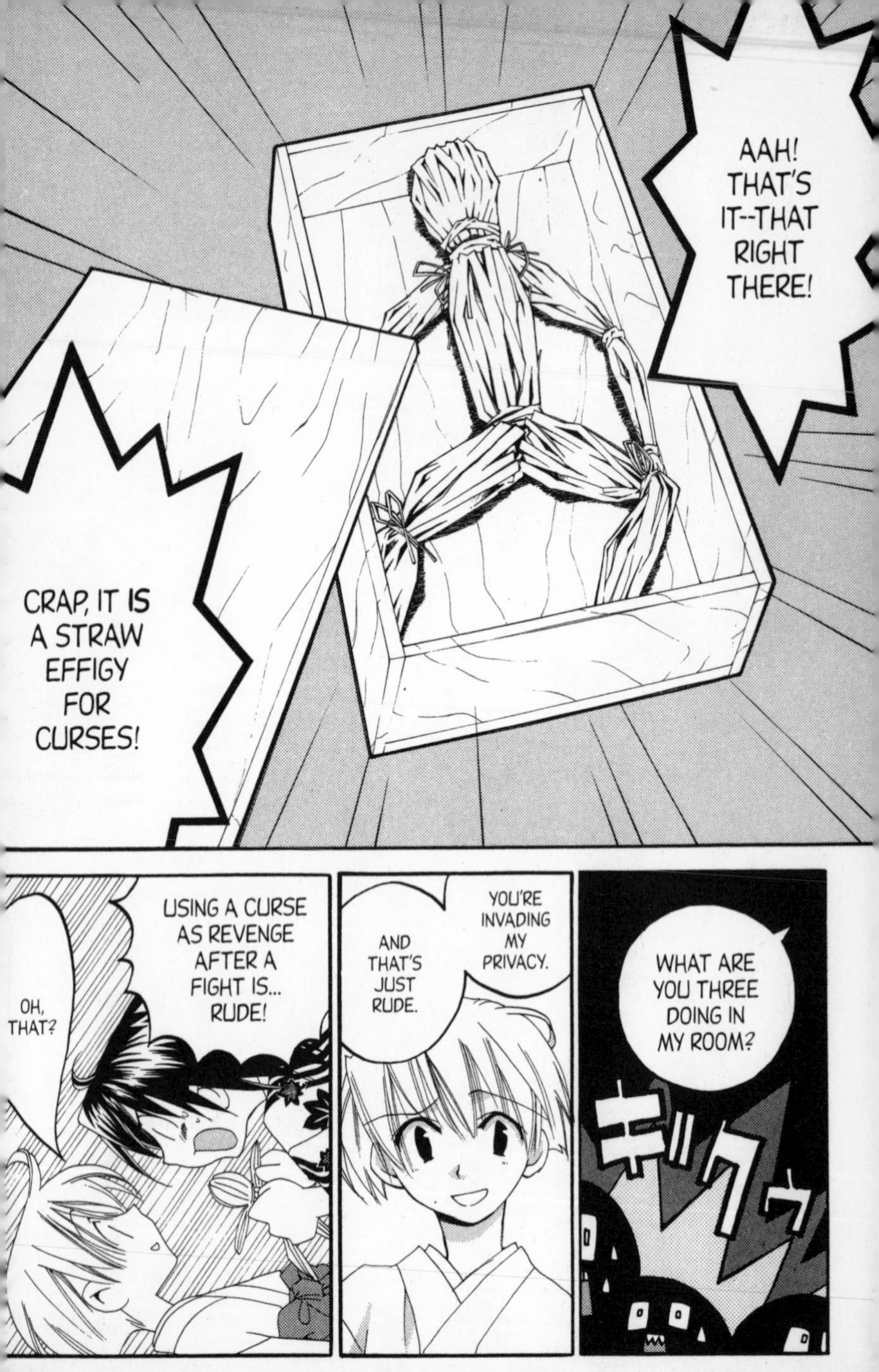
AAH! THAT'S IT--THAT RIGHT THERE!
CRAP, IT IS A STRAW EFFIGY FOR CURSES!
WHAT ARE YOU THREE DOING IN MY ROOM?
ギクゥ
YOU'RE INVADING MY PRIVACY.
AND THAT'S JUST RUDE.
USING A CURSE AS REVENGE AFTER A FIGHT IS... RUDE!
OH, THAT?

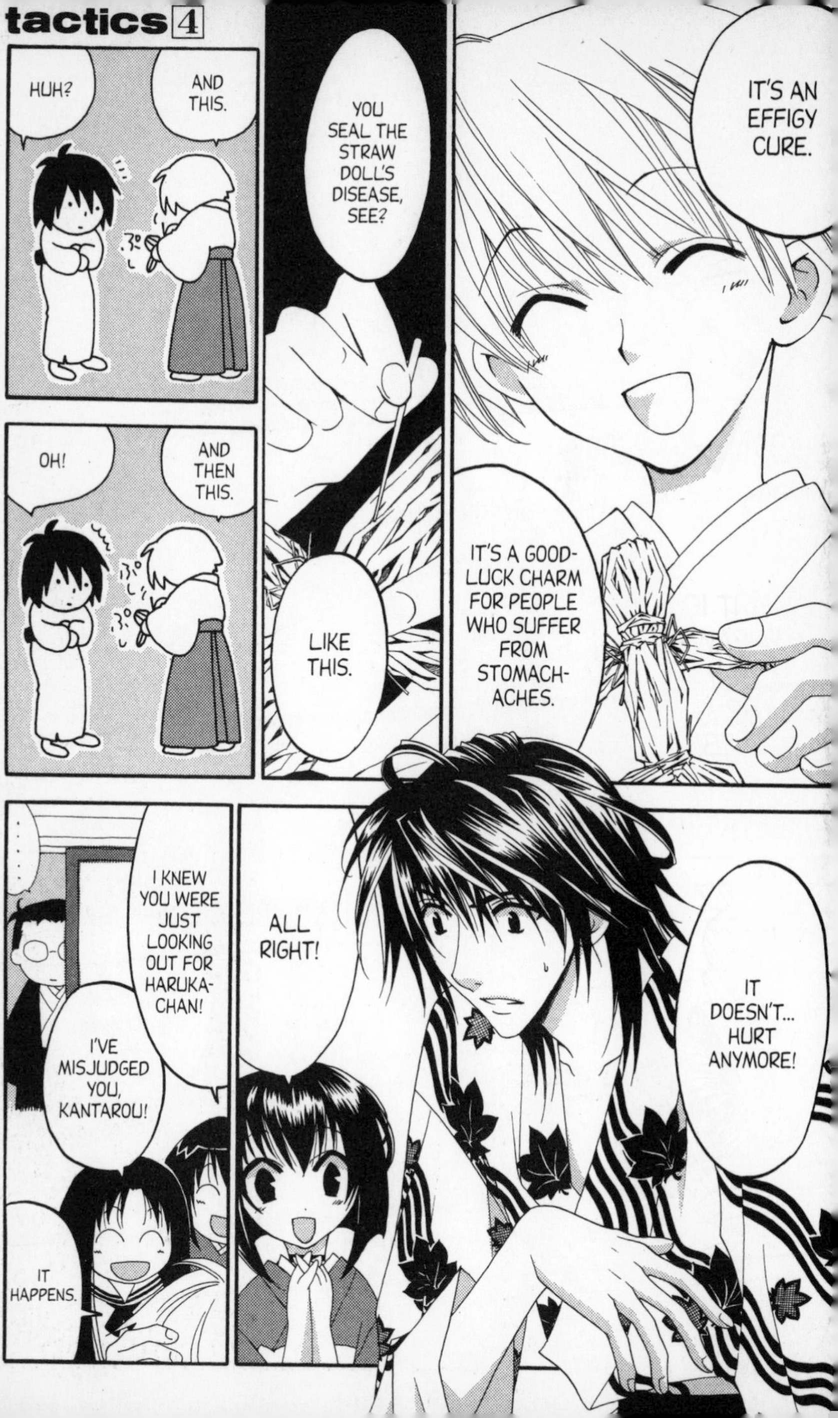
IT'S AN EFFIGY CURE.
IT'S A GOOD-LUCK CHARM FOR PEOPLE WHO SUFFER FROM STOMACH-ACHES.
YOU SEAL THE STRAW DOLL'S DISEASE, SEE?
LIKE THIS.
AND THIS.
HUH?
ぷし
AND THEN THIS.
OH!
ぷし
ぷし
IT DOESN'T... HURT ANYMORE!
ALL RIGHT!
I KNEW YOU WERE JUST LOOKING OUT FOR HARUKA-CHAN!
I'VE MISJUDGED YOU, KANTAROU!
......
IT HAPPENS.

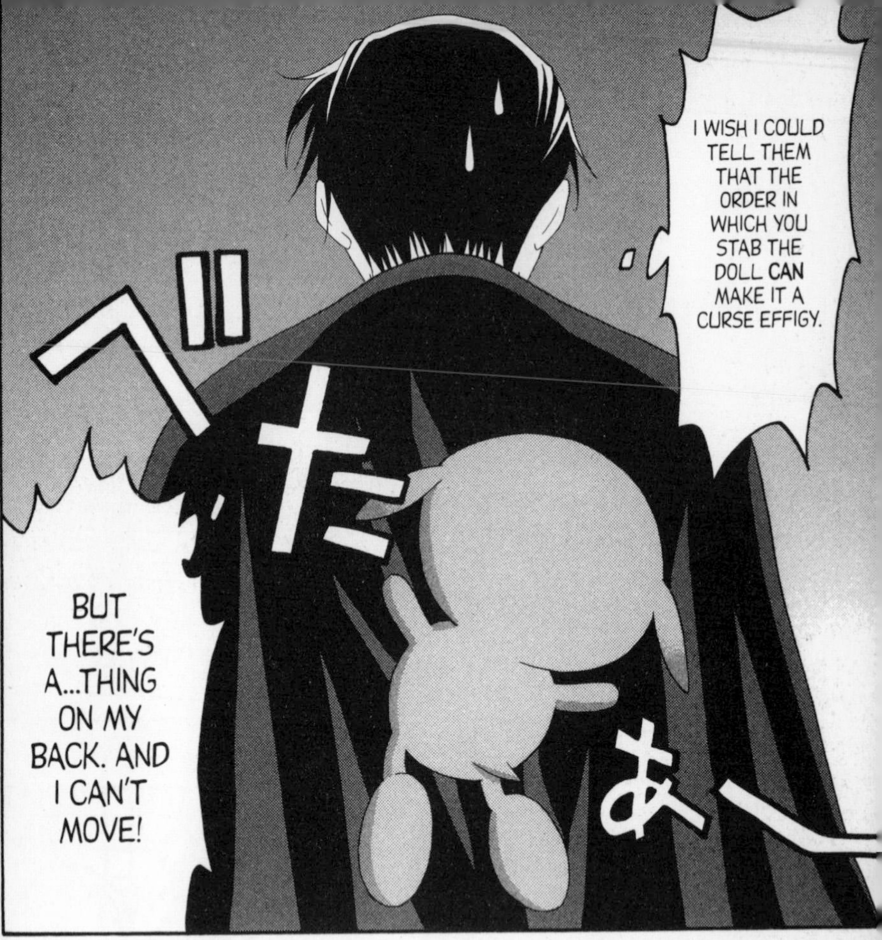
I WISH I COULD TELL THEM THAT THE ORDER IN WHICH YOU STAB THE DOLL **CAN** MAKE IT A CURSE EFFIGY.
BUT THERE'S A...THING ON MY BACK. AND I CAN'T MOVE!

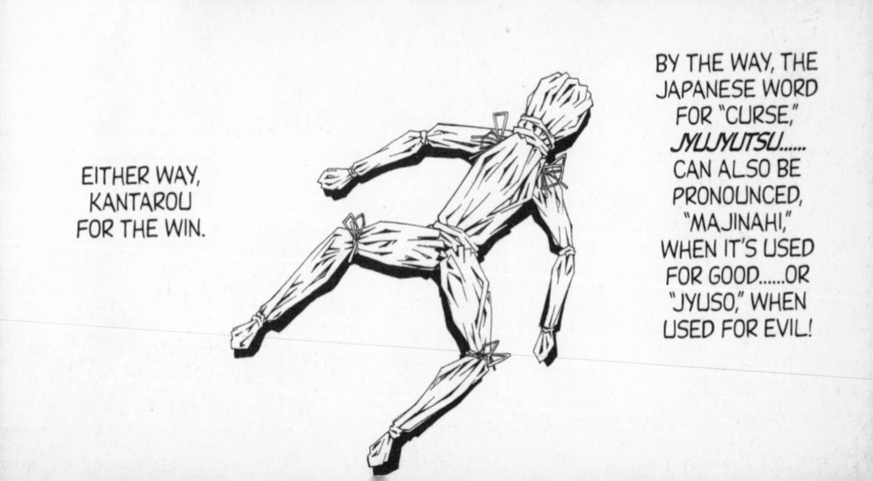
BY THE WAY, THE JAPANESE WORD FOR "CURSE," ***JYUJYUTSU***...... CAN ALSO BE PRONOUNCED, "MAJINAHI," WHEN IT'S USED FOR GOOD......OR "JYUSO," WHEN USED FOR EVIL!
EITHER WAY, KANTAROU FOR THE WIN.

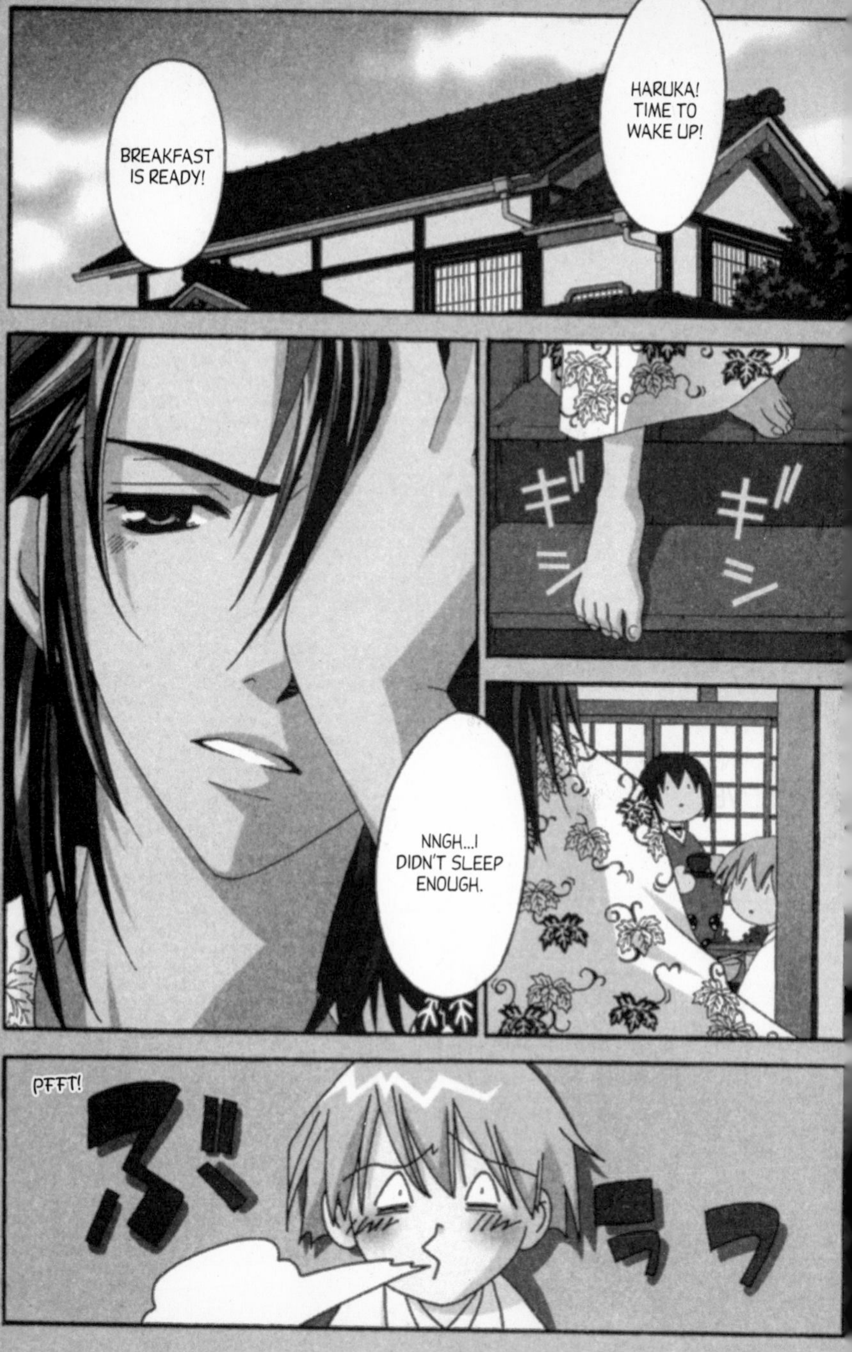
HARUKA! TIME TO WAKE UP!
BREAKFAST IS READY!
ギシ
ギシ
NNGH...I DIDN'T SLEEP ENOUGH.
PFFT!

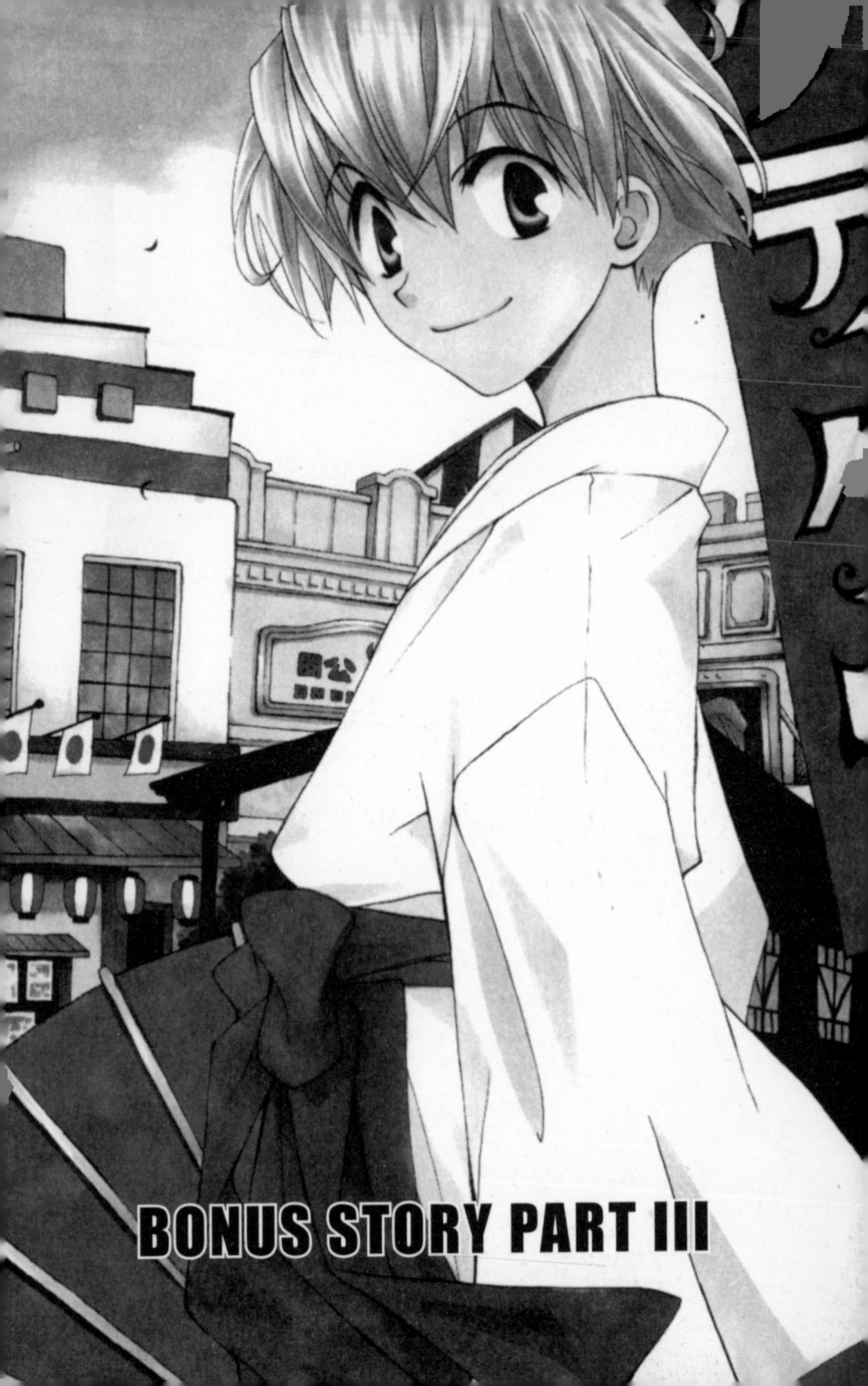

BONUS STORY PART III

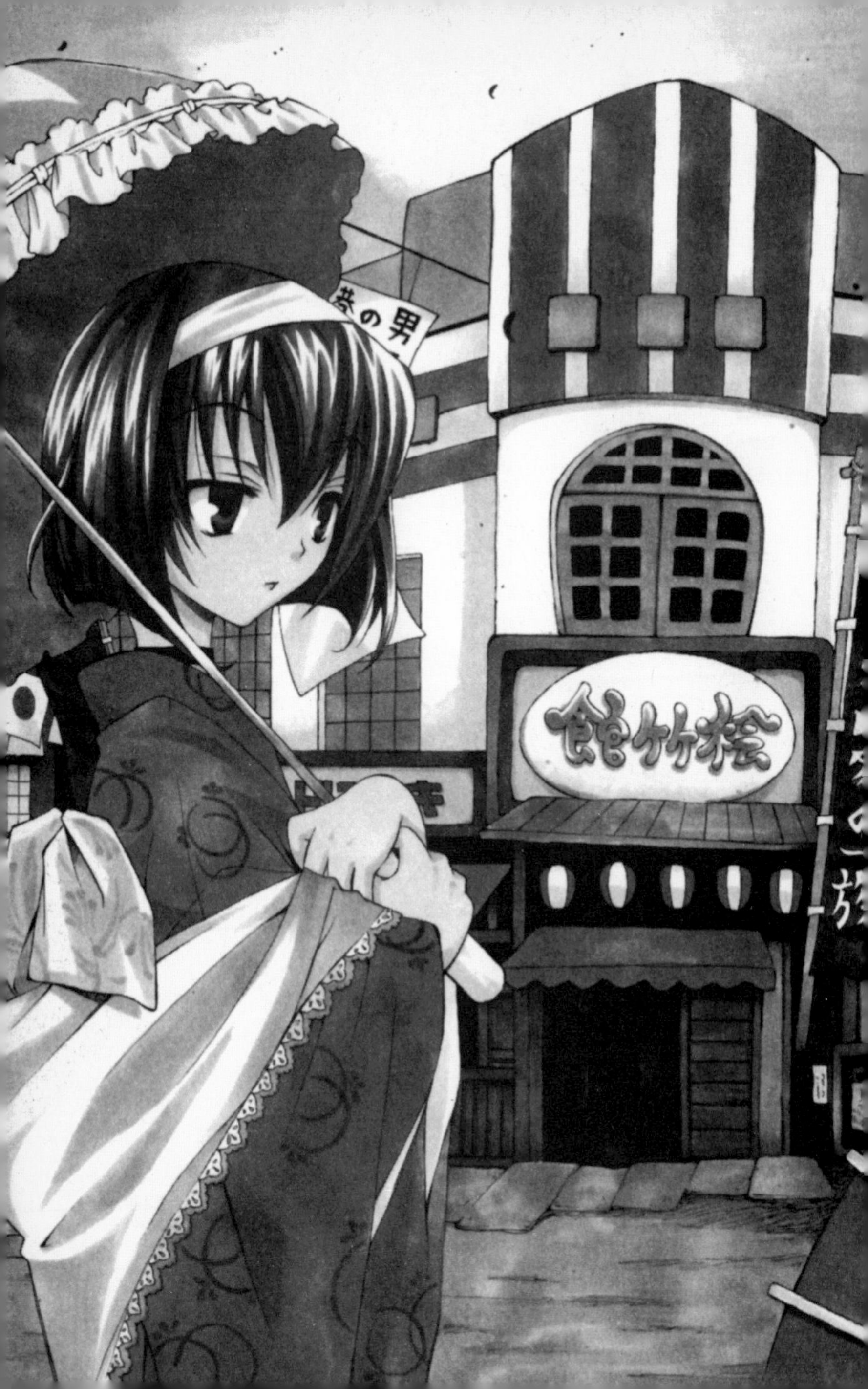

Hello, this is Sakura Kinoshita!

Thank you very much for buying tactics Volume 4.

It's finally Volume 4... Wow, we're moving at a slow pace.

But we'll do our best! Volume 5 is coming out soon!

This time around, we got to see the new character Raikou-san.

He's my favorite kind of villain. (Actually, this manga's full of villains.)

I'm looking forward to how he'll develop from now on.

Well, let's meet up again in Volume 5!

It's coming up right around the corner!

2004 . KINOSHITA SAKURA

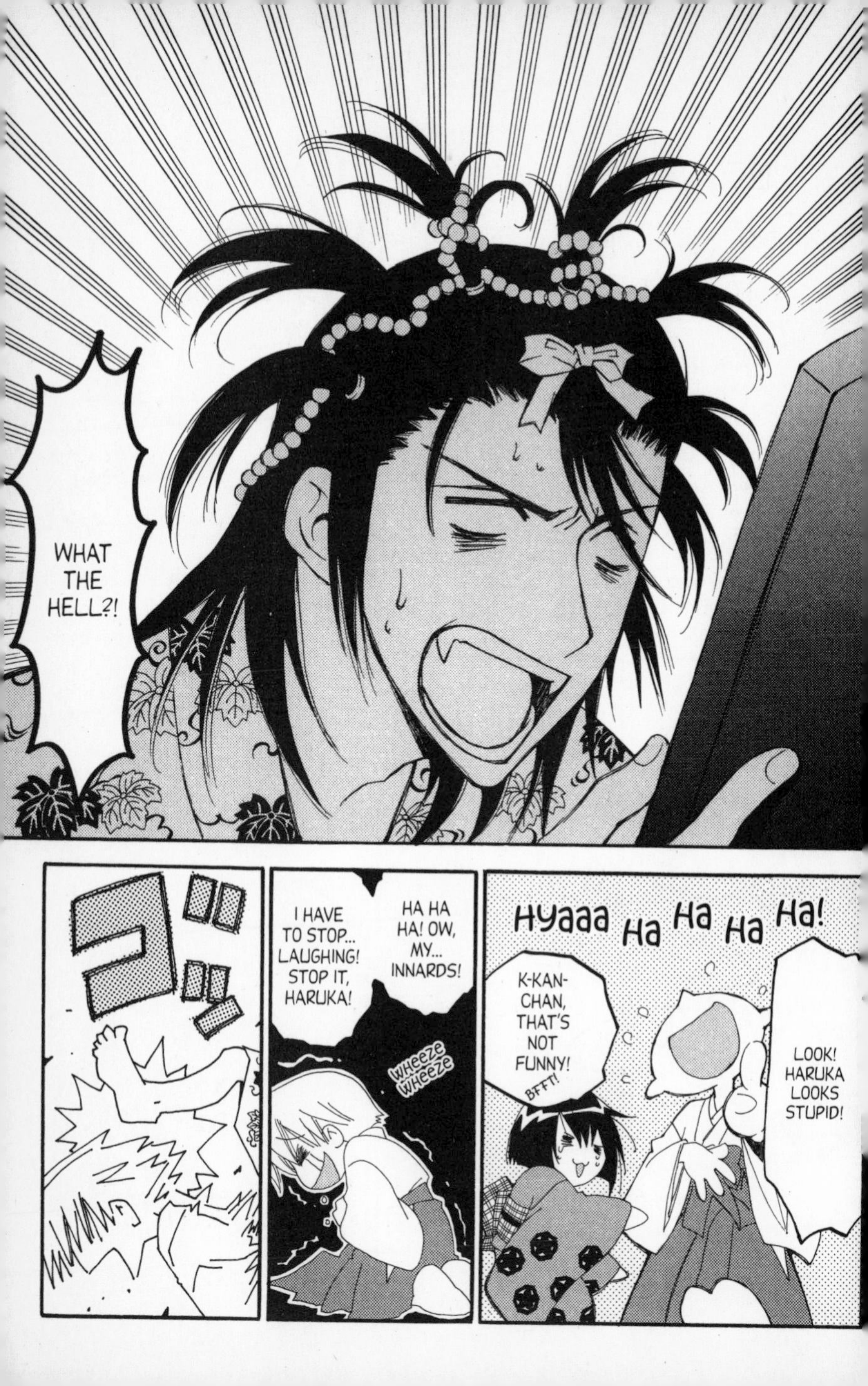
WHAT THE HELL?!
Hyaaa Ha Ha Ha Ha!
LOOK! HARUKA LOOKS STUPID!
K-KAN-CHAN, THAT'S NOT FUNNY!
BFFT!
HA HA HA! OW, MY... INNARDS!
I HAVE TO STOP... LAUGHING! STOP IT, HARUKA!
WHEEZE WHEEZE

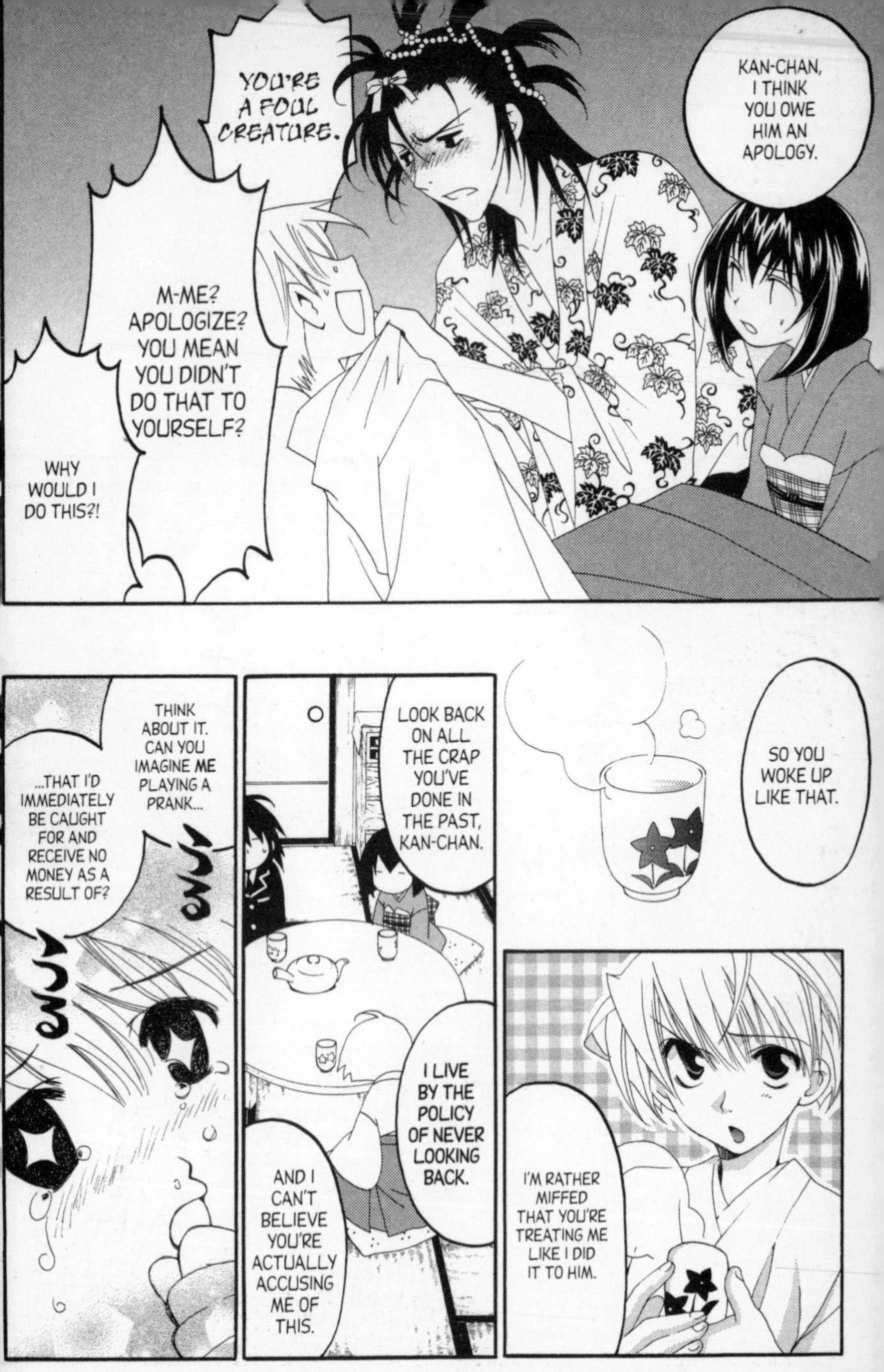
KAN-CHAN, I THINK YOU OWE HIM AN APOLOGY.
YOU'RE A FOUL CREATURE.
M-ME? APOLOGIZE? YOU MEAN YOU DIDN'T DO THAT TO YOURSELF?
WHY WOULD I DO THIS?!
SO YOU WOKE UP LIKE THAT.
I'M RATHER MIFFED THAT YOU'RE TREATING ME LIKE I DID IT TO HIM.
LOOK BACK ON ALL THE CRAP YOU'VE DONE IN THE PAST, KAN-CHAN.
I LIVE BY THE POLICY OF NEVER LOOKING BACK.
AND I CAN'T BELIEVE YOU'RE ACTUALLY ACCUSING ME OF THIS.
THINK ABOUT IT. CAN YOU IMAGINE **ME** PLAYING A PRANK...
...THAT I'D IMMEDIATELY BE CAUGHT FOR AND RECEIVE NO MONEY AS A RESULT OF?

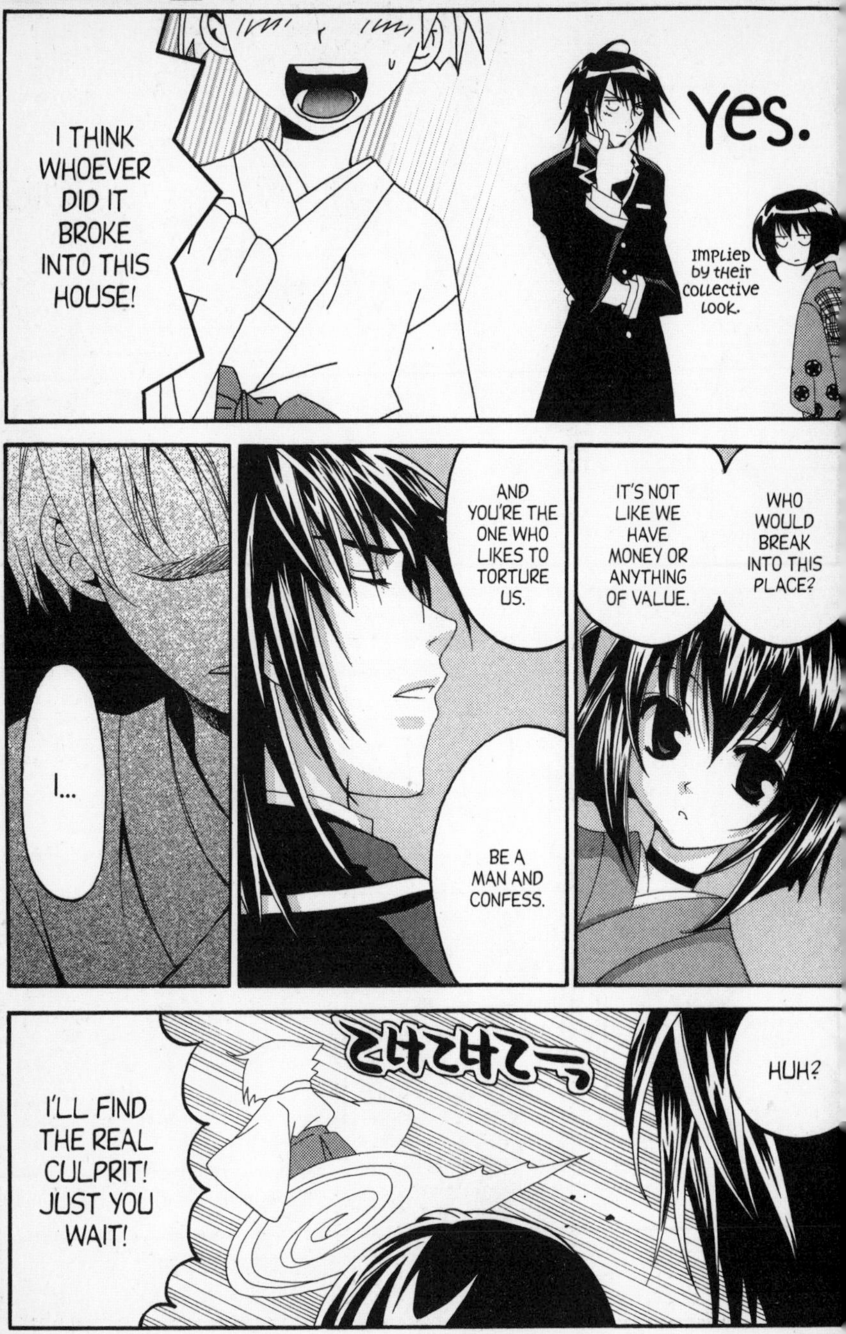
Yes.
Implied by their collective look.
I THINK WHOEVER DID IT BROKE INTO THIS HOUSE!
WHO WOULD BREAK INTO THIS PLACE?
IT'S NOT LIKE WE HAVE MONEY OR ANYTHING OF VALUE.
AND YOU'RE THE ONE WHO LIKES TO TORTURE US.
BE A MAN AND CONFESS.
I...
HUH?
I'LL FIND THE REAL CULPRIT! JUST YOU WAIT!

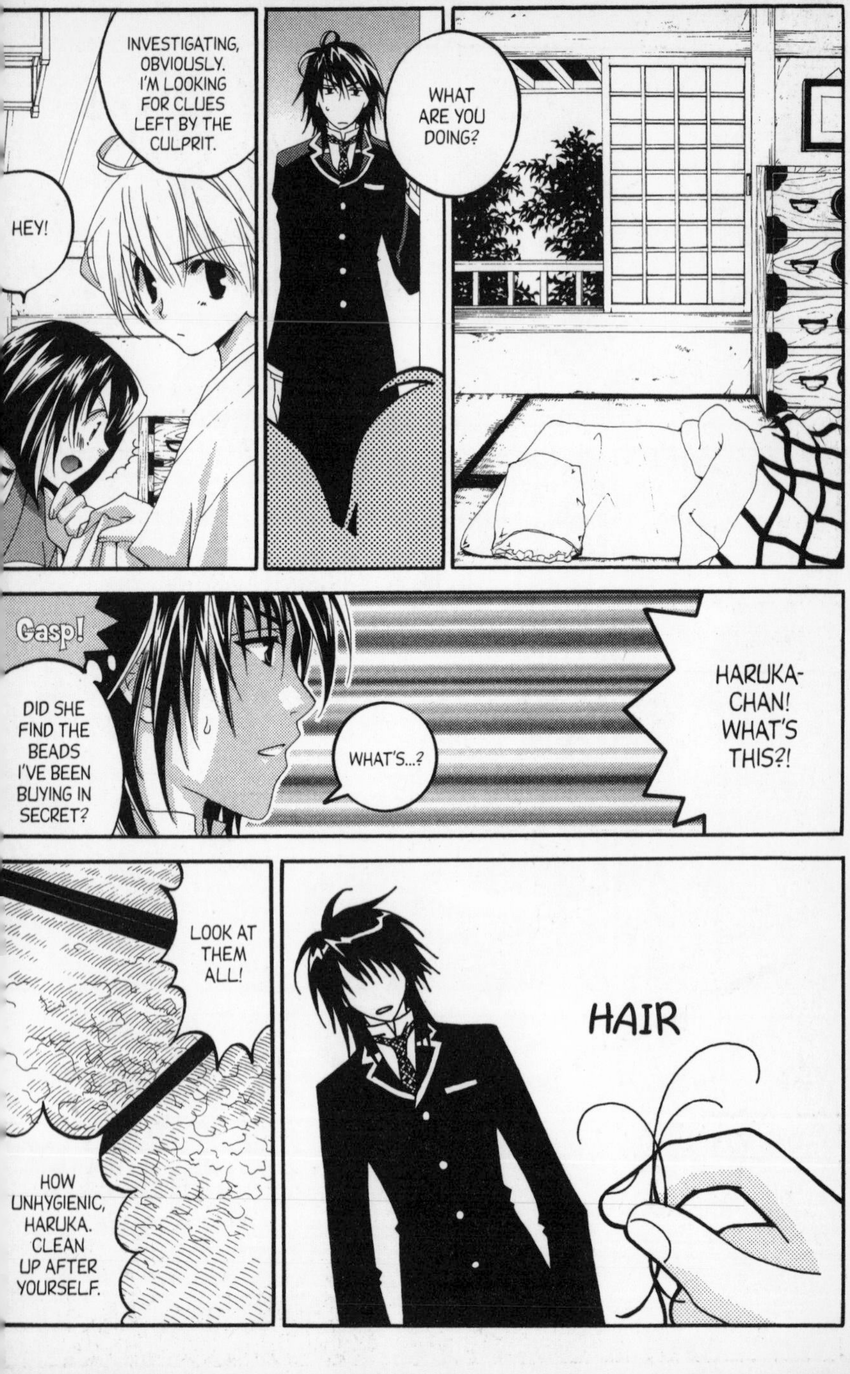
WHAT ARE YOU DOING?
INVESTIGATING, OBVIOUSLY. I'M LOOKING FOR CLUES LEFT BY THE CULPRIT.
HEY!
HARUKA-CHAN! WHAT'S THIS?!
WHAT'S...?
Gasp!
DID SHE FIND THE BEADS I'VE BEEN BUYING IN SECRET?
HAIR
LOOK AT THEM ALL!
HOW UNHYGIENIC, HARUKA. CLEAN UP AFTER YOURSELF.

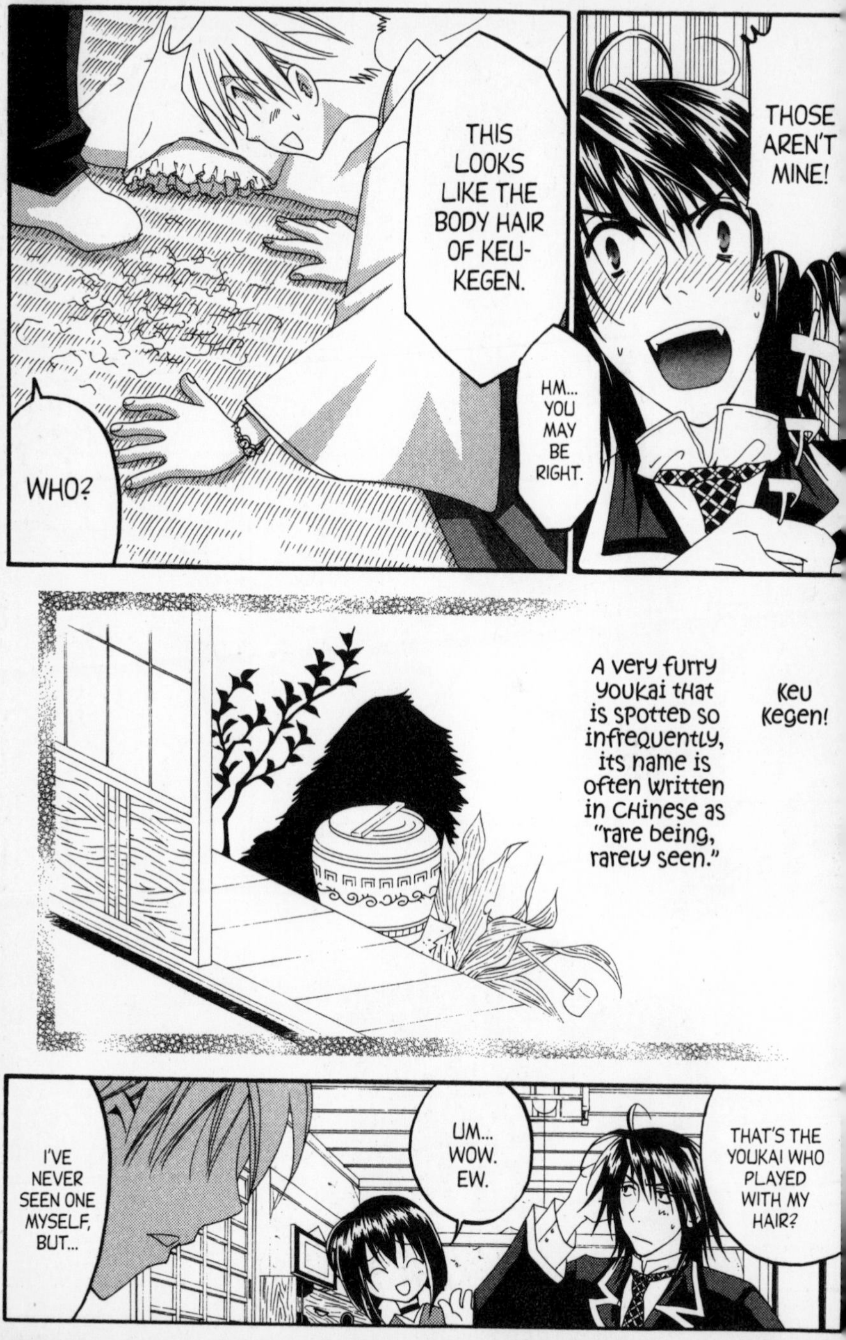
THOSE AREN'T MINE!
THIS LOOKS LIKE THE BODY HAIR OF KEU-KEGEN.
HM... YOU MAY BE RIGHT.
WHO?
Keu Kegen!
A very furry youkai that is spotted so infrequently, its name is often written in Chinese as "rare being, rarely seen."
THAT'S THE YOUKAI WHO PLAYED WITH MY HAIR?
UM... WOW. EW.
I'VE NEVER SEEN ONE MYSELF, BUT...

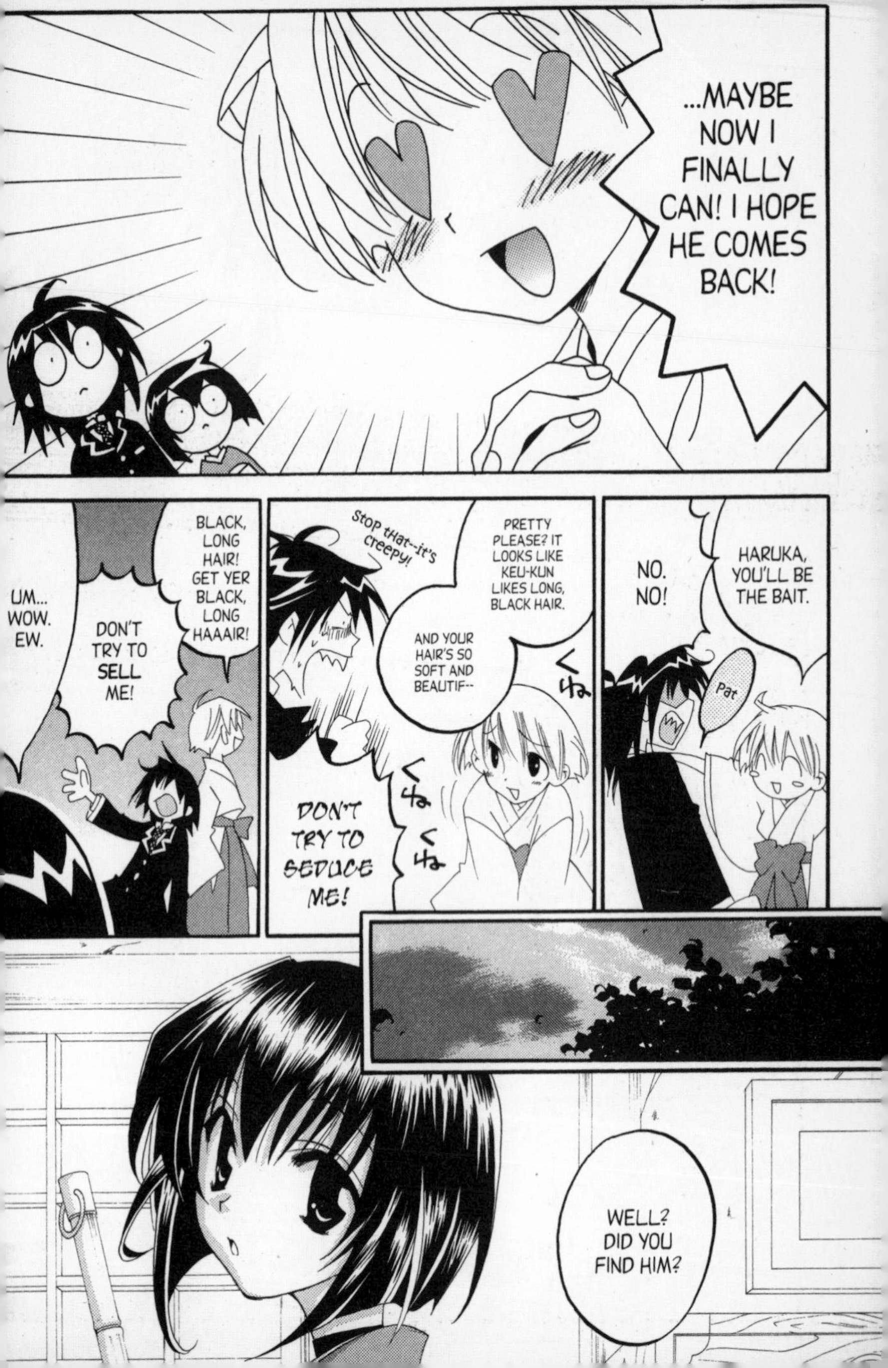
...MAYBE NOW I FINALLY CAN! I HOPE HE COMES BACK!
HARUKA, YOU'LL BE THE BAIT.
Pat
NO. NO!
PRETTY PLEASE? IT LOOKS LIKE KEU-KUN LIKES LONG, BLACK HAIR.
Stop that--it's creepy!
AND YOUR HAIR'S SO SOFT AND BEAUTIF--
くね
くね くね
DON'T TRY TO SEDUCE ME!
BLACK, LONG HAIR! GET YER BLACK, LONG HAAAIR!
DON'T TRY TO SELL ME!
UM... WOW. EW.
WELL? DID YOU FIND HIM?

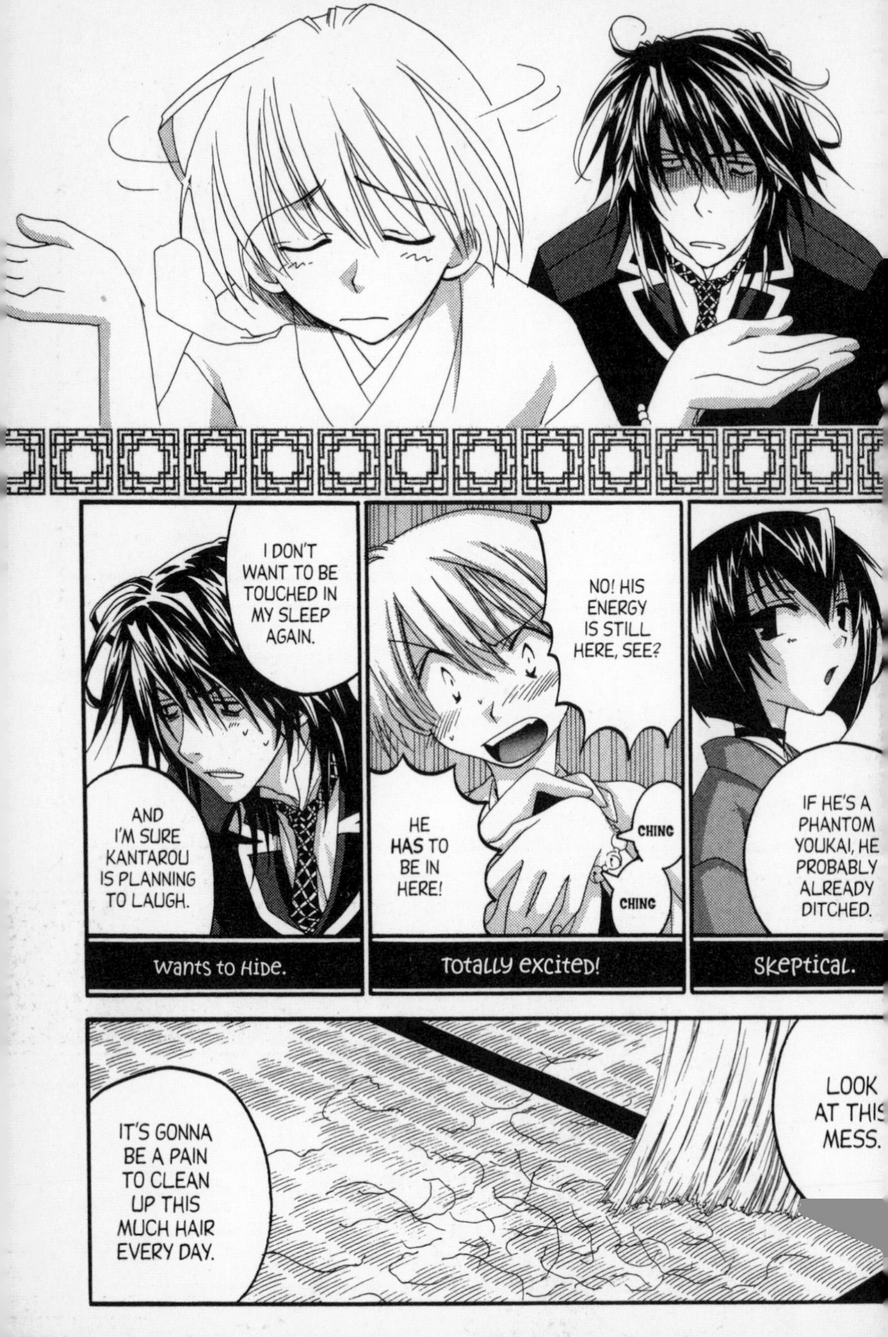
IF HE'S A PHANTOM YOUKAI, HE PROBABLY ALREADY DITCHED.
Skeptical.
NO! HIS ENERGY IS STILL HERE, SEE?
CHING
HE HAS TO BE IN HERE!
CHING
Totally excited!
I DON'T WANT TO BE TOUCHED IN MY SLEEP AGAIN.
AND I'M SURE KANTAROU IS PLANNING TO LAUGH.
Wants to Hide.
LOOK AT THIS MESS.
IT'S GONNA BE A PAIN TO CLEAN UP THIS MUCH HAIR EVERY DAY.

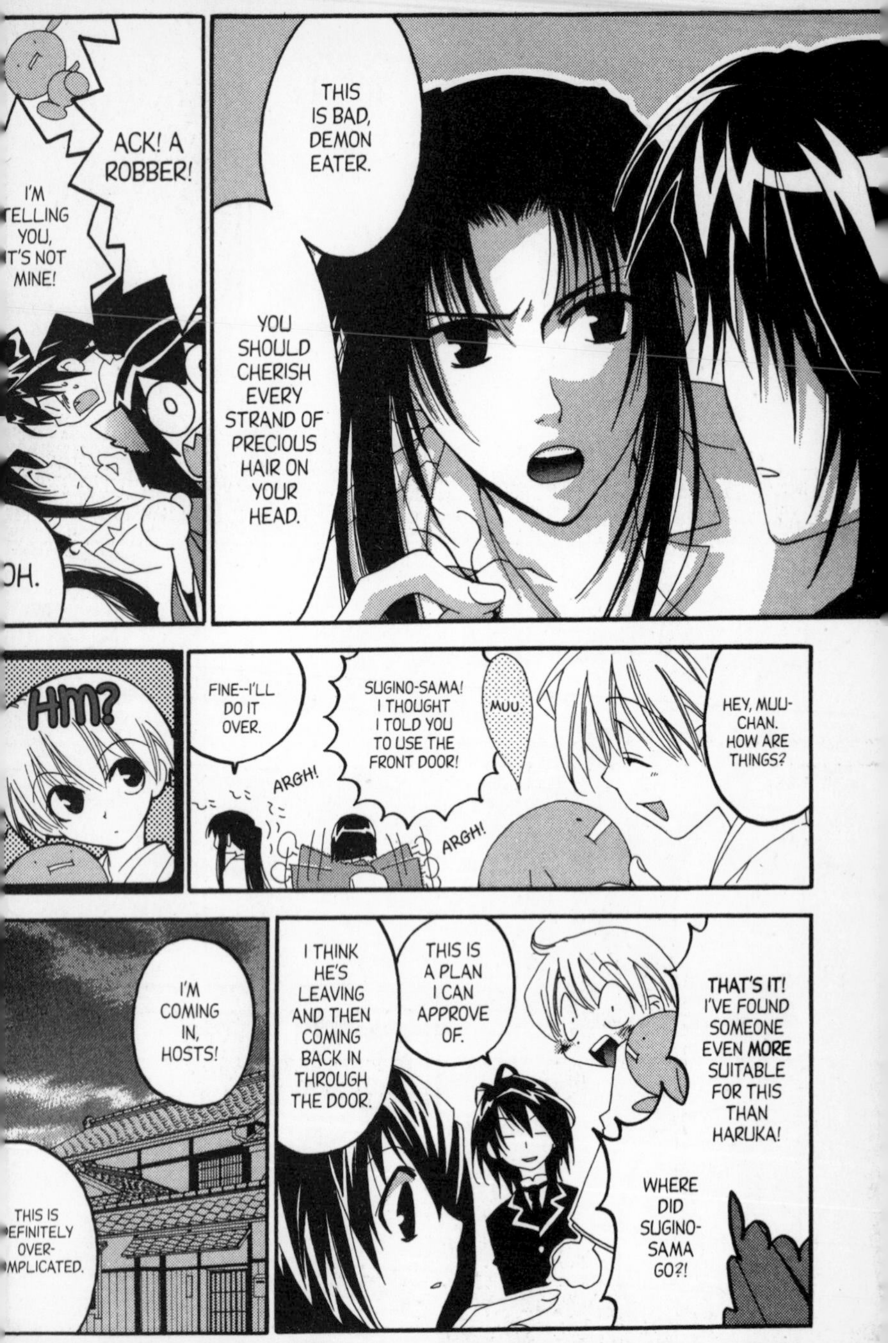
THIS IS BAD, DEMON EATER.
YOU SHOULD CHERISH EVERY STRAND OF PRECIOUS HAIR ON YOUR HEAD.
ACK! A ROBBER!
I'M TELLING YOU, T'S NOT MINE!
OH.
HEY, MUU-CHAN. HOW ARE THINGS?
MUU.
SUGINO-SAMA! I THOUGHT I TOLD YOU TO USE THE FRONT DOOR!
ARGH!
ARGH!
FINE--I'LL DO IT OVER.
HM?
THAT'S IT! I'VE FOUND SOMEONE EVEN **MORE** SUITABLE FOR THIS THAN HARUKA!
WHERE DID SUGINO-SAMA GO?!
THIS IS A PLAN I CAN APPROVE OF.
I THINK HE'S LEAVING AND THEN COMING BACK IN THROUGH THE DOOR.
I'M COMING IN, HOSTS!
THIS IS EFINITELY OVER-MPLICATED.

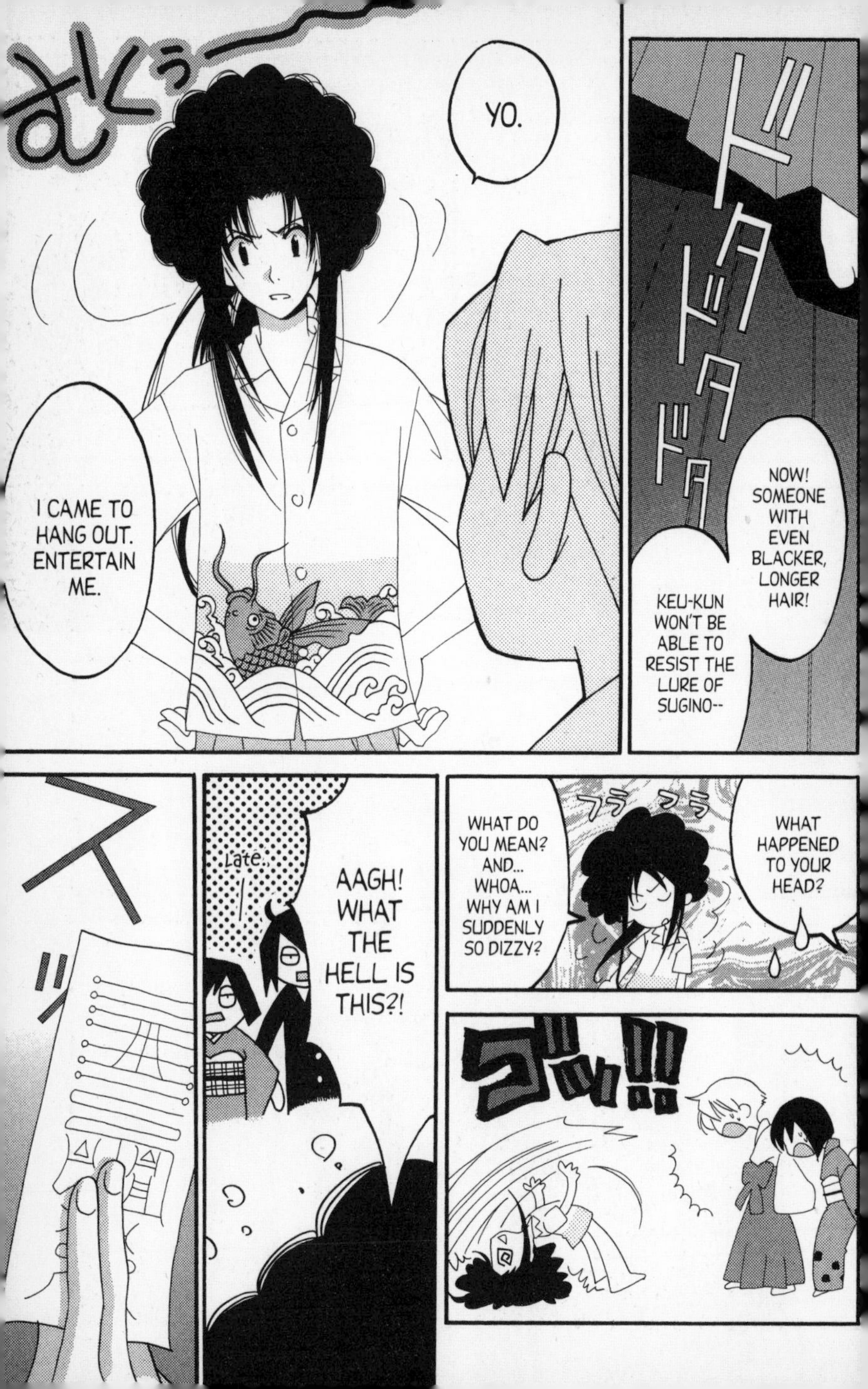
ドタドタドタ
NOW! SOMEONE WITH EVEN BLACKER, LONGER HAIR!
KEU-KUN WON'T BE ABLE TO RESIST THE LURE OF SUGINO--
むくぅー
YO.
I CAME TO HANG OUT. ENTERTAIN ME.
WHAT HAPPENED TO YOUR HEAD?
フラ フラ
WHAT DO YOU MEAN? AND... WHOA... WHY AM I SUDDENLY SO DIZZY?
ゴッ!!!
Late..
AAGH! WHAT THE HELL IS THIS?!
スッ

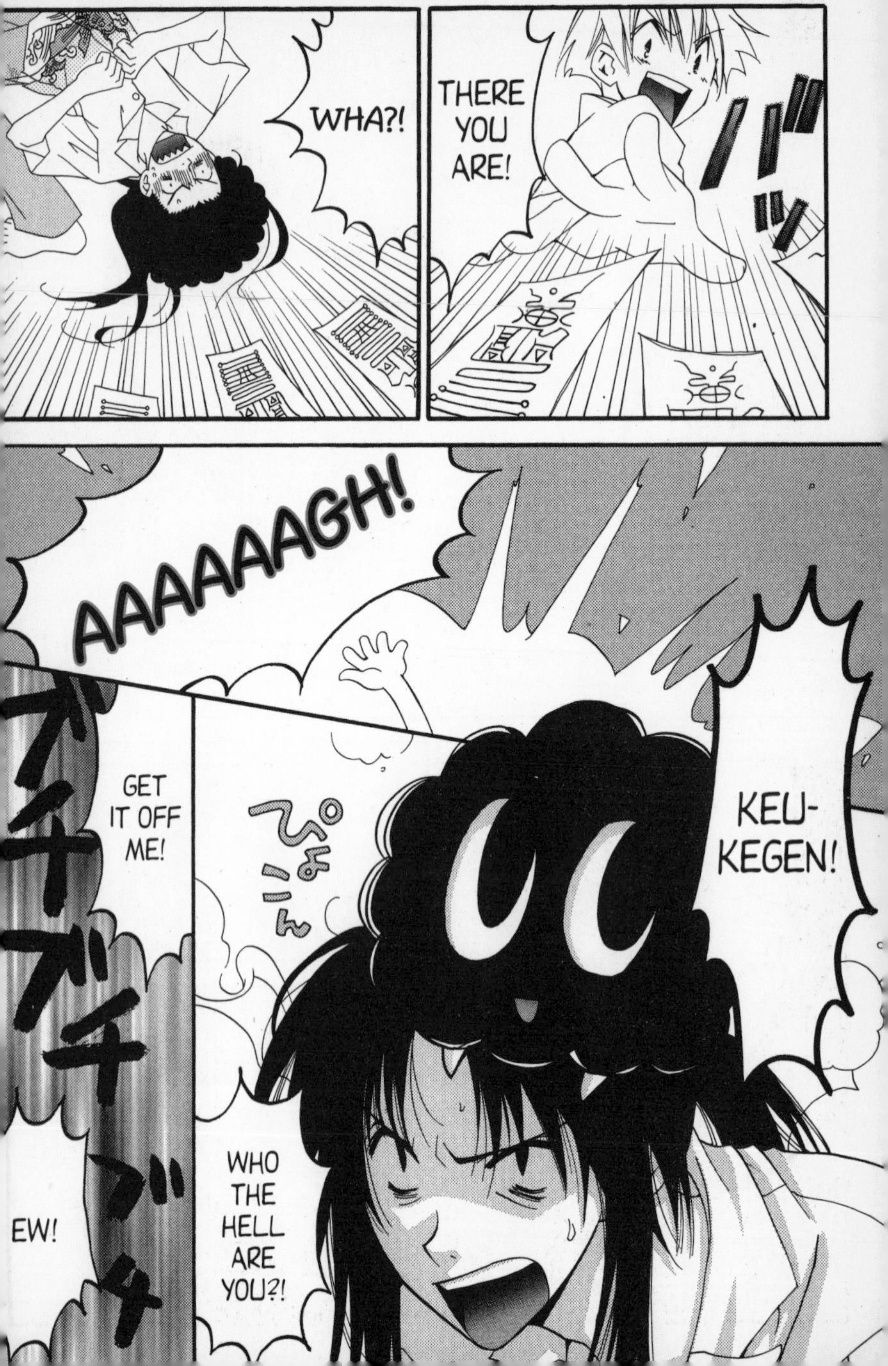
THERE YOU ARE!
WHA?!
AAAAAAGH!
KEU-KEGEN!
ぴょこん
GET IT OFF ME!
WHO THE HELL ARE YOU?!
EW!

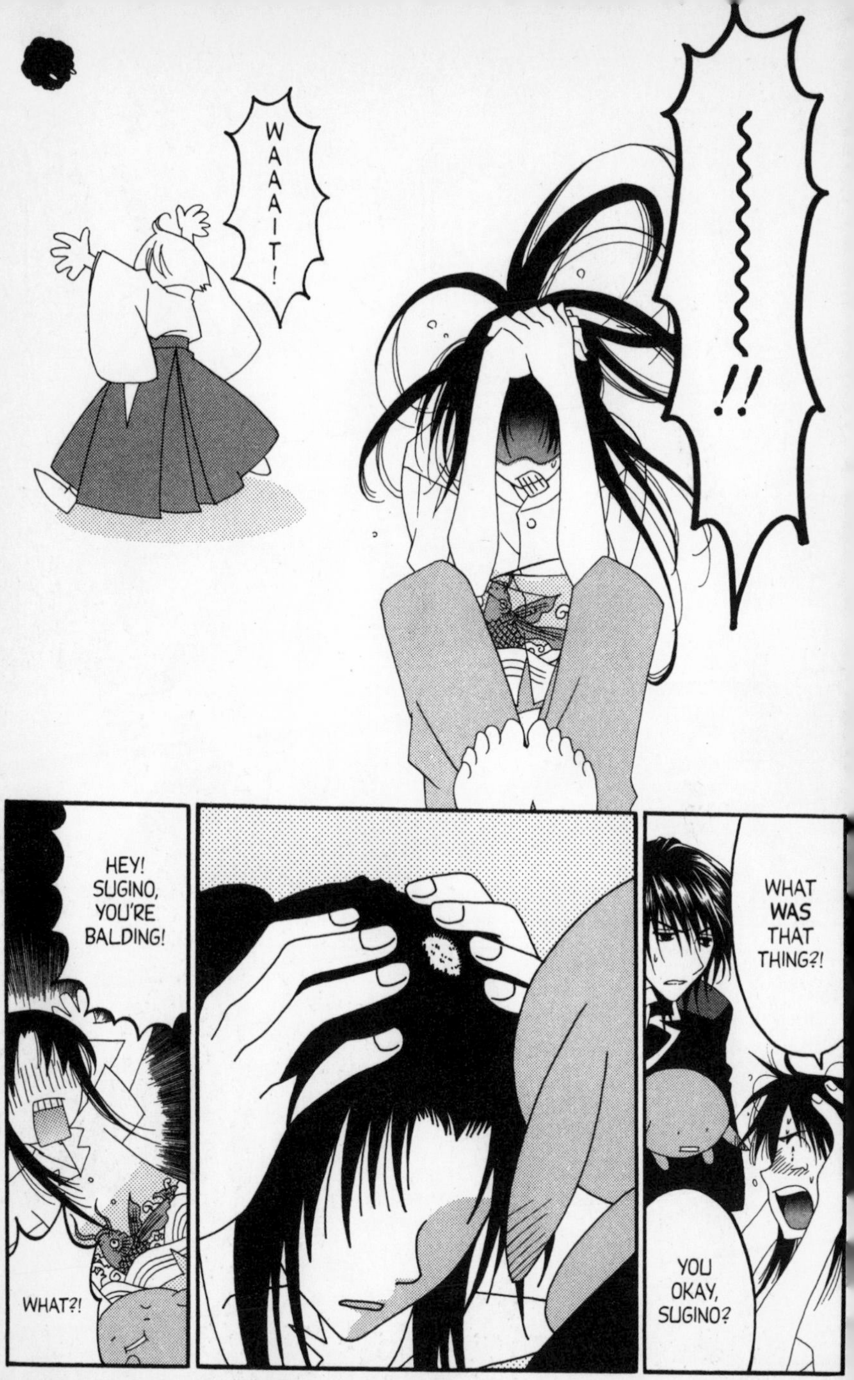

!!
WAAAAIT!
WHAT WAS THAT THING?!
YOU OKAY, SUGINO?
HEY! SUGINO, YOU'RE BALDING!
WHAT?!

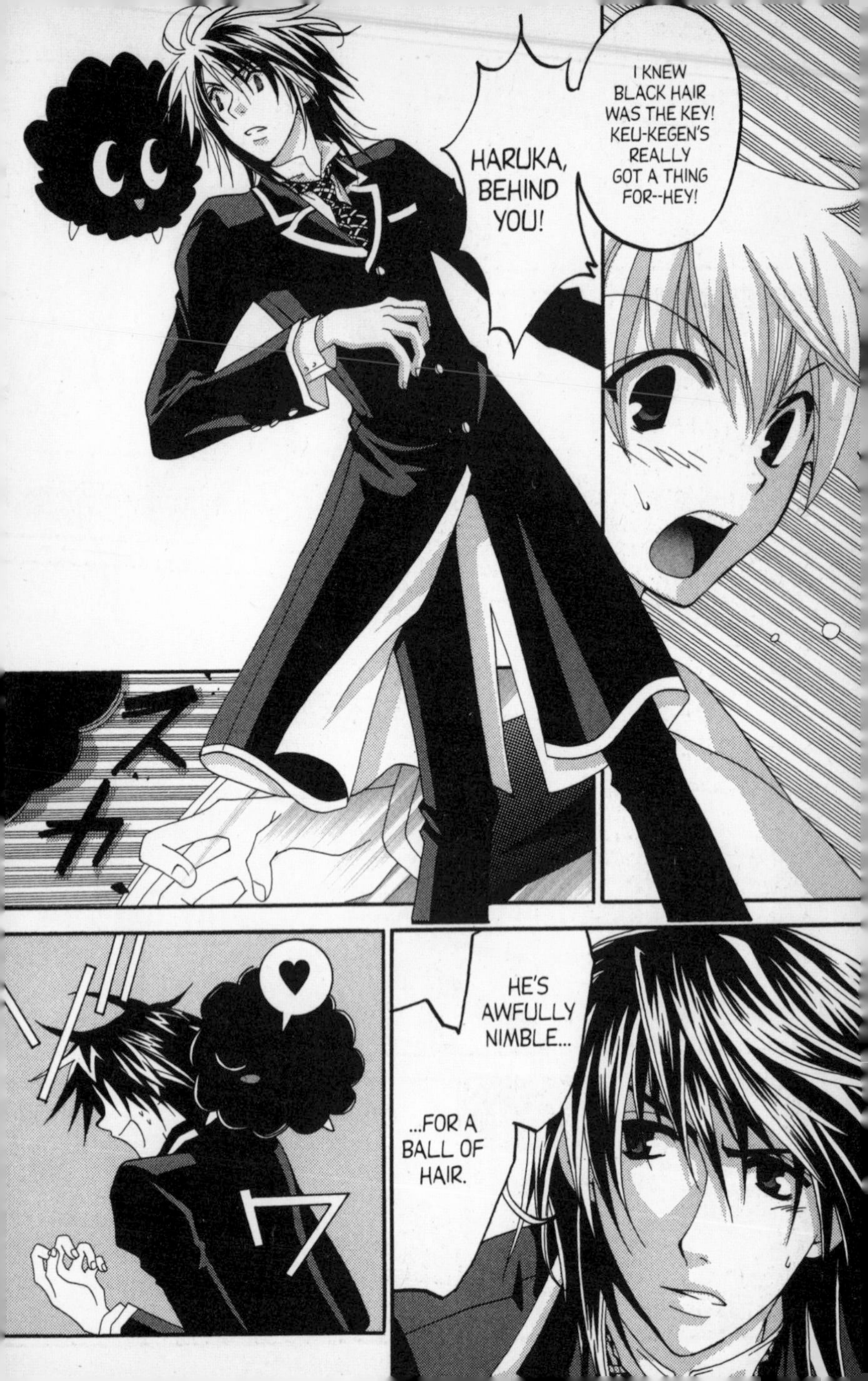
I KNEW BLACK HAIR WAS THE KEY! KEU-KEGEN'S REALLY GOT A THING FOR--HEY!
HARUKA, BEHIND YOU!
HE'S AWFULLY NIMBLE...
...FOR A BALL OF HAIR.

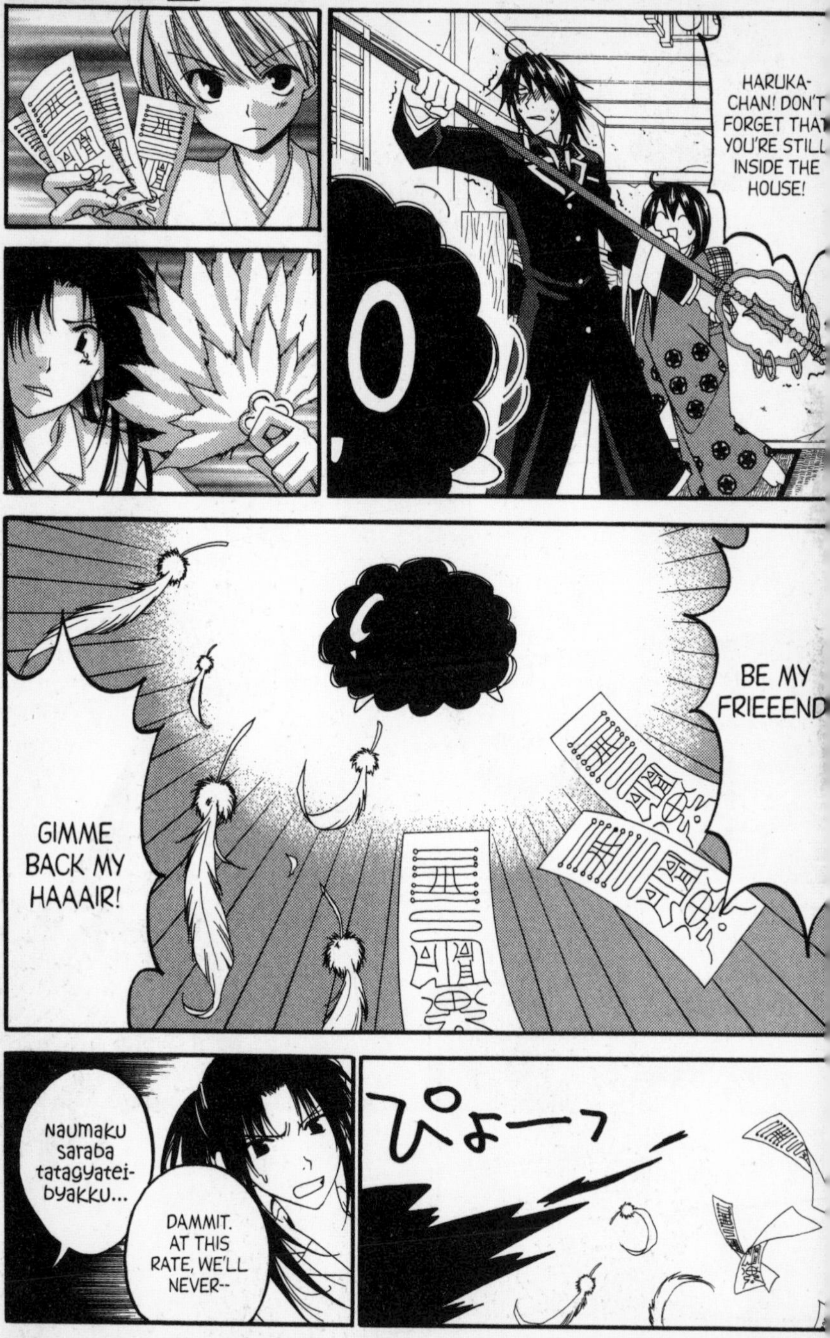
HARUKA-CHAN! DON'T FORGET THAT YOU'RE STILL INSIDE THE HOUSE!
BE MY FRIEEEND
GIMME BACK MY HAAAIR!
ぴよーっ
Naumaku saraba tatagyatei-byakku...
DAMMIT. AT THIS RATE, WE'LL NEVER--

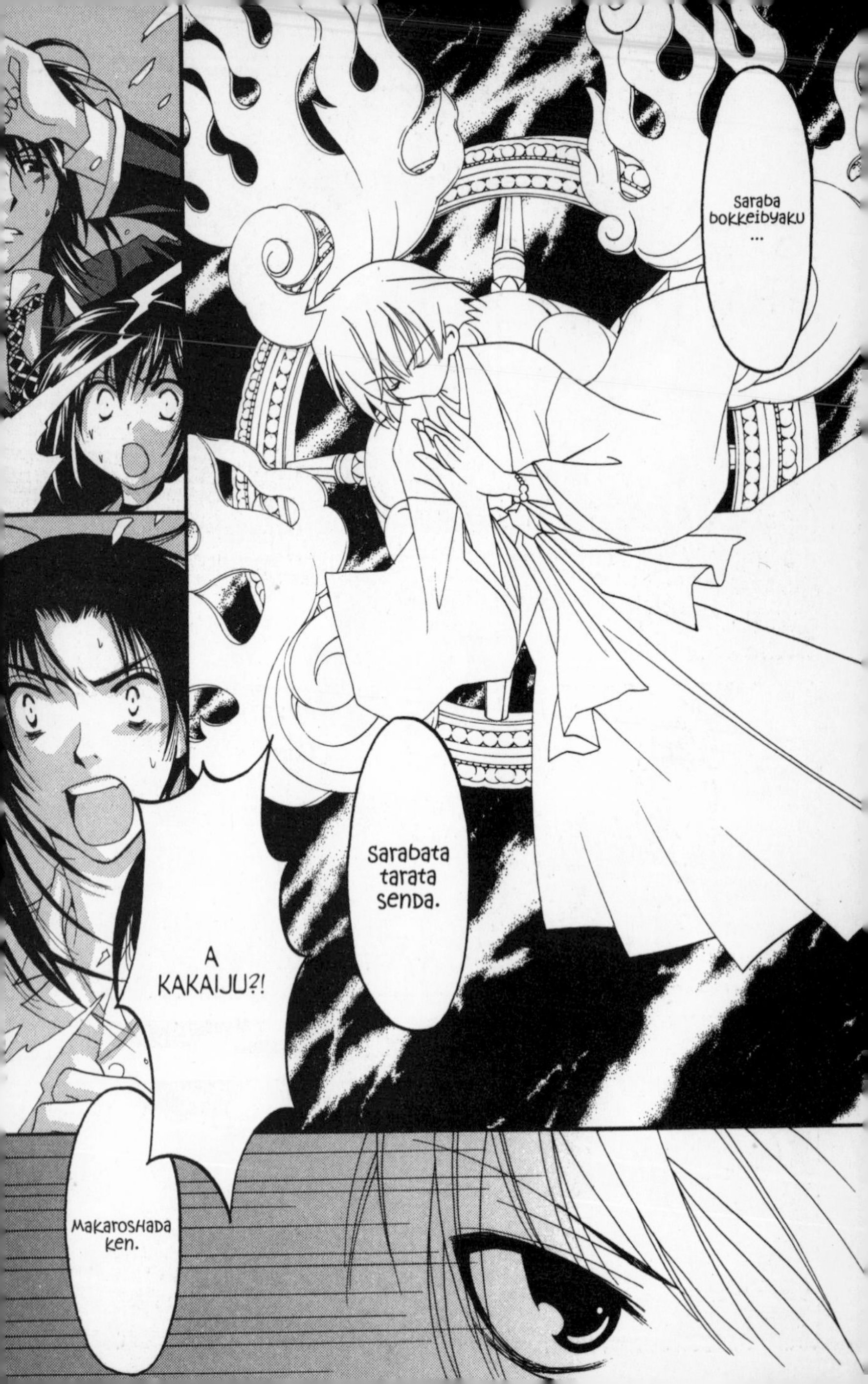
Saraba bokkeibyaku ...
Sarabata tarata senda.
A KAKAIJU?!
Makaroshada ken.

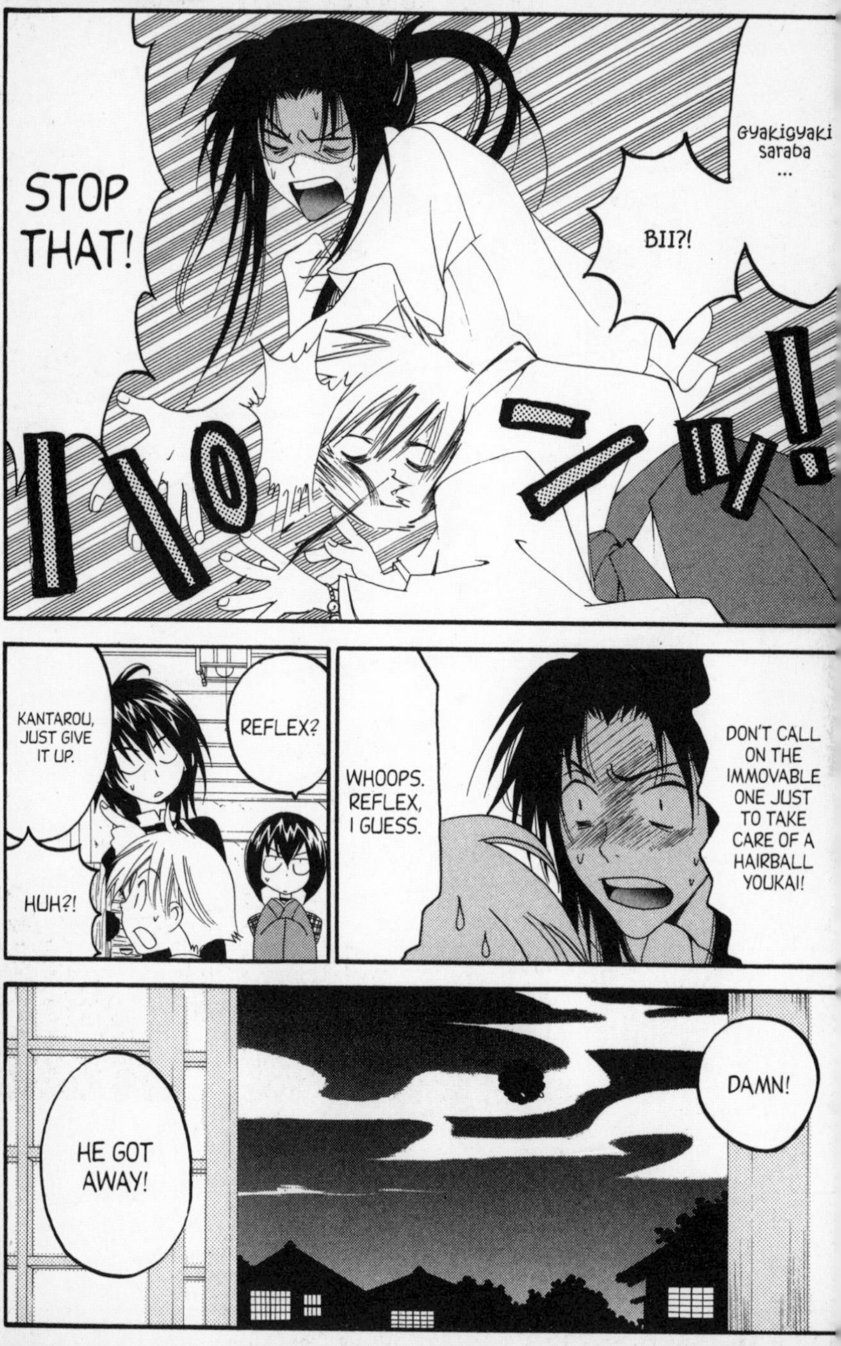
Gyakigyaki saraba ...
BII?!
STOP THAT!
DON'T CALL ON THE IMMOVABLE ONE JUST TO TAKE CARE OF A HAIRBALL YOUKAI!
WHOOPS. REFLEX, I GUESS.
REFLEX?
KANTAROU, JUST GIVE IT UP.
HUH?!
DAMN!
HE GOT AWAY!

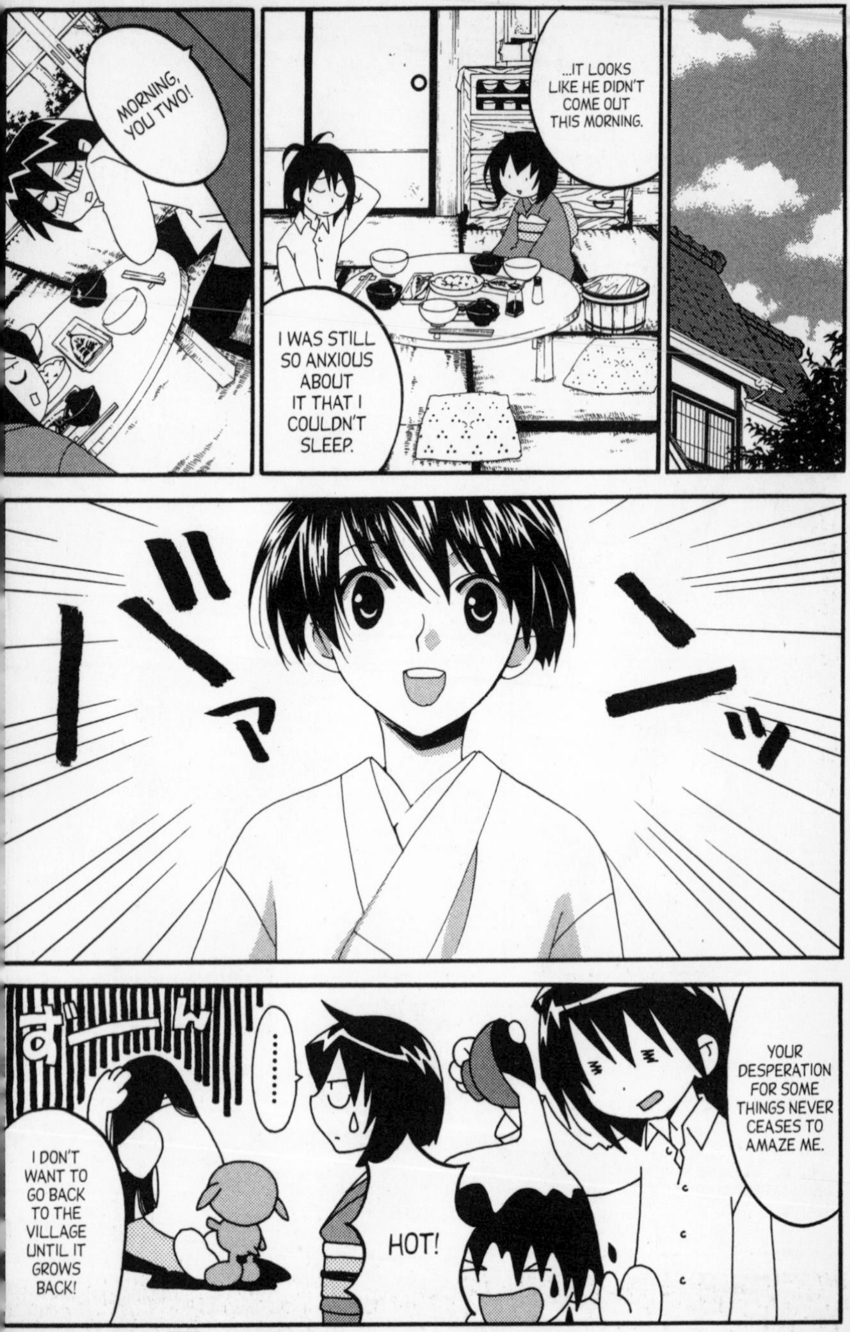
...IT LOOKS LIKE HE DIDN'T COME OUT THIS MORNING.
I WAS STILL SO ANXIOUS ABOUT IT THAT I COULDN'T SLEEP.
MORNING, YOU TWO!
YOUR DESPERATION FOR SOME THINGS NEVER CEASES TO AMAZE ME.
HOT!
......
I DON'T WANT TO GO BACK TO THE VILLAGE UNTIL IT GROWS BACK!
ずーん

tactics 4 THE END

Kantarou Ichinomiya Figure – Front

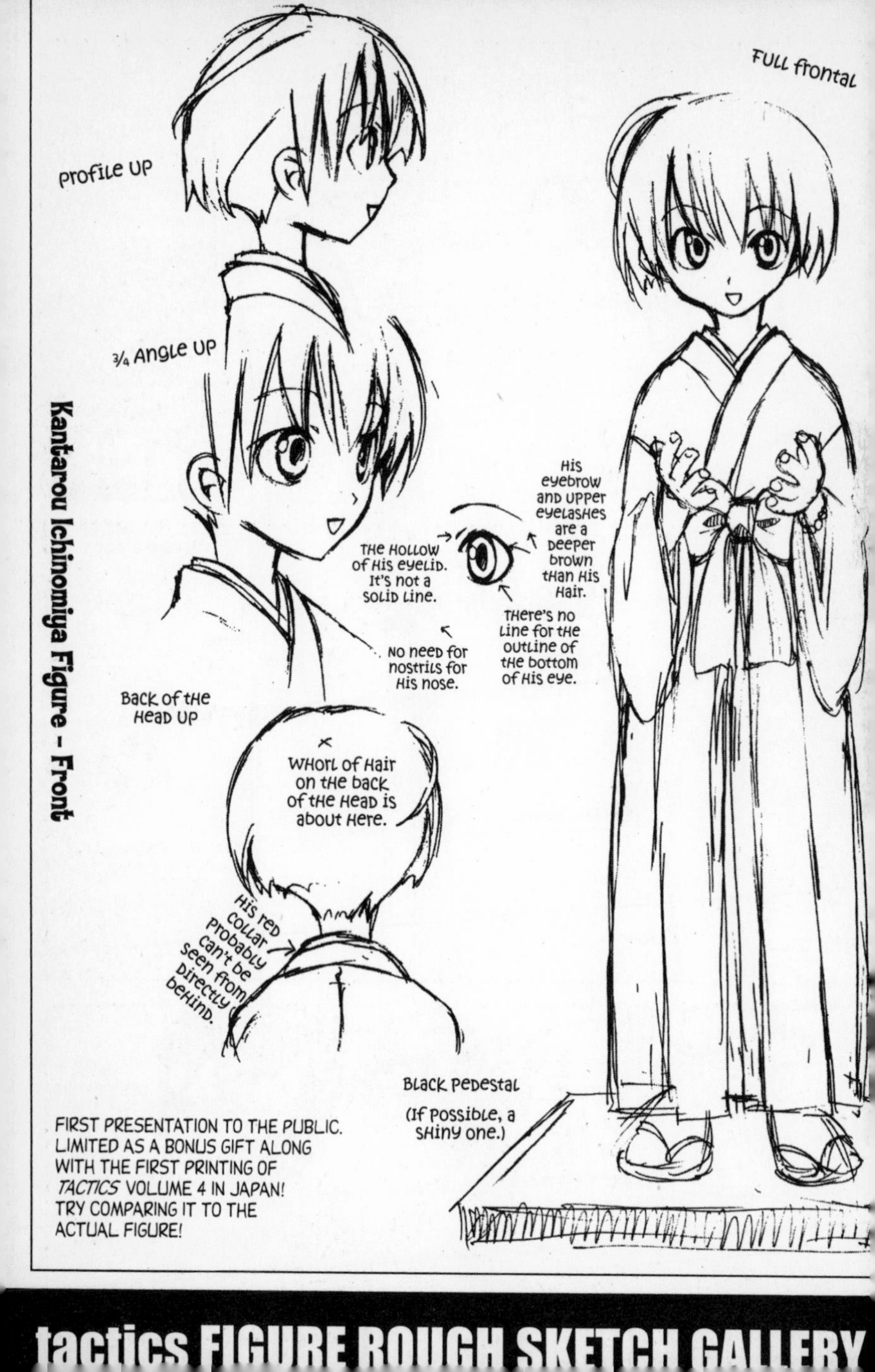

FULL frontal
profile up
3/4 Angle up
His eyebrow and upper eyelashes are a deeper brown than his hair.
The hollow of his eyelid. It's not a solid line.
There's no line for the outline of the bottom of his eye.
No need for nostrils for his nose.
Back of the head up
Whorl of hair on the back of the head is about here.
His red collar probably can't be seen from directly behind.
Black pedestal
(If possible, a shiny one.)

FIRST PRESENTATION TO THE PUBLIC. LIMITED AS A BONUS GIFT ALONG WITH THE FIRST PRINTING OF *TACTICS* VOLUME 4 IN JAPAN! TRY COMPARING IT TO THE ACTUAL FIGURE!

tactics FIGURE ROUGH SKETCH GALLERY

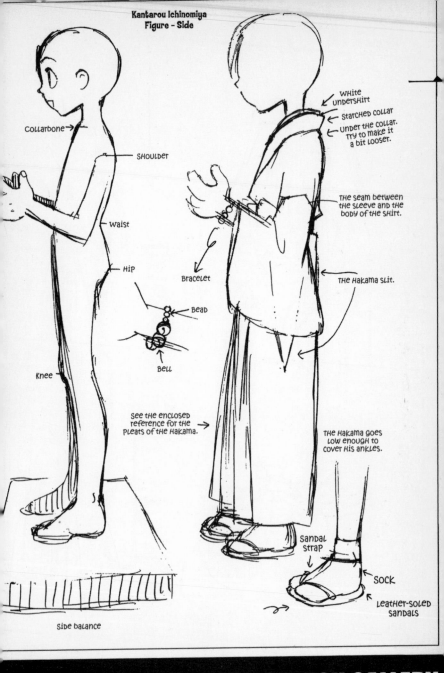

Kantarou Ichinomiya
Figure – Side

Collarbone →

← WHITE
   UNDERSHIRT

← STARCHED COLLAR

← UNDER THE COLLAR.
   TRY TO MAKE IT
   A BIT LOOSER.

SHOULDER

WAIST

THE SEAM BETWEEN
THE SLEEVE AND THE
BODY OF THE SHIRT.

HIP

Bracelet

← THE HAKAMA SLIT.

Bead

Knee

BELL

SEE THE ENCLOSED
REFERENCE FOR THE
PLEATS OF THE HAKAMA. →

THE HAKAMA GOES
LOW ENOUGH TO
COVER HIS ANKLES.

SANDAL
STRAP

→ SOCK

← LEATHER-SOLED
   SANDALS

SIDE BALANCE

Kantarou Ichinomiya Figure – Clothing

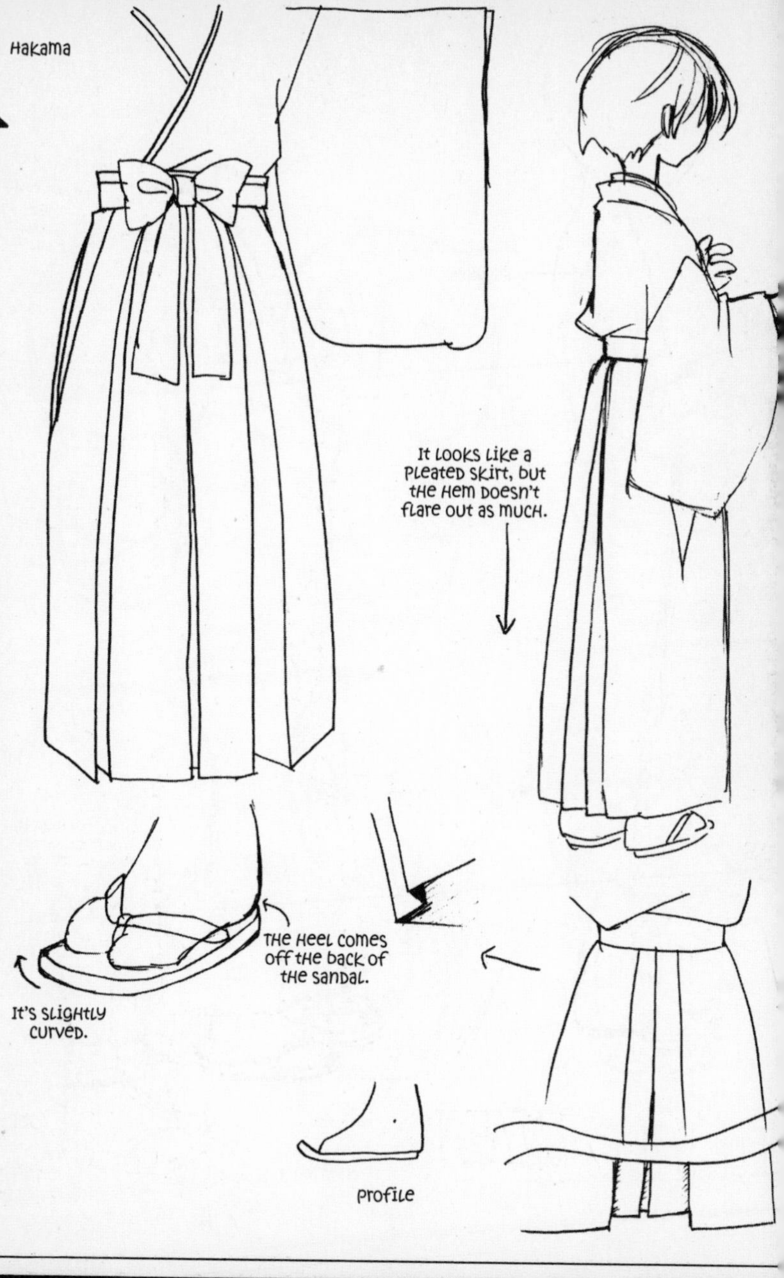
Hakama
It looks like a pleated skirt, but the hem doesn't flare out as much.
The heel comes off the back of the sandal.
It's slightly curved.
Profile

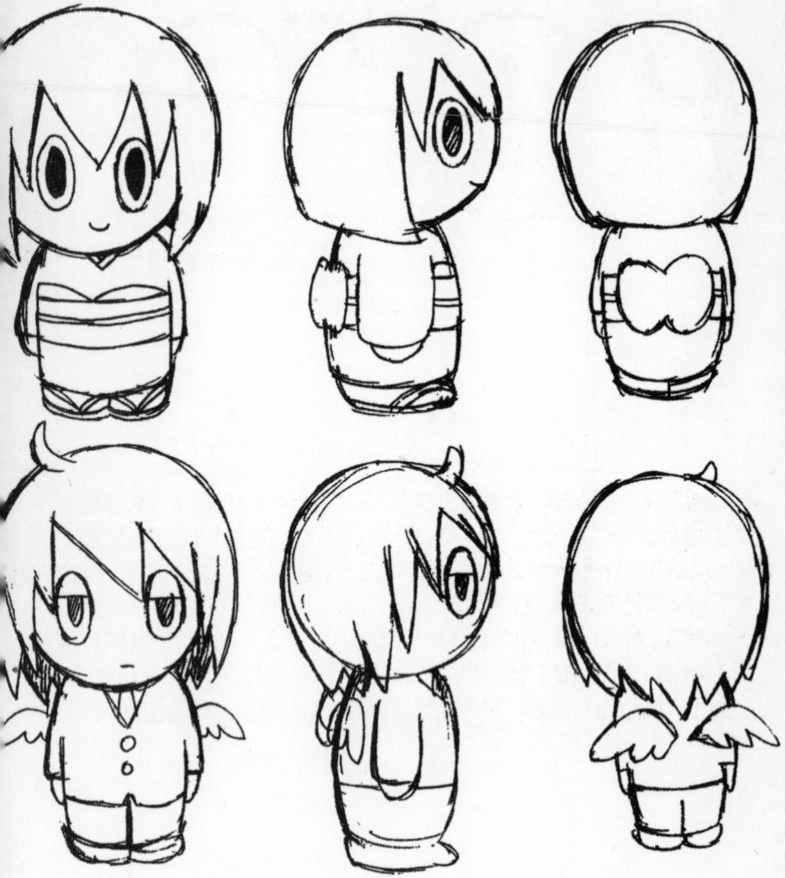

His subordinate youkai.

IN THE NEXT VOLUME OF

tactics

Kantarou's struggle against the mysterious Raikou Minamoto and his strange band continues as the even more mysterious Father Edwards returns to the fray! Facing off against possessed actresses and demons from the great beyond, Haruka and Kantarou are up to their necks in trouble, especially when Minamoto's true motives are finally revealed....

Language and Culture Notes on *tactics* vol. 4!

Chapter 9:

~Kan-chan's opening mantra: a fire spell of purification known as the Mantra of Acalanatha Vidya-raja (Japanese: "Fudou-Myou-ou"), meaning roughly, "Pay homage to Buddha or begone, leave or be punished and purified, destroy, Oh Wrathful One, turn away and begone!"

~The spell continues: roughly translated, "Devils and the dark path, in everything is Buddha. The four devils (hindrances caused by the five components, obstructions caused by one's mental and physical function, hindrances of earthly desire, hindrance of death, hindrance of the Devil of the Sixth Heaven) and the three obstacles (obstacles of earthly desires, obstacles of karma, obstacles of retribution), all come on Buddha's path. The world of the devils and the world of Buddha live according to the same principles. In all ways directly, without a difference."

~Gidayuu reciters: performers of a classic Japanese ballad drama, who use their voices and special theatrical instruments.

~Bunraku theater: very sophisticated traditional puppet theater, originating in Osaka, and closely associated with kabuki, to the extent that several famous playwrights wrote for both mediums. Puppeteers appear on stage with the puppets, but often robed in black, so as to be "invisible" to the audience.

~Kantarou's heihaku incantation: Your editor fails! This prayer starts with the traditional "namu amida butsu" of many Buddhist incantations, and I never managed to find the specific one (if there is a specific one) that matches this. Help!

~Heihaku: a Shinto offering of cloth.

~Kan-chan lays the smack down: This is all a part of a incantation that roughly means "Demons and heretical doctrine, monsters and fierce gods, venomous beasts and malicious dragons, and venomous insects, hear the voice of the khakkhara, hide from the harm of poison, awaken your aspiration for Buddhahood, undertake many journeys and quickly gain enlightenment."

Chapter 10:

~The return of the Kuji! See previous volume for note.

~Shugendou: a Japanese mountain asceticism-shamanism incorporating Shinto and Buddhist concepts.

~A note on turn of the century Japanese religious practice: Those visiting modern Japan may be surprised by how easily the traditional Shinto and Buddhist practices meld together (tactics uses both fairly equally), but there was a time when this was not the case. As part of the political decision to promote the Emperor over the shogun during the Meiji Restoration, "State Shinto," which revered the Imperial family as descendants of the gods, was instituted and promoted heavily, to the denigration of Buddhism and other practices. The political background of Hasumi's role in this chapter reflects the government's insistence on the separation of faiths, especially ones that were deemed insufficiently "modern," even as the State itself pushed one particular religion.

~Doujigiri-Yasutsuna: the name of Raiko's sword roughly translates to "child-slaying quiet rope."

~Koushin: this concept in the Japanese zodiac points to a day of misfortune. It's comprised of two terms: "kou," the term from the Chinese zodiac system associated with metal and planet Venus, and "shin," meaning painful. But what exactly this means in regards to Haruka had yet to be revealed...

~Shakujyou: Haruka's staff is also known as a khakkhara in Sanskrit. Often translated as "alarm staff" or "sounding staff," this object is carried by many a monk from India to Tibet to Japan, be they Buddhist or Hindu. As an attribute of the Bodhisattva Ksitigarbha (known in Japan as "Jizo"), it is sometimes called "Jizo's staff" and features six rings, signifying that this bodhisattva is prepared to help the beings of all six realms of existence. In other cases, the number of rings is four, reminding those who hear the staff's jingling sound of the Buddhist Four Truths.

Bonus stories:

~Jizo statues: as mentioned above, Jizo is the Japanese name for the Bodhisattva Ksitigarbha. These statues are seen all over Japan, and are often wearing little knit hats or shawls donated by worshipers. Jizo is the guardian of travelers and of children.

~Keu-Kegen: the Chinese characters for Keu-kegen are "hair-feather-hair-exist" but in this second instance of Keu-kegen they are replaced with "rare-being-rare-sighting."

~Kakaijuu: this is the third mantra to Acalanatha Vidya-raja, or Fudou-Myou-ou, "The Immovable One." The mantra roughly translates as, "Everything becomes Tathagata, so pay respect to all the different facets of existence."

~Fudou-Myou-ou: coming from ancient Hindu philosophy, but important in Esoteric Japanese Buddhist practice, The Immovable One carries a demon-subduing sword in one hand, and a rope in the other. A god of fire, a destroyer of ignorance and illusion, and very powerful, you can see why Kantarou's youkai would be so dismayed that he would be so casually invoked! Your humble editor is a big fan of Fudou-Myou-ou.

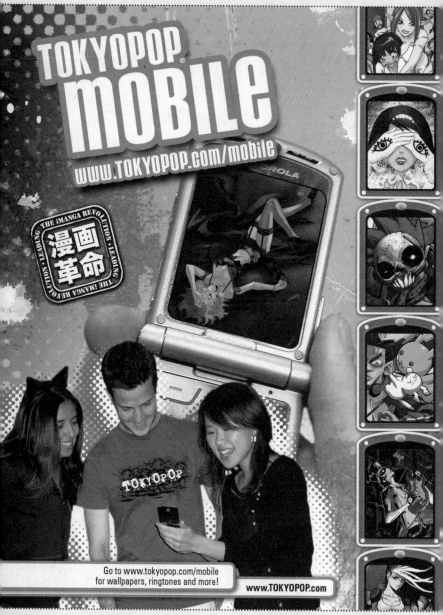

STOP!

This is the back of the book. You wouldn't want to spoil a great ending!

This book is printed "manga-style," in the authentic Japanese right-to-left format. Since none of the artwork has been flipped or altered, readers get to experience the story just as the creator intended. You've been asking for it, so TOKYOPOP® delivered: authentic, hot-off-the-press, and far more fun!

DIRECTIONS

1
2
3
4
5
6
7
8
9
10

If this is your first time reading manga-style, here's a quick guide to help you understand how it works.

It's easy... just start in the top right panel and follow the numbers. Have fun, and look for more 100% authentic manga from TOKYOPOP®!

THE MANGA REVOLUTION · LEADING · 漫画革命